THE SURPRISE OF RECONCILIATION
IN THE CATHOLIC TRADITION

The Surprise of Reconciliation in the Catholic Tradition

Edited by
J. J. Carney and
Laurie Johnston

Paulist Press
New York / Mahwah, NJ

Cover image: Sassetta (Stefano di Giovanni) (c. 1400–1450). *The Wolf of Gubbio*, 1437–44. © National Gallery, London / Art Resource, NY. Used with permission. Cover and book design by Lynn Else

Library of Congress Cataloging-in-Publication Data
Names: Carney, J. J., editor. | Johnston, Laurie (Professor of theology), editor.
Title: The surprise of reconciliation in the Catholic tradition / edited by J.J. Carney and Laurie Johnston.
Description: New York : Paulist Press, [2018] | Includes bibliographical references.
Identifiers: LCCN 2018018807 (print) | LCCN 2018038615 (ebook) | ISBN 9781587687532 (ebook) | ISBN 9780809153800 (paperback :alk. paper)
Subjects: LCSH: Reconciliation—Religious aspects—Catholic Church. | Christian sociology—Catholic Church.
Classification: LCC BX2260 (ebook) | LCC BX2260 .S87 2018 (print) | DDC 261.8—dc23
LC record available at https://lccn.loc.gov/2018018807

ISBN 978-0-8091-5380-0 (paperback)
ISBN 978-1-58768-753-2 (e-book)

Published by Paulist Press
997 Macarthur Boulevard
Mahwah, New Jersey 07430

www.paulistpress.com

Printed and bound in the
United States of America

To Eileen Burke-Sullivan and Mike Griffin,
for your enthusiastic championing
of this book at its genesis.

And to all laboring for peace, justice, and
reconciliation around the world.

Contents

Contents

Acknowledgments

If reconciliation is ultimately a journey rather than a destination, much the same could be said for this book. As a doctoral student in church history at The Catholic University of America who had been immersed in the theology of Christian reconciliation and peacebuilding at Duke Divinity School, I found myself frustrated at the lack of dialogue between these two scholarly worlds. The field of church history focused on historical theology, church-state relations, sacramental history, and the social history of Christian peoples, among other key loci. But rarely did I encounter explicit reflection on how our historical forebears dealt with questions of social violence, peace, or restorative justice. Likewise, the theology of reconciliation offered inspiring contemporary examples of Christian peacebuilding that at times drew on biblical sources. But the historical Christian tradition did not seem to register in most of this literature. It was as if Enlightenment imagination had succeeded in convincing even Christian scholars that the history of Christianity was solely about war, conflict, and religious persecution—with no counterresponse.

The inspiration for the book also germinated in the field where I saw seemingly ancient ritual practices incorporated into modern social reconciliation work. In the summer of 2014, I had the opportunity to return to Rwanda to conduct interviews with local Catholic peacebuilders twenty years after the 1994 genocide. One of the most powerful initiatives was run out of Mushaka Parish in southwestern Rwanda. Here Catholic priests and lay ministers coordinated a program known as *gacaca nkirisitu* or "Christian *gacaca*." In this process, former genocide perpetrators were ritually excommunicated from the sacraments so that they could undertake a six-month penitential process. During this time, they participated in weekly catechetical programs examining the connections between human rights, sacramental practice, and the work of the Holy Spirit. Perpetrators were asked to share the full truth about their actions during the genocide, and they were encouraged to overcome their shame and seek forgiveness from victims. They participated in retreats, both on their own and with victims. At the end of the six-month process, they were given the opportunity to receive the sacrament of reconciliation, and victims were asked if they were ready to forgive them. If so, at the subsequent Sunday Mass each perpetrator knelt in front of a representative of the victim's family, who in turn placed a hand on the perpetrator's shoulder. Echoing early church penitential traditions, the priest and/or bishop performed a ritual rite of reincorporation including the sprinkling of baptismal water. Victims and perpetrators then received the sacrament of the Eucharist together, signaling the reincorporation of the perpetrators into the community. After Mass, the entire community shared a celebratory feast with the perpetrator, victim, and their families, symbolizing the community's desire to once again "live together" in peace and harmony.[1] This project further convinced me of the potential relevance of ancient church practices for contemporary reconciliation efforts.

If the original idea for the book germinated in both the classroom and the field, many gardeners helped bring the seeds of this book to fruition. First and foremost, I am grateful to Eileen Burke-Sullivan, vice provost and head of Creighton's Office of Mission and Ministry, for supporting and underwriting this project. It was Eileen who suggested bringing all of the contributors together for a September 2016 weekend at the Creighton retreat center in Griswold, Iowa. This retreat was facilitated beautifully by Eileen's brother, Kevin Burke, SJ, and Bill O'Neill, SJ, around the theme of Johann-Baptist Metz's "dangerous memory." More than anything else, this retreat helped this volume's contributors become a community of Christian scholars pursuing a common theological project rather than a disparate group of academics contributing to a collection of edited writings. At Creighton I also thank John

O'Keefe, director of the Center for Catholic Thought, and Carol Krajicek in the Office of Mission and Ministry, for their unflagging support and logistical coordination for both the retreat and the September 2017 academic conference.

Beyond Creighton, I would like to express a particular word of thanks to Michael Griffin at Holy Cross College (Notre Dame, IN). It was Mike who first volunteered to collaborate with me on this book back in 2014, and he had great influence in the initial envisioning of the project. Ultimately, Mike was not able to participate in the project due to a health crisis in his family. But his passion and imagination helped set the tone for this book.

All of the contributors to this volume have been heavily invested in this project. Over the course of two years, they worked on their research, attended a weekend retreat, presented at an academic conference, and finished their chapters on time. Each has demonstrated an impressive level of personal commitment, and it has been a joy to work with all of them.

I would also like to thank Donna Crilly at Paulist Press for her faith in this project. Donna and Paulist accepted this project before we even had a manuscript together, and she came to our conference to express support, learn about our vision, and offer guidance to the group. We hope this book will live up to Paulist's tradition of publishing outstanding theological works that seek to make a pastoral difference in the church and world alike.

Last but not least, I express a major debt of gratitude to my coeditor, Laurie Johnston, of Emmanuel College. Laurie helped envision the structure of this book and took on the lion's share of editing duties (while pursuing a Fulbright fellowship in Belgium no less)! This book is far better because of her incisive eye for detail complemented by her holistic vision that never confused the forest for the trees.

Jay Carney
Omaha, Nebraska, USA
March 17, 2018
Feast of St. Patrick, Victim and Peacebuilder

Notes

1. The story of *gacaca nkirisitu* is explored in more depth in J. J. Carney, "A Generation after Genocide: Catholic Reconciliation in Rwanda," *Theological Studies* 76, no. 4 (2015): 797–800.

Introduction

A *Ressourcement* of Reconciliation: Mining the Catholic Tradition for Social Visions of Peace, Justice, and Healing

J. J. Carney and Laurie Johnston

The wolf shall live with the lamb,
 the leopard shall lie down with the kid,
the calf and the lion and the fatling together,
 and a little child shall lead them.
The cow and the bear shall graze,
 their young shall lie down together;
 and the lion shall eat straw like the ox.
The nursing child shall play over the hole of the asp,
 and the weaned child shall put its hand on the adder's
  den.
They will not hurt or destroy
 on all my holy mountain;
for the earth will be full of the knowledge of the Lord
 as the waters cover the sea.

Isaiah 11:6–9

saiah's vision of a world in which the wolf lives peacefully with the lamb can feel very far away from the world of division and violence we know so well. Yet Christian faith teaches us that the divine gift of reconciliation is already breaking into the world, even now. The grace of reconciliation comes as a surprise—when St. Paul writes about it in 2 Corinthians 5, he remarks, "See, everything has become new!" This book is an account of some of those surprising moments when, in partial and incomplete ways, reconciliation has emerged in societies. But it is also an account that reveals just how deep and universal is the need for reconciliation in our world.

One particularly surprising moment of reconciliation appears on the cover of this book. Sassetta's altarpiece, from San Sepolcro in Italy, may well be the earliest depiction of St. Francis with the wolf of Gubbio. According to this beloved story from the Fioretti of St. Francis, the wolf had been terrorizing the people of Gubbio for some time. Like many today who live in situations of endemic violence, they feared to leave their houses. But St. Francis came and spoke directly to the wolf, and arranged a remarkable inter-species peace treaty. Knowing that the wolf was merely hungry, St. Francis asked the people of Gubbio to agree to leave food for him. In exchange, the wolf agreed to stop attacking them and their animals. St. Francis convinced the wolf to come meet the villagers face to face, and the wolf placed his paw in Francis's hand as a sign of assent. The peace treaty appears to have brought a genuine reconciliation:

> The wolf lived two years at Gubbio; he went familiarly from door to door without harming anyone, and all the people received him courteously, feeding him with great pleasure....At last, after two years, he died of old age, and the people of Gubbio mourned his loss greatly; for when they saw him going about so gently amongst them all, he reminded them of the virtue and sanctity of St. Francis.[1]

Not all peacemakers are as successful as St. Francis; not every community experiences relief from the wolves that terrorize them; and not every perpetrator receives empathy and reintegration into the community, like the wolf of Gubbio did. Still, it is our belief that there is much we can learn from this and other moments of reconciliation in the Catholic tradition.

Christians in history have often faced complicated questions about reconciliation that resonate with our contemporary contexts as well. For example, can people who have deeply betrayed their own community ever be reintegrated and reconciled? That was a question for the third-century bishop Cyprian of Carthage, dealing with Christians who had denied their faith under Roman persecution. But it is also a question for twenty-first-century Ugandans attempting to reintegrate former child soldiers—children who in many cases were forced to kill members of their own families and communities. It is also a question facing Americans when former gang members are released from prison—young people who have not only carried out violence in their own communities but have also been deeply betrayed by a society that does not uphold their full humanity. Reconciliation requires attending to human relationships in all of their complexity.

It is our hope that this book can offer both theological wisdom and practical insights by drawing upon concrete experiences of Christians, past and present, who have wrestled with reconciliation. Whether it is through symbol, sacrament, or speech, these cases offer fresh ways to think about how we might respond to violence in our own contexts. They can also lend new layers to the ways that analysts are thinking about the relatively recent phenomenon of political reconciliation.

Theological writings on social reconciliation—defined here as the journey to restore social peace and right relations in the context of sociopolitical violence and conflict—emerged out of the post-Cold War prevalence of intrastate conflict and Christian churches' increasingly prominent roles in peacebuilding and post-conflict reconciliation. This was especially evident in communities with large Christian populations such as Northern Ireland, Colombia, South Africa, and the African Great Lakes region.[2] Many of the most important theologians of reconciliation have written out of their own sociopolitical contexts, the most famous being Anglican archbishop Desmond Tutu, chair of the Truth and Reconciliation Commission in South Africa in the late 1990s.[3] Lived public theology accompanied further scholarly reflection on questions of reconciliation and forgiveness in contexts of social conflict.[4] In addition, political scientists and other theorists working on questions of "political reconciliation" have also drawn deeply on Christian themes of forgiveness, ritual, and restorative justice.[5]

In the modern Catholic tradition, the Second Vatican Council (1962–65) reframed the Catholic sacrament of penance and/or confession as a "sacrament of reconciliation," emphasizing how the sacrament restores both "vertical" right relations between the human subject and God and "horizontal" right relations between humans. This sparked a renewed engagement with the history of sacramental reconciliation, a history that revealed the deeply communal roots of the sacrament in the early church.[6] At the same time, documents such as Vatican II's *Gaudium et Spes* (1965) and Pope John XXIII's *Pacem in Terris* (1963) moved beyond speaking of peace primarily as social order, instead calling it the fruit of social justice, and something that "must be built up ceaselessly" (*GS* 78). In addition, post–Vatican II Catholic social ethics has also been marked by a turn to reconciliation and peacebuilding. Most prominent in the recent literature would be the Catholic Peacebuilding Network's 2010 volume, *Peacebuilding: Catholic Theology, Ethics, and Practice.*[7] The theme of reconciliation has also been echoed recently in ecclesial contexts, such as the papal World Day of Peace messages as well as the 2009 Second African Synod of Bishops.[8]

Oddly missing in all of the aforementioned literature are explicit connections between the Catholic historical tradition, on the one hand, and questions of sociopolitical violence and conflict on the other. Scholars have investigated the history of the sacrament of reconciliation; biblical visions of reconciliation, justice, and peace; and contemporary cases of Christian peacebuilding. But in large measure, the eighteen-hundred-year history between the New Testament era and the late twentieth century has been ignored when it comes to case studies of reconciliation. And few scholars have examined how explicitly Catholic practices, sacraments, and imagination can contribute to social reconciliation. This volume seeks to address both of these lacunae.

We do so in a spirit of *ressourcement*, a French term coined by Charles de Péguy that can be roughly translated as "returning to the sources."[9] In the decades preceding Vatican II, French Catholic theologians such as Henri de Lubac, Yves Congar, M. D. Chenu, and Jean Danielou mined biblical and patristic sources to renew a twentieth-century theological tradition that had become ossified in an arid neo-Scholasticism.[10] *Ressourcement* entailed shifting from an ahistorical to a more historical methodology in theology, and de Lubac's and Danielou's *Sources Chrétiennes* series recovered and translated hundreds of ancient works. However, the purpose of the movement was never strictly historical. Rather, the aim of this historical mining was to draw on the church's roots to help renew the church in the modern day. This spirit of "returning to the sources to renew in the present" became a hallmark of Vatican II's vision of *aggiornamento*—"updating" the church by drawing on the deepest wellsprings of its roots.

It is with a similar spirit that we approach this book. The cases presented herein are not meant to be chronologically exhaustive or thematically encyclopedic. Such a task would likely be impossible, and readers looking for a broader historical survey of the Catholic tradition's engagement with questions of peacebuilding should be directed to Ronald Musto's outstanding corpus of work on the subject.[11] Rather, we present these cases as illustrative. We believe they offer particular and largely unknown insight into the various dimensions of social reconciliation in our current context, including forgiveness, truth-telling, limiting violence, the healing of memories, and the pursuit of justice. We hope in turn that this project will inspire church historians, theologians, and social ethicists to explore the countless other historical cases of social reconciliation and peacebuilding not mentioned in this book, including cases from well beyond the Roman Catholic tradition that we privilege here.

We acknowledge that the term *reconciliation* has been used in problematic ways in the past. In particular, many white Christians in the United States have spoken about "racial reconciliation" in ways that fail to acknowledge the full, ongoing effects of racial injustice in our society.[12] And there are certainly examples in other contexts in which powerful perpetrators have called for "reconciliation" as a way of evading true justice. Yet it is our conviction that this book, by examining these cases of reconciliation, will illustrate just how demanding real reconciliation is, thereby helping to reveal the flaws in hasty or superficial calls for reconciliation. Genuine reconciliation is not a shortcut; it *includes* truth-telling, reparations, and justice. This is powerfully illustrated by the image on the cover of this book. In the reconciliation that Francis brokers, there is no denial of what the victims have suffered. In fact, their bloody limbs remain in the picture. And Francis directly confronts both the wolf for having "dared to devour men, made after the image of God." At the same time, Francis also preaches a sermon in Gubbio, in which he calls upon the people of Gubbio—the seemingly innocent parties—to repent and do penance for their sins. It is on account of these sins, he explains, that God has allowed them to suffer the attacks of the wolf. The story reminds us, therefore, of both the complexity and the exigency of true reconciliation.

We have organized the book into three broad sections. The first four chapters focus on Christian reconciliation cases from the New Testament and patristic period (first through sixth centuries AD). The next four chapters examine historical and theological examples from the medieval and early modern eras (roughly tenth through eighteenth centuries AD). The final six cases unfold within our recent historical context in the late twentieth and early twenty-first centuries. This chronological approach respects the vast differences in historical and social context between, for example, the late patristic world of desert monks and the late twentieth-century world of Peruvian base communities. We hope that this broadly chronological organization will lend itself to teaching, but readers are not obliged to read these chapters in the exact order outlined here. One can certainly observe the themes of social reconciliation, such as forgiveness, justice, or truth-telling, in a variety of different historical contexts. And in the spirit of *ressourcement*, all of our authors conclude their chapters by connecting their case studies to key dimensions of a theology of social reconciliation, with intended applications in today's world. Each author has also included guiding questions at the end of their chapters designed to facilitate deeper reflection and discussion.

Thomas Stegman, SJ, begins this volume with an analysis of Paul's theology of reconciliation as presented in 2 Corinthians, Romans, and Ephesians. Stegman argues that reconciliation lies at the heart of Paul's theology, and it is Paul in turn who gives reconciliation its uniquely "Christian" stamp. For Paul, reconciliation begins with God's initiative, namely through the saving person, work, death, and resurrection of Jesus Christ. Followers of Jesus are called to be ministers of reconciliation who take the initiative to love and forgive others even as they await the unfolding of God's "new creation."

Introduction

John O'Keefe narrates how the second-century theologian Irenaeus of Lyons's deeply material vision of creation countered the "anti-materialistic" worldview of early Christian "Gnostic" movements. Irenaeus called humans to "reconcile with their own materiality," loving this material world while also anticipating God's ultimate transformation of it. For O'Keefe, this message has striking resonance in our own context of ecological crisis in which modern people are literally "at war with the material creation," unwilling to accept that we, too, are earthly bodies intrinsically tied up in the "dust" of the earth. In sum, the reconciliation with the environment so urgently needed in the twenty-first century entails human reconciliation with our own materiality.

Scott Moringiello examines the third-century bishop Cyprian of Carthage. Cyprian ministered in the midst of the Novation dispute, a bitter division that broke out in the 250s over whether to reintegrate lapsed Christians who had denied the faith in the face of Roman persecution. In allowing apostates back into eucharistic communion after a period of penance, Cyprian took a middle path between "rigorists," who permanently excommunicated the lapsed, and "laxists," who readmitted them without preconditions. For Moringiello, Cyprian's envisioning of reconciliation through the Pauline lens of *dilectio*, or "mutual love," entails virtues much in demand in today's world: unity, humility, mercy, and respect for one's opponents. For postconflict communities that are trying to balance justice and mercy as they reintegrate ex-combatants, this case may offer insights.

Zachary Smith's exploration of monastic practices of silence in the fourth and fifth centuries reveals the dangerous, even uncontrollable power of words to both build up and tear down, to paraphrase the prophet Jeremiah. For Smith, monastic practices were inherently violent in trying to reform and/or mold the mind and body of the self and one's brother monk. Monks recognized the power of words to inflict spiritual, emotional, and physical harm, often reflecting a spirit of anger and pride far removed from the gospel. For these reasons, they practiced contemplative silence, creating the time and space necessary to listen, reflect, lament, and meditate on both their words and actions. In a twenty-first-century world drowning in a cacophony of virtual words, hateful

xix

speech, and demonization of opponents, the monastic practices of silence and "selective speech" are needed now more than ever.

Moving to the medieval period, **Jay Carney** analyzes the Peace of God movement of tenth- and eleventh-century France. Amid escalating social violence in the late Carolingian period, Catholic bishops, monks, and peasants reached agreements with local lay nobility to establish sacred boundaries of time and space designed to curb the violence being inflicted on clerics and peasants. Fueled by millennial expectations surrounding the thousandth anniversary of Christ's birth and death, the Peace of God movement involved the Catholic Church to an unprecedented degree in political and social questions of war and peace. The church's blessing of "protective force" and the inexorable trend from the Peace of God's "holy peace" to the Crusades' "holy war" also leave ambiguous legacies that linger to the present day.

Laurie Johnston examines an issue with striking resonance for the twenty-first century—the relationships between Muslims and Christians in Iberia and beyond during the medieval period. In contrast to the well-known violent voices of the Crusades or even the Spanish martyrs of Cordoba, Johnston examines a range of "alternative voices" for interreligious coexistence, including James of Aragon, Juan of Segovia, Nicholas of Cusa, and even Martin Luther. She ultimately argues that coexistence—recognizing the "other's" right to exist at all—is the foundation for any process of social reconciliation. In turn, Johnston shows how Muslims and Christians were able to coexist on the common ground of respect for God, mutual rationality, and a shared political community. The more they learned about each other, the more they learned a kind of "humble agnosticism"—namely that no one community has "the whole story about God."

Kristin Haas analyzes the 1427 peacemaking sermons of Bernardino of Siena, a Franciscan who became renowned for his efforts to reconcile warring city-states in Italy. In a divisive culture of factions, Bernardino reminded his hearers of the "dangerous memory" of the city's original life of peace. Exhorting his hearers that they "belonged to Christ" rather than their political factions, Bernardino challenged individuals to convert their hearts, take responsibility for their actions, and freely choose peace in the face of social pressure demanding vengeance. For Haas, this message of moral responsibility and personal freedom remains resonant in the face of a twenty-first-century illusion that social and environmental problems can be resolved solely through political policies or technical means.

In a probing essay on the eighteenth-century Italian moral theologian Alphonsus de Liguori, **Julia Fleming** examines Liguori's understanding of "restitution." For Liguori, restitution is an act of reparation that seeks to repair damage done through an unjust action perpetrated on a victim. Fleming breaks down the complexities of the debate, including the fact that restitution is both morally obligatory in the Catholic tradition, yet, strictly speaking, impossible in cases where "life, limb, reputation, or bodily integrity" have been damaged or lost. Ultimately, Liguori's thought underlines the importance of justice and human dignity for all parties, including resisting the temptation to place undue harm on the penitent. Fleming's essay also underscores a pressing challenge in contemporary arguments over, for example, reparations for slavery: how to make restitution generations after the initial violence.

Moving to the twentieth century, **John Kiess** examines how the sacrament of anointing helped restore the dignity of the body during Northern Ireland's "Troubles" era of violent conflict between Catholics and Protestants (c. 1972–98). Drawing from an array of first-person testimonies, Kiess demonstrates how the sacrament of anointing served as a "sign of contradiction" in the highly ritualized environment of social violence in Northern Ireland. Rather than just project ideological meaning on a political martyr, anointing reclaimed the ordinary dignity of the human body. Kiess reminds us that social reconciliation is always about bodies and spaces and the willingness to cross "enemy lines" to touch human flesh.

Likewise, **Steven Judd, MM**, looks at how person-to-person contact helped "heal the breaches" that threatened to tear apart southern Peru during the violent Shining Path insurgency of the 1980s and early 1990s. Drawing on his witness as a missionary in Peru during this period, Judd argues that indigenous Catholic communities and lay-led "vicariates of solidarity" helped to literally and figuratively "embody" liberation theology and the preferential option for the poor. These communities were ultimately able to maintain their unity and resist both Shining Path and government violence. All the while, they advocated for land reform, documented human rights violations, organized community protests, and drew on indigenous spirituality to celebrate their Catholic patronal feast days.

Shifting focus from South America to North America, **William O'Neill, SJ**, examines the worldview that has led to the mass incarceration of over 2.2 million prisoners in the prisons of the United States. Drawing from his years of ministry as a chaplain in a federal women's prison in California, O'Neill calls for the transformation of America's "retributive quint," emphasizing the punishment and dehumanization of the prisoner, to a "restorative squint" that seeks to heal victims, communities, and perpetrators. Highlighting his fellow Jesuit Greg Boyle's "Homeboy Ministries" in Los Angeles, O'Neill argues that Boyle's vision of "kinship"— taking the victim's side as your own—ultimately enables the restoration of a shared human identity, seeing perpetrator and victim alike as "just like me."

Ashley Hall also examines a by and large successful case of modern reconciliation: Lutheran–Catholic ecumenism. Over the past fifty years, this dialogue has focused on healing the originating division of the Reformation, bringing these two communities from "conflict to communion." If differences in eucharistic theology and practice undergirded the sixteenth-century divisions between Lutherans and Catholics, today's conflicts stem from disagreements over who can be ordained to celebrate the Eucharist. Hall's essay offers valuable insights for journeys of social reconciliation—the need to seek unity without losing one's authenticity; the importance of working toward "reconciled difference" rather than forced conversion; and ultimately a vision of reconciliation as "writing a new story together."

The themes of story and memory similarly mark **Emmanuel Katongole**'s chapter on the Catholic activist Maggy Barankitse and her ministry of Maison Shalom (house of peace) in Burundi and Rwanda. Katongole shows how the memory of a 1993 massacre witnessed by Barankitse motivated her work for reconciliation, leading Barankitse to establish a network of homes, hospitals, schools, and employment centers for over thirty thousand orphaned children. Drawing again on Johann Baptist Metz's notion of "dangerous memory," Katongole demonstrates how Barankitse's memory of the violence of the cross intersects with her memory of God's salvific love and the hope of the resurrection. For Barankitse, this act of "remembering the future" is embodied in her devotion to the Eucharist, a devotion that sends her out into the world in a spirit of hope that God's love will always have the final word.

Daniel Philpott also explores East Africa as a central milieu for the recent emergence of political forgiveness as a key dimension of postconflict social reconciliation. Philpott first describes the surprising turn to political forgiveness in Catholic magisterial teaching, especially in the writings of Pope John Paul II, Pope Benedict XVI, and Pope Francis. The church's call for political forgiveness has come as a (somewhat unpleasant) surprise to what Philpott describes as "the liberal peace," the post–World War II international consensus predicated on human rights and a generally retributive vision of justice. Countering these critics, Philpott marshals impressive data to demonstrate how the practice of forgiveness has helped heal both individuals and communities in postwar Uganda.

Finally, **Robert Schreiter, CPPS**, one of the true trailblazers in the modern Catholic theology of social reconciliation, offers a conclusion that weaves together the insights of the volume's contributors. Schreiter further locates this conversation within the recent turn to reconciliation in both Christian practice and Catholic social thought. He shows how the volume's authors all contribute to key dimensions of a "spirituality of social reconciliation," including themes of new creation, eschatological hope, the healing of memory, truth-telling, the pursuit of justice, and forgiveness. Ultimately, the spirituality of social reconciliation is a call to contemplate and imagine a world whose determinative story is the story of God's love. On the long, painful, and uneven journey toward social reconciliation and peace, it is this "dangerous hope" that keeps Christians moving toward Isaiah's holy mountain.

Notes

1. Roger Hudleston, trans., *The Little Flowers of Saint Francis of Assisi* (New York: Heritage Press, 1930).

2. See Gregory Baum and Harold Wells, eds., *The Reconciliation of Peoples: Challenge to the Churches* (Maryknoll, NY: Orbis Books, 1997); David Little, ed., *Peacemakers in Action: Profiles of Religion in Conflict Resolution* (Cambridge: Cambridge University Press, 2007); Raymond Helmick and Rodney Petersen, eds., *Forgiveness and Reconciliation: Religion, Public Policy and Conflict Transformation* (Philadelphia: Templeton, 2001).

3. See Desmond Tutu, *No Future Without Forgiveness* (New York: Doubleday, 1999). Other notable South African voices would include John de Gruchy, *Reconciliation: Restoring Justice* (Grand Rapids, MI: Eerdmans, 2002); and Charles Villa-Vicencio, *Walk with Us and Listen: Political Reconciliation in Africa* (Washington, DC: Georgetown University Press, 2009).

4. See Miroslav Volf, *Exclusion and Embrace: A Theological Exploration of Identity, Otherness, and Reconciliation* (Nashville: Abingdon Press, 1996); and *The End of Memory: Remembering Rightly in a Violent World* (Grand Rapids, MI: Eerdmans, 2006); Donald Shriver, *An Ethic for Enemies: Forgiveness in Politics* (Oxford: Oxford University Press, 1995); L. Gregory Jones, *Embodying Forgiveness: A Theological Analysis* (Grand Rapids, MI: Eerdmans, 1995); Robert J. Schreiter, *The Ministry of Reconciliation: Spirituality and Strategies* (Maryknoll, NY: Orbis Books, 1998); Emmanuel Katongole and Chris Rice, *Reconciling All Things: A Christian Vision for Justice, Peace, and Healing* (Downers Grove, IL: InterVarsity, 2008).

5. See Howard Zehr, *The Little Book of Restorative Justice* (Intercourse, PA: Good Books, 2002); John Paul Lederach, *The Moral Imagination: The Art and Soul of Building Peace* (New York: Oxford University Press, 2005); Daniel Philpott, *Just and Unjust Peace: An Ethic of Political Reconciliation* (New York: Oxford University Press, 2012).

6. See Karl Rahner, *Theological Investigations Vol. XV. Penance in the Early Church* (New York: Crossroads, 1982); James Dallen, *The Reconciling Community: The Rite of Penance* (New York: Pueblo, 1986); Kenan Osborne, *Reconciliation and Justification: The Sacrament and Its Theology* (Mahwah, NJ: Paulist Press, 1990); Frank O'Loughlin, *The Future of the Sacrament of Penance* (Mahwah, NJ: Paulist Press, 2007).

7. Robert J. Schreiter, R. Scott Appleby, and Gerard F. Powers, eds., *Peacebuilding: Catholic Theology, Ethics and Praxis* (Maryknoll, NY: Orbis Books, 2010).

8. See Agbonkhianmeghe Orobator, ed., *Reconciliation, Justice, and Peace: The Second African Synod* (Nairobi: Acton Publishers and Maryknoll, NY: Orbis Books, 2011).

9. Gabriel Flynn, "Introduction: The Twentieth-Century Renaissance in Catholic Theology," in *Ressourcement: A Movement for Renewal in Twentieth-Century Catholic Theology*, ed. Gabriel Flynn and Paul D. Murray (New York: Oxford University Press, 2012), 4.

10. "Neo-Scholasticism" refers to the dominant stream of Catholic theology in late nineteenth-century and early twentieth-century Europe. From the pontificate of Pope Leo XIII (1878–1903), Catholic seminary training was reframed around the thought of Thomas Aquinas as viewed through a particular neo-Scholastic interpretive tradition. This movement broadly reflected the Catholic magisterium's opposition to modern streams of intellectual and political thought in the aftermath of the Enlightenment and the French Revolution.

11. Ronald G. Musto, *The Catholic Peace Tradition* (Maryknoll, NY: Orbis Books, 1986, reprinted 2002 by Peace Books); *The Peace Tradition in the Catholic Church: An Annotated Bibliography* (New York: Garland, 1987); *Catholic Peacemakers: A Documentary History* (Maryknoll, NY: Orbis Books, 1996).

12. See Jennifer Harvey, *Dear White Christians: For Those Still Longing for Racial Reconciliation* (Grand Rapids, MI: Eerdmans, 2014).

I

NEW TESTAMENT AND PATRISTIC CASES

CHAPTER I

A Pauline Foundation for Social Reconciliation

Thomas D. Stegman, SJ

When looking to the New Testament for foundations for social reconciliation, one encounters, at first glance, what might seem to be formidable obstacles. First, reconciliation terminology does not appear as frequently as one might expect—only fifteen instances, all but two of which occur in the Pauline Letters. And most of these instances refer explicitly to what is often called the vertical axis of reconciliation, the reconciliation between God and human beings, rather than to the so-called horizontal axis, the reconciliation between and among peoples. Second, the New Testament writings are largely concerned with *intracommunity* issues rather than sociopolitical ones. This should come as little surprise since the authors wrote to relatively small numbers of Christ-believers, many of them Gentiles who were struggling to mature in the new life to which they had been called. The authors thus focused inwardly on their nascent communities, whose existence was precarious and vulnerable in the face of external forces. Third, the New Testament evinces in several places the expectation that the *parousia*, the return of the Lord Jesus in glory to usher in the fullness of God's kingdom, was imminent; this expectation would seem to render moot a concern for the sociopolitical order.

These obstacles, however, are more apparent than real. The New Testament does in fact have something significant to say about reconciliation—especially concerning its theological basis and implications for the church. While it is essential to start with the explicit references to reconciliation, we will see that proper exegesis requires that we expand our consideration beyond them. Although the New Testament writings are concerned in large part with the formation of communities of faith, they also make clear that the life of faith is conducted in the world and has transformative witness value. In fact, the latter is all the more urgent in light of the eschatological outpouring of God's Spirit, an outpouring that enables the beginning of the enactment of the restoration of relationships as part of the new creation foretold in the prophets (especially Isaiah).

In this essay, I narrow the focus to the question, what does the *Pauline* corpus say about reconciliation, including its social dimension? There are a number of reasons for so limiting the scope of study, one of which is consideration of space. As already noted, the vast majority of references to reconciliation occur in the Pauline Letters. Zeroing in on key passages will allow for more exegetical analysis, the careful investigation of the biblical texts themselves. Moreover, a critical social situation Paul dealt with, the relationship between Gentile and Jewish believer, can suggest some interesting analogues in today's context.

It is also appropriate to focus this investigation on Paul because he is the one who is generally recognized as giving reconciliation language its particular Christian stamp. Prior to him, the verbs *diallassō* and *katallassō* ("reconcile") and the noun *katallagē* ("reconciliation") were used in Hellenistic literature mostly with reference to *interpersonal* relations. Presuming a prior condition of enmity between parties, they expressed the change of condition from enmity and division to one of peace and friendship. They were thus typically employed in political and diplomatic contexts (e.g., treaties between warring factions),[1] as well as in contexts of conflicts between citizens and in marital disputes. In short, Hellenistic usage pointed to the horizontal axis of reconciliation. A different application, from Hellenistic Judaism, appeared in the second century BCE when the author of 2 Maccabees used *katallassō* to express *God's* being reconciled with his people (1:5;

5:20; 7:33; 8:29) following a period of divine anger. In this case, God is the one who is reconciled in response to his people's suffering (even martyrdom) and to their supplication in prayer.

The *novum* introduced by Paul is his insistence that *God* is the agent of reconciliation. God is the one who reconciles people to himself, not vice versa; in fact, *only* God could so act and, through Christ, defeat the enslaving powers of sin and death. Even more, God does so as an expression of divine mercy and love. Paul thus highlights the vertical axis of reconciliation. But, as we will see, he still draws on the Hellenistic understanding of reconciliation as involving the amelioration of interpersonal relationships—within the *ekklēsia* and beyond. This horizontal axis of reconciliation is not always appreciated by Pauline commentators, many of whom concentrate solely on the vertical axis.[2] The vertical and horizontal axes of reconciliation go hand in hand for Paul. There is not one without the other, though the vertical axis does play the primary role: it is the reconciliation God has brought about through Christ that makes possible the restoration of social relations and subsequent peace in the "new creation" (2 Cor 5:17; Gal 6:15).

A final reason for limiting our study to the Pauline corpus is the growing recognition of the crucial importance of reconciliation in his theology. The question of what is the center of Paul's theology—justification by faith? Christ mysticism?—has long been debated. We need not enter into that debate here. Ralph P. Martin has been a leading proponent for the centrality of reconciliation in Paul's theology.[3] Whether or not Paul's theology has one center around which all else pivots, N. T. Wright gives voice to a growing sentiment among Pauline scholars when he claims, "Paul's aims and intentions can be summarized under the word *katallagē*, 'reconciliation.'"[4] This scholarly emphasis is no accident, as social reconciliation is among the greatest needs today in our world that is marked by violence and displacement of millions of peoples. Hence, to the Apostle's treatment of reconciliation we now turn. In what follows, I examine at some length his understanding of reconciliation in 2 Corinthians and Romans, the two undisputed letters where he explicitly takes up the topic. Next, I turn briefly to the treatment of reconciliation in Ephesians, considered by some scholars to have been written after Paul's death. In the final section, I summarize the findings in a series of bullet points.

I. Reconciliation in 2 Corinthians

Daniel J. Harrington observed that "many biblical scholars regard 2 Corinthians as the most difficult document in the New Testament. Paul is often emotional and elliptical and so the reader needs to supply what Paul left unsaid in his hurry to express himself."[5] The challenge to interpret 2 Corinthians includes the reconstruction of events that led to its writing.[6] For our purposes, it is sufficient to note that the relationship between some in the community and its founding Apostle had broken down. Paul's apostolic credentials had been called into question, as well as his way of preaching the gospel. One member of the community had challenged his authority, which led, ultimately, to this person's ostracization by the majority of the assembly (see 2 Cor 2:5–6; 7:11). Paul's work on a relief collection for the Jewish Christ-believers in Rome had come to a standstill (8:10–11), possibly because of suspicions of financial improprieties (12:17–18). In short, the Apostle felt compelled to clear the air, to defend his ministry, and to rebuild bridges.

Paul insists that God has made him a minister of a new covenant (2 Cor 3:6), a ministry characterized by the Spirit's empowerment (3:8) and by righteousness (3:9). Later on in his impassioned apologia (2:14—7:4), he introduces reconciliation language. In fact, 5:18–20 contains the most concentrated use of reconciliation language in Paul's letters. There he announces that, through Christ, God has reconciled people to himself and has given to "us" the ministry of reconciliation (5:18). He then explains what God's act of reconciliation involves: the forgiveness of sins ("not counting their trespasses against them"; 5:19)[7]. Similar to the bestowal of the ministry of reconciliation, Paul claims that God now entrusts to "us" the message of reconciliation (5:19). He goes on to announce that "we" are ambassadors through whom God makes the appeal: "Be reconciled to God" (5:20). Although the first person plural pronouns in these verses refer minimally to the Apostle and those like him who have been called to proclaim the gospel, we will see that the logic of the passage entails a wider reference to all those who are in Christ.

The next verse (2 Cor 5:21) is a theologically loaded statement. Paul declares, "For our sake [God] made the one [i.e.,

Christ] who did not know sin to be sin, so that in him we might become the righteousness of God" (au. trans.). In the words of one commentator, this verse "invites us to tread on sacred ground."[8] It is enough to highlight here Paul's insistence on *God's* activity throughout this passage: God is the one who has taken the initiative to act on behalf of the world. And God has done so through his Son. More specifically, God's work of reconciliation has taken place through Jesus's death, as the phrase "made to be sin" is an allusion to the sin offering described in Leviticus 4:1—5:13, a sacrifice of an unblemished animal that restored one's relationship with God.[9] Notice, too, that Paul reveals that God has so acted that "we"—here, a reference to all who open themselves to God's gift of reconciliation—might become "the righteousness of God." We will return to this point shortly.

A key to understanding 2 Corinthians 5:18–21 is to recognize the clues in the preceding verses that suggest that Paul's understanding of reconciliation was influenced by personal experience, namely his experience on the Damascus road.[10] Prior to his encounter with the risen Christ, Paul was a persecutor of the followers of Jesus. As a Pharisee zealously devoted to the Jewish law, he regarded Jesus as a lawbreaker and as one whose death on a cross was one cursed by God (Deut 21:23; see Gal 3:13). The claims made by Jesus's followers—that he was Messiah and Lord—sounded like blasphemy to Paul the Pharisee's ears. Then came his dramatic encounter with the risen Jesus, whom he experienced not only as living but also as imbuing the glory of God. Moreover, the risen Lord called him to proclaim the gospel to Gentiles (Gal 1:16). To say the least, Paul's world was turned upside down. He alludes to these things in 2 Corinthians 5:14–16. Though Paul once regarded Jesus from "a fleshly point of view" (au. trans.; i.e., as a false messiah), he does so no longer. Jesus *is* the Messiah and Lord (5:16). Indeed, the Apostle has come to the determination that Jesus's death was "for all," so that people might live not for themselves (i.e., for self-aggrandizement) but in service of others, as did Jesus (5:15). Most significantly, his experience revealed Jesus's love for him, which has become a compelling force in his life and ministry (5:14; see also Gal 2:20).

Paul's Damascus experience lies just underneath the surface in two other passages in 2 Corinthians. In 4:6, Paul names

God as the one "who has shone in our hearts to give the light of the knowledge of the glory of God in the face of Jesus Christ," a description that evokes a christophany, the revelation of "the image of God" (4:4). In 2:14–16, he employs imagery from the Roman triumph, an elaborate procession that was celebrated following a great military victory.[11] Interestingly, Paul depicts God as the conquering general and himself as one of the captured prisoners who was being paraded in the triumphal procession. This striking imagery—used in the context of the Apostle's expression of thanksgiving!—conveys, among other things, his keen awareness that, in his persecution of Jesus's followers, he was conducting himself as God's enemy. In that context, God reached out to him through the risen Lord Jesus.[12]

At this point, it will be helpful to take stock of what can be gleaned from the allusions to Paul's Damascus experience in relation to his understanding of reconciliation. Typically, the offending person is the one who must initiate the process of reconciliation. In this case, however, God—the offended party—is the one who takes the initiative.[13] God does so toward one who had made himself God's enemy, forgiving his sins. It is little wonder that a recurring theme in Paul's letters is *grace*, which he himself had so profoundly experienced. The divine outreach came at great cost, the death of God's Son Jesus. Yet this self-giving unto death was in actuality an expression of love, a love whose power overcame death (recall that it is the *risen* Lord who appeared to Paul). Finally, God has now called Paul to be an "ambassador for Christ" through whom God continues to make his appeal to people to be reconciled. But before pursuing this latter theme, there is another underlying feature of the reconciliation passage in 2 Corinthians that will be fruitful to explore.

Commentators have long noted the presence of allusions and echoes from the prophet Isaiah in 2 Corinthians 5:17—6:2. In 5:17, Paul declares, "So if anyone is in Christ, there is a new creation: everything old has passed away; see, everything has become new!" The language of old things passing and new things coming to be recalls Isaiah 43:18–19 and 65:17. The latter passage, with its reference to God's making new heavens and a new earth, is also evocative of "new creation." The sinless one's sacrifice in 5:21 has been linked to the fourth Isaian servant song (Isa 52:13—53:12),[14]

including the notion that the servant "shall make many righteous" (53:11; see also Paul's "we might become the righteousness
of God"). And in 2 Corinthians 6:2, Paul quotes and appropriates
Isaiah 49:8—"At an acceptable time I have listened to you, / and
on a day of salvation I have helped you." This line follows the
third Isaian servant song, where God bolsters the discouraged servant and confirms his vocation not only to restore Israel but also
to extend God's salvation to the nations.

These allusions and echoes come from the part of Isaiah
(chaps. 40—66) in which the prophet announces that God is acting to redeem and restore Israel after her captivity in Babylon. The
exile is over, not because of anything Israel has done, but because
of God's loving mercy. And in bringing back Israel from exile, God
is transforming the people and all of creation so that peace and
reconciliation abound among peoples. Indeed, God's outreach of
salvation will extend "to the end of the earth" (Isa 49:6), even to
the Gentiles.[15] Finally, at the heart of this outreach are the min-
istrations of the mysterious figure of the servant, whose suffering
has borne the sins of the many.

In echoing and appropriating texts from Isaiah, Paul suggests
that the Prophet's vision is now being fulfilled in what God has
done through Christ's suffering and death.[16] This is in line with the
allusions in 2 Corinthians 2:3–6 to Ezekiel 11:36 and Jeremiah 31
concerning the new covenant and the outpouring of God's Spirit
in human hearts. Paul regards the Christ-event and the gift of the
Spirit as the fulfillment of the great prophetic promises. Perti-
nent to our topic is how the Isaian vision of restoration and peace
between people gives meaning and texture to the ministry of reconciliation. According to Corneliu Constantineanu, "the 'great
new thing' God has done in Christ, the reconciliation of the world,
is not something that affects only [people's] relationship with God
but also their living together, as reconciled people, in the midst of
concrete historical circumstances."[17] Moreover, the *ekklēsia* is to be
an agent of reconciliation beyond itself so that it touches upon
the world (i.e, "to the end of the earth").[18] So will the great Isaian
vision of restoration and peace be fulfilled (e.g., Isa 60:18–22).

Although Paul makes clear in 2 Corinthians 5:18—6:2 the primacy of God's activity, that is, of the vertical axis of reconciliation,
the message/ministry of reconciliation must still be proclaimed

and enacted. While this entails the fundamental proclamation "Be reconciled to God" (5:20), it also involves effort along the horizontal axis of reconciliation. We are now better positioned to appreciate Paul's role as ambassador, even as God's coworker (6:1), in this project. While Jesus is the principal referent of the Isaian servant, recall that the Apostle has also appropriated this role to himself. God has encouraged Paul that his toil among the Corinthians has not been in vain (cf. Isa 49:4). Paul in turn encourages the community (2 Cor 5:21b—6:2), as all the members of the church have important roles to play. Those who have been reconciled by God's grace are called and empowered to be reconcilers. Indeed, the new covenant ministry (3:6) is actualized in a preeminent way through the ministry of reconciliation (5:18), which is a manifestation of the outreach of "the righteousness of God" (5:21), that is, of God's covenant faithfulness.[19]

That Paul's understanding of reconciliation entails the horizontal axis is evident from various elements of 2 Corinthians. The letter itself has as its main purpose the inculcation of reconciliation between the Apostle and the community: "Our heart is wide open to you [Corinthians]. There is no restriction in our affections, but only in yours. In return—I speak as to children—open wide your hearts also [to us]" (6:11–13; see also 7:2–4). Paul is passionate that the Corinthians appreciate and accept his manner of exercising his apostleship, for it embodies the gospel he proclaims. Rejection of him is rejection of the gospel; that is why he pleads with them "not to accept the grace of God in vain" (6:1). Reconciliation begins at home. In addition, Paul models reconciliation and forgiveness in 2:5–10, where he takes the initiative to forgive the person who had offended him and encourages the entire assembly to do the same and restore this person to fellowship in the community. What is striking is that Paul does not wait for this person to apologize or repent. He thereby imitates God's way of dealing with him. (We will return to the issue of forgiveness at the end of the essay.) The Apostle's statement that Satan's designs are served by divisions in the community speaks to the importance of reconciliation (2:11).

The need for reconciliation goes beyond Corinth, however. In 2 Corinthians 8:1—9:15, Paul gives a lengthy exhortation to the mostly Gentile Corinthian *ekklēsia* to be generous in giving to the collection for the members of the church in Jerusalem. It is significant that he calls the collection a "ministry to the holy ones" (au. trans. of 8:4; 9:1), which hints that it is an expression of the ministry of reconciliation. While the collection responded to economic need, it also expressed for Paul the reconciliation between Gentile believers and Jewish believers—in fulfillment of Isaiah's vision (see Isa 56:1–8)—as well as their new identity as brothers and sisters in Christ (see Rom 15:26–27).[20] The liturgical language at the end of the passage (2 Cor 9:11–15) points to the *koinōnia* between churches and how God is praised by generosity. Admittedly an implicit theme in 2 Corinthians 8—9, reconciliation between Gentile and Jewish believers will become prominent in Romans.

II. Reconciliation in Romans

Paul wrote this letter from Corinth not long after penning 2 Corinthians. Romans is unique among the undisputed Pauline Letters in that it was written to communities the Apostle did not found. It contains his most sustained and systematic treatment of the gospel he proclaims. Although he had not yet been to Rome, his farewell greetings reveal that he knew several people who now lived there (Rom 16:1–16). These friends and coworkers are likely the source of Paul's knowledge of the various challenges and tensions faced by the house churches in the capital of the empire. It is widely accepted that the gospel first came to Rome through Jews who were Christ-believers, though by the time Paul wrote, Gentiles were in the majority. Some of the challenges and tensions involved food regulations and observance of religious feast days (14:1–6), issues pertaining to synagogue practice.[21] Another tension was the result of the recent return of some Jewish believers from the exile of leading Jews imposed by the emperor Claudius.[22] The expulsion had created a leadership vacuum in some of the house churches, a vacuum that had since been filled. The returning exiles thus came back to a different situation than the one they had left.[23] In short, Jewish–Gentile relations loom large in Romans.

Paul raises the theme of reconciliation in Romans 5:10–11. He does so following his lengthy treatment of the figure of Abraham

(4:1–25), where he insisted that the latter is the father of the family of faith consisting of both Gentile and Jewish believers (4:11b–12). In 5:10–11, Paul refers to the reconciliation to God that has been effected through "the death of his Son," now raised from the dead. He insists on the gratuitous nature of God's act of reconciliation: God acted "while we were enemies" (5:10; see also Col 1:21–22)—recall the Apostle's personal experience—in the condition of being "ungodly" (Rom 5:6) and "sinners" (5:8).[24] Reconciliation is linked closely with justification (see the parallel structure in vv. 9 and 10), and thus involves the forgiveness of sins. Moreover, God's act demonstrated his love, the love revealed in that "Christ died for us" (5:8). Paul's condensed formulation requires unpacking. God shows the extent of divine love by holding nothing back from us, not even God's Son (see 8:32, where God is described as one "who did not withhold his own Son, but gave him up for all of us"). Jesus reveals this love by giving his life for us (see Gal 2:20; Eph 5:2). And this love has been poured into human hearts through the gift of the Spirit (Rom 5:5). This is the nucleus of the Pauline gospel.

As was the case in 2 Corinthians, so now in Romans, Paul's initial emphasis is on the vertical axis of reconciliation. But Romans 5:1–11 contains two clues that the horizontal axis is also involved. The first clue is the main clause of 5:1, which is rendered by the NRSV: "since we are justified by faith, we have [*echomen*] peace with God through our Lord Jesus Christ." However, there is stronger textual attestation for reading the main verb as a hortatory subjunctive, that is: "since we have been justified by faith, *let us have* [*echōmen*] peace with God."[25] The second clue is in 5:10, where Paul offers a lesser to greater argument: "For if while we were enemies, we were reconciled to God through the death of his Son, much more surely, having been reconciled, will we be saved by his life." Here the reconciliation effected through Christ's death is one (albeit essential) step on the way to salvation. The risen life of Jesus, mediated through the Holy Spirit,[26] then empowers a new way of life that leads to the fullness of salvation.

This new way entails the horizontal axis of reconciliation. To have peace with God in an ongoing manner (suggested by the exhortation "let us have peace") involves the outworking of reconciliation in the lives of individual believers and in the *ekklēsia*. For Paul, the gift becomes the task; the "indicative" of God's saving action and the "imperative" of the Christian moral life are two sides of one coin. God's reconciling people to himself through Christ—a costly yet quintessential expression of divine love—makes possible and calls for the ongoing work of reconciliation in the social sphere. In Romans, the horizontal axis largely involves reconciliation between Gentile and Jewish believers.

While Paul does not take up this theme until Romans 12:1—15:13, he lays the foundation for it in the paragraphs following 5:1–11. In 5:15–19, he evokes the "new creation" by portraying Christ as the new Adam through whose obedience to God's will "many will be made righteous." In 6:3–14, he sets forth his teaching that, through baptism, believers participate in the death and resurrection of Christ, becoming members of his Body (see also 12:5; 1 Cor 12:12–13), empowered to become obedient "instruments of righteousness." The references to righteous/ness here recall 2 Corinthians 5:21, where becoming the righteousness of God is linked to reconciliation. Finally, in Romans 8:1–30, Paul discusses the outpouring of the Spirit, which, recall, is the sign that the time of fulfillment of the prophetic promises has arrived (including Isaiah's vision of peace and reconciliation). The Spirit conforms recipients into the likeness of Christ, the "firstborn" of the family of faith (8:29), and enables them to fulfill "the just requirement of the law" (8:4), which the Apostle will soon explicate as the way of love (13:8–10).

The way of love laid out in Romans 12:1—15:13 can be captured, in large part, by the notion of reconciliation. Here I anticipate a possible objection, namely that reconciliation language does not appear in these chapters. Constantineanu rightly counters, however, arguing "for the need to consider the larger symbolism that Paul is employing and by which he gives expression."[27] This symbolism includes concepts like love, generosity, hospitality, mutual welcome, peace, and unity. Moreover, Paul begins this entire unit by appealing to "the mercies of God" (12:1), which recalls God's initiative, out of love, to reconcile sinners to himself (5:6–11). His use of the body metaphor—"we, who are many, are one body in Christ" (12:5)—emphasizes the communal arena in which the life of faith is enacted and suggests the interdependence of all the members.

Paul then exhorts the believers in Rome to a number of "reconciling practices"[28] (Rom 12:9–13, 15–16). In practicing "genuine" love, they are to be magnanimous in showing honor to one another. This counteracts the competition and envy that often result when people seek first their own honor. Paul encourages generosity in response to the needs of fellow believers, who are to be regarded as brothers and sisters. He calls for the practice of hospitality, opening the door in welcome to others—a particularly apt call in the context of a network of house churches. Paul also exhorts his readers to "live in harmony" with one another, which entails being aware of and sensitive to the plight of others ("rejoice with those who rejoice, weep with those who weep"; 12:15). He thus summons the Roman believers to a strong sense of solidarity with one another, especially with the poor and marginalized ("associate with the lowly"; 12:16).

Paul's exhortations in Romans 12 are general. Beginning at 14:1, they become more specific, dealing with particular issues that threaten to rend apart the community. The issues involved the observance of kosher food laws and religious festivals. Although the issues were grounded in Jewish practices, it is too simplistic to place the fault line rigidly between Jewish and Gentile believers (observe that Paul aligns himself with those who are free with regard to such practices). What is important to appreciate is that the issues impinged upon table fellowship and worship. Paul's initial response is twofold. First, he places the disagreements—ones that did not have clear resolutions—within the context of God's inclusive mercy. Each member on both sides of the debate has already been welcomed by God (14:3). Thus they should learn to handle areas of disagreement in ways that do not divide.[29] Second, he condemns two attitudes that have no place within a reconciled community: on the one hand, passing judgment in condemnation of others; on the other hand, holding in contempt those considered to be "weak" (14:10).

While Paul initially takes no sides in the debate (Rom 14:1–12), he goes on to admonish one side—the so-called "strong," who, in good conscience, considered themselves free regarding Jewish food laws (14:13—15:6). In short, he admonishes them to realize that it is more important to love than to insist on one's rights. They are to look upon other community members not only as brothers and sisters, but as brothers and sisters *for whom Christ died*" (14:15; italics added).[30] Paul reminds the "strong" that

God's kingdom concerns "righteousness and peace and joy in the Holy Spirit" (14:17)—all marks of reconciliation—and that this calls forth the commitment to "pursue what makes for peace and for mutual upbuilding" (14:19). And they are to imitate Christ, who did not seek to please himself but to serve and give his life for others (15:3). The Spirit's empowerment to be conformed to Christ, the firstborn of many brothers and sisters (8:29), means growing more and more to resemble the "family likeness." This means setting aside insistence on one's ways in order to act for the good of others, to seek what makes for peace.

Paul ends his lengthy exhortation with a simple plea in Romans 15:7–13: "Welcome one another, therefore, just as Christ has welcomed you." Here he refers explicitly to Gentiles and Jews, and states that the coming together of Gentiles and Jews in the family of faith is for the glory of God.[31] We will return to this image when we look at Ephesians 2. But one other feature of this paragraph is worth pointing out, namely the chain of Scripture passages Paul employs. The concluding citation, regarding the root of Jesse, is from Isaiah 11:10. Once again, Paul draws on the prophet Isaiah. Significantly, the citation's broader context (11:1—12:6) describes the renewal of the created order, the restoration of Israel, and the summons to the "nations" (the same term in Greek that is rendered "Gentiles") to join the community of salvation. But for this more universal vision to be realized, the scope of the practices of reconciliation must widen.

Paul has already widened the scope in a passage that we momentarily passed over, Romans 12:14, 17–21. The fact that this passage is interspersed with intracommunity concerns (vv. 15–16) suggests the all-encompassing scope of practices of reconciliation. The passage consists of four paired contrasting exhortations:[32]

> Do not curse your persecutors // Call God's blessing on them
> Do not retaliate // Take forethought of how to live nobly + live peaceably with all
> Do not avenge yourselves // Give food and drink to your enemies
> Do not be overcome by evil // Overcome evil with good

While it is not clear whether the believers in Rome were experiencing hostility from outsiders at the time Paul wrote, he was certainly aware of the opposition that the gospel provoked (see, e.g., 2 Cor 1:8–10; 4:8–12; 6:5). His exhortation in Romans 12:17 to "think beforehand" (au. trans. of *pronoeō*) shows that he expects the community to be prepared for how they will act in the face of enmity.

In these verses, Paul proposes three practices of reconciliation concerning outsiders, including one's enemies: words of blessing, nonretaliation, and charitable actions. In exhorting the believers in Rome to "bless those who persecute you," he intends that they pray for their enemies, calling on God to bestow his gracious blessing upon them. Commentators are divided on whether this prayer includes asking God to show them mercy and forgiveness, though the fact that the Apostle himself offers no caveat suggests (at least to me) that the prayer for blessing be completely magnanimous. The call to nonretaliation means no personal revenge or quid pro quo retribution. Positively, Paul advises loving actions (e.g., feeding the hungry enemy), acting so as to bring no disapprobation to the community, and doing what is in one's power to live peaceably with all. He insists on leaving vindication and vengeance to God. Now, whether Paul's teaching has literal applicability in modern situations he did not envision, such as genocide, can rightly be called into question. But in general terms vis-à-vis the commitment to social reconciliation, his fundamental conviction stands: "Christians are called to the unilateral pursuit of peace."[33] In doing so, they imitate God's reconciling action through Christ.

III. Reconciliation in Ephesians

Reconciliation language also appears in Ephesians. Because of some stylistic[34] and theological differences, many scholars consider this writing as coming from another hand after Paul's death. Even if that is the case, its Pauline character is not in dispute. A circular letter directed to Gentile Christ-believers, Ephesians is regarded as an apt epitome of Paul's theology. A key theme in it is the revelation of the *mystērion* of the gospel, the eternal plan of

God to unite all things in Christ (Eph 1:9–10). God, who is "rich in mercy, out of the great love with which he loved us," has brought about salvation through Christ (2:1–10) and bestowed "the promised Holy Spirit" as a seal and down payment, as it were, of our salvation (1:13–14).

In Ephesians 2:13–18, the author employs the language and imagery of reconciliation. While the vertical axis of reconciliation is maintained—through the cross, both Gentiles and Jews have been reconciled to God (2:16)—the focus is on the horizontal axis, the reconciliation between Gentiles and Jews. The imagery is dramatic. Christ Jesus, "our peace…has made us [i.e., Jews and Gentiles] both one, and has knocked down the dividing wall of hostility" (au. trans. of 2:14). The latter is an allusion to the wall in the Jerusalem temple complex beyond which Gentiles could not pass, which symbolized for the author deeply engrained social division and hostility. Through his death (and resurrection), Christ has broken the barrier in order "that he might create in himself one new humanity [*anthrōpos*]…, thus making peace" (2:15). Now, as William S. Campbell points out, not only is the dividing wall a metaphor; so, too, "the new *anthrōpos* image is a metaphorical representation of the reconciliation effected by Christ between Jew and gentile."[35] The point of the metaphor is not that differences are done away with. Rather, through Christ and the transforming power of the Spirit, the ways that differences—whether ethnic, social, economic, gender, etcetera—tend to divide can be overcome (see also Gal 3:28).

It is no accident that in Ephesians 2:17 the author evokes the prophet Isaiah when he writes that Christ "proclaimed peace to you who were far off and peace to those who were near" (Isa 59:17; see also 52:7).[36] Once again, the prophetic vision of reconciliation is being fulfilled through Christ and the outpouring of the Spirit (Eph 2:18). Taking up the temple imagery from Ephesians 2:14, the author then states that the members of the *ekklēsia*, consisting of Jews and Gentiles, are growing into a "holy temple," "a dwelling place of God in the Spirit" (2:19–22 RSV). This entails a *process*.[37] The indicative of divine reconciliation calls forth and enables the diverse membership of the *ekklēsia* to grow in unity and love. Indeed it is the church's primary vocation to reveal to the world the outworking of God's reconciling power—"the mystery hidden for ages" but now

17

revealed in Christ—by embodying unity in diversity among its members (3:9–10). The reconciled family of faith that is the church is to be an alternative community in contrast to the world's ways of violence and division.[38]

With this latter observation, we finally arrive at why reconciliation is so important for Paul. For him, the greatest "proof" of the efficacy of the Christ-event is the *ekklēsia*—especially in its local instantiations—bearing witness to reconciliation. When Gentiles and Jews, rich and poor, slaves and free come together and truly regard and treat one another as brothers and sisters in Christ, they manifest the ongoing power of resurrection life. Paul's passion for his churches giving such witness can be seen in his virtue and vice lists. The vices against which he rails most vehemently are those that cause division and break down communities (e.g., Rom 1:29–31; Gal 5:19–21). Conversely, the qualities to which he exhorts his followers are those that build up the community and inculcate peace. One of the best examples, if not *the* best one, is the list of qualities delineated in Colossians 3:12–14:[39]

> As God's chosen ones, holy and beloved, clothe yourselves with compassion, kindness, humility, meekness, and patience. Bear with one another and, if anyone has a complaint against another, forgive each other; just as the Lord has forgiven you, so you also must forgive. Above all, clothe yourselves with love....

The virtues enumerated here are the marks of being conformed more and more into the likeness of Christ (Rom 8:29). Observe, moreover, the reference to forgiveness. The stress on forgiveness makes clear Paul's insistence that forgiveness is what makes reconciliation along the horizontal axis truly possible.

IV. Concluding Reflections

What can be gleaned from the preceding analysis of Paul's teaching on reconciliation? I offer the following bullet points to provide a foundation from which to reflect on the broader issue of social reconciliation. While the Apostle cannot be made to speak for the whole New Testament (not to mention the entire Bible), the importance of the theme for him merits our attention to what he sets forth:

- Reconciliation is, first and foremost, a gift from God who, through love and mercy, extends the offer of forgiveness of sins through the death (and resurrection) of Christ. This vertical dimension makes possible and calls forth the horizontal axis of reconciliation.

- Reconciliation and peace among peoples are central to God's promises of the "new creation" as set forth in the Old Testament, especially in the prophet Isaiah. These promises have been (at least initially) fulfilled through Christ, and God's Spirit continues to animate their fulfillment. Devotion to God's word and openness to the Spirit's empowerment and lead are sine qua nons for the work of social reconciliation.

- Paul's understanding of reconciliation is grounded in a profound personal experience of God's love and mercy, an experience that compelled his work for reconciliation. While the Apostle's particular experience was unique, ways exist for people to inculcate personal appropriation of God's merciful love (e.g., the First Week exercises of St. Ignatius Loyola's *Spiritual Exercises*).

- Like charity, the work and ministry of reconciliation begins at home, that is, within local communities of the Body of Christ. The church's embodiment of unity in diversity not only bears witness to the possibility of reconciliation; it provides credibility for the outreach of the ministry of reconciliation beyond itself.

- Reconciliation as Paul proposes it entails not only the willingness to forgive others, but even more, taking the initiative to do so. Love trumps insistence upon one's own ways. Crucial to this way of living is regarding and treating one's fellows as "brothers and sisters for whom Christ died."

- Generosity, hospitality, and sensitivity to the plight of the poor and suffering are essential practices of reconciliation.
- Members of the Body of Christ are to be committed to nonretaliation in the face of hostility. Rather than take vengeance, they are to bless their enemies and act for their benefit, taking the initiative in working for peace.

Reflection Questions

1. Why is it important to appreciate that reconciliation, as understood by Paul, is fundamentally *God's* work?
2. What experience(s) of mercy and compassion do I have out of which I approach the ministry of reconciliation?
3. What difference does it make that forgiveness of others is at the heart of Paul's teaching about reconciliation?
4. How can the perception of others as "brothers and sisters for whom Christ died" inculcate transformed relationships?
5. Who are contemporary analogues of the Jews and Gentiles to whom Paul ministered?

Notes

1. See Cilliers Breytenbach, *Versöhnung: Eine Studie zur paulinischen Soteriologie*, WMANT 60 (Neukirchen-Vluyn: Neukirchener, 1989).

2. Two exceptions are Corneliu Constantineanu, *The Social Significance of Reconciliation in Paul's Theology: Narrative Readings in Romans*, LNTS 421 (London: T & T Clark, 2010); and William S. Campbell, "'Let Us Maintain Peace' (Rom 5:2): Reconciliation and Social Responsibility," in *Unity & Diversity in Christ: Interpreting Paul in Context: Collected Essays* (Eugene, OR: Cascade, 2013), 169–86.

3. As expressed most thoroughly in his *Reconciliation: A Study of Paul's Theology*, New Foundations Theological Library (Atlanta: John Knox, 1981).

4. N. T. Wright, *Christian Origins and the Question of God*, vol. 4, *Paul and the Faithfulness of God* (Minneapolis: Fortress Press, 2013), 1487.

5. Daniel J. Harrington, *Who Is Jesus? Why Is He Important? An Invitation to the New Testament* (Franklin, WI: Sheed & Ward, 1999), 91.

6. See, e.g., Margaret E. Thrall, *A Critical and Exegetical Commentary on the Second Epistle to the Corinthians*, 2 vols. (Edinburgh: T & T Clark, 1994–2000), 1:49–74.

7. Quotations from the Bible are from the NRSV, unless otherwise indicated. My own translations are signaled by "au. trans." (for "author's translation").

8. Murray J. Harris, *The Second Epistle to the Corinthians*, New International Greek Testament Commentary (Grand Rapids, MI: Eerdmans, 2005), 456.

9. See Linda L. Belleville, *2 Corinthians*, IVP New Testament Commentary Series (Downers Grove, IL: InterVarsity, 1996), 159.

10. See also, e.g., Seyoon Kim, "2 Cor. 5:11–21 and the Origin of Paul's Concept of 'Reconciliation,'" *Novum Testamentum* 34 (1997): 360–84; and Constantineanu, *The Social Significance of Reconciliation in Paul's Theology*, 65–73.

11. The relief panel on the Arch of Titus in Rome both depicts the procession that celebrated Titus's victory in the Jewish War and shows the spoils from Jerusalem.

12. See also Frank J. Matera, *II Corinthians: A Commentary* (Louisville: Westminster/John Knox, 2003), 72. "Paul is presenting himself as God's captive, whom God conquered in order to be his apostle and ambassador. Paul himself is deeply aware that he was God's enemy (1 Cor 15:9) and that he is now under a divine obligation to preach the gospel."

13. See John T. Fitzgerald, "Paul and Paradigm Shifts: Reconciliation and Its Linkage Group," in *Paul beyond the Judaism/Hellenism Divide*, ed. Troels Engberg-Pedersen (Louisville: Westminster/John Knox), 241–62.

14. See, e.g., Thomas D. Stegman, *Second Corinthians*, Catholic Commentary on Sacred Scripture (Grand Rapids, MI: Baker Academic, 2009), 144.

15. The same Greek word, *ethnē*, is rendered "nations" and "Gentiles."

16. See G. K. Beale, "The Old Testament Background of Reconciliation in 2 Corinthians 5–7 and Its Bearing on the Literary Problem of 2 Corinthians 6:14—7:1," *New Testament Studies* 35 (1989): 550–81.

17. Constantineanu, *The Social Significance of Reconciliation in Paul's Theology*, 87.

18. Constantineanu, *The Social Significance of Reconciliation in Paul's Theology*, 87.

19. For reading the phrase *dikaiosynē theou* as God's covenant faithfulness, see A. Katherine Grieb, "The Righteousness of God in Romans," in *Reading Paul's Letter to the Romans*, ed. Jerry L. Sumney (Atlanta: Society of Biblical Literature, 2012), 65–78.

20. See David J. Downs, *The Offering of the Gentiles: Paul's Collection for Jerusalem in Its Chronological, Cultural, and Cultic Contexts*, Wissenschaftliche Untersuchungen zum Neuen Testament 2/248 (Tübingen: Mohr Siebeck, 2008).

21. See, e.g., Joseph A. Fitzmyer, *Romans: A New Translation with Introduction and Commentary*, Anchor Bible 33 (New York: Doubleday, 1993), 26–36.

22. Claudius's edict occurred in 49 CE; it was rescinded when Nero became emperor in 54 CE. Scholars typically date Paul's letter to the Romans to ca. 57 CE.

23. For a full study on the early churches in Rome, see Peter Lampe, *From Paul to Valentinus: Christians at Rome in the First Two Centuries*, trans. M. Steinhauser (Minneapolis: Fortress Press, 2003).

24. See Rom 1:18–32; 2:17—3:20; 7:7–25 for Paul's assessment of the condition of humanity apart from Christ.

25. See also, e.g., Robert Jewett, *Romans*, Hermeneia (Minneapolis: Fortress Press, 2007), 344. The difference in Greek is one letter, omicron (short "o") or omega (long "o").

26. For more on the connection between the resurrection of Jesus and the bestowal of the Spirit, see Luke Timothy Johnson, *The Writings of the New Testament: An Interpretation*, 3rd ed. (Minneapolis: Fortress Press, 2010), 95–109.

27. Constantineanu, *The Social Significance of Reconciliation in Paul's Theology*, 21. See also Campbell, "'Let Us Maintain Peace' (Rom 15:2)," 174–75.

28. I take the term from Constantineanu, *The Social Significance of Reconciliation in Paul's Theology*, 145.

29. See Brendan Byrne, *Romans*, Sacra Pagina 6 (Collegeville, MN: Liturgical Press, 1996), 406.

30. Recall the transformed way of thinking in 2 Cor 5:16 mentioned earlier, now with reference to how one looks at other members of the community.

31. As was the case with the conclusion of 2 Cor 8:1—9:15, so here Paul employs much liturgical language.

32. I follow here Gordon Zerbe's structural analysis. See his "Paul's Ethic of Nonretaliation and Peace," in *The Love of Enemy and Nonretaliation in the New Testament*, ed. Willard M. Swartley (Louisville: Westminster/John Knox, 1992), 181–82.

33. Zerbe, "Paul's Ethic of Nonretaliation and Peace," 204.

34. E.g., *apokatallassō* for "reconcile" rather than *katallassō* as in 2 Corinthians and Romans.

35. William S. Campbell, "Unity and Diversity in the Church: Transformed Identities and the Peace of Christ in Ephesians," in *Unity & Diversity in Christ: Interpreting Paul in Context: Collected Essays* (Eugene, OR: Cascade, 2013), 134.

36. The statement in Eph 2:14 that Christ "is our peace" alludes to the "prince of peace" in Isa 9:5.

37. See Campbell, "Unity and Diversity in the Church," 138–43.

38. See Wright, *Paul and the Faithfulness of God*, 1484–1504.

39. Colossians is the other letter in which the theme of God's reconciliation through Christ is explicit (1:20, 22).

CHAPTER 2

Reconciliation with Material Creation

LESSONS FROM THE SECOND CENTURY

John J. O'Keefe

More than any other time in the history of the human race we stand in need of reconciliation with the material world, or, to cast this need in the language of Christian theology, we stand in need of reconciliation with creation. Our civilization is literally at war with the planet, and we citizens of this time are increasingly at war with our own materiality.

Such a statement may seem extreme or even wrongheaded. After all, when one considers the long swath of human history, it would be difficult to find a culture more interested in material prosperity and the physical dimension of human thriving than the late capitalist culture we now inhabit. We invest billions in the care of our enfleshment, we are obsessed with the extension of life, and we are convinced that this physical life is all there is. We profess to love it more than all things. Yet, despite our professions of devotion, we secretly hate the world we inhabit. We hate the limitations our bodies impose on us. We despise the material limits of the Earth. We want a bigger planet, a new planet, a planet that yields to our will, one that does not insist on killing

24

us and recycling our matter to make space for new life. We detest our creaturehood, and our destructive rage is manifest all over the very Earth we profess to love so much.

As a scholar trained in the world of ancient Christianity, it strikes me that there is a surprising resemblance between our contemporary attitudes toward the material creation and the attitudes of ancient anti-materialist Christians, whom Christian scholars usually refer to collectively as "Gnostics." I will explain shortly some problems associated with the term *Gnostic*. For the moment, let it suffice to say that these anti-materialist Christians were convinced that there was something wrong with the world in which we find ourselves. This world was far from spirit, subject to decay, and destined for destruction. God, they hoped, through Christ, would lead them out of this world into one more consistent with their desires, a world of spirit and bliss, a world unfettered by the dense weight of bodies.

On the surface, these ancient anti-materialists would appear to have little in common with twenty-first-century, body-loving, late capitalists, but I would like to suggest that both share a deep dissatisfaction with the material creation as it actually exists and long for one more consistent with their fantasies. We, like them, want to live in a different world, one not subject to limitation, decay, and death. We may not want a world of pure spirit, but we do want a world that is more like that than we care to admit; we want a material existence purged of suffering, where matter does our bidding and where we are free to enjoy all its pleasure with none of its pain. We are, paradoxically, materialistic anti-materialists.

In this paper I would like to suggest that a reconsideration of the second-century Christian struggle to defend the material creation can provide a helpful framework for contemporary Christians who are attempting to foster a deeper and more intimate communion with the Earth.

As a point of entry, it might be helpful to turn to an often-misquoted passage from *Against the Heresies*[1] by Irenaeus of Lyons. Irenaeus was one of the most important theologians of the second century, and he spent his career in a protracted battle with other Christian groups whose teachings included a systematic denigration of the material creation. Searching for Irenaeus on Google, however, does not yield this impression. According to the search engines, Irenaeus is the one who said, "The glory of God is the human person fully alive." In general, this text and translation are attached to statements expressive of contemporary spirituality, which emphasizes God's desire to foster the emotional flourishing of God's followers. However, a close look at the passage in the surviving Latin suggests that Irenaeus meant something quite different when he wrote this. What Irenaeus actually wrote was this: "For the glory of God is the living man, and the life of man is the vision of God."[2] While this translation removes the possibility of thinking Irenaeus was the progenitor of a contemporary spirituality of self-care, it does get us closer to the concerns that dominated his theological life.

Here is what I mean. This quotation appears at the end of an extended meditation on the significance of Genesis 2:7, which he interpreted through statements by Paul in 1 Corinthians 15.[3] According to the text from Genesis, "the LORD God formed man *from the dust of the ground*, and breathed into his nostrils the breath of life; and the man became a living being" (emphasis added). In 1 Corinthians, Paul builds on this story, explaining how Christ, as the new Adam, fulfills the promise of this first creation by re-creating the living man (Adam) into an imperishable being through the resurrection of Christ (the new Adam). Irenaeus, in turn, builds upon Paul to make a point about how "the dust man"—the earthling, if you will—gives glory to God precisely by being an embodied spiritual being. This claim contrasts with the position of Irenaeus's opponents who think that the creation of the dust man was an error and an affront to the dignity of God.

Irenaeus goes on to insist not only that the one true God made the dust man, but he also made *this world* for him to live in, and he made it intentionally. This God, Irenaeus explains,

> created and adorned and contains everything. This "everything" includes *us and our world*. We too, with everything the world contains, were made by him. Of him scripture says, "And God formed man, taking dust of the earth, and he breathed in his face a breath of life."

Irenaeus goes on to say that this same Creator God "assigned *this world* to the human race," and through the incarnation will

26

deliver it and them to their imperishable potential. For Irenaeus, "this world" is an intentional project of God, just as the higher, spiritual parts of the cosmos were also God's project; this world, too, gives glory to God. Thus Irenaeus is arguing that in this "living man," this man of dust, this earthling, is "the Glory of God." Far from being a vague reference to psychospiritual maturation, the phrase "the glory of God is the living man" exposes the earthy center of Irenaean thought.

The presence of this promaterialist vision, however, can be difficult to see for several reasons. First, the biblical texts Irenaeus discusses are very familiar. Because of this, it can be easy to read past them and miss their contextual significance. Second and more significantly, we do not understand the significance of their cosmological references. To understand their concerns about matter and materiality, we must take their cosmological references literally. After all, we take our own cosmological references literally. When we say, for example, that the Earth is a planet in the Milky Way galaxy, we believe that the earth is indeed located in that place; the Milky Way is not a symbolic or metaphorical reference to a state of being or to an existential horizon. To understand the ancients here, we need to grasp that for them the universe literally was divided into the higher and lower. The spirit world was literally "up there" above the path carved by the moon, and most fully realized up even higher—literally up—beyond the fixed stars. Our part of the universe was literally "here below" in the sublunar world, the realm of dense matter, physicality, and change. Again, the spiritual and the material worlds were to them literal locations in the cosmos in that same way that our sun, Sol, and the star Alpha Centauri are cosmic loci, not spiritual states. To focus our attention on the thicker meaning of ordinary words and to help us to remember to take cosmological references literally, I have added italics in previous and subsequent paragraphs. In this way, we will discern more easily the promaterial core that runs through the entire Irenaean project, a project that will have a significant impact on the later emergence of Christian Orthodoxy.

Irenaeus and Anti-Materialist Christians

Most students of the Christian tradition are familiar with the term *Gnostics*, which was invented in the nineteenth century to describe a set of ancient texts and ideas that seemed to coalesce around a dualistic and anticosmic worldview, a worldview that stood in contrast to Orthodoxy. According to this perspective, one recognized Gnostics by the fact that they were both not Orthodox and probably a little crazy. Recent scholarship has questioned this paradigm, with many scholars suggesting that the word *Gnostic* as a description of an ancient category or a group should be abandoned.[4] Arguments in favor of abandonment revolve around deepening scholarly convictions about the pluralist character of earliest Christianity. That is, scholars are increasingly aware that there were many varieties of Christianity in the first few centuries, and that only gradually did the tradition coalesce around what we now call "Orthodoxy," or the mainstream Christian tradition.[5] Many scholars worry that the term *Gnostic* evokes images of an original pristine "Orthodoxy" confronted by demonic heretical "Gnostic" sects. These images are historically false—there was no pristine *Orthodoxy* fighting a pristine *Heresy*; instead, they argue, there were diverse Christianities, one of which—the one scholars now call "proto-Orthodoxy"—would eventually dominate and become standard.[6] I am generally persuaded by the arguments in favor of abandoning the term *Gnostic* as a reference to an ancient category and have opted in this paper to refer instead to the opponents of Irenaeus as "anti-materialist Christians" rather than as "Gnostics."[7]

Theologian Stephen Webb accurately describes the anti-materialist impulse that captured the imaginations of many of these Christians when he observes that they were preoccupied with figuring out the value and purpose of the material part of the universe, the lower world in which we humans find ourselves embedded. These thinkers "found it unthinkable that God could have dirtied his hands directly in the lowly miasma of matter." As a corrective, "they turned Plato's Demiurge into an evil creator in order to preserve the goodness (that is, the immateriality) of the one true God." With their multileveled cosmos populated by layer after layer of intermediary powers, anti-materialists "are what you get when Neo-Platonism becomes philosophically eclectic and theologically fundamentalist." The visible world is no longer just a "pale shadow" of the real world, as it was for Plato and later Plotinus; it "must be fought to the death because it threatens to smother all our attempts to penetrate to the intelligible realm."[8]

As an example of this anti-materialist impulse among early Christians, let us consider the text *The Gospel of Truth*, a Valentinian homily[9] known to Irenaeus and, fortunately for us, preserved in the Nag Hammadi codices that were discovered in 1945.[10] "The gospel of truth," the author writes, "is joy for those who have received from the Father of truth the gift of knowing him through the power of the Word that came forth from the pleroma."[11] This Word is Jesus, who brings us knowledge of the true nature of things *in our world* and, in delivering this knowledge, offers us a means of escape from the material world.

Early in the homily, the author gives a brief account of the origins of the material world, which is especially apt here: "Ignorance of the Father brought about anguish and terror. And the anguish *grew solid like a fog* so that no one was able to see. For this reason, error became powerful; it fashioned its own matter foolishly, not having known the truth."[12] Clearly the Valentinian mythic narrative has little hope for bodies or materiality. They are a part of the cosmos that should not exist and that we must vacate as soon as we can. In the Valentinian myth presented here, the Platonic and Neoplatonic distinction between matter and spirit has been radicalized in precisely the ways that Webb suggests; the lower cosmos, the world of embodiment, is evil and must be overcome.

Irenaeus and Rhetoric

Scott Moringiello has pointed out that as a student of rhetoric, Irenaeus used all the tools available to him to oppose this worldview.[13] Thus, one of the best ways to approach the positions expressed in *Against the Heresies* is to see them as a form of persuasive speech, Irenaeus's preferred approach to theological reasoning. To understand Irenaeus, then, we need to remember that his arguments are primarily rhetorical rather than philosophical. Although Irenaeus was familiar with philosophical reasoning,[14] he was also quite suspicious of it, and even calls it at one point the "progenitor of the gnostic heresies he opposes."[15] Irenaeus wants his readers to be swept into accepting his vision of the gospel more by the persuasive power of his words than by the inevitability of his logic. So, we could say that in *Against the Heresies*, he presents to us a list of Gnostic foes who serve as foils to his own position. The rhetoric may exaggerate the difference, but the difference exists nonetheless.

The differences between Irenaeus and his Gnostic opponents surface most concretely around discussion of *our material world*. Like his opponents, Irenaeus believed that the cosmos was arranged hierarchically on a continuum stretching from mind and spirit down through levels of being to the sublunar, material, and changing world where we dwell. Irenaeus, however, also believed that this entire system had been designed by—and was under the direct control of—God. The whole cosmos was blessed, intentionally made, and ultimately good. In contrast, his opponents described a universe in conflict. For them, the conflict was located in the lower region of the cosmos. The material world was like a dark and dystopian future city that, having been severed from the control of the rightful authorities, is zealously guarded by malevolent forces, and now entraps many citizens of the spirit world above.

Consider the following from book 1 of *Against the Heresies*, where Irenaeus describes some key Valentinian doctrines. Here Irenaeus says the Valentinians believe the material world originated from the suffering and emotional distress of a being named Achamoth. This Achamoth, "together with her passion" became separated from the original "fullness," and in that separation "suffered grief." The passion of Achamoth, "they say became the origin and substance of matter from which this world is formed." Moist things come from her tears, "luminous substances" from her laughter, and from grief derive "the corporeal elements of the world."[16]

While modern readers may see in the mythic language of the Valentinians only an arcane artifact of a long-dead mythology, many people in the second century found in that same mythology solace and comfort. The knowledge that material life was not real life resonated deeply. As David Brakke reminds us in a discussion of Valentinian doctrine, for them, "the material world has its origin in error or ignorance" and is for that reason "ultimately not real." For them, "the only true reality is God." The myth promised a way out of the ignorant and unreal fog of our material density back to our true spiritual home with God. For Valentinians and others, waking up to the truth of our entrapment in *this world* was to wake up to the truth of our existence and thereby to open a path to liberation.[17]

The Divine Economy

Another way to understand the tension between Irenaeus and his Gnostic foils is to see it as a collision of metanarratives. In modern thought, metanarratives are the master stories that govern the way cultures "construct" the world. Often, particular metanarratives are so dominant in a culture that they escape the possibility of critique, or even the possibility of being recognized as cultural constructions. When this occurs, a metanarrative is said to be "totalizing." For example, in the modern Western world, most people fail to notice that ideas we have about economic growth and the limitless expansion of markets are human cultural constructions. We tend to speak of the "economy" as if it were emergent from nature, and we see it as a way of organizing society that has been discovered rather than fabricated. To the extent that we resist seeing capitalist economics as a metanarrative, we resist putting our heads above the totalizing discourse of capitalism and seeing it for what it is: one among many possible ways of organizing human communities. Some metanarratives have clearly been more destructive than others, and it is not unreasonable to think that some are more delusional than others. However, the existence of such narratives seems beyond doubt, and constructing them does appear to be a fact of human life and culture.

Beginning in the fourth century, what we now call "Orthodox" Christianity emerged as a totalizing metanarrative. Averil Cameron explains this process persuasively in her book *Christianity and the Rhetoric of Empire*,[18] where she traces the development

31

of the imperial church. Christendom, the cultural expression of this metanarrative, would last fifteen hundred years before it began its long and ongoing decline. However, in the second century, when Irenaeus was writing *Against the Heresies*, the arrival of the totalizing metanarrative of the Christian empire was still more than two hundred years in the future, and Christian groups were still arguing over the elements that would comprise this future totalizing discourse. In *Against the Heresies* we encounter a record of this argument, which Irenaeus was attempting to win by telling what he thought was a better metanarrative of Christianity. He referred to his narrative as the "Divine Economy."

The phrase "Divine Economy" contains many layers of meaning that are, for the most part, inaccessible to modern readers who have not been exposed to this theological language. For us, the word *economy* inevitably evokes images of markets and money because, unsurprisingly, that is what the word *economy* has come to mean in our culture. Etymologically, the word *economy* derives from the Greek word *oikonomia*, which originally meant "household management." Thus the meaning could push toward our modern usage in the sense of financial markets, but that was not the meaning in antiquity. Confusingly, the word *economy* could also mean "the inhabited world," which is the meaning behind the word *ecumenical*. Thus an ecumenical council is a council of the whole world. Finally, the word also contained the idea of a "plan" or an "arrangement." In ancient theology this third usage was quite common; the word *economy* designated "the divine ordering of things" or "the divine plan." When Irenaeus referenced the "Divine Economy," he meant the overarching narrative describing God's plan for the world. For him, the Divine Economy was the master story of Christianity.

In *Against the Heresies*, then, we encounter a collision of economies, or a collision of metanarratives. Here Irenaeus claims that Valentinians and others are wrong because they have utterly failed to understand the true nature of the Divine Economy. They are like "someone who would take the beautiful image of a king, carefully made out of precious stones by a skillful artist, and would destroy the features of the man on it and change around and rearrange the jewels, and make the form of a dog, or of a fox."[19] For Irenaeus, the Valentinians and others used the components of scriptures (the tesserae of the mosaic) to tell the overall story of the Scriptures in a distorted way. They were, in short, bad storytellers who did not understand the true essence of Christianity. In contrast, Irenaeus insisted that the story he and his community were teaching was in fact the true Christian story; they were the ones who had correctly assembled the mosaic of scripture to reveal the true narrative of the gospel. His version told a radically pro-materialist story, which contrasts dramatically with the anti-material narrative of his opponents.

For Irenaeus, the phrase "Divine Economy" references a story whose outline goes something like the following. It begins with the creation of the heavens and the earth, as attested in the Book of Genesis. Into this new creation God placed all the creatures of the earth, including humans. Drawing upon a distinction in Genesis 1:26, Irenaeus says these first humans were made in God's "image," but they were at the same time spiritual babies who lacked "likeness" to God and would have to grow into that likeness over time. Thus, because humans were created as immature beings, there was an inevitability to the fall. Indeed God knew that when tempted by the fruit from the tree of knowledge, these baby humans would likely eat it and die. After Adam and Eve did what God expected and ate, they eventually died. As a result, they and the material creation they inhabited became subject to suffering, death, and decay.

However, God had already planned a way to redeem the decaying humans and the decaying creation. By means of the incarnation, God both leads broken humanity to maturity and reverses the powers of death and decay. Borrowing language from Paul, Irenaeus understood Christ to be the "new Adam," the first inhabitant of the new creation. Christ was not, as the anti-materialists claimed, a revealer of knowledge, but a force of divine stability in a destabilized creation. Christ stabilized the material world by divinizing it, not by replacing or destroying it. In short, God through Christ unleashes the spiritual potential of the material creation.

For Irenaeus, this new and divinized creation will be physically manifest in the appearance of the new heaven and the new earth promised in the Book of Revelation. There will also be a New Jerusalem physically populated by resurrected material humans who share the new creation with other earth creatures. However, in the new creation, many things that characterize the old will pass away, such as prey and predation, which are artifacts of an old world subject to decay. Commenting on the prediction in Isaiah 65:25 that "the wolf and the lamb shall feed together, / the lion shall eat straw like the ox; / but the serpent—its food shall be dust," Irenaeus insists that these things will literally happen at the time of the resurrection: Eden will be restored.[20]

In the time between now and the advent of the New Jerusalem, we live in a world of already and not yet. We still suffer with the impact and decay, but, at the same time, the community of the just is already experiencing the transforming power of the new creation in the liturgy and through the Eucharist. This, Irenaeus insisted, is the true "economy" of the scriptures. It is the correct "master story."

These themes are present throughout *Against the Heresies*, but they all come together in the rhetorically dense pages of book 5. Here Irenaeus describes how Christ takes up the entire story of human self-destruction since Adam and reorders it so that it becomes instead a story of salvation. Throughout, he never presents the material creation as evil or as a cause of our problems, and creation remains intact even in the solution. Thus, in chapter 33, he writes with deep passion about the resurrection of the just:

> When the just rise from the dead and reign; when also the creation renovated and freed will abundantly produce a multitude of all foods out of the rain from the heaven and the fertility of the earth; as the presbyters who had seen John, the Lord's disciple, remembered hearing from him how the lord used to teach about times and say, The days will come when vines come up each with ten thousand branches and on each branch ten thousand twigs and on each twig ten thousand shoots and on each shoot ten thousand grapes, and each grape when pressed will give twenty-five measures of wine. And when one of the saints picks a cluster, another will shout, "I am a better cluster; pick me, bless the Lord through me." Similarly a grain of wheat will produce ten thousand ears, and each ear will have ten thousand

grains, and each grain ten pounds of pure flour; and the other fruits and seeds and herbs in like proportions; and all the animals, using those foods which are taken from the ground, will become peaceful and harmonious, subject to men with all subjection.[21]

A creation renewed and ruled over by Christ will characterize this new order. Irenaeus emphasizes that these things will literally come true; "none of us," he writes,

can take this allegorically, but everything is solid and substantial, made by God for the enjoyment of men.... Since men are real, their transformation must also be real, since they will not go into non-being but on the contrary will progress in being. For neither the substance nor the matter of the creation will be annihilated.[22]

These words—*solid*, *substantial*, *true*, and *transformed*—together encapsulate Irenaeus's hope for the future of the thickly material part of the cosmos, a hope that clearly distinguishes him from his opponents.

Creation from Nothing and Apostolic Authority

In textbook summaries of second-century Christianity, however, this aspect of Irenaeus is often ignored or misunderstood. Instead, scholars tend to point to his contribution to the development of the idea of apostolic succession and episcopal authority, or to his significance as an early example of a theologian embracing the theological idea of creation from nothing. However, if we look carefully at how both ideas are used in his work, it is clear that the reason Irenaeus appeals to apostolic authority and affirms that God created the world from nothing is that he is seeking to strengthen his core arguments in defense of the material world.

As an illustration, consider a series of passages appearing early in book 2 of *Against the Heresies*. Here Irenaeus argues against those who believe that the material reality characteristic of the lower cosmos was fashioned by mediating angels or "other world-maker," apart from the intention of God. He insists instead that God the Father made everything intentionally through his Word. Indeed, all of reality is God's reality. God "did not need Angels as helpers to make the things that are made," Irenaeus explains. "On the contrary, he predetermined in himself all things in advance," and God's preplanning included all levels of the cosmos, extending all the way down to the low places, thick and densely material. Irenaeus insists that this one God gave everything its proper form—"giving to spiritual beings a spiritual and invisible substance; to super celestial, a super celestial, to Angels, an angelic; to animals, an animal, to swimming creatures, an aquatic; to land creatures, one fitted for land."

To prove his point, he turns to the scriptures. "John, the Lord's disciple, says of him: *All things* were made by him and without him was made nothing." Then, as if for great emphasis, Irenaeus insists, "*Now in 'all' is contained also this world of ours. It, too, was made by his Word, as Scripture tells us in Genesis, he made all things around us by his Word.*" Clearly, Irenaeus wished to validate the material creation by unequivocally defending *this world* as one of God's intentional projects. This world did not come into existence through the malevolent intention of mediating beings or through the gradual erosion of higher mind (or spirit) into the chaotic mess of matter barely formed: it came about because God wanted to create it.[23]

As the discussion in book 2 continues to unfold, Irenaeus fends off the competing views of his opponents. He insists that they have misconstrued the Divine Economy and have failed to grasp the noble place of the material creation in God's plan. His arguments culminate in chapters 9 and 10, where he finally appeals to apostolic authority and where he affirms the idea of creation from nothing. Thus, in chapter 9, he asserts the apostolic pedigree of his teaching; our teaching, he says, has roots as old as Genesis: "the ancients guard [our position] as a tradition coming from the first-formed man, and they hymn the one God as the Creator of heaven and earth." God's people were reminded of this by the prophets, and gentiles can learn it by reading the book of creation, for the "creation itself manifests him who created it." Indeed, "the whole church throughout the world received this tradition from the apostles." This, "the heretics" do not grasp.[24]

Next, in chapter 10, Irenaeus insists that his opponents are bad readers who have no understanding of the scriptures: "[Because they] wish to explain ambiguous scriptural passages… they fabricated another God." And in doing so, "they braid ropes out of sand and add a bigger difficulty to a smaller one." In contrast, Irenaeus says, the Father through his Word created a unified cosmos that is "credible and acceptable and stable." In fact, he says, God made this world by calling it into *existence out of nothing*. God "himself invented the matter of his word, since previously it did not exist." The materiality of the creation, he concludes, does not come from the passion of Achamoth[25] or from any lower being but from God alone. Indeed, God made it and everything else out of nothing and according to God's own will.

Here Irenaeus invokes apostolic authority not to advance a doctrine about episcopal power but to strengthen the theological position he has been relentlessly arguing. Similarly, his statements about God creating everything from nothing are contextual and not systematic. Irenaeus probably did not envision God radically transcending the cosmos and creating all reality from nothing as later iterations of the doctrine would insist. Irenaeus seems to have in mind a being who calls into existence the various creatures and materials of the cosmos, but he stops short of exploring the full metaphysical implications of this idea. Irenaeus's statement about God's radical power to create from nothing has more to do with the goodness of the material world and its right to exist in the cosmos than with understanding God's transcendental perfection.

If we read Irenaeus's appeals to apostolic authority and creation from nothing out of context, this distracts from what he was actually worried about: the redemption of the physical creation. For Irenaeus, the perfection of the material creation would be realized not in the movement of the material toward the immaterial, but rather in the movement of the material toward its own perfection, precisely as matter. Irenaeus's insistence that the world was good did not prevent him from acknowledging that things "down here" were broken. Like his opponents, he, too, lived in a realm of suffering, decay, death, and change. However, for Irenaeus, the creation was not finished and would not be until the unveiling of the new heaven and the new earth promised in the Book of Revelation. In other words, for Irenaeus, eschatology and the future fulfillment of the world pressed far more powerfully on his theological imagination than did images of ascent toward an idealist platonic perfection.

Toward a Contemporary Christian Deep Ecology

At this point, readers of this somewhat long excursus into the arcana of an ancient Christian debate may be wondering what this has to do with us and our time. At the beginning of this essay, I suggested that a reconsideration of Irenaeus's defense of matter could provide a helpful framework for contemporary Christians who are attempting to foster a deeper and more intimate communion with the Earth. In the pages that remain, I would like to flesh out this proposal more concretely. That is, I am now asking how Irenaeus's battle with ancient anti-materialist Christians can inform our own efforts to overcome the paradoxical anti-materialism of this moment.

It may be tempting for contemporary Christians with an ecological disposition to take a path of least resistance. Many Christians who think environmentally believe that embracing a theology of "stewardship" is the proper response to our environmental situation. Indeed, it is fair to say that if a contemporary Christian community has an environmental commitment, it is extremely likely that this commitment will be justified with appeals to stewardship. In their approach to ecology, Roman Catholics, Eastern Orthodox Christians, Mainline Protestants, and Evangelicals tend to agree: God has appointed humans to be good caretakers of the Earth and we are duty bound to do so.

This view is good as far as it goes, but it does not go very far. First, it is very difficult to construct a theology of stewardship from Christian Scripture. The entire argument is based upon an implausible reading of Genesis 1:28, where God gives humans "dominion over the fish of the sea and over the birds of the air and over every living thing that moves upon the earth." Defenders of stewardship attempt to translate the word *dominion* as *stewardship*, but the Hebrew word *kabash* does not mean that; it means "subdue." While it is possible to make an exegetical argument that pushes the meaning of the Hebrew *kabash* toward a softer translation like *dominion*, *stewardship* is a real stretch.

Many biblical scholars have argued that contrary to exulting the human role in the world, the Old Testament as a whole suggests human tininess and lack of power in the face of God's creation, adding weight to the argument against stewardship theology.[26] Moreover, it is difficult the take seriously claims that humans have been appointed "stewards" over a planet that existed for billions of years without us and will exist for billions more when we are gone. In the face of cosmic vastness, the idea of stewardship sounds delusional. Finally, theologies of stewardship do not sufficiently challenge the paradoxical anti-materialism of contemporary culture. We cannot hope to respond to this planetary crisis if we continue to think that we are being good stewards by recycling plastic and turning off lights all the while continuing to burn fossil fuels and consume like locusts binging on summer wheat.

Instead of theologies that give us permission to continue business as usual, we need a theology that can help us confront directly the anti-materialist impulses that linger in our tradition. The same forces that allow us to think that deep down we are spirits dwelling *in* a body, allow us to pretend that our food is replicated in the back of the grocery store, that there is no material limit to our energy supply, and that we really exist independent of nature, in a virtual matrix detached from any mooring in matter.

As we have seen, this ambiguous relationship to matter is an old problem dating back to Christian origins, and one could easily argue that despite the best efforts of Irenaeus and his peers, the anti-materialist tendencies of Christianity were never fully mastered. In a famous passage of *Confessions*, Augustine muses that the saints in heaven eat "truth for food,"[27] and Aquinas explains that in beatitude there will be no room for animals and plants because humans will live on knowledge of God.[28] Many environmental critics of Christianity never tire of directing attention to this anti-materialism, and they have a point.

Here a recovery of Irenaean materialism can help by complicating this historical narrative. Irenaeus never forgot the profound limits on the power of the creatures dwelling in the sublunar world. At the same time, Irenaeus and the strand of early Christianity he represents loved *this world* and stressed that, despite the suffering and difficulty associated with this place, we humans were made to dwell here. He and they never thought that salvation meant escape to the celestial heavens. Instead, they hoped and longed for the spiritualization of their materiality. It seems to me that Christian ecological thinking can and should learn from this forgotten past as we attempt to think again and more deeply about the ultimate purpose of our bodily and creaturely existence.

Still, many religious environmentalists, Christians among them, have little confidence that this old religion has the capacity to deliver an ecological vision thick enough to respond to the urgency of now. Instead they and we turn with increasing frequency to deep ecology for ecospiritual consolation. Deep ecology responds to modern ecological alienation from this earth in many ways that are compelling and attractive. As an environmentalist, I admit to being moved by the ecomysticism expressed in a film like James Cameron's *Avatar*, where evil, earth-hating, consumptive humans are thwarted by biophelic natives of the planet Pandora, who live in harmony with the dark green mother goddess spirit of their world. In the world of deep ecological religious scholarship, the names David Abram and Bron Taylor stand out as accomplished exemplars of intellectuals attempting to reawaken the religious imagination of our time with appeals to intentional engagement with embodiment. Abram's efforts to reconnect us to the animal and material centers of our existence are especially noteworthy.[29]

These deep ecological approaches, however, suffer from a serious inability to respond in a meaningful way to the problem of evil and suffering. They are prone to romanticism and tend to ignore the reality that nature is "red in tooth and claw." For example, in his book *Dark Green Religion*, Taylor suggests that we need to stop thinking about the existence of prey and predation as a form of natural evil and come to celebrate it as part of the joy of being in this world,[30] a position that only the most committed deep ecologist would be willing to embrace. In addition, deep ecological approaches are tinged with a utopian hope for an earthly paradise where nature is purged of all its harshness. The deep ecological vision of the film *Avatar* is a fantasy. In the deep past, humans, like pandorans, lived as hunters and gatherers who were certainly more deeply connected to the physical world than we are, but their world was no Pandora and their lives were hard.

A contemporary Christian ecological vision inspired by Irenaeus can reclaim, with the deep ecologist, a robust affection for the material creation. It can also own fully the material character of the human person and affirm that we are deep down creatures of this planet. We are earth dwellers, not star dwellers, and our fate is tied to this place. At the same time, this Christian vision can affirm that our spiritual consciousness gives us access to awareness of reality, an awareness that includes knowledge that all is not well. This knowledge rightly compels us to ask deeper questions about the final end or purpose of both this world and the creatures that dwell here. A Christian deep ecology will embrace both a furious love for *this world* and an Evangelical hope that, in the fullness of time, God will reveal ever more clearly the mysterious necessity of our embodiment and the suffering associated with it. Living with this hope as a guide is, I think, the best path for us to follow if we seek to live lives reconciled with *this* creation.

Reflection Questions

1. In what ways can a recovery of our own identity as material creatures who are native to *this* world help us to lead lives of deeper reverence for *this* creation? What concrete practices can we embrace to help foster this awareness? How can we live in a way that is reconciled to both the goodness and the limits of *this* creation?

2. Irenaeus urged his readers to be reconciled with creation by regarding it as both good and broken. Is this a way of describing a reconciliatory attitude more generally? Does seeing other people as "good but broken" help us to be reconciled to them as well?

Notes

1. Irenaeus, *Against the Heresies*, 4.20.

2. This translation is found in Robert M. Grant, *Irenaeus of Lyons* (London: Routledge, 1997), 153.

3. English translations of book 4 are found in *Irenaeus of Lyons: Against the Heresies*, in *The Ante-Nicene Fathers*, vol. 1, ed. Alexander Roberts and James Donaldson (New York: Christian Literature Publishing Co., 1885). The Latin text is available in the series *Sources Chrétiennes*, vol. 100 (Paris: Cerf, 1965).

4. See, e.g., David Brakke, *The Gnostics: Myth, Ritual, and Discovery in Early Christianity* (Cambridge: Harvard University Press, 2010); and Karen L. King, *What Is Gnosticism?* (Cambridge: Harvard University Press, 2003). Somewhat confusingly, Brakke thinks that there was indeed a religious group in antiquity called "The Gnostics," but that they were one of many anti-materialist groups whose distinctiveness is lost when we use the term *Gnostic* in the modern way to designate a collective.

5. Walter Bauer first argued the case for pluralism in his influential book *Orthodoxy and Heresy in Earliest Christianity* (Philadelphia: Fortress Press, 1971). Most scholars in the field working today accept the reality of original pluralism.

6. The transition of "Proto-Orthodoxy" into "Orthodoxy" is long and complicated, but was largely in place by the middle of the fourth century with the arrival of the Christian empire inaugurated by the Roman emperor Constantine.

7. Readers should note that the term *Gnostic* is still very prevalent in academic discussion and that arguments in favor of abandoning it have not been universally accepted.

8. Stephen H. Webb, *Jesus Christ, Eternal God: Heavenly Flesh and the Metaphysics of Matter* (Oxford: Oxford University Press, 2012), 40–41.

9. Antti Marjanen, "Gnosticism," in *The Oxford Handbook of Early Christian Studies*, ed. Susan Harvey and David Hunter (Oxford: Oxford University Press, 2008), 203–20.

10. Scholarly understanding of ancient Christianity was greatly enhanced by this discovery, which included forty-one ancient texts that had previously been unknown to scholarship.

11. The "pleroma" is a reference to the nonmaterial, upper part of the universe from which humans had fallen.

12. See the translation in James M. Robinson, ed., *The Nag Hamadi Library in English* (Leiden: Brill, 1996), 38–51.

13. Scott Moringiello, *Irenaeus Rhetor* (PhD diss., University of Notre Dame, 2008).

14. Anthony Briggman, "Revisiting Irenaeus' Philosophical Acumen," *Vigiliae Christianae* 65 (2001): 115–24.

15. *Against the Heresies.*

16. *Against the Heresies*, 1.4.1–2, in *St. Irenaeus of Lyons against the Heresies*, bk. 1, trans. Dominic J. Unger (New York: Paulist Press, 1992).

17. See Brakke, *The Gnostics*, 100.

18. Avril Cameron, *Christianity and the Rhetoric of Empire: The Development of Christian Discourse* (Berkeley: University of California Press, 1991).

19. *Against the Heresies* 1.8.1.

20. Grant, *Irenaeus of Lyons*, 179.

21. Grant, *Irenaeus of Lyons*, 178–79.

22. Grant, *Irenaeus of Lyons*, 184.

23. *Against the Heresies* 2.2.1–6, in *St. Irenaeus of Lyons against the Heresies*, bk. 2, trans. Dominic J. Unger (New York: Paulist Press, 2012). Emphasis added.

24. *Against the Heresies*, 2.9.1.

25. *Against the Heresies*, 2.10.1–2.

26. Ronald A. Simkins, "Anthropocentrism and the Place of Humans in the Biblical Tradition," in *The Greening of the Papacy*, *Journal of Religion and Society*, Supplement 9 (2013): 16–29.

27. *Confessions*, 10.10 (24).

28. *Summa Theologica*, Supplement, question 91.

29. David Abram, *Becoming Animal: An Earthy Cosmology* (New York: Pantheon Books, 2010).

30. Bron Taylor, *Dark Green Religion: Nature Spirituality and the Planetary Future* (Berkeley: University of California Press, 2010), 127–28.

CHAPTER 3

Caritas, Correction, Communion

CYPRIAN OF CARTHAGE ON THE
READMISSION OF THE LAPSED

Scott D. Moringiello

Jesus Christ, the Word of God made flesh, reconciled human beings to the Father through his life and his work. But Christ's reconciliation does not only connect human beings to God. It also reconciles human beings with each other. All the essays in this volume discuss examples of Christian responses to Christ's life and work of reconciliation. In this chapter, I will focus on Cyprian of Carthage, a North African bishop whose community suffered persecution at the hands of the Roman Empire in the mid-third century. For Cyprian, the basis of Christian reconciliation is love (*caritas* or *dilectio*). Now our task will be to explore what Cyprian means when he uses the words *caritas* or *dilectio*. Love, as we will see, makes the community a community, and it does so through the Christian Eucharist. Cyprian helps us to think about social reconciliation through the lens of Christian love. Indeed, for Cyprian, there is simply no other way to reconcile people except through Christian love.

Immediately, then, we must ask, how do we know what Christian love is? Like all bishops, and indeed like all Christians, Cyprian knew about God through God's revelation in the scriptures. Christians learn about Christian love in the Christian community that protects and proclaims (in word and deed) the scriptures that describe that love. And I think we can understand much of his argument on this connection by thinking about how he understands the Johannine corpus and the Letter to the Ephesians.

I want to divide my discussion into three main sections. In the first part of my essay, I will address the historical circumstances in which Cyprian wrote. The second part of the essay is the most important part. Here I will focus on how Cyprian discusses love in his letters and in his treatise *On the Unity of the Catholic Church*. In the third part of my essay, I will offer some thoughts on what Cyprian's writings and his method might have to say to Christians today who want to draw on the history of the church for insights into meditating conflicts. Cyprian's time is not our time, and Cyprian's answer to the foregoing question turns out to be something of a minority report in the history of Christian theology. But his voice is worth considering.

Before turning to my main argument, I want to say a word about several scriptural precedents for Cyprian's views on love.[1] Perhaps the most important scriptural passage for this discussion is Ephesians 4:15–16. There we read, "But speaking the truth in love, we must grow up in every way into him who is the head, into Christ, from whom the whole body, joined and knit together by every ligament with which it is equipped, as each part is working properly, promotes the body's growth in building itself up in love." The author's focus on love here is instructive. Christ is the head of the whole body, and we ought to understand *body* here in the corporate sense. This corporate body can only be the corporate body of Christ if it acts in love.

The other important passage comes from 1 John 4:8, which proclaims that God is love. The Greek for *love* in this passage is *agape*, a word meaning "self-giving love," and a word relatively unknown before the writings that became the New Testament. In his Vulgate, Jerome translated *agape* as *caritas*, but it seems that the Bible Cyprian used has *dilectio* rather than *caritas*. If we bring these two texts together, we see that not only does love bind the church together, but it does so because God is love.[2]

Before I get any further, I should note that my own reading of Cyprian is also something of a minority report. He does not offer a treatise on love, and the words *caritas* and *dilectio* do not obviously jump off the page as you read his writing. My own argument, of course, is that love plays an important role in Cyprian's thinking on the church and communion, but I want to acknowledge that this role can only become clear in context. I hope to provide that historical context here. Thus if we view Cyprian's writings on love in the right way, we can see how important they are for him. And if we understand how important they are for him, we can then consider how important they could be for us.

I. Historical Background

In Christian theology, historical knowledge almost always enriches our understanding of an author's argument. In the case of Cyprian, however, knowledge of the history is essential. It's common knowledge that Christianity did not become officially tolerated in the Roman Empire until the Edict of Milan in 313 under Constantine, and Christianity did not become the official religion of the empire until the Edict of Thessalonica in 380 under Theodosius. It is also common to discuss ages of persecution within the church. I would not go so far as to claim that persecution was a myth, but we should note that for much of its first three hundred years, Christianity did not face constant or widespread assault at the hands of the Empire.

Christians in the Roman Empire in 250, however, did suffer a widespread and systematic persecution under the emperor Decius, who had come to power in 249. Decius wanted to revive the past glories of Rome, and he believed proper piety was essential to achieving that goal. The way to ensure proper piety was to have everyone in the empire sacrifice to the gods. They would do this by burning incense to the gods for the well-being of the emperor, and they had to offer this sacrifice in the presence of a Roman magistrate, who would give the worshipper a *libellus*, which was an official document to show that he or she had sacrificed.

Christians at the time responded in various ways, as you would expect. Some offered the sacrifice voluntarily and indeed willingly. Others were able to pay for the *libellus* without having to sacrifice. Still others offered the sacrifice but did so under coercion. There was a minority of Christians who refused to offer the sacrifice and who refused to pay for a *libellus*.[3] And finally, some Christians were able to leave their homes and property in the city. Cyprian was one such person. While he was the bishop, he went into voluntary exile.

Once the persecution ended, Christians throughout the empire began to wonder how to treat those Christians who had offered sacrifices to the emperor. Those who offered sacrifices came to be known as the "lapsed" or the "fallen" because they had fallen away from the community through the sin of idolatry. Because Christians saw themselves in the corporate Body of Christ, these idolatrous sacrifices wounded the whole Body. The bishops, too, were divided among themselves. Some shared the Eucharist with the lapsed, while others did not. And among the lapsed, some undertook a form of penance and waited for their bishop to return, and others never left the church and felt at home in the empire.[4] For Cyprian, these disagreements among the bishops cut to the very issue of how they understood their communities bound in love, and it cut to the very issue of the love among the bishops.

Let me highlight now some key players and dates. During the persecution, Pope Fabian was martyred. Cornelius was then elected Pope in 251, but a priest named Novatian opposed his election because Cornelius allowed the lapsed back into communion. Novatian was himself consecrated bishop by three other bishops in Italy, and he said he was the true bishop of Rome. Novatian and his allies came to be known as the "rigorists." On the other side, there was a presbyter in Carthage named Novatus, who during Cyprian's exile, freely readmitted the lapsed to communion. Novatus was never consecrated bishop, but Cyprian believed he acted as though he were a bishop.[5] Novatus and his allies came to be known as the "laxists." In Cyprian's mind, these divisions led to schism and heresy.[6]

The examples of Novatian and Novatus demonstrate that the issues surrounding the Decian persecution extended far beyond Carthage. It also shows that Christians understood unity beyond their own geographical area. What occurred in the church in Rome affected the church in Carthage and vice versa. The church was set *in* a particular location, but it was not confined *to* that location. To the laxists, Cyprian insisted that the lapsed must submit to the community and its rituals of forgiveness to remain in the peace of the church and the forgiveness of Christ. To the rigorists, in turn, he insisted on the efficacy of reconciliation and the forgiveness of Christ.[7] Cyprian led a series of councils in Carthage, and these councils determined that the lapsed should be allowed to reenter communion after a period of penance. They also decided that if a bishop had committed the sin of idolatry or had broken away from the community in any other way, the sacraments received from him were invalid and did not transmit God's grace. Such a bishop was no longer in the communion of God's love that the sacraments shared.

Two issues arose because of these disagreements. First, the bishops needed to discern the conditions for readmitting the lapsed to the reception of the Eucharist. Second, they needed to decide whether baptism in a heretical church was valid. That is, was there only one baptism among Christians, or was baptism conditional on the right set of beliefs in the community doing the baptizing? An in-depth discussion of the history and the major players is beyond the scope of this essay, but we might think of these questions in this way: What are the conditions necessary for love to exist in the Christian community? Can a person renounce his community and still love it? Do people need to agree on fundamental things in order to love each other? And if they do, who decides what those fundamental things are? Cyprian refused to separate practice and belief, so he came to see that those Christians who understood and practiced forgiveness and the Eucharist differently were in fact not united to all other Christians.[8]

The various responses put a strain on the unity of the church. One such strain was organizational. The presbyters of Carthage believed Cyprian had abandoned his responsibilities as bishop. Besides the presbyters, there were confessors, who because they had suffered, took an outsized role in the community. A "confessor" was simply one who had suffered for the faith but had not been killed. The confessors, who were freed from prison, acted as conduits between the people and Christians who were awaiting martyrdom. Those who had apostatized believed that if the martyrs pled their case before Christ in heaven, the lapsed would be forgiven and would be allowed to return to the sacraments of the Christian community.

After the persecution, the church in Carthage was roughly divided into three groups: the laxists, the rigorists, and the moderates. Now, as soon as we set up the divisions this way, it is clear who the winners are. But it's important to make the stakes in the debate clear. Part of the problem here is that rival traditions were in place that offered the first two groups reasons to believe they were following Christ's desire. There was one early tradition that the church could not forgive three sins committed after baptism. These three sins were murder, adultery, and idolatry. Tertullian, who wrote in Carthage a generation before Cyprian, claimed that not even bishops had the power to forgive these sins. Tertullian believed that a lifetime of repentance outside eucharistic communion was the proper form of penance for such sins. The martyr tradition, especially in North Africa, was just as strong. Building on Matthew 10:32–33, these Christians believed that Christ would consider the martyrs' petitions. And if the martyrs promised that they would intercede for the lapsed, the lapsed would be judged favorably by Christ and so should be able to reenter communion. The confessors, then, ended up seeing themselves as beyond the discipline of the church community. They, who were the conduits to the martyrs, also saw themselves as beyond the church.[9] Because the martyrs were outside the organizational structure of the church, they provided a perfect entrée for the lapsed to reenter the church. Thus the lapsed reinforced the authority of the martyrs and upheld the authority of the confessors.[10]

This picture, then, presents a church with multiple centers of authority. The most important part of that authority comes from the power to reconcile members of the community back into the community. Cyprian insisted that only the bishops could readmit the lapsed to communion. Thus he disagreed with the laxists, who believed a confessor could.[11] In Cyprian's view, to be a member of the universal church, one had to be in communion with a validly ordained presbyter who was in communion with a bishop who was in communion with all the bishops in the world.[12] In Cyprian's day, the bishop played the role that a priest of a large parish would today. That is, the bishop would know his congregants and, most importantly, he would preside over the Eucharist. And the Eucharist, after all, was the sacrament of God's love. Thus we see that a dispute among bishops wasn't simply political or organizational. The dispute among bishops was a dispute about how one ought to be prepared to receive the sacrament of God's love. This preparation, in turn, addressed the very structure of the Christian community. In some ways, of course, Cyprian was himself part of the problem. It was difficult for him to make an argument for the importance of bishops while he himself was in exile. Many of his presbyters saw him as a fugitive from his responsibilities.[13]

Traditionally, one participated in Christ's salvation through corporate membership in the Body of Christ, the church. Cyprian is an important case study because he helps us think through membership in the church, and analogously membership in any body. In a series of letters and in *On the Unity of the Catholic Church*, Cyprian lays out a position that tries to navigate the Scylla of laxism and the Charybdis of rigorism. Love is the rudder that guides this navigation.

2. Cyprian's Theology: Love as the Key to Reconciliation

One of the problems with discussing how Cyprian understands love is that we do not find a discourse of love in Cyprian's letters. He does not offer a sustained exegesis of scriptural texts that involve *caritas* or *dilectio*. Nor, frankly, does Cyprian offer a sustained argument on the church in his letters. (We do find such an argument in *On the Unity of the Catholic Church*). Cyprian's letters are occasional pieces written in specific circumstances. I want to argue, though, that Cyprian has an overriding concern in his letters and in *On the Unity*. He wants Christians to be unified because unity is the manifestation of God's love. In order to have unity the members of the community must be reconciled to each other and to God, and the sign of that reconciliation is sharing the Eucharist. Cyprian talks of the body of love that is the Eucharist in the church. He is clear that Christian love can only be manifested in the community that is gathered under a properly ordained bishop.[14] After all, the bishop is the one who presides over the Eucharist. And finally, the unity that Cyprian desires transforms the individual believer by making him or her more like the God who is love. If the believer has not been transformed by the love of God in the community, then he does not truly take part in that love.

What I find striking—and compelling—about Cyprian's view of love is that it is so different from our own. Obviously, Cyprian isn't talking about romantic love, but he isn't even talking about love in relationship to knowledge in a way akin to Paul's famous 1 Corinthians 13 or the Johannine corpus.[15] Cyprian builds on both pictures. For Cyprian, love is the mark of the community as such; love is embodied in the cohesiveness and unity of the community. The heretics and schismatics have done worse than separate themselves from the community as if the community were some sort of voluntary association. They have separated themselves from a community based in God's love. Thus they have separated themselves from what comes with love. Cyprian associates this love with peace and concord. For example, he writes, "Now assuredly you have kept in the peace of the Lord and the law of undivided love [*caritas*] and of concord." In return, "you have given…an example of love [*dilectio*] and peace to others."[16] In the pages of Cyprian's letters, you can hear how deeply he feels his concern for love in the community. When someone returns to the community, he writes, "I confess that I both greatly congratulate you, and I glory more than others in your peaceful return and love [*caritas*]. For you ought to hear simply what has been in my heart. I grieved vehemently, and I was greatly distressed because I was not able to be in communion with those whom I had begun to love [*diligo*]."[17] This love, this *caritas*, reconciles "the broken body to the unity of the Catholic Church."[18] Indeed, Cyprian goes so far as to say that Christians "owe" and should show "mutual love [*dilectio*]" to each other.[19]

Letters 55 and 57 give representative views on how Cyprian sees love in the church. In both letters, Cyprian is concerned about the unity of the church and the readmission of the lapsed. That unity is marked, for Cyprian, by the love of the church. Cyprian is especially concerned with the idea that one could somehow pass over the unity of the church thanks to the prayers of the martyrs. "If he is rejected by the Church, he should go over to the heretics and schismatics. From there, although he should afterwards have been killed for the Name, because he has been put out from the Church and divided from unity and love [*caritas*], he could not be crowned in death."[20] But, as I have noted, Cyprian was concerned to bring the lapsed back into the love of the church. He believed that outside the community and the Eucharist they could not be transformed by God's love. The church should "encourage them as much as we can with the aid and solace of our love [*dilectio*], and to be not so severe and pertinacious in blunting their repentance nor again, free and easy in rashly relaxing communication."[21] This love, we need to remember, requires penance. Cyprian wants the lapsed to return, but he wants them—and all Christians—to know what God's love requires.

Bishops should especially know what God's love requires, and to Cyprian Novatian's actions against the unity of the church are actions against love. Novatian is Cyprian's focus in Letter 55. Novatian, according to Cyprian, "could not keep the episcopate even if he was made a bishop earlier. He withdrew from the body of his fellow bishops and from the unity of the Church."[22] Cyprian reminds his addressee about Paul's words on love and unity in Ephesians: "Bearing with one another in love, taking sufficient care to preserve the unity of the Spirit in the bond of peace."[23] Novatian might well have been an intelligent and eloquent speaker, but Cyprian reminds his audience that "he who has not kept brotherly love or ecclesiastical unity has lost even what he formerly had been."[24] After all, Cyprian wants the heretics to be reunited to the church. According to Cyprian, the rigorist position cuts people off from who God is. "Inasmuch as He is merciful and devoted, peace can be given through his priests."[25] Because the church is bound by God's love, it reaches out to sinners because of God's mercy.

Cyprian discusses mercy in letter 57 because mercy allows for unity to be repaired. "For it was not right, and the affection of the Father and divine clemency did not permit the Church to be closed to those who knock and the help and hope of salvation denied."[26] God's love welcomes the heretic back. "Peace is necessary," Cyprian writes, "not for the sick, but for the strong; nor is communion to be given by us to the dying but to the living."[27] Cyprian wants to make an offer of peace to those he considers schismatics because he wants the church to be unified. "Lest, then, the sheep entrusted to him by the Lord be demanded back from our mouth by which we refuse peace, by which we oppose rather the harshness of human cruelty than the Spirit of divine and fatherly piety." Cyprian wants to examine each case and "give peace to the lapsed."[28]

God's love also forms the person who accepts it. This love, of course, formed Cyprian's own view. "Because it was fitting to faith and love and solicitude, we made known those things which were in our conscience."[29] Cyprian fears that bishops have not been formed in God's love as he has. If they have not, then they cannot be symbols of unity in the churches and markers of unity with other churches.

Let me end this brief exploration of love in Cyprian's letters by stressing a few other places where he connects love and unity in the church. Cyprian recognizes that the church is, to borrow a phrase from Augustine, a *corpus permixum*. He can acknowledge the "tares" in the church and still note "neither our faith nor our love [*caritas*] ought to be hindered so that because we see there are tares in the Church we ourselves should withdraw from the Church."[30] The weakness of members of the church should not rend the unity of the church. This chimes with Cyprian's stress on the close relationship between humility and love. Unity needs humility because humility recognizes that one's love is not one's own but comes from God. All priests must be humble. Everyone, he says, "knows best and love[s] [*diligo*] my humility, and you also knew and loved [*diligo*] it when you were still in the Church and in communion with me."[31] The humility of which he speaks is the humility of God who humbled himself in Christ. And Christ, of course, loves the church. "If there is one Church, which is loved [*diligo*] by Christ and that alone is purged by his washing, how can he who is not in the Church either be loved by Christ or washed or purged by his washing?"[32] Without the church one cannot be formed in God's love. And because it is so essential to be formed in God's love, the lapsed need to be able to reenter communion.

In letter 54, Cyprian underscores how love drives his work. He tells his addressee, "You may look into all of these matters thoroughly by reading the treatises which I had read recently here and for the sake of our mutual love [*dilectio*], had sent to you likewise to be read." Here he refers to the *Unity of the Catholic Church*. This treatise, he writes, "will please you more and more since you already read it in such a manner that you may approve and love [*diligo*] because, what we have written in words you fulfill in deed when you return to the Church in the unity of love [*caritas*] and peace."[33] Let us now turn to *On the Unity of the Catholic Church* and further explore Cyprian's remarks on love, peace, unity, and communion.

For Cyprian, as I've said, love binds the community, and this love chides both the rigorists and the laxists. Ultimately, Cyprian believed that the lapsed *could* be readmitted to the Eucharist if they underwent a period of penance. And the lapsed can be admitted after this penance because the love of God is found in the properly ordered church. This order comes from the love of the Spirit, and this order is marked by the presence of the bishop. I'll note, too, that the presence of a martyr or a confessor is *not enough* to mark the unity of the church.

In *On the Unity of the Catholic Church*, we find many of the same themes we found in the letters. I will focus on love, unity, and peace. Cyprian even quotes Ephesians 4:3, just as he did in letter 55. Love, unity, and peace also need simplicity and humility. A sign of the peace of God is the same simplicity one found in the dove that descended on Jesus after his baptism. "This is the simplicity that ought to be known, this is the love [*caritas*] that ought to be attained, so that the love [*dilectio*] of the brotherhood may imitate the doves, so that their gentleness and meekness may be like the lambs and sheep."[34] Cyprian's point, obviously, is that neither the rigorists nor the laxists have this simplicity. This simplicity is only found in the church. Division is a mark of pride because when one divides himself from the community, he divides himself from the *caritas* that is God. And only that love can properly humble a person.

He who does not have love does not have God, Cyprian makes clear. For God is love, and he who remains in God remains in love, and God remains in him (see 1 John 4:8, 16). But for Cyprian to remain in love is to remain in the visible church. Not even martyrdom is enough of a sign of one's identity within the church. "The one who is not in the Church cannot be a martyr. He cannot attain the kingdom who forsakes what will reign there." Christ "gave us peace. He ordered us to be in agreement, and of one mind. He charged the bonds of love [*dilectio*] and charity [*caritas*] to be kept uncorrupted and unviolated. He cannot show himself to be martyred who has not maintained brotherly love [*caritas*]."[35] Today, we would never think of questioning a Christian martyr, and sadly our age knows even more martyrs than the era of Cyprian. But Cyprian reminds us that the martyr dies as a *Christian* martyr because he or she is a member of the Body of Christ. Just after this passage, Cyprian goes on to quote Paul's famous passage about love being patient, kind, and all the rest. For Cyprian, clearly the only way to remain in God's love is to remain in the church. There can be no martyr-shaped loophole that will allow people to be part of God's love without the church. To say that there could be such a loophole is to say that one can be formed in the love of God outside the community. To say this, of course, would be an act of pride.

But, Cyprian would stress, one can go too far in the other direction. If the laxists rely too heavily on the martyrs rather than the church, the rigorists divide the church because they forget that the church is the church because of love, unity, and peace. As Cyprian writes, "But what unity does he keep, what love [*dilectio*] does he maintain or consider, who, angry with the furor of discord, divides the Church, destroys the faith, disturbs the peace, dissipates love [*caritas*], profanes the sacrament?"[36] Notice how faith, peace, *caritas*, and the sacrament go together in Cyprian's mind. His target here is Novatian, who in his zeal for purity ended up sowing discord. Novatian divided himself from faith, peace, *caritas*, and the Eucharist. Love and unity must be the priority over purity. Indeed, if there is no unity, those who need to purify themselves will not have the community they need to do so.

Through the community Christ forms the individual believer in love. If you are outside the community because of past sin— and if you therefore lack the love and unity and peace that came with being in the community—then you do not have access to the Eucharist that guards against sins, especially the sin of pride. Christ "humbled Himself upon earth," and so "how can He love [*diligere*] arrogance?" Cyprian then comes to confessors. "Someone is a confessor of Christ only if the majesty and dignity of Christ be not afterwards blasphemed by him."[37] The fact that Cyprian mentions confessors here suggests that he has them in his sights as those who need humility. And we can imagine the power they wielded. Their work—not the work of a bishop—enabled a person to return to communion. But that power, in turn, could easily have led to pride. As we can see, Cyprian believes that both the rigorists and the laxists misunderstand the church because they misunderstand unity and love.

Given what I have discussed thus far, it's obvious that Cyprian's understanding of love differs greatly from the understanding of love that most would hold today, even most Christians. Part of our difficulty in appreciating Cyprian comes from the fact that it is difficult for people today to envision love as first coming from the community. We might think of love in erotic terms or perhaps think of love in terms of the family. Even those who love their country would not say that the country is the origin of that love. Cyprian challenges our view. According to Cyprian, "The son of peace ought to seek peace and follow it. He who knows and loves the bond of love [*diligit vinculum caritatis*] ought to hold his tongue from the evil of dissension."[38] He continues, "The sons of God ought to be peacemakers, gentle in heart, simple in speech, of one heart in affection."[39] Love, for Cyprian, is found in the community, not just between two people. Indeed, we can go so far as to say that love is only found within a group of people. That's why membership in the church is so important. And it's why the Eucharist is so important. Love leads to unanimity—being of one soul—and as Cyprian reminds his readers, "This unanimity once was among the apostles and so the new assembly of believers, who keep the Lord's commandments, maintained its love [*caritas*]."[40]

In one of the quotations above, Cyprian said that the son of peace should love the bond of love—*diligit vinculum caritatis*. This phrase, which Cyprian also uses in Letter 45, nicely sums up Cyprian's approach to unity. Any reconciliation and any unity in the church can only be in the church because it is a unity based on God's love. Cyprian pleaded with his fellow bishops that they readmit their lapsed brothers and sisters to the eucharistic feast. He wanted the Christian community to be marked with *caritas*, and that *caritas* could lead to communion if there were unity and peace, humility and simplicity.

3. Lessons for Today

All the examples in our volume were chosen because the specifics of each example transcend its time and place. I take five lessons away from the way Cyprian dealt with the rigorists and the laxists.

First, Cyprian takes his opponents seriously. All too often we can demonize those who disagree with us, and such demonization prohibits reconciliation. Cyprian recognizes that Novatian and the rigorists on the one hand, and Novatus and the laxists on the other, have substantive arguments and that they are trying to help people follow God's will. He disagrees with them, of course, but he seeks to understand their points.

Second, Cyprian shows us that reconciliation does not always occur by meeting others halfway. Cyprian didn't try to give a few things to one side and a few things to the other side. Instead, he changed the conversation. He realized that the crux of the conversation was about God's love and mercy and how people could only be formed in that love in the Christian community. We are accustomed to entrenching ourselves in our own arguments and points of view. Sometimes we need someone to help us re-view our situation and change the underlying terms of the debate.

Third, Cyprian believes that unity is the precondition for reconciliation, not vice versa. I take this as one of his fundamental points. We cannot do the work of reconciliation if we do not first see that we are already unified. Telling the truth, though, is an essential ingredient to unity. Cyprian made clear that the rigorists and the laxists were not unified to the church because they were not being truthful to God's love. Pretending that separated Christians were not in fact separated fails to advance the cause of unity. Cyprian reminds us that we must tell the truth in our struggles to be reconciled. The ultimate truth, however, is that human beings are reconciled because of God's love in Christ. Once human beings respond faithfully and truthfully to that love, they will see that reconciliation is less *achieved* than it is *recognized*.

Fourth, in order to recognize that unity, we need humility—a humility that Cyprian found lacking in both the rigorists and the laxists. This, too, is difficult for us. Ours is an age—especially in the United States of America—where people see themselves first as individuals and second as members of a community. Everything Cyprian writes stands against this tendency. Humility implies that you understand that you are who you are because of your membership in a community. Our day needs the lesson of the early church to remind us of our dependence on our community. The only way we can have humility is to reform ourselves in God's love in the church. Again, love and unity are paramount.

Fifth, this unity only comes about because of God's love, and Christians come to experience this love through the celebration of the Eucharist. Cyprian wants all Christians to partake in the Eucharist if they are willing to undergo penance for their sins. Christians partake in *Christian* practices of reconciliation by understanding reconciliation in light of God's love, and the way to understand God's love is through Christian practices of prayer. The Eucharist, of course, is the source and summit of Christian prayer and therefore of Christian life. The practice of the Eucharist reminds people that their love and their unity are gifts from God. Through the Eucharist they recognize themselves as members of the community. *Caritas* leads to correction, which leads to communion.

Reflection Questions

1. What in Stegman's article about reconciliation in Paul resonates with Cyprian's understanding of reconciliation? Where does Cyprian follow Paul, and where does he go his own way?
2. How does Cyprian's understanding of love differ with or agree with understandings of love that you know? Is his view compelling? Are there ways we can incorporate the kind of humility Cyprian discusses into our understanding of love?
3. This article has stressed how Cyprian connects reconciliation with individual formation. How do you see that connection at work in other articles in this volume?
4. Can Cyprian's discussion of love and reconciliation lend insight into geopolitical contexts, such as the cases that Carney and Philpott analyze?

Notes

1. I would recommend that readers consult Thomas Stegman's essay in this volume for a fuller description of Paul's theology of reconciliation in Ephesians.

2. For a thorough account of Cyprian's use of Scripture, see Michael Andrew Fahey, *Cyprian and the Bible: A Study in Third-Century Exegesis* (Tuebingen: J. C. B. Mohr, 1971). Unfortunately, he does not discuss Cyprian's use of 1 John 4:8.

3. Robert Mayes, "The Lord's Supper in the Theology of Cyprian of Carthage," *Concordia Theological Quarterly* 74, nos. 3–4 (2010): 307.

4. J. Patout Burns, *Cyprian the Bishop* (New York: Routledge, 2002), 23.

5. Cyprian of Carthage, *On the Church, Selected Treatises*, trans. Allen Brent, Popular Patristics Series (Crestwood, NY: St. Vladimir's Seminary Press, 2006), 11.

6. Although *schism* and *heresy* mean two different things today, for Cyprian they were synonymous. See Geoffrey D. Dunn, "Heresy and Schism according to Cyprian of Carthage," *The Journal of Theological Studies* 55, no. 2 (2004): 566.

7. Burns, *Cyprian the Bishop*, 29.

8. For how Cyprian connected practice and belief, see Dunn, "Heresy and Schism according to Cyprian of Carthage," 559.

9. See Burns, *Cyprian the Bishop*, 21. See also Allan Brent, *Cyprian and Roman Carthage* (Cambridge: Cambridge University Press, 2010), 257–73, where he argues that the martyrs played a more important role historically than Cyprian gives them credit for.

10. Burns, *Cyprian the Bishop*, 22. It is probably clear that I have found Burns and Brent (*Cyprian and Roman Carthage*) essential for navigating the historical issues in Cyprian.

11. Brent, *Cyprian and Roman Carthage*, 254.

12. Brent, *Cyprian and Roman Carthage*, 287.

13. Burns, *Cyprian the Bishop*, 21.

14. As Laurence puts it, "It consists in each Christian's giving his or her obedience according to the Gospel to the one properly ordained bishop, gathering with the rest of the Church at the common Eucharist, and in everything manifesting Christ's 'inseparable

love' for his 'body' the Church" (John D. Laurance, "Eucharistic Leader according to Cyprian of Carthage: A New Study," *Studia Liturgica* 15, no. 2 [1984]: 71).

15. For Cyprian's Johannine view of the church, see Cyprian of Carthage, *On the Church, Selected Treatises*, 32. For Cyprian's Pauline view of the church, see *On the Church, Selected Treatises*, 29.

16. Letter 54.1. Hereafter, I will use the abbreviation Ep for "epistle." For Latin text of letters, see *Opera Omnia Corpus Christianorum Series Latina* (New York: Johnson Reprint Company, 1965). Translations are my own, but also see *Letters (1–81)*, trans. Sister Rose Bernard Donna, Fathers of the Church (Washington, DC: Catholic University of America Press, 1964).

17. Ep 54.2.

18. Ep 45.1. For more on *unitas* in Cyprian, see Juan Antonio Gil-Tamayo, "La iglesia como sacramentum unitatis en Cipriano de Cartago," *Scripta Theologica* 39, no. 2 (2007): 345.

19. Ep 59.19. For the practice of the Eucharist in the church in Carthage around 250, see Andrew Brian McGowan, "Rethinking Agape and Eucharist in Early North African Christianity," *Studia Liturgica* 34, no. 2 (2004): 172.

20. Ep 55.17.

21. Ep 55.19.

22. Ep 55.24.

23. Ep 55.24.

24. Ep 55.24.

25. Ep 55.29.

26. Ep 57.1.

27. Ep 57.2.

28. Ep 57.5.

29. Ep 57.5.

30. Ep 54.3.

31. Ep 66.3.

32. Ep 69.2; Eph 5:25; see also Ep 74.6.

33. Ep 54.4.

34. *De unitate* 9. For Latin text, see Cyprian of Carthage, *L'unité De L'église = De Ecclesiae Catholicae Unitate*, vol. 500, Sources Chrétiennes (Paris: Cerf, 2006).

35. *De unitate* 14.

36. *De unitate* 15. For an explanation of "sacramentum" in Cyprian, see Laurance, "Eucharistic Leader according to Cyprian of Carthage," 70.

37. *De unitate* 21.

38. *De unitate* 24.

39. *De unitate* 24.

40. *De unitate* 25.

CHAPTER 4

Early Monastic Practices of Strategic Speech and Selective Silence to Limit Violence

Zachary B. Smith

One morning in the late fourth century, a demoniac entered a church in Scetis, the southernmost collection of monastic establishments in Lower (northern) Egypt. The monks praying there—forty miles from the nearest village—tried to cast the demon out of the man, but it was beyond their ability. They realized that only one monk nearby, Bessarion, was powerful enough to cast out this demon; they also realized that Bessarion's humility prevented him from demonstrating his gift for exorcism. So the monks planned a "drive-by" exorcism in which they would trick Bessarion into casting out the demon by asking him to "wake" the "sleeping" man. Bessarion entered the church the next morning, and the monks asked him to wake the demoniac, who was sleeping at the front of the church. Bessarion told the man, "Arise, go out," and immediately the demon interpreted the command "go out" to apply to him and left the afflicted man.[1]

The story of Bessarion and the accidental exorcism encapsulates a truth in early monasticism—the words spoken by monks were powerful and performed actions beyond the intentions of the speakers. Early monastic thought held that because the words of monks were powerful to the point of sometimes being danger-ous, monks should exercise great discretion when speaking and should consider whether silence is preferable to speech in some circumstances. In this chapter, I offer an overview of the idea of dangerous speech and instructive silence in monastic thought, along with some suggestions for incorporating these ideas into modern reconciliation, peacemaking, and reformative activities.

Background, Context, and Approach

Modern academic discourse recognizes the dangers of speaking. The late twentieth- and early twenty-first-century Slovenian philosopher and social critic Slavoj Žižek argues that naming violence is the same as performing violence. The individ-ual who performs the naming applies her own standard of "nor-mal" against which she names the actions she deems violent. In so doing she forces the actions into her own conceptual frame and thus forces the actor into the role of perpetrator. Because lan-guage forces conceptual changes, it is necessarily violent.[2] Žižek relies partly on the twentieth-century French psychoanalyst Jacques Lacan to argue that language is violent and the human subject is stuck—tortured even—in language.[3] Words enter into the mind and force the speaker's ideas into the hearer's corpus of internal reference. And indeed Lacan is very aware that the sub-ject changes as a result of speaking and being spoken to, which is part of the problem that psychoanalysis encounters in try-ing to use language to explore the subject.[4] Twentieth-century French philosopher Michel Foucault spent his last three years working, in large part, on the process and dangers of *parrhesia*—truth-telling or plain-speaking.[5] Language and speech perform violence on the speaker and on the hearer. The hearer's mind shifts as a result of the vocalization of language. Because it forces a change in her perception, speaking becomes an act of violence to at least the mind of another person.

These contemporary ideas on speech and violence find close correspondences with the ascetic tradition, which operates care-fully when it comes to speaking. The monastic tendency toward silence is more than just an effort by monks to avoid distraction. Literary sources from the late antique, Byzantine, and medieval periods demonstrate that monks practiced strategic speech and selective silence to limit the possibilities of violence inherent in even corrective discourse. The monks seem willing to concede the idea that all speech is violent, whether it is instructive or simply words in passing. While modern philosophers limit the effects of verbal violence to the mind, the landscape for violence in the ascetic tradition stretches beyond the mind to the hearer's soul and body. Stories from early monasticism recount that words—just words—did violence to the bodies of demons; that monks not infrequently refused to speak lest their words be misconstrued; and that monks spoke only about certain topics like their own sins because other topics (the spiritual life, for instance) were considered too dangerous.

I focus here on the three primary concerns of monastic discourse: inappropriate speech, appropriate speech, and silence. My reading of speech, silence, and violence centers on two primary sources: a fourth- and fifth-century sayings text that records the teaching of and stories about important Egyptian monks (titled *Sayings of the Fathers*[6]), and the writings of John Cassian,[7] who trained in Egypt to be a monk. Pairing these two texts makes sense, as Cassian's *Conferences* purportedly records his conversations with Egyptian monks (similar to the *Sayings of the Fathers*) and his *Institutes* summarizes what he learned about the theory and practice of Egyptian-style monasticism. European monasticism was profoundly shaped by its Egyptian origins and returning to these sources illuminates the Eastern Christian traditions that influenced Catholicism.[8]

The Power of Language in Egyptian Monasticism

When the Egyptian monk Pambo declared that a monk's lips are holy, he drastically understated the common understanding of the power of a monk's words.[9] The words of monks exorcised demons, healed people, and raised children from the dead[10]—all by accident. While most stories about the healing words of monks find them speaking with intention,[11] the power of words delivered without specific miraculous intention demonstrates the perceived power of monastic speech, both inside and outside monastic communities. Another way of thinking about monastic speech is that it may be dangerous. These accidental words performed actions on the bodies and souls of other people beyond the intentions of the speakers. In one story, the verbal condemnation from one monk to another monk for a simple transgression nearly condemned the mildly transgressive monk to hell.[12] With all this power pouring from the lips of holy men in popular late antique imagination, it is no wonder that the monks preferred to keep silent.

Even beyond the popular conception of the power of a monk's words, there was significant power in their seemingly banal instructive utterances. Speech in monasticism came in two forms: inappropriate or worldly speech, and appropriate or heavenly speech. Inappropriate speech was violent because it tore the listener from her or his presence before the divine—by breaking concentration, introducing heresy, distracting the practitioner, confusing the worldly and heavenly realms, or removing personal peace. Even seemingly neutral speech such as a greeting or praise for spiritual devotion drove God away from the monk's mind and was thus inappropriate.[13] In the latter case, the monk John the Short exclaimed, after three interruptions by a visitor, "After coming here, you pushed God away from me!"[14] Hearing another person speak interrupted John's contemplative cycle of work, removing God from his mind.

Even appropriate speech, however, could prove violent by virtue of its transformative power over the hearer. The basic didactic element of monastic utterances was the simple verbal instruction to perform or not perform specific bodily or thought actions. The simplest example comes in the opening saying when Apa ("Father") Antony struggled to perform his asceticism and prayed for help. The divine responded by sending an angel to demonstrate the relationship between work and prayer; the angel concluded his lesson by saying simply, "Do this, and be saved."[15] The small instructive sayings necessarily transformed the hearer, even when rejected. The hearers understood the words in relation to themselves and made subjective judgments about their ability to perform the directives, their position in relation to the divine, and their understanding of their place in the afterlife. Since the speech-act precipitated these thoughts, it performed violence on the mind of the hearer by forcing self-examination in the terms of the speaker's instructive saying.

An even more violent action took place if the hearer put the words into action. Not only was the hearer forced into self-examination in the speaker's terms, but the hearer was forced into actions of bodily and mental violence in order to transform the self into a new subject. From Žižek, Lacan, and the monastic tradition, I understand violence to mean a causal relationship in which one person performs a forcible action that alters the recipient. One may perform violence on another person and on oneself. The key elements are the employment of force and the alteration in the subject receiving the application of force.

Violence may be as grotesque as Perpetua, an early third-century martyr from Carthage who died in an arena, guiding the gladiator's sword to her throat when he failed to kill her with the first stroke—here each performed a violent act, Perpetua against herself and the gladiator against Perpetua.[16] But violence may be as subtle as transmitting a thought to another person through a speech-act, such that the recipient cannot view a person (including herself) or situation in the same way that she did before the speech. Even an activity as seemingly banal as speech forces an alteration in the hearer's mind and in her subjective experience of reality.

The most obvious violent speech-act in monastic literature is the violence that a monk's words perform on demons. Besides instances of monks' words confounding the plans and actions of Satan and his demonic hordes, the words of monks performed actual violence on demons and were sometimes described as causing the demons physical pain.[17] In one story, when Apa Xanthias wanted to cast out a demon, he simply said that the demon would be cast out by the time Xanthias had finished a small glass of wine. As he drank, the demon screamed repeatedly, "You burn me!" Xanthias's pronouncement of exorcism burned the demon until it was cast out.[18] The idea that words can harm demons demonstrates the power of language in the monastic world—if even appropriate speech against demons was physically harmful, then inappropriate speech was even more dangerous.

Violence of Inappropriate Speech

Violence performed on another through inappropriate speech was one of the vices of monasticism. If the goal of asceticism was self-transformation (or self-recreation) of body, mind, and soul with the purpose of union with the divine, then anything that subverted that goal, such as inappropriate speech, was considered destructive. Speech became inappropriate in various ways. Simply speaking poorly of another person was considered inappropriate speech because it forced a change in how the hearer perceived the person discussed.[19] In other instances, speech was inappropriate because it stirred up vice in the hearer or distracted the hearer from his or her ascetic practice.[20] In these cases, the inappropriate speech forced a change in the mind of the hearer from the object of their intentional contemplation. One monk even called the distraction of speaking dangerous: "If you are unable to remain silent, it is much better [to talk] about the sayings of the fathers than about scripture. Because it [i.e., speaking] is no small danger."[21] Whatever the form, inappropriate speech received strong condemnation.

Uncontrolled speech was considered the worst passion in some monastic circles,[22] a vice so bad that it is the hardest one for righteous persons to remove.[23] John Cassian, in a saying recorded in the *Sayings of the Fathers*, said that inappropriate speech is a tool of Satan,[24] and the great Egyptian monk Antony said that scandalizing one's fellow monks through word or deed is a sin against Christ.[25] Monks developed a whole body of techniques involving intense focus on God in order to remove the possibility of distracting speech that harmed the hearer.[26] Inappropriate speech—snatching the hearer from the very presence of the divine and from the contemplation of higher things, creating vice, passion, and sin in the heart and mind of the hearer, forcing the hearer to think things that she or he does not wish to think—was seen as particularly destructive. Macarius the Great said that "a single evil word makes even the good, evil."[27]

Reformative Violence of Instructive (Appropriate) Speech

Conversely, Macarius said in the same breath that "a single good word makes even the evil, good."[28] Appropriate speech could have a reforming quality, changing the bad into good. Nevertheless, even appropriate speech in the monastic context was seen as violent because it did two things. First, appropriate speech transformed the mind of the hearer by placing it in the context of the speaker's utterance. If a monk corrected, adjusted, or taught through speaking, he (or, on occasion, she) necessarily transformed the mind of the hearer with spoken words. Even if the hearer did not put these words into effect, the act of hearing the spoken words transformed the subjective experience by placing it in the categories, judgments, and language of the individual speaking. Such a transformation was not voluntary and could be seen as violent.

Therefore, the monks could say that instruction and reproach were the same thing, because in telling another person how to perform his asceticism, the speaker necessarily cast judgment on the hearer's current practices.[29] The judgment then forced an alteration in the hearer's self-conception. Instead of the *self*-accusation and *self*-recrimination that monks saw as preferable, accusation and recrimination were forced onto the ascetic practitioner by the instructive words of another.[30] While reformative, the words of monastic instruction were necessarily violent because they forced the hearer to change thought or deed.

The monastic texts record the effect that these instructions had on the hearer, casting them in terms of internal and external pain. Antony's words are twice described as piercing another person's heart.[31] After many years, the teachings of one monk to his disciple shifted the disciple's perception of his teacher—the reformative violence of instruction made the teacher "Satanic" to the disciple, such that even his encouragement was as hard and piercing as metal.[32] Another teacher's way of life was described as too difficult by his disciple, which led the teacher to retort that the disciple was too soft.[33] Occasionally, following the teachings of older monks exposed the disciples to real physical harm; in one instance following Antony's teachings led to a monk being mauled by wild dogs.[34] In a story that recalls Abraham's near sacrifice of Isaac in the Torah, a senior monk tested a would-be ascetic practitioner by telling him to cast his son into a river so that he could become a monk unencumbered.[35] Fortunately, a third monk stopped the man just as he was about to murder his son. The words of monks created internal pain and external suffering even when carried out appropriately, because asceticism is necessarily performing violence on oneself.

Thus, even when a monk's speech advocated self-reformation, it could be regarded as violent speech. Advanced monks who wished to teach others knew that speech needed to be performed selectively, because it was a violent action. If the hearer could not perform the necessary actions of self-reforming asceticism, then the teacher either remained silent[36] or modified the speech to something that the hearer could perform[37]—still violent, but not so violent that the hearer might become discouraged through inability to carry the violent speech into violent self-reformation.[38] The work of a monk was self-destruction for the purpose of self-reformation.[39] Teaching others this process of self-reformation through speech performed violence on the hearer by forcing a change in his internal orientation and by causing him to perform ascetic violence on his body.

Verbal Violence in the Egyptian Desert

Given that even reformative speech could be violent, silence was the only way to prevent the violence of speech. And so the monks strove for silence, even to the point of training other monks entirely by example, in silence.[40] The monk Arsenius received divine instruction on how to achieve sinlessness, including the directive to remain silent: "Arsenius! Flee, maintain silence, and be still [in prayer]. For these are the foundations of sinlessness."[41]

Another monk spent three years with a rock in his mouth learning to keep silent.[42] Part of the reason that monks attempted solitude was that it aided their quest for silence.[43] And yet even the instructive silence that prevented violence was occasionally painful in itself.[44] Sometimes monks practiced silence in order to create space for the would-be hearer to self-reflect and thereby self-reform. This disturbing silence in the face of questions and requests made petitioners uncomfortable, even upset, and created these necessary conditions for reflection on the request for speech. Depending on the situation, monks sometimes found this approach more instructive than teaching verbally. No matter what precautions a monk took, asceticism was inherently violent in all its performances.

Cassian on Speech and Silence

Cassian's fifteen years in Egypt included a formative period in Scetis, the home of many of the monks in the *Sayings of the Fathers*.[45] Therefore it is not surprising to find the same ideas in Cassian that we find in the pages of the *Sayings*. The *Conferences* record his recollections of conversations with monks in Egypt, including several in Scetis, and the *Institutes* are the collected and distilled wisdom from his time there, written to form monks in Europe. Cassian recognized the power of words and encouraged caution when speaking.

Near the end of his conference with Daniel of Scetis, Cassian recorded Daniel's condemnation of those who speak frivolously because, in their pride, they considered themselves better than their ascetic peers.[46] Pride—one of the primary ascetic vices—expressed itself through speech. Likewise, the vice of anger was expressed, in some instances, through speech.[47] Severe speech, accidental speech, and intentionally provocative speech (even if the goal of the provocative speech was to create ascetic suffering for the speaker at the hands of others) were all likewise condemned in Cassian's *Conferences*.[48] So the monks of Cassian's conferences advocated for care in speech, especially instructive speech, because there were ample opportunities for abuse and

70

because speech could destroy the virtues.[49] Lack of care in even a single word opened one monk to demonic possession.[50]

Speech additionally had the power to create, making it even more dangerous. In a section discussing salvation, Cassian's speaker Chaeremon pointed out the healings of Jesus and the apostles—with emphasis on the words spoken in the healings.[51] The words of powerful people created health where before there was none. The words of monks, likewise, held great power: they moved their hearers to action, worked miracles, and created virtue in their hearers.[52] These words of practitioners of the virtuous life amazed and produced intense emotions of desire in the listeners to the point that such speech could be called heavenly.[53] At the most fundamental level, the instruction contained in the *Institutes* and *Conferences* came from speech—instructive speech, carefully delivered, exhibiting discretion and the wisdom of ascetic practitioners reproduced in written form intended to be read to early practitioners of European-style monasticism.[54] Cassian remained deeply aware of the power of speech throughout his two works, a power both to create and to destroy.

Given the awesome power of speech, the monk Theonas, when exploring the words of Qohelet, reminded Cassian that silence and speaking are only appropriate when performed at their appropriate times and in their appropriate ways.[55] Silence held as firm a place in teaching others as speaking; throughout the *Conferences*, Cassian noted the times when his speakers silently contemplated the questions that started the conferences. The emphasis on silence is clear in a metaphor for the ascetic journey that Cassian repeated throughout the *Conferences*. Each person is on a boat, and the open seas represent the appropriate speech of monks—deep but dangerous. On the other hand, there is the safe, deep harbor of silence, where the ascetic may anchor safely.[56] Silence was necessary for prayer and contemplation, and was a virtue greatly desired by the monks.[57] The monks practiced eating in silence, keeping silent on unimportant matters, and even keeping silent when insulted.[58] Silence was a primary good that was broken mainly to teach, but even silence served as instructive.

Silent work served as an example for other monks to imitate—the silence was as instructive as the spoken words of the monk.[59] A kind of indirect silence, in which a more advanced monk speaks in general terms in order to move a specific novice to proper action, served to correct gluttony.[60] In one story, recounted by Apa Serapion about his time training at the feet of Apa Theonas, Serapion remembers secreting bread from the meals to eat later in the day. After one such meal, Theonas taught his students about gluttony, and the generic words moved Serapion to confess and strive for more virtuous actions. Similarly, attaining the virtue of patience required direct silence to create interior peace, and this silence joined the monk to God.[61]

Because of the power of words to create and destroy, monks found it better to keep silent and develop the interior connections between themselves and God. The *intention* of the silence was important, however, because silence could be weaponized to harm others.[62] One of the best teachings on weaponized silence comes from Apa Joseph, who explained that the silence deployed against the anger of another speaker, even when used to keep oneself from speaking angrily, still conveys the anger of the non-speaker and can provoke the original speaker further.[63] The intention to remain silent required purity to be considered righteous silence. Ultimately, the message of the desert of Scetis was that silence and interiority—no matter how advantageous—were very difficult.[64]

Like the Egyptian monks, Cassian understood the dangerous nature of speech and held that silence was preferable. Silence created interiority and a connection with God and could even instruct other monks. Speech had the power to create and destroy (remember, God pronounced Creation in Genesis 1, and Word was the organizing and creating principle in John 1), so all speech, including instruction, required great care. Speaking was a violent act that forced changes in the hearer, either changes of mind or changes of behavior, and speaking could be weaponized through intentional malice or unintentional carelessness, making it even more violent. Cassian, drawing on the deep tradition of the Egyptian desert in which he trained, recognized the value of strategic speech and selective silence to limit violence.

Reclaiming Techniques of Speech and Silence

What, then, can we take from the monastic traditions of speech and silence for our discussion of reconciliation and limiting violence? First, the monks teach that corrective speech requires tempering. Humanity in modernity is told that solving and healing conflict starts with dialogue. "Truth and justice" or "truth and reconciliation" commissions, twelve-step programs, and counseling are examples of reformative activities that open with dialogue, discussion, and verbal discovery. While these are useful tools for reconciliation, they are not the only tools. As the monks demonstrate, sometimes silence and the space for an individual to correct herself (or to receive divine correction) are more instructive than didactic censure. Practicing selective silence allows others to learn more deeply through mistakes and contemplation, whereas verbal correction sometimes creates the desire to respond defensively or shut down internal dialogue in the face of external critique. Bringing people together sometimes requires shutting one side up.

Most important here is the place of internal dialogue. Contemplative practices, including prayer, made up a major portion of a monk's time. These practices occur in the silent spaces created by the intentional choice not to speak and thus not to force changes into the minds of hearers. Instead, their own internal voices fill the silence and form new modes of thinking, without the force of the other voice. Reconciliation efforts might benefit from some of these monastic modes of contemplation by creating the spaces and times for participants to reflect on the situation themselves and the other persons with whom they are in conflict. Peacemaking dialogues could include the process of internal reflection on the *logos* ("utterance," "reckoning," and "explanation," among others) part of the *dialogos* ("through speaking"). Indeed, related to *logos* is *logismos*—one's reasoning power, or the internal *logos* that creates the spoken *logos*. Allowing evidence, victim statements, impact reports, and other materials to penetrate the minds of participants could be a powerful tool in reconciliation and peacemaking. This tool of contemplation requires silence, and in the quiet, words can echo even more loudly than when shouted by an angry horde.

Emmanuel Katongole explores some of the issues of silence in his reflection on the silence of Rwanda post-genocide. He understands that the failure of *words* (*logos*) is not a failure of *thoughts* (*logismos*):

> This silence is not an empty silence but a silence that bubbles with a lot of unanswered questions about the meaning, dignity, and sacredness of the human person. Who am I? What does it mean to be a human being? Are we indeed different from cows? Is it true that we are created in the image of God? What does that mean? Is that true for the killers as well? Who is my neighbor, and what does it mean to be a neighbor? Whom can I trust?[65]

He concludes by invoking Ezekiel 37 (Ezekiel in the valley of dry bones) and suggesting that lament is the only expression remaining after words cease. The monks see something similar in their silences—the space for internal questions and answers, and more importantly (as in Cassian's story about the monk who hid bread in his robe) the space for interior movement toward lament over current or past events and the movement toward a better subjectivity. This bettered subjectivity creates the necessary conditions for reconciliation—the ability inside oneself to change.

On the other hand, there are instances in which the potential evils of not speaking outweigh the violence performed by speaking. In such cases, strategic speech requires assessing the situation and determining the most effective approach to the desired outcome. Selective speech is not reactionary; it is careful, deliberate, situational, reflective, and perhaps violent. It seeks to bring about a change in the mind and behavior of the hearer, and as such should be deployed very carefully. Selective speech is necessarily both instructive and destructive, removing other ways of thinking, being, and acting in order to replace them with the reformed ideas, existences, and actions. In reconciliation and peacemaking, selective speech is perhaps the only way to dialogue. Words have an impact often far beyond what the speaker intends, so the best message is the one briefly conveyed.

Another aspect of the monastic tradition that might offer insights for contemporary reconciliation efforts is the "conference" model of instruction, in which an older monk was designated the teacher, but younger monks set the topic of the occasion's monologue. The older monk would speak briefly in response to a question, and the younger monks could then ask for clarification or expansion on the teacher's words. Effectively, while one person is the primary speaker, it is the listeners who set the domain of speaking. This is not a standard dialogue; each side receives the space to speak, but that speech is guided by the other side such that neither is placed solely in the passive, listening position. When combined with the space for contemplation, this strategy could produce more effective responses than days of prepared statements and counterstatements.

Ultimately, though, these are all examples of alternative discursive modes that serve to break the expectations of the observer/listener/learner. Instead of verbal instruction, silence allows the hearer to become the self-speaker interiorly in the absence of expected discourse (again, the relation of *logos* and *logismos* is key to the monastic tradition). We see a shift in how and why the speech occurs (inside the person, driven by the discomfort of silence when expecting speech). Importantly, the effect is often the same—a change on the part of the hearer—though without the force and violence associated with verbal utterances by an Other. When one monk visited another in the Egyptian desert, he often greeted his host with the phrase, "Give me a word." These were open invitations by the speaker to have his mind altered by the instructions of another. When the monk failed to answer, the empty space between the two hung heavy with the anticipation of instruction. The silence forced the original speaker into the position of answering himself within his own mind.

Often, though, monks answered each other when asking for "a word" and provided carefully measured instruction. Another alternative discursive mode occurs in the strategic speeches of monks. Knowing the power of words to create (ideas and actions) and destroy (relationships, motivation, etc.), monks used them sparingly. Because of their relative paucity of speaking, and their aversion to certain topics, the force of their words intensified. When monks spoke words of instruction, the necessity to speak was so great as to override their aversion to using force and performing violence. Particularly in the *Sayings* and parts of Cassian's works, the question-oriented approach predominates in monastic vocalization, with their answers appearing almost like Zen koans. The hearer is nearly engulfed by the power of the words. While the listener may not have understood these words at the time, the force of hearing them out of the silence and then meditating on them in the ensuing silence dramatically disrupted the hearer's subjective reality. Words worked because they were rarely used.

Conclusion

Just as Lacan and Žižek argued that speech could be violent, the desert fathers understood that their words held significant power to destroy and create. Their creation of a monastic subject first required the destruction of the old subject, so speech—even instructive speech—in monasticism was performing violence on the hearer. In a way, every story about a monk keeping silent is an example of a monk trying to prevent violence against another person or trying to create the space for the subject to learn from himself. Similarly, in actions of reconciliation and peacemaking, we are trying to create a new subjectivity by destroying the old subject. Speaking is not just about arguments and ideas, but about undertaking the process of subject making through strategically destroying and rebuilding others and their ideas and action. Silence provides individuals the space to start this literally self-destructive process on their own. The alternative to practicing strategic speech and selective silence is sometimes the ultimate form of violence: personal or social damnation. Asceticism, the making of new subjects, was a violent undertaking, and the monks learned the hard way, living among the sticks and stones of the desert, that words could hurt them.

Reflection Questions

1. What can we apply from ancient monastic practices of speech and silence to modern reconciliation and peacemaking activities?
2. What things can help facilitate the internal dialogue created by silence?
3. What kinds of situations necessitate breaking silence? What ethical boundaries, when transgressed, always require speech?
4. How does one know when the time for silence is over and the time for dialogue begins?

Notes

1. Bessarion 5 (*Sayings*); edition citation in n. 6, below. All translations in this chapter are my own.

2. Slavoj Žižek, "Language, Violence, and Non-violence," *International Journal of Žižek Studies* 2, no. 3 (2008): 1–12, at 2. He explores this concept at great length in *Violence* (London: Profile Books, 2008), especially in chap. 2.

3. Žižek, "Language," 3–4.

4. Jacques Lacan, "The Function and Field of Speech and Language in Psychoanalysis," in *Écrits*, trans. Bruce Fink (New York: Norton, 2006), 197–268 (237–322 in the French edition).

5. Michel Foucault, *The Hermeneutics of the Subject: Lectures at the Collège de France, 1981–1982*, ed. Frédéric Gros, trans. Graham Burchell (New York: Picador, 2005); Foucault, *The Government of Self and Others: Lectures at the Collège de France, 1982–1983*, ed. Frédéric Gros, trans. Graham Burchell (New York: Picador, 2010); Foucault, *The Courage of Truth: The Government of Self and Others II: Lectures at the Collège de France, 1983–1984*, ed. Frédéric Gros, trans. Graham Burchell (New York: Picador, 2011).

6. The text is Jacques-Paul Migne, *Patrologia Graeca* 65:71–440 (Paris: J.-P. Migne, 1864), with additions by Jean-Claude Guy, *Recherches sur la tradition grecque des* Apophthegmata Patrum, Subsidia Hagiographica 36 (Brussels: Société des Bollandistes,

1962), 13–58. The most recent English translation is by John Wortley, *Give Me a Word: The Alphabetical Sayings of the Desert Fathers*, Popular Patristics Series 52 (Yonkers, NY: St. Vladimir's Seminary Press, 2014).

7. John Cassian, *Conferences*, ed. and (French) trans. E. Pichery, *Conférences*, 3 vols., Source Chrétiennes 42, 45, 64 (Paris: Éditions du Cerf, 1955–59); Cassian, *Institutes*, ed. and (French) trans. Jean-Claude Guy, *Institutions cénobitiques*, Sources Chrétiennes 109 (Paris: Éditions du Cerf, 1965). Good, standard English translations are Boniface Ramsey, *John Cassian: The Conferences*, Ancient Christian Writers 57 (New York: Paulist Press, 1997); Boniface Ramsey, *John Cassian: The Institutes*, Ancient Christian Writers 58 (New York: Newman Press, 2000).

8. On the development of Western monasticism from Egypt, see Marilyn Dunn, *The Emergence of Monasticism: From the Desert Fathers to the Early Middle Ages* (Oxford: Blackwell, 2003).

9. Pambo 7 (*Sayings*).

10. Bessarion 5, Macarius the Great 15, Sisoes 18 (*Sayings*).

11. E.g., Longinus 3–4, Milesius 1, Poimen 7 (*Sayings*).

12. Isaac the Theban 1 (*Sayings*).

13. John the Short 32 (*Sayings*).

14. Ἀφ' οὗ εἰσῆλθες ἐνταῦθα, ἔβαλες τὸν Θεὸν ἀπ' ἐμοῦ

15. Antony 1 (*Sayings*), Οὕτως ποίει, καὶ σώζῃ.

16. *Passion of Perpetua and Felicity* 21.9–10 (trans. Maureen A. Tilley, "The Passion of Saints Perpetua and Felicity," in *Religions of Late Antiquity in Practice*, ed. Richard Valantasis [Princeton: Princeton University Press, 2000], 387–97). See also Maureen A. Tilley, "The Passion of Perpetua and Felicity," in *Searching the Scriptures*, vol. 2, *A Feminist Commentary*, ed. Elisabeth Schüssler Fiorenza (New York: Crossroads, 1994), 829–58, at 850–51.

17. Macarius the Great 3, 11; Elias 7; Longinus 4; Xanthias 2 (*Sayings*).

18. Xanthias 2 (*Sayings*), Καίεις με, καίεις με. With the semantic range of καίω from "kindle" to "consume with fire," it is possible that the exorcism destroyed the demon entirely by burning him up.

19. John the Short 6 (*Sayings*).

20. John the Short 5 (vice of anger), Antony 18 (constantly talking younger monks distracted the peace of the silent older monk),

Ammoes 1 (walked out of church ahead of everyone else to prevent irrelevant speech from interrupting his contemplation of the service), Achilles 4 (heard something that bothered him but did not confront the speaker about it, so the words he wanted to say turned into blood and he spat them out) (*Sayings*).

21. Amoun of Nitria 2 (*Sayings*), Εἰ οὐ δύνασαι σιωπᾶν, καλόν ἐστι μᾶλλον ἐν τοῖς λόγοις τῶν γερόντων, καὶ μὴ ἐν τῇ Γραφῇ. Κίνδυνος γάρ ἐστι οὐ μικρός. The saying here plays off the dual ideas that both inappropriate speech and discussions about Scripture are dangerous. The danger of speaking about Scripture or "heavenly" things is a common trope in Egyptian monastic literature.

22. Agathon 1 (*Sayings*).

23. Epiphanius 12 (*Sayings*).

24. Cassian 6 (*Sayings*).

25. Antony 9 (*Sayings*).

26. Theodora 8 (*Sayings*).

27. Macarius the Great 39 (*Sayings*).

28. Macarius the Great 39 (*Sayings*).

29. Poimen 157 (*Sayings*).

30. Theophilus the Archbishop 1 (*Sayings*).

31. Antony 13, 29 (*Sayings*).

32. Ammoes 2 (*Sayings*).

33. Sisoes 51 (*Sayings*).

34. Arsenius 24, Antony 20 (*Sayings*).

35. Sisoes 10 (*Sayings*).

36. Arsenius 7 (did not speak to a magistrate except to tell him never to return), Isaac Priest of Kellia 2 (lived with Theodore of Pherme, who refused to order him and instead taught by example) (*Sayings*).

37. Ares 1, Joseph of Panephysis 3, Poimen 22–23 (*Sayings*).

38. Hence Sisoes 33 (*Sayings*), in which hanging oneself over a cliff to avoid sleep was prohibited by an angel because of the potential for harm; the angel also prohibited Sisoes from teaching such an activity.

39. E.g., Alonius 2 (*Sayings*).

40. Isaac Priest of Kellia 2, Theophilus 2 (Pambo believed that silence was instructive and would not speak to the archbishop) (*Sayings*).

41. Arsenius 2 (*Sayings*), Ἀρσένιε, φεῦγε, σιώπα, ἡσύχαζε· αὗται γάρ εἰσιν αἱ ῥίζαι τῆς ἀναμαρτησίας.
42. Arsenius 2, Agathon 15 (*Sayings*).
43. Antony 11, Longinus 1 (*Sayings*).
44. John the Theban 1 (*Sayings*).
45. On Cassian's time in Egypt, see Columba Stewart, *Cassian the Monk* (Oxford: Oxford University Press, 1998), 7–12, 133–40. On the *Sayings of the Fathers* as a Scetis-centered text, see Zachary B. Smith, *Philosopher-Monks, Episcopal Authority, and the Care of the Self: The* Apophthegmata Patrum *in Fifth-Century Palestine*, Instrumenta Patristica et Mediaevalia 80 (Turnhout: Brepols, 2018), 28, 31–35.
46. Cassian, *Conferences* 4.20.1–3.
47. Cassian, *Conferences* 5.11.7.
48. Cassian, *Conferences* 2.13.4–9; 17.29; 16.20.
49. Cassian, *Conferences* 14.9.4–7. Sometimes the failure of speech lies not in the speaker but in the hearer, though both may be at fault (Cassian, *Conferences* 14.18).
50. Cassian, *Conferences* 7.27.
51. Cassian, *Conferences* 13.14–16.
52. Cassian, *Conferences* 8.25.5; 2.11.1–5; 1.20.6–8.
53. Cassian, *Conferences* 1.23; 7.7.
54. Instruction becomes a two-way communication because the learner must tell the teacher all his thoughts (Cassian, *Institutes* 4.9).
55. Cassian, *Conferences* 21.12.3–4.
56. Cassian, *Conferences* Praef. 3; 8.25.5; 24.26.18.
57. Cassian, *Institutes* 4.12; 2.10.1–2; 10.3; Cassian, *Conferences* 9.25; 9.27; 9.35–36; 10.11; 24.18.
58. Cassian, *Institutes* 4.17; 4.15.2; 4.41.1–2; Cassian, *Conferences* 16.26.2.
59. Cassian, *Institutes* 10.11; 10.14.
60. Cassian, *Conferences* 2.11.1–4.
61. Cassian, *Conferences* 18.12; 14.13.5; 14.4.1.
62. Cassian, *Institutes* 12.27.4–6, 12.29.2–3.
63. Cassian, *Conferences* 16.18.
64. Cassian, *Conferences* 24.4.

65. Emmanuel Katongole, "Justice, Forgiveness, and Reconciliation in the Wake of Genocide: The End of Words," *The Other Journal* (August 16, 2012), https://theotherjournal.com/2012/08/16/justice-forgiveness-and-reconciliation-in-the-wake-of-genocide-the-end-of-words/.

II

MEDIEVAL AND EARLY MODERN CASES

CHAPTER 5

The Medieval Peace of God Movement

J. J. Carney

On Christmas Eve 1914, several months after the outbreak of World War I, soldiers initiated a truce on the Western Front. As the guns fell silent, British, French, and German soldiers exchanged gifts with each other and joined in an impromptu soccer match. The truce continued through Christmas Day until superiors on both sides ordered their soldiers back to their trenches.

In 2002, the United Nations deployed the United Nations Organization Mission in the Democratic Republic of the Congo (MONUC, later renamed MONUSCO), an international force that eventually grew to over 23,000 soldiers. The UN's largest ever peacekeeping deployment came in response to "Africa's World War," an internecine conflict that took the lives of an estimated 4 million civilians, soldiers, and militia between 1996 and 2003. Even as MONUSCO struggled to keep the peace while doing business with the corrupt, authoritarian regime of President Joseph Kabila, the Catholic Church stepped into the void left by the absentee government, providing social services, building bridges, monitoring elections, and attempting to broker a peaceful political succession.

In February 2017, Jeannette Vizguerra, an undocumented Mexican immigrant who had lived in the USA for over twenty years, took sanctuary in a Unitarian and later a Baptist church in Denver, Colorado, to avoid deportation by the U.S. government's Immigration and Naturalization Services (INS).

What do these three disparate modern stories have in common? All three resonate with key dimensions of the medieval Peace of God movement and its successor the Truce of God, two little-remembered social and ecclesial movements that swept through western parts of the Carolingian Empire around the turn of the first millennium. In an effort to limit escalating local violence, Catholic bishops reached agreements with feudal nobles to protect clerics and peasants from violence, establish sanctuary for church property, limit the days on which armies could fight, and combine temporal and spiritual sanctions to keep the peace. Although movements related to the Peace of God lingered through the late Middle Ages, they have been largely overshadowed in popular memory by the Holy Land Crusades. In stark contrast to the Crusades, awareness of the Peace of God is limited to select medieval historians and a smattering of theologians and ethicists working on questions of just war and the Catholic peace tradition.[1]

In this chapter, I hope to recover this little-known medieval movement for a broader audience. I will first place the Peace of God movement in its historical context in the early medieval period before tracing its explicit development in the late tenth and eleventh centuries. In keeping with this volume's overall spirit of *ressourcement*, I dedicate the second half of this essay to four key resonances of the Peace of God movement for our contemporary world. First, this movement offers a case study in how ecclesial imagination and the church's storehouse of ritual, juridical, and sacramental traditions can be applied to contexts of peacekeeping and violence. Second, the Peace of God movement offers an important example from the Christian tradition of closely linking peace and justice. Third, the Peace of God movement reminds us that we are always limiting rather than eliminating violence, and this often entails the necessary yet dangerous use of force in protective peacekeeping. Finally, the juxtaposition of the Peace of God movement with the Crusades raises uncomfortable but necessary questions concerning the nature of Christian identity, the "othering" of the non-Christian outsider, and the connection between "holy peace" and "holy war."

Historical Overview of the Peace of God Movement, 979–1095 AD

The Peace of God movement originated in the late 900s in the Burgundy and Aquitaine region of modern-day France, then part of the western provinces of the Frankish Carolingian kingdom.[2] Founded by Charles Martel and his son and successor Charlemagne in the late eighth century, the Carolingian Empire dominated central and western Europe through the 800s AD. By the tenth century, however, the empire had fragmented, with Carolingian royal authority giving way to power struggles between rival local nobles. In turn, Frankish and Germanic society's clan-based feuding culture exacted a growing toll on local communities that were themselves undergoing a boom in population, agriculture, and mercantile commerce. Finally, religious revival was on the rise in light of monastic reform movements at Cluny, growing lay interest in pilgrimages and relics, and fervent millennial expectations surrounding the year 1000 AD.[3]

These factors combined to bring the church more centrally into the business of making peace. On one level, the rhetoric of "Peace of God" was not wholly innovative in the tenth century. The language of *pax ecclesiae*, or "peace of the church," appears in the Christian tradition as early as the sixth century. In this context, Christians who were faithful to God's law as handed down through the church were embodying the *pax ecclesiae*. In contrast, those who broke the peace were cast out and could only be readmitted after substantial penance.[4] In the Carolingian period, peacemaking had primarily been regarded as within the purview of the king. He served as a *mediator cleri et plebis*, a mediator among the clergy and the people, charged with maintaining public peace and social order.[5] Peace here was understood as protection against outside invasion and the maintenance of internal security and order. But with the increasing impotence of Carolingian royal authority—especially in outlying regions like southwestern France—local nobles jockeyed with each other for power, undermining collective security. In this context, the tenth-century Peace of God movement emerged as an explicitly ecclesial effort to restore a measure of social order. In the words of Tomaz Mastnak, "the *pax Dei* [peace of God] replaced peace made and defended by the king, *pax regis*."[6]

The first Peace of God Council occurred at La Puy in the Burgundy region of Auvergne around 979 AD. The lyrically named Bishop Guy of Le Puy assembled hundreds of *rustici* (peasants) and local *milites* (mounted soldiers or knights) "so that they might give him their advice on the correct way to assure the peace."[7] In an open field surrounded by the very clerics and peasants they had abused, the assembled *milites* swore an oath of peace and promised to return goods they had stolen from churches. Bishop Guy's armed relatives—namely his nephews and their respective militias—stood with the bishop as these oaths were pronounced, lending a measure of military threat to the bishop's religious sanction.

A basic pattern in the Peace of God councils emerged as Bishop Guy called subsequent councils at Aurillac in the 980s and again at Le Puy in 993–94. First, the bishop organized what could be termed a "popular council," gathering a large number of clergy, monks, nobility, and laity in open fields near the episcopal see. Second, monks brought saints' relics to these gatherings, introducing elements of divine sanction and intercessory healing. Third, on pain of excommunication, local *milites* swore oaths to respect church property as well as the lives and property of unarmed peasants and clergy. Finally, the presence of the bishop's "family militia" offered a measure of military force to reinforce these spiritual and legal oaths.[8] It also reflected an early medieval context in which the "kin-group" was responsible for "bringing to justice anyone who had wronged a member of the kin."[9]

Bishop Le Puy proved to be a trendsetter. Fellow bishops in the nearby region of Aquitaine gathered at the councils of Charroux (989), Limoges (994), and Poitiers (1000). Regional peace councils continued in France throughout the first half of the eleventh century, including a flurry of nearly twenty peace councils in the 1020s and 1030s as Christians prepared for the millennial anniversary of Christ's death in 1033. In Aquitaine, the gatherings typically happened in open fields where large numbers of local laity, clerics, and monks could witness the oaths of the *milites*. The oaths banned knights from taking ecclesiastical property by force, invading churches, plundering peasant agricultural fields, and/or attacking unarmed clerics, *pauperes* (the poor), and *agricolae* (farmers).[10] If these oaths were broken, penance and restitution of stolen goods were expected.[11] In the absence of such satisfaction, the bishops excommunicated the offender, denying him the sacraments or burial in holy ground. Thomas Head, a leading historian of the Peace of God, argues that the movement was most successful in protecting church property, preserving clerics and bishops from violence, and reestablishing principles of ecclesial sanctuary. It was rather less successful in actually protecting the poor.[12]

Both lay and clerical elites played prominent roles in helping to "keep the peace."[13] As noted, bishops could threaten peacebreakers with spiritual sanctions of excommunication and interdict (namely, refusing to allow sacramental celebrations in a local area). Some went further. In one notorious case in Burgundy in the late 1030s, Archbishop Aimon of Bourges assembled a militia of peasants and clerics to punish peacebreaking *milites*. In general, though, the enforcement of the peace was left to sympathetic lay lords. In western France, this role was played by the Dukes of Aquitaine, William IV Iron Arm and his son William the Great. Revealingly, the former preferred to be called "lay abbot," reflecting the blurring of lay and clerical authority that would become such a prominent point of contention during the bitter eleventh-century disputes between Pope Gregory VII and German king Henry IV.[14]

Enthusiastic popular support was no less important to the success of the Peace of God. Peasants and clergy typically connected the Peace of God movement to physical healing from disease and divine deliverance from natural disaster, epidemics, and famine. Such events were seen as revelatory signs of God's judgment at the turn of the millennium.[15] In response to the perceived wrath of God, penitent communities embarked on multiple days of fasting. Monks would then bring saints' relics to the Peace of God councils. According to local belief, these relics facilitated healing miracles that attested to the flowering of "God's peace," precipitating popular euphoria and facilitating the acquiescence of local lords and knights.[16] The popular dimension of the Peace of God movement is captured in the eleventh-century historian Rodulphus Glaber's recounting of the 1033 council commemorating the millennial anniversary of Christ's death. "Such enthusiasm was generated that the bishops raised their croziers to the heavens, and all cried with one voice to God, their hands extended: 'Peace! Peace! Peace!' This was the sign of their perpetual covenant with God."[17]

Between the 1020s and the 1040s, the Peace of God evolved into a related but distinct movement known as the "Truce of God." If the Peace aimed to protect certain categories of property and persons from abuse, the Truce looked to limit all violence through an expanded sense of "holy time."[18] For example, following an older Carolingian tradition, the 1027 Council of Toulouges declared that the Lord's Day of Sunday should be preserved from fighting. At the 1041 Council of Toulouges, the bishops expanded their proscription of warfare from sunset on Wednesday until dawn on Monday (in honor of Holy Thursday, Good Friday, Holy Saturday, and Easter Sunday).[19] These bans were later extended to include many saints' feast days and the liturgical seasons of Lent and Easter. An underlying *mythos* here concerned the perpetual peace that should exist between baptized Christians. This ambition is perhaps best captured in the 1054 Council of Narbonne's declaration that "no Christian should kill another Christian, since whoever kills a Christian doubtless sheds the blood of Christ."[20] As the church increasingly condemned violence between Christians, the question arose as to where the church could direct Christian knights or *milites*. One of the key outlets became the Crusades themselves, initiated by Pope Urban II in 1095 to underwrite "perpetual peace within the whole of Christendom" through a new "dedication of arms to a salutary war against the heathen."[21] Thus the "holy peace" that began the eleventh century culminated with "holy war" at the end. Peace of God canons were reaffirmed at the first three Lateran councils of the twelfth century,[22] but the energy of Christendom was now directed outward toward the propagation of war in the name of Christian expansion.

Ressourcement: Four Key Resonances of the Peace of God for Today

A thousand years is a long time, and much has changed from the early second millennium to the early third millennium. Sadly, however, our world is no less conflictual and violent. Yet there is more to the story, both then and now. Modern stereotypes of Catholic history often highlight the violence of the Crusades, the intolerance of the Spanish Inquisition, and post-Reformation religious conflicts. Such episodes should not be papered over in an apologetic effort to defend the Catholic Church. But recovering the memory of movements like the Peace of God helps broaden our awareness of an alternative trajectory in Catholic history— one committed to making peace rather than making war. More specifically, I would point to four areas where the Peace of God movement offers particular insight for today's world.

Marshaling Local Catholic Resources to Limit Violence

The Peace of God movement offers a unique historical example of the local church marshaling a large and diverse array of ecclesial resources in an effort to reduce and limit violence. First, much of the power of the Peace of God movement stemmed from the medieval sense of the church as an "eschatologically conceived phenomenon."[23] In other words, the church was both an earthly and eternal reality, initiated by Christ in historical time, yet pointing to, awaiting, and even tasting the dawning of God's eternal kingdom. In turn, early medieval Christians lived with a keen sense of the permeability between the spiritual and physical worlds.[24] Within this worldview, one can understand what Thomas Head calls the "eschatological weight" of excommunicating peacebreakers, thus denying them the sacramental means of receiving God's grace (from Eucharist to burial).[25] At the time of the Peace of God, this

91

eschatological sense was only heightened by the millennial celebrations of Christ's birth and death. World events appeared to confirm these expectations, such as the appearance of Haley's Comet in 989, the 992 juxtaposition of Good Friday with the Feast of the Annunciation to Mary, the Saracens' sacking of the Holy Sepulchre in Jerusalem (1009), a major flood in Aquitaine (1028), and a famine in Bourgogne (1031–33).[26] Christian commentators saw these events as underscoring the inbreaking of Christ's millennial kingdom with concomitant signs of divine judgment, calls for repentance and good works, and a promise of social peace. Sadly, such events also led to persecutions of Jews, heretics, and others associated with the impending reign of the antichrist.[27]

Second, the Peace of God movement brought together an impressive range of Christian actors with the shared goals of limiting violence and furthering social peace. Bishops stepped into the void of declining Carolingian authority to call a series of peace councils, facilitating the rise of the political stature of the medieval church. In Tomas Mastnak's words, "the peace council regulations gave the Church the authority to determine who could employ arms, for what purpose, on whose command, against whom, and when."[28] Unlike today, however, these councils were not exclusively hierarchical forums but unfolded in the presence of hundreds of laity, monks, and clerics. For their part, monks served as feudbreakers and peace mediators. For example, during one peacemaking episode on the Feast of the Pentecost, monks called feuding nobles out by name outside of church, challenging them to make peace with their enemies.[29] Lay nobles played a critical role in both enforcing social peace and forswearing violence against clerics, churches, and peasants. And even the saints through their relics played key mediating roles, facilitating the popular healings seen as God's ratification of the movement. The Peace of God thus represented a major effort by nearly all sectors of the Latin Church to collectively engage in what moderns would term "peacebuilding." Glaber's contemporary recounting of the 1033 councils in Burgundy captures the spirit of this collective move to peace, with a certain amount of hagiographical hyperbole:

> But at the millennial anniversary of the passion of the Lord (1033), the clouds cleared in obedience to divine

mercy and goodness....In the region of Aquitaine bishops, abbots and other men devoted to holy religion first began to gather councils of the whole people. At these gatherings the bodies of many saints and shrines containing holy relics were assembled. From there through the provinces of Arles and of Lyon, then through all of Burgundy, and finally in the farthest corners of France, it was proclaimed in every diocese that councils would be summoned in fixed places by bishops and by the magnates of the whole land for the purpose of reforming both the peace and the institutions of holy faith. When the news of these assemblies was heard, the entire populace joyfully came.[30]

How might the contemporary church seek to marshal a similar array of resources for the cause of peace today? Part of the success of the Peace of God movement was its concrete response to local problems, using church networks to communicate and convene people across long distances. In this vein, American dioceses could organize local "synods on violence" to discuss the root causes of violence in their local communities. This could include discussion forums on issues like gun control, radicalism, and mental health; more coordinated collaboration with Christian, public, and nonprofit groups tackling these problems; and ritual services and Masses to pray for the victims and perpetrators of the violence. Parishes could be encouraged to organize reading and discussion groups on the Christian response to the challenge of violence in the contemporary world, from domestic abuse to international conflict. Here the Catholic Church could learn from ecumenical grassroots initiatives already happening around the country, such as Boston's annual "Mother's Day Walk for Peace," the Christian prayer walks held at the site of every violent homicide in Omaha, or the nationwide student campaigns against gun violence.

Linking Peace and Justice

The Peace of God movement also challenges us to think more carefully about the meaning of our language of "peace." As Thomas Renna has argued, medieval Christians generally divided peace into three types: the monastic peace of serenity and a pure heart dedicated to prayer; the ecclesial peace that referred to a free, unified, and properly functioning church; and the worldly peace, stability, and order that kings were supposed to ensure.[31] Early medieval Christian notions of peace were indebted to Book XIX of Augustine of Hippo's *City of God*, especially Augustine's emphases on hierarchical order and rightful authority. In Augustine's words, "Peace between mortal man and God is an ordered obedience, in faith, in subjection to an everlasting law...the peace of the whole universe is the tranquility of order."[32] One sees echoes of this rhetoric in the Peace of God movement's calls for "reconciling or punishing the quarrelsome or the evildoers."[33]

Yet the notion of peace was not limited to "order" and obedience. In the medieval mind, God's peace also entailed components of justice, righteousness, and healing. For example, the 989 Council of Charroux proclaimed that "these bishops, as well as clerics and monks, not to mention laypeople of both sexes, have beseeched the aid of divine justice."[34] Ademar of Chabannes's account of the 994 Council of Limoges spoke of the "pact of peace and justice concluded by the duke and his lords."[35] And in the famous opening words of the acts of the Council of Poitiers in the millennial year 1000, "Handsome indeed is the name of peace, and beautiful the belief in unity, which Christ ascending to heaven left to his disciples...the duke and other princes swore this restoration of peace and justice [*iustitia*] by providing hostages and by accepting the threat of excommunication."[36] As Thomas Head has noted, this juxtaposition of peace and justice blurred the lines between the church's association with peace and the state's association with justice. Such blurring—as well as the movement's implicit challenge to local nobility to clean up their acts—comforted the afflicted but also afflicted the powerful. For example, the influential monastic commentator Andrew of Fleury feared that the Peace of God movement posed a revolutionary threat to the established, tripartite feudal order between the priestly and monastic *oratores* (pray-ers), the knightly *bellatores* or *pugnatores* (fighters), and the working *laboratores* (laborers, peasants, and farmers).[37] For its critics, the Peace of God councils' decrees on peace and justice thus overstepped the lines between the church's spiritual power and the king's temporal control of the sword—thus potentially threating the *tranquillitas ordinis*.

The idea that peace must be based not just on order but upon justice is one that remains resonant for Catholic peacebuilding efforts today. From liberation theology to Pope Francis, modern Catholicism has embraced this close linking of peace and justice. The Jesuits themselves recast their mission in the 1970s as the "service of faith, of which the promotion of justice is an absolute requirement."[38] Most American Catholic universities—including my own school Creighton—have established academic programs in justice and peace studies. In this sense, the Peace of God movement does not so much introduce something new as remind us of the deeper historical roots of our contemporary commitment to linking peace and justice. Over a millennium before Pope Paul VI stated in 1972 that "if you want peace work for justice," Burgundian bishops decreed that "all men should be constrained by an oath, themselves as well as others, that they should become servants of peace and justice."[39]

The Dangerous Necessity of Protective Violence in Peacekeeping

The medieval historian T. B. Lambert has argued that "for humans to live together there has to be some force acting as a deterrent to violence."[40] In this vein, the Peace of God movement reminds us that violent force is built into the structures of peace. As the Carolingian kings failed to fulfill their traditional duty as "arbiters of peace,"[41] this responsibility increasingly fell to local political and military leaders. The military support of Bishop Guy's relatives in Burgundy and of William IV Iron Arm in Aquitaine undergirded the peace councils of the 980s and 990s. Not surprisingly, declining support for the project from the nobility led to a lull in ecclesial peace councils in the 1000s and 1010s. In addition to local lay lords, Catholic bishops also stepped into the vacuum of centralized political authority. For example, the Council of Poitiers warned that if an offending party should fail to "do justice" and restore stolen possessions, "let all [the princes and bishops who ordained this council] unanimously set out to destroy and trouble him, and let him endure this persecution and troubling until he returns to the rectitude of justice."[42] This shift toward a more decentralized system for adjudicating war and peace helped legitimize the rising authority of the "spiritually powerful" bishops and the "physically powerful" dukes.[43]

There were examples, however, of peacekeeping spinning out of control. The most infamous case was that of Archbishop Aimon of Bourges's "war on war" in 1038. Frustrated at the refusal of several local nobles to honor the terms of a recent peace council, Archbishop Aimon gathered a "peace militia" of over two thousand peasants and priests, pledging to "wholeheartedly attack those who steal ecclesiastical property, those who provoke pillage, those who oppress monks, nuns and clerics, and those who fight against holy mother church, until they repent."[44] The size of Aimon's army initially had its desired effect of shock and awe. In the words of the eleventh-century commentator Andrew of Fleury, "Their hearts fell so that, forgetting their status as knights and abandoning their fortified places, they fled from the humble peasants as from the cohorts of very powerful kings."[45] However, this ostensibly peaceful march soon turned violent as Aimon's peasant army set fire to one recalcitrant lord's castle, killing nearly all of the fourteen hundred men, women, and children sheltering inside. In a subsequent retaliatory campaign, a noble named Odo of Deol gathered his own militia and routed Archbishop Aimon's peace army, killing over seven hundred clerics in the process. The entire episode not only discredited the warrior bishop but also demonstrated the risk of overzealous violence in the name of peace. Not surprisingly, the Truce of God saw bishops and nobles collaborate more closely to forestall peasant rebellion.

Just as the Peace of God rested partly upon the threat of force, the use of military force for peacekeeping remains critical in today's world. In 2017 alone, the United Nations operated fifteen separate peacekeeping missions in thirteen countries. It is easy to point out the flaws of these missions, but it is harder to argue that our world would somehow be less violent without protective force. In fact, there are cases that point the exact opposite way, such as the UNAMIR mission in Rwanda in 1993–94 in which peacekeepers were not allowed to utilize protective force, facilitating a genocide that killed nearly one million Rwandese. Rather, the excesses of the eleventh or even twenty-first centuries point to the importance of teaching *jus in bello* requirements (ethical behavior within conflict) and holding soldiers accountable for abuses. Given the dominance of civilian casualties in recent conflicts in countries like DRC, Syria, Myanmar, or South Sudan, an especially important *jus in bello* teaching is the principle of noncombatant immunity.[46] I would also highlight the importance of training soldiers in just war teaching, such as Creighton's required course in military ethics for ROTC students. Of course the violent abuses of peacekeeping forces in the eleventh or twenty-first century also point to the need for nonviolent alternatives to transform conflict such as Christian Peacemaker Teams in recent conflicts in Iraq and South Sudan.[47]

The Trajectory from Holy Peace to Holy War

In terms of community identity, the Peace of God movement also signified the rise of distinctively Christian metaphors such as the mystical Body of Christ. Peace rested on a shared sense of Christian family or kinship, and Christendom was increasingly envisioned as "one large family united in peace."[48] This culminated with the 1054 Council of Narbonne's famous command that "no Christian should kill another Christian" (a call to intra-Christian peace in the same year, ironically, as the Great Schism between Latin Catholics and Eastern Orthodox). Obviously this is an aspirational ideal; the lion did not suddenly lie down with the lamb in eleventh-century Christian Europe. Nevertheless, such discourse represented an important rhetorical shift in church teaching toward limiting intra-Christian violence and "Christianizing" Europe's warrior class. But at the same time, earlier, more universal strictures against violence fell away. In other words, the preeminent ethical question no longer revolved around the act of killing itself. Rather, the key question was *whom* you killed (Christian or non-Christian) and *why* you killed (for personal gain or for the good of Christendom).

If Christians could not commit violence against Christians, where could the Christian *milites* channel their violent energies? Who could serve as the unifying external enemy for Christendom? In the eleventh century, one common answer to this question was

"Muslims in the Holy Land." Within a decade of Narbonne, Pope Alexander II issued a proclamation approving violence against the Muslim Saracens as "punishment for their crimes and to counter hostile aggression."[49] Pope Urban II went further in his famous 1095 call for the First Crusade at the "universal peace council" of Clermont.[50] At Clermont, Pope Urban juxtaposed his calls for a crusade to retake the Holy Land with a corresponding call for perpetual peace within Christendom, anathematizing knights who continued to "seize or despoil monks, priests, nuns and their servants, or pilgrims or merchants" and calling the assembled to "reenact the law made by our holy ancestors long ago and commonly called 'the Truce' [of God]."[51] At the same time, he exhorted the faithful to channel their violent passions on the Muslim infidel. "Let those who have hitherto been robbers now become soldiers of Christ. Let those who have formerly contended against their brothers and relatives now fight as they ought against the barbarians."[52]

With the rise of the Crusades, one sees the dark side of the calls for peace within Christendom. Namely, sociopolitical violence was ultimately directed outside Christendom to the religious other. The ancient practice of soldiers seeking the church's "permission" to engage in violence became in the Crusades a church-sanctioned "mission" to fight on behalf of Christianity. The *milites Christe*, or "soldiers for Christ," were no longer monks struggling to live disciplined lives for Christ; they were now Christian knights fighting to protect Christendom and regain the Holy Land.[53] Or in the twelfth-century words of Bernard of Clairvaux, "The Knights of Christ may safely fight the battles of their Lord, fearing neither sin if they smite the enemy, nor danger at their own death; since to inflict death or to die for Christ is no sin, but rather, an abundant claim to glory."[54]

For all the laudable modern distaste for the Crusades themselves, the crusading mentality is hard to dislodge. In the case of the United States, the external enemy—whether Nazi Germany or the Soviet Union—served a unifying purpose throughout the "American century" from World War I through the end of the Cold War. Today one sees a resurgence in the "othering" of Muslims within modern Western societies, fed by the stereotypical collapsing of all Muslims into fringe jihadist groups like al-Qaeda and ISIS. In turn, since at least the First World War, nearly all U.S. military interventions have been launched with the goal of restoring peace (and often democracy). Such noble ideals have justified almost any means, from the nuclear bombing of Hiroshima and Nagasaki to drone attacks in contemporary Yemen. The "cult of the soldier" undergirds an American civil religion predicated around the ideal of "freedom is not free," implying that violent force is the key linchpin in the preservation of American democracy. This worldview echoes the Crusades mentality that peace is only ensured by war. In the words of medieval historian Carl Erdmann, "Until recently, every organization of peace has simultaneously been an organization of war, since mankind hitherto has not wished to believe in a peace that was not guaranteed by the possibility of war."[55]

In response, I would argue for the restoration of an earlier legacy of the Christian tradition: the church's and soldier's respective obligations to lament, cleanse, and do penance for any type of war killing. This would acknowledge the cost of killing, no matter the perceived justness of the cause. Such rituals could be integrated into existing liturgical celebrations of national holidays such as Memorial Day or Veterans' Day, helping to transform these services from mere props in the edifice of American civil religion to a broader reckoning with the human costs of war. As Michael Griffin advocates, such efforts could include ecclesial statements of lament and the encouragement of participation in reparation efforts such as the Veterans for Peace Iraq Water Project.[56] In other words, one could admit the tragic reality of war in a fallen world without glorying in it.

Overall, the Peace of God movement demonstrates the myriad ways—social, political, economic, sacramental, and eschatological—in which the church can constructively contribute to communal peace and limit social violence. There is no magic bullet here; we cannot directly transpose the medieval church's actions or worldview to the twenty-first century. In addition, the Peace of God warns us how the promotion of peace in one area can displace violence to another. But in its bold and innovative responses to the violence of its era, the eleventh-century Peace of God movement offers historical inspiration for similarly creative and ambitious peacebuilding efforts in the midst of our own troubled world.

Reflection Questions

1. How would you define or imagine "peace" and "justice"? What do you see as the relationship between the two concepts?
2. What do you see as the proper role(s) for the institutional church in situations of armed conflict and peacebuilding? Why?
3. To what extent is protective force a necessary element in the preservation or restoration of civil peace?
4. What types of local Christian peacebuilding initiatives can you imagine that could draw on the Christian tradition's "storehouse" of rituals, practices, and vision?
5. Should the church ever withhold or suspend sacraments in contexts of armed violence or human rights violations? Why or why not?

Notes

1. See, e.g., the brief overviews offered in Ronald G. Musto, *The Catholic Peace Tradition* (New York: Peace Books, 2002), 71–75; and Mark J. Allman, *Who Would Jesus Kill? War, Peace, and the Christian Tradition* (Winona, MN: Anselm Academic, 2008), 85–86. For an excellent overview of Peace of God scholarship in the nineteenth and twentieth centuries, see Frederick S. Paxton, "The Peace of God in Modern Historiography: Perspectives and Trends," *Historical Reflections/Réflexions Historiques* 14, no. 3 (1987): 385–404.

2. On the general contexts that gave rise to the movement, see Thomas Head and Richard Landes, "Introduction," in *The Peace of God: Social Violence and Religious Response in France around the Year 1000*, ed. Thomas Head and Richard Landes (Ithaca, NY: Cornell University Press, 1992), 10–16.

3. On the fervent millennial expectations in western Europe during this era, see Richard Landes, Andrew Gow, and David C. Van Meter, eds., *The Apocalyptic Year 1000: Religious Expectation and Social Change, 950–1050* (New York: Oxford University Press, 2003).

4. Elisabeth Magnou-Nortier, "The Enemies of Peace: Reflections on a Vocabulary, 500–1100," in Head and Landes, *Peace of God*, 59–60.

5. Gerd Tellenbach, *The Church in Western Europe from the Tenth to the Early Twelfth Century* (Cambridge, MA: Cambridge University Press, 1993), 38–42.

6. Tomaz Mastnak, *Crusading Peace: Christendom, the Muslim World, and Western Political Order* (Berkeley: University of California Press, 2002), 8.

7. Thomas Head, "Peace and Power in France around the Year 1000," *Essays in Medieval Studies* 23 (2006): 3. See also H. E. J. Cowdrey, "The Peace and Truce of God in the Eleventh Century," *Past and Present* 46 (1970): 43.

8. Head, "Peace and Power," 4–5.

9. Hunt Janin, *Medieval Justice: Cases and Laws in France, England and Germany, 500–1500* (London: McFarland, 2004), 12.

10. Head, "Peace and Power," 5–6. Lawrence Duggan highlights the important distinction between "armed" and "unarmed" clerics. The former would not be protected under most Peace or Truce of God canons with the important exception of bishops themselves (Lawrence G. Duggan, *Armsbearing and the Clergy in the History and Canon Law of Western Christianity* [Woodbridge, UK: Boydell and Brewer, 2003], 100).

11. To take an example from Charroux, "Anathema against those who break into churches. If anyone breaks into or robs a church, he shall be anathema unless he make satisfaction. Anathema against those who rob the poor. If anyone robs a peasant or any other poor person of a sheep, ox, ass, cow, goat, or pig, let him be anathema unless he makes satisfaction" ("Synod of Charroux, Proclamation of the peace of God, 989," in Musto, *Catholic Peacemakers*, 437).

12. Head, "Development of Peace of God," 685.

13. See Cowdrey, "Peace and Truce of God," 44–45.

14. Thomas Head, "The Development of the Peace of God in Aquitaine (970–1005)," *Speculum* 74, no. 3 (1999): 660. On the church-state struggle between Pope Gregory VII and German Emperor Henry II, see Tellenbach, *Church in Western Europe*, 222–52.

15. On the major impact of apocalyptic imagination among both elites and the masses, see Johannes Fried, "Awaiting the End of Time around the Turn of the Year 1000," in Landes, *Apocalyptic Year 1000*, 17–63.

16. Richard Landes traces this pattern to the Council of Limoges in 994. See Landes, "Between Aristocracy and Heresy: Popular Participation in the Limousin Peace of God, 994–1033," in Head and Landes, *Peace of God*, 189–90. The most common disease was described as *ignis sacer*, or "St. Anthony's Fire," a burning and gangrenous form of ergotism that stemmed from eating bread with tainted rye-flour (Cowdrey, "Peace and Truce of God," 48; Head, "Development of Peace of God," 676).

17. Ralph Glaber, "Histories Book IV," quoted in Ronald G. Musto, *Catholic Peacemakers: A Documentary History Vol. 1* (New York: Garland Publishing, 1993), 435.

18. In the words of H. E. J. Cowdrey, the Truce moved from "protecting certain classes/goods at all times" to "stopping all violence at certain times" (Cowdrey, "Peace and Truce of God," 44).

19. "The Council of Toulouges," in Musto, *Catholic Peacemakers*, 442. See also "Rodulphus Glaber on the Truce of God (1041)," in Head and Landes, *Peace of God*, 342.

20. Head and Landes, "Introduction," 7–8; Cowdrey, "Peace and Truce of God," 53.

21. Quoted in Cowdrey, "Peace and Truce of God," 57. Duggan notes that the Peace/Truce of God did not end at Clermont. The conciliar renewed in the twelfth-century councils.

22. Duggan, *Armsbearing and the Clergy*, 122.

23. Tellenbach, *Church in Western Europe*, 23.

24. Tellenbach, *Church in Western Europe*, 94.

25. Head, "Peace and Power," 7. Thomas Gergen agrees that "this punishment [excommunication] was the main weapon of the Peace of God" (Thomas Gergen, "The Peace of God and its legal practice in the Eleventh Century," *Cuadernos de Historia del Derecho* 9 [2002]: 26).

26. Dominique Barthélemy, "La paix de Dieu dans son context (989–1041)," *Cahiers de civilisation medieval* 157 (1997): 32; Richard Landes, "Between Aristocracy and Heresy: Popular Participation

in the Limousin Peace of God, 994–1033," in Head and Landes, *Peace of God*, 188; Fried, "Awaiting the End of Time," 37.

27. Fried, "Awaiting the End of Time," 60.

28. Mastnak, *Crusading Peace*, 10. For similar sentiments, see Isnard Wilhelm Frank, *A Concise History of the Mediaeval Church*, trans. John Bowden (New York: Continuum, 1995), 119.

29. Gregory Koziol, "Monks, Feuds and the Making of Peace in Eleventh-Century Flanders," in Head and Landes, *Peace of God*, 244–45. In Koziol's words, monks successfully created situations in which knights would be "publicly shamed if they denied peace and publicly praised if they accepted it" (245).

30. "Rodulphus Glaber on the events in the year 1033," in Head and Landes, *Peace of God*, 338.

31. Cited in Lambert, *Peace and Protection*, 8. See Thomas Renna, "The Idea of Peace in the West," *Journal of Medieval History* 6 (1980): 143–67.

32. Augustine of Hippo, *City of God*, trans. Henry Bettenson (New York: Penguin, 2003), 19.13, 870. On the connections between Augustinian theology and the Peace of God movement, see Amy G. Remensnyder, "Pollution, Purity and Peace: An Aspect of Social Reform between the Late Tenth Century and 1076," in Head and Landes, *Peace of God*, 282; and Barthélemy, "La paix de Dieu," 17.

33. Tellenbach, *Church in Western Europe*, 137.

34. "Acts of the Council of Charroux (989)," in Head and Landes, *Peace of God*, 327.

35. "Ademar of Chabannes on the First Council of Limoges (994)," in Head and Landes, *Peace of God*, 330.

36. "Acts of the Council of Poitiers (1000/14)," in Head and Landes, *Peace of God*, 330. Hunt Janin notes that *iustitia* "included not only the police power of arrest and punishment but also the financial power to authorize markets, tax transactions taking place in them, and levy tolls on the use of public highways" (Janin, *Medieval Justice*, 47).

37. Thomas Head, "The Judgment of God: Andrew of Fleury's Account of the Peace League of Bourges," in Landes and Head, *Peace of God*, 228.

38. These famous words are taken from Decree 4 of the 1974–75 General Congregation 32 of the Society of Jesus, accessed February 21, 2018, https://www.scu.edu/ic/programs/ignatian

-tradition-offerings/stories/decree-4-gc-32-service-of-faith-and
-the-promotion-of-justice.html.

39. "Excerpts from the *Gesta episcoporum Cameracensium* (1024–36)," in Head and Landes, *Peace of God*, 336.

40. T. B. Lambert, *Peace and Protection in the Middle Ages*, 15.

41. R. I. Moore, "The Peace of God and Social Revolution," in Head and Landes, 314.

42. "Acts of the Council of Poitiers (1000/14)," in Head and Landes, *Peace of God*, 330.

43. Claire Taylor, "Royal Protection in Aquitaine and Gascony by c. 1000: The Public, the Private and the Princely," in Lambert, *Peace and Protection*, 56, 59.

44. "Andrew of Fleury: Activities of the Peace League of Bourges in 1038," in Head and Landes, *Peace of God*, 340.

45. "Andrew of Fleury: Activities of the Peace League of Bourges in 1038," 340.

46. On *jus in bello* requirements and contemporary challenges to them, see Allman, *Who Would Jesus Kill?* 200–204.

47. See Glen H. Stassen, *Just Peacemaking: Ten Practices for Abolishing War* (Cleveland: Pilgrim, 1998); and Greg Barrett, *The Gospel of Rutba: War, Peace, and the Good Samaritan Story in Iraq* (Maryknoll, NY: Orbis Books, 2013).

48. Lambert, *Peace and Protection*, 9.

49. Mastnak, *Crusading Peace*, 21.

50. Mastnak, *Crusading Peace*, 49.

51. Pope Urban II, "The Call to the First Crusade, 26 November 1095," in *Readings in Church History Vol. 1*, ed. Colman J. Barry (New York: Newman Press, 1960), 327.

52. Pope Urban II, "The Call to the First Crusade, 26 November 1095," 328.

53. Mastnak, *Crusading Peace*, 23–26, 44. Mastnak notes that prior to the eleventh century, the church typically used the Latin term *milites saeculi* (mounted warriors of the world) to refer to soldiers, reserving the title of *milites Christe* to monks.

54. Bernard of Clairvaux, "In Praise of the New Knighthood," in *Treatises III: The Works of Bernard of Clairvaux, Vol. 7*. Trans. Conrad Greenia, Cistercian Fathers Series 19 (Kalamazoo, MI: Cistercian Publications, Inc., 1977), 134. Bernard wrote this treatise

for the Knights Templar in the lead-up to the Second Crusade in 1147–49.

55. Erdmann quoted in Duggan, *Armsbearing and the Clergy*, 111. Carl Erdmann's *The Origin of the Idea of Crusade* (Princeton: Princeton University Press, 1977) offers a fuller explication.

56. Michael Griffin, *The Politics of Penance: Proposing an Ethic for Social Repair* (Eugene, OR: Wipf and Stock, 2016), 151–59.

CHAPTER 6

Encountering Islam

MEDIEVAL CHRISTIAN PERSPECTIVES FROM THE CORDOBAN MARTYRS TO JUAN OF SEGOVIA

Laurie Johnston[1]

One of the fundamental aspects of reconciliation is a minimal one—the task of merely acknowledging the other's right to *be*. This requires recognizing the existence of the other and consenting to live in some proximity with the other without trying to kill or expel them. It is a very limited form of reconciliation; one might consider it simply "reconciling oneself to the existence of the other." And yet it is vital, and not easy, particularly in a context of violence, where proximity to the enemy is precisely what most people would prefer to avoid.

For some in the United States and Europe today, there is a deep reluctance to reconcile themselves to the presence of Muslim "others." Nationalist politicians build support upon perceptions that Islam is inherently violent, sexist, and incompatible with liberal democracy and Western culture. Rather than providing real moral leadership, many politicians pander to the most fearful and racist tendencies among their constituents. Visa bans to prevent entry and veil bans to prevent public presence have garnered striking levels of public support.[2] The strain of mass migration is, for many European countries, creating a backlash against migrants generally, and Muslim migrants in particular. Violent terrorist attacks contribute to a perception that Islam is incompatible with Western society—and sometimes these attacks appear to be motivated by the desire to cultivate precisely that perception of incompatibility. In this context, one of the key ethical challenges for citizens of the United States and Europe today is how to live up to their own commitment to human rights and human dignity when it comes to their Muslim neighbors.

For theological ethicists, the task is even more specific: to explain how and why loving our Muslim neighbors is constitutive of Christian discipleship and the ministry of reconciliation. *Ressourcement* can help with this task; broadening our sphere of experiences to include those of the past can bring fresh ideas to contemporary problems. While it would be entirely anachronistic to expect our medieval forbears to use modern human rights language, there is nevertheless wisdom in the tradition that can help us to understand how we should—and should not—approach the question of the Muslim "other."

A look back at the ways Europeans in past centuries have responded to the presence of Muslims may not seem like the most promising way to address contemporary challenges. Studying history with an eye to the present holds many pitfalls, not least of which is simply allowing a contemporary agenda to lead to a misapprehension of the history. In addition, the history of Muslim-Christian relations is filled with harsh polemic, misunderstanding, and violence—many occasions, one might say, of failures to reconcile. But there are also some contexts in which one can find other forms of engagement, moments of complexity, and departures from the polemics and polarization. At various times in various places, Muslims and Christians have found a *modus vivendi*, learned from one another, and collaborated to some degree in the tasks of government and society. Often this was the result simply of political and practical necessity. Yet there were also occasions in which various Christian thinkers reflected on their encounters with Muslims and sought to either justify these or reject them on various theological and practical grounds. Those moments in medieval society when writers suggested that a degree of social and political accommodation with Islam might be possible are by no means representative. The vast majority of

Christians who wrote about Islam did so in negative, hostile, and profoundly ignorant ways. But that makes it all the more interesting to uncover the exceptions and seek to understand how, at least in some cases, more irenic perspectives toward Islam might be justified. What we will find is that these more reconciliatory perspectives begin from the assumption of some form of common ground with Muslims.

This chapter will examine three forms of that common ground. First, some Christians found common ground with Muslims based on their shared worship of one God. Second, some Christians argued that it was possible to find intellectual common ground with Muslims; for this reason, they regarded it as worthwhile to engage Muslims in reasoned debate and dialogue. Finally, some Christians found political common ground with Muslims, regarding them as citizens of a shared political community. All three of these areas of common ground offer interesting possibilities to consider today as well.

Does Monotheism Invalidate Martyrdom? The Debate over the Martyrs of Cordoba, Killed at the Hands of Those Who "Venerate Both God and a Law"

Do Muslims worship the same God as Christians? Should sharia—Islamic law—be regarded as legitimate in any way? If so, what are the implications for how Christians should relate to Muslims? If we regard their faith as legitimate, does that imply a threat to the truth of ours? These are questions that remain controversial today, but they were also asked by medieval Christians many centuries ago. Then, as now, different Christians drew very different conclusions. These differing opinions come through clearly in one of the earliest records we have of the encounter between Western Christians and Muslims: the set of texts that describe the Martyrs of Cordoba.[3] At the time these texts were written, the Ummayad dynasty had been in control of southern Spain—which they called Al-Andalus—for more than one hundred years. Cordoba was their capital. And it was there, during the years 851–59, that forty-eight Christians were executed, accused of public blasphemy.

Eulogius, a priest and member of the Christian elite in Cordoba, has provided us with an account of these martyrdoms. His work *Liber apologeticus martyrum* was written not long before his own martyrdom in 857. As he and other sources tell us, these martyrdoms began when a monk, Isaac, came to Cordoba from his monastery in the mountains and publicly insulted the Prophet Muhammad. Strictly speaking, it was not illegal for a Christian to disavow faith in Muhammad. Under the Ummayad caliph, Abd-Rahman II, Christians, as *dhimmi,* had the right to practice their religion as long as they paid the *jizya,* or tax. However, it seems that the highly public and provocative nature of Isaac's action was problematic, and he was executed in 851. Over the next decade, other Christians imitated him in a variety of ways, resulting in nearly fifty deaths.

What is most interesting about the case of the Cordoban martyrs is how they divided opinion within the Christian community of Cordoba. Eulogius feels the need to present his apology for the martyrs' cause in order to address fellow Christians who do not share his enthusiastic—and eventually participatory—support for these martyrs. In his view, too many Cordoban Christians are assimilating to Arab culture and adopting dangerously positive views of Muslims. Eulogius urges them, therefore, "to resist this lost and very filthy prophet [Muḥammad]…and…demolish the religion of such a scoffer." He goes on to exclaim, "It is absolutely the duty of Christians to separate from [Muslims'] destruction… to break [Muḥammad's] poisonous dogma, to curse his sect [and] to detest his thoughts which are bringing a great multitude to perdition."[4] This duty of separation and opposition is so important, Eulogius says, that it outweighs any duty to "do good to the enemies of Christ." Christians would even be justified in murdering Muhammad, should he be alive in contemporary Cordoba.[5]

Clearly, reconciliation was not on Eulogius's mind. And his friend Alvarus took a similar stance. Alvarus held up the example of the martyrs as an important witness to "lukewarm" Christians.

Who are such lukewarm Christians? Those "who failed to perform their prayers in public before Muslims, Christians who neglected to bless themselves with the sign of the cross after yawning, and those who did not *explicitly* affirm the divinity of Christ before Muslims." As Charles Tieszen writes, Alvarus's concern was that "this tepid brand of Christianity arrested the spread of the gospel because it turned the martyrs into 'mute dogs unable to bark.'"[6] The martyrs, on the other hand, are precisely those who refuse to be mute.

What is interesting for our purposes, though, is how concerned Eulogius and Alvarus are to draw stark lines between Christians and Muslims. They clearly condemn Islamic doctrines, and, as Norman Daniel points out, Eulogius's work may well be the first instance in history of a Christian clearly identifying Islam as a distinct religion rather than just a Christian heresy.[7] Along the way, though, Eulogius reproduces some of the arguments of his Christian opponents in order to refute them. And here is where we catch a glimpse of social reconciliation between Christians and Muslims in Cordoba.

Many Christians in Cordoba apparently saw these martyrdoms as utterly unnecessary. They argued that the situation was *not* analogous to that of the early Christians. Cordoban Christians faced no persecution comparable to that experienced under some of the Roman emperors. So, many Christians refused to see the martyrs as genuine martyrs—instead they were unnecessarily reckless, provocative, and perhaps even suicidal. How could these be genuine Christian martyrs when they had "suffered at the hands of men who venerated both God and a law?"[8] As Kenneth Wolf writes,

> This is a remarkable, one-sentence window into the minds of the more assimilated Cordoban Christians. As they saw it, the Muslims were monotheists who worshiped the same God as they, though on the basis of a distinct, revealed law. As far as they were concerned, this religious common denominator not only rendered inappropriate the radical actions of the martyrs but also presumably legitimated the cooperative attitudes that governed their own day-to-day relations with the

Muslims. Where did the Christians get such an … "ecumenical" perspective? From the Muslims. The same Qur'anic perspective that allowed Muslims to tolerate Christians as monotheists and recipients of a revealed law, provided Christians with a ready-made justification for their participation in Islamic society.[9]

In other words, Christians were learning from Muslims about the possibilities—and perhaps some of the limits—of religious tolerance and coexistence. But to Eulogius, such an assimilationist view of Islam was utterly unacceptable: "Those who assert that [these martyrs] were killed by men who worship God and have a law, are distinguished by no prudence with which they might at least give heed to cautious reflection, because if such a cult or law is said to be valid, indeed the strength of the Christian religion must necessarily be impaired."[10]

This debate over the Cordoban martyrs, then, raises some issues that are strikingly contemporary. First is the question of Islamic law—sharia. When sharia is discussed in the United States today, it is rarely in the sense of "these Muslims have a valid law that they follow," as the Cordobans' opinions would seem to imply. On the contrary, sharia is frequently regarded with hysteria, as by those U.S. politicians who propose "laws banning sharia"—an odd phrase, given that it is logically rather difficult to create a "law banning law."[11] There is no doubt that some interpretations of sharia are not compatible with contemporary human rights norms. But all legal systems require revision and innovation, and many of the criticisms commonly leveled at sharia might well have applied to U.S. or European law only a few generations ago, when, for example, corporal punishment and the disenfranchisement of women were the norm. In any case, the primary threat to the rule of law is not another system of law, but lawlessness. Eulogius's Christian opponents valued the Ummayads' respect for the rule of law and for the sovereignty of God—a prudential judgment with which Eulogius disagreed.

The second issue that Eulogius's criticism raises is a more theological question. He writes that "the strength of the Christian religion" is impaired by the idea that the Islamic "cult" may be valid. He was concerned about the problem of those who might choose to convert from Christianity to Islam—indeed a temptation faced by the Christian community under Muslim rule in Spain and elsewhere, often because conversion led to increased social and economic standing. But one may imagine that Eulogius's concern for "the strength of the Christian religion" is about more than just demographics. For many Christians, in both Eulogius's time and ours, an acknowledgment that there may be validity in another belief system appears to be a threat to the distinctive truth of the Christian gospel. This is a complex issue; the problem of religious pluralism is one that perplexes theologians and believers alike. Yet if, as some of the Cordobans did, we point out that Muslims, too, believe in God and seek to obey his will, perhaps space can emerge for forms of theological and social reconciliation.

This is difficult, however, when the idea that Christians and Muslims both worship the one God remains controversial. It is common, today as well as in the past, for Christians to draw stark divisions between their community and the Muslim community by asserting that Muslims do not worship "the same God." Muslims, on the other hand, reject the notion of the Trinity. Nevertheless, the idea that both religions worship the God of Abraham is one that both Muslims and Christians have repeatedly acknowledged throughout history.[12] In fact, many Christian polemicists—particularly those with actual knowledge about Islam—have treated Islam as a Christian heresy rather than a form of paganism. That did not make their attacks on the tenets of Islam any less harsh, but this choice nevertheless reveals a sense that this was an internal rather than an external squabble. And sometimes the acknowledgment of a shared commitment to God has produced a remarkable degree of rapprochement in Christian-Muslim dialogues.

A remarkable—if rare—example is found in the writings of the eighth-century East Syriac Patriarch Timothy I. Writing about his dialogue with the caliph al-Mahdi in 781, he declares himself to have said,

> Muhammad deserves the praise of all reasonable men because his walk was on the way of the prophets and of the lovers of God. Whereas the rest of the prophets taught about the oneness of God, Muhammad also

taught about it. So he too walked on the way of the prophets. Then, just as all the prophets moved people away from evil and sin, and drew them to what is right and virtuous, so also did Muhammad move the sons of his community away from evil and draw them to what is right and virtuous. Therefore, he too walked on the way of the prophets.[13]

Timothy goes on to compare Muhammad to Moses and other prophets and, as Daniel Madigan points out, "seems to have much less difficulty than Christians do nowadays with the Prophet of Islam's military campaigns; after all, he observes, this is one of the roles of the genuine prophet—to wield the sword, as Moses did, in defense and propagation of the truth."[14]

Patriarch Timothy's irenic tone may have been quite unusual, but he is not unique in his willingness to acknowledge a shared commitment to God, even while disagreeing on key elements of doctrine. Some centuries later, Thomas Aquinas, in a short work entitled "Reasons for the Faith against the Saracens, Greeks, and Armenians, to the Cantor of Antioch," repeats many of the common medieval criticisms of Islam, for example, that Muhammad was a false prophet given over to sensuality. Yet Thomas also notes that "we argue presently against those who say they are worshippers of God, whether Muslims or Christians or Jews."[15] Thus he acknowledges that Muslims are at least attempting to worship the God of Abraham. And he clearly believes that it is worthwhile to engage in rational argumentation about theological topics with Muslims, since he is writing the essay to serve as a resource for such debates.[16]

Is There Enough Common Ground to Make Intellectual Engagement Possible and Worthwhile?

Thomas Aquinas's work is an example of a recurring pattern in medieval discussions of Islam: even harsh polemic against Islam is sometimes accompanied by a clear acknowledgment of partial common ground and the possibility of intellectual engagement. Such a willingness to engage in conversation with the other is one of the most basic prerequisites for reconciliation. Even if the motive for dialogue or intellectual engagement is purely to convert the other, there is nevertheless a basic level of respect inherent in the effort itself: dialogue assumes that conversation with the other is somehow worthwhile, and that they have the intellectual capacity to participate. But there have been many Christians, both in the Middle Ages and today, who would reject any such dialogue with Muslims. Eulogius urged Christians to stay away from the polluting influence of Muslims, whom he called "God-haters." In his mind, they were not even worthy of receiving the gospel, and therefore any form of dialogue or reconciliation with them was impossible. There was no point in even attempting to learn about what Muslims believe, because to Eulogius, it was "poisonous dogma." But other medieval Christians saw value in intellectual engagement with Islam and criticized the ignorance of the many Christian polemicists who repeated gross inaccuracies about Muslim doctrine.[17]

A century after Thomas Aquinas, Paul of Burgos was willing to engage intellectually with the ideas of Islam. He was a *converso* Jew who became an archbishop. He wrote powerful polemics against Islam but moderated them with an acknowledgment that one historian describes thus: "If one were to look at [Islam's] positive aspects, one could understand God's ways. Although Islam could be found in the images of Revelation 13, it was not like other pagan religions: the Saracens were not idolatrous; they did not force Christians to apostatize, but only to pay taxes; there were many Christians in Islamic territories; and Islam considered Jesus to be the most excellent of all creatures."[18] Few in the United States and Europe today are aware that Muslims, too, revere Jesus—yet this was something Paul asserted matter-of-factly.

Another Spanish convert to Christianity, Juan Andres, wrote about Islam a century after Paul. Juan produced a strong polemic against Islam that nevertheless preserved the possibility of finding some good in the person of Muhammad: "Juan's Muhammad is portrayed as one seeking God, with a capital 'D' ('Dios'), and rejecting idols….a human being who sought truth comes forth.

The polemical purpose remains clear, but the detail with which the author describes this episode and others relates individuals and human intentions in a history independent of Christianity, a history of Islam."[19] In addition, Muslims themselves are portrayed as genuinely seeking God: "the original Muslim community may have been 'lacking in all understanding,' but it nonetheless left paganism in search of something better. Most notable, then, is not so much Juan's portrayal of Muslims as simple or stupid, but as sincerely devoted to God, even if wrongly oriented."[20] This portrayal of Muslims as well-intentioned is a striking departure from other portrayals of Muslims—common both then and now—as demon possessed and debauched. Overall, both Paul of Burgos and Juan Andres provide a reminder that humans do not exist in spaces of pure conflict or pure reconciliation—either on a practical or a theological level. What we find in these thinkers is not a simple pattern of either *pure intolerance* or *pure tolerance* in the ways we would use those terms today. But the opening to the possibility of common ground with Muslims is an important beginning. Without hope that there might be some common ground, there is no point in seeking dialogue or reconciliation.

One of the most basic forms of intellectual engagement with the "other" is reading their sacred texts, of course—notably, the Qur'an. Thus it is interesting to see that a number of medieval Christian scholars lamented the lack of reliable information about Islam and also advocated for translation of the Qur'an so that intellectual dialogue and missionary efforts might be founded on actual knowledge of the other's tradition. At the dawn of the Reformation, Martin Luther was a strong advocate for the publication of the Qur'an and other key texts in Latin—a controversial stance at the time. He wrote a preface for the publication of one book, *Libellus de ritu et moribus Turcorum*, which he judged to be far more accurate than most other Christian works on Islam. In his preface he makes a strong argument for genuine, intellectual engagement with Islam. Too many authors, he complains,

> Eagerly take pains to excerpt from the Qur'an all the most base and absurd things that arouse hatred and can move people to ill-will, at the same time they either pass over without rebuttal or cover over the good things

it contains. The author of this book, however…relates details so as not only to recount the evils of the Turks but also to exhibit alongside them the best things….His writing certainly bears the clear signs of a forthright and sincere heart that writes nothing from hatred, but sets forth everything out of love of the truth. Indeed, those who only censure and condemn the base and absurd characteristics of the enemy but remain silent about matters that are honest and worthy of praise do more harm than good to their cause. What is easier than to condemn things that are manifestly base and dishonest (which in fact refute themselves)? But to refute good and honest things that are hidden from sight, that is to further the cause….[21]

In the current day, when it is common to see the most violent portions of the Qur'an quoted selectively and without context, Christians in the West would do well to heed Luther's advice. Intellectual dishonesty serves no one's best interest, and genuine, intellectual dialogue is the surest way to approach both truth and reconciliation.

Beyond Intellectual Dialogue to Shared Citizenship

Besides the question of whether it is possible to find common ground intellectually or theologically, there are also practical political questions that arose during medieval encounters with Islam. For instance, did Muslims under Christian rule deserve political protection, and was Muslim-Christian coexistence possible in society? Should Muslims be regarded as citizens and legitimate subjects of a Christian ruler? In many circumstances of Muslim-Christian encounter in both East and West, leaders on both sides have created different classes of citizenship or sought to keep the populations geographically or socially separate. In the past this may have looked like laws banning intermarriage; more recently it is due to immigration and citizenship restrictions. Yet there are also examples of political and social cooperation and collaboration at many levels of society. The degree of this cooperation is a frequent topic of scholarly debate. For example, there is a lively debate among historians about the extent to which Al-Andalus should be described as either a model of interreligious tolerance or merely a situation of begrudging truce and fraught coexistence.[22] Nevertheless, even when coexistence was less than ideal, there are many examples of collaboration that belie modern narratives about an inevitable "clash of civilizations."[23]

There were, indeed, many conflicts between Muslim and Christian rulers and peoples; Muslims living under Christian rulers fared poorly in many circumstances. But there were also exceptions. The traveler Ibn Jubayr, for instance, was surprised to find in 1185 that Muslims living in Norman Sicily under William II enjoyed very good treatment.[24] And one Christian ruler who spoke clearly about his Muslim subjects as possessing important political rights, including the right to worship as they saw fit, was James I of Aragon.

In the thirteenth century, James succeeded in significantly expanding his territory into lands previously controlled by the Almohads, and thus gained control of territories with significant Muslim populations. He wrote an autobiography, *Llibre des Feyts*, in which he shows ambivalence about Islam, but also clearly takes pride in his role as the protector of his Muslim subjects. On multiple occasions he negotiated surrender treaties with Muslim populations in which he promised "to keep and defend them as…[his] subjects and vassals."[25] The Muslims then retained a degree of self-government, and in most cases "they were to be judged by their own officials in accordance with Islamic 'custom' [*sunna, çuna*] that the Crown considered to be 'the privileges and customs that the Saracens were accustomed to have.'"[26] In attempting to protect the rights of his Muslim subjects, however, James sometimes ran into trouble with the Christian population. For instance, there was the problem of "Christian hotspurs such as Guillem de Aguilo, who though freely admitting that he had robbed and murdered many of the king's Muslim vassals, could not see that he had done any 'disservice' to the Crown since, to him, Islam and its adherents were still the enemy."[27] Nevertheless, "Even into his old age…the sovereign continued to intercede for the defeated Muslims. At times, as in the Murcian campaign of 1265–6, James' reputation as a 'good lord' helped bring on the Muslim surrender of whole districts."[28] James also had his Muslim vassals swear their allegiance to him on the Qur'an, recognized Muslim marriage ceremonies as legal, exempted mosque properties from taxes, and permitted swearing on the Qur'an in Christian courts of law in Valencia and elsewhere.[29]

James also wanted to ensure that Muslims could continue to worship as they were accustomed and allowed the *adhan* to continue to be proclaimed from the minarets of mosques. The one exception was a mosque quite near his castle in Murcia. After James was repeatedly awakened by the call to prayer from that mosque, he ordered that mosque—and that mosque alone—to be closed. As he explained, "The cry of the muezzin 'close to my head while I am sleeping, though you may think it good, is not a pleasant thing.'"[30] Though James was not, certainly, a model of perfect respect for religious liberty, it is still interesting to see that in this example, he was far more enlightened than most political leaders in Europe today, where it is difficult to imagine a public *adhan* being permitted anywhere.

There is much more that could be said about the context and nuances of James's rather self-congratulatory autobiography. James is certainly not broadly representative of the attitudes of his contemporaries; within a few short centuries his successors would carry out massive expulsions of both Muslims and Jews from the Iberian peninsula. And James shared many of the anti-Islamic prejudices typical of his time and place. Yet he balances those attitudes with a practical, pragmatic approach to dealing with actual Muslims. As Burns summarizes, "In his autobiography the king is at pains to proclaim himself an enemy of Islam, a bloody expeller of pagans, a Christian champion repelled by the vileness of Mudejar Islam's encumbrance of his realms. Merely in telling where he went and what he did, however, he unwittingly betrays his real self as possessing a shrewder humanity and a deeper Christianity."[31] In the midst of an era of Crusade and Reconquista, he reveals a remarkable sense of the basic humanity of Muslims. Whether this is more a case of ethical commitment or of mere political necessity, it nevertheless illustrates the possibility of a certain degree of reconciliation even when the overall context is that of political and religious conflict.

Dialogue as an Alternative to Violence against Muslims

It is one thing to be gracious toward your enemies when, like James I, you have defeated them militarily. Yet it is another matter to preserve a reconciliatory impulse when one is on the defensive and fears further attacks. The fall of Constantinople to the Ottomans in 1453 was a frightening and painful moment for many Christians—not only those directly affected, but also Western European Christians watching from further away. Not surprisingly, many called for quick and forceful military action. But for others, the fall of Constantinople provoked soul-searching and inquiry about the possibilities of some form of reconciliation and dialogue with Muslims. Two of the most interesting figures of the period in this regard were Nicholas of Cusa and Juan of Segovia. The two were friends and correspondents who both played important roles in church politics of the day, particularly at the Council of Basel in the 1430s.

Juan of Segovia was a theologian at the University of Salamanca. Though he was one of the most important intellectuals of the fifteenth century, his work fell into disfavor for political reasons and is therefore not as well-known as it ought to be. Most relevant for our purposes is that after the fall of Constantinople, he strongly opposed any form of violence against the Ottomans. Like many of his contemporaries, he was deeply opposed to Islam as a religion—and yet he completely rejected the idea of another crusade against Muslims. He believed that the proper stance of the Christian was to convert Muslims by demonstrating the love of Christ. Otherwise, how could Muslims "possibly come to love and welcome Christ if Christians had been killing them in his name?"[32] Anne Marie Wolf, author of a recent biography of Juan, explains his unusual perspective in the following terms:

> Faced with the recent Ottoman conquest of Constantinople and responding to Jean Germain's call for a military campaign, Segovia noted that, in the Bible, God had freed plenty of faithful from various predicaments, but it was never by the sword. When Germain protests that the

danger from the Turks was real, Segovia reminded him that Christ had indicated on the cross how Christians should respond to threats just as real: "With a loud cry and tears, he begged the Father to forgive them, since they did not know what they were doing."[33]

Juan wrote to many major figures of the day, including Piccolomini, the future Pope Pius II, to urge them not to support a crusade. Instead, he proposed a reconciliatory dialogue. Like some of the thinkers we have already seen, he believed that reasonable dialogue with Muslims was possible and desirable. And he also believed, unlike Eulogius, that it was appropriate to hope for Muslims' conversion. In fact, he believed that this goal of conversion was all the more urgent after the fall of Constantinople because, he argued, the surest way to put an end to Muslim hostility was to convert them to Christianity. Thus he "proposed that a high-level delegation be sent to Muslim leaders in order to 'invite them to peace.'"[34] Violence against Muslims, on the contrary, would lead to neither conversion nor peace and thus he staunchly opposed it.

Juan's argument for dialogue with Muslims was not only theoretical, however. During the last years of his life, he worked closely with a leading Islamic scholar, Iça Gidelli, to produce a trilingual edition of the Qur'an (Arabic, Latin, and Castilian). Like Martin Luther in later years, Juan saw serious engagement with the text of the Qur'an as an important prelude to evangelizing Muslims. This was tactical; he did not regard the Qur'an as having any revelatory power. On the contrary, Juan called the Qur'an a cursed, demonic law and Muhammad a prophet of the devil. But, as Wolf writes,

> Nevertheless, the fact that one who harbored such views could also argue for dialogue and against war, and even carry on conversations with Muslims that Muslims themselves sought to prolong rather than escape, suggests one lesson that his story offers for the modern observer...[Juan] remained curious, and not convinced that he had the full story.[35]

To remain curious about the other, and "not convinced that we have the full story"—these are some of the basic prerequisites to any form of reconciliation, whether in Juan's era or our own.

Furthermore, Juan perceived that his Muslim interlocutors may have been genuinely seeking the truth and thus open to rational dialogue. Writing about a series of dialogues he had with an ambassador from Grenada, he says that the "ambassador, out of the love of truth or for some other reason, on several occasions came to see me." Juan writes modestly about how he explained doctrines such as the Trinity to his interlocutor:

> Having heard the explanation that is commonly used by theologians, [the ambassador] marveled and said these words, in effect: "And by God, there is not one among the Christians who knows how to explain these things except for you." I responded, "Do not believe that the Christian religion is so lacking in scholarly men, since even today in this very town there are twenty people who know how to explain these things."[36]

Juan describes this conversation in the context of arguing that many conflicts between Muslims and Christians are caused by a lack of mutual understanding. He suggests that having a real dialogue with Muslims could correct the misunderstandings that are leading them to make war against Christians. In such a dialogue,

> there can be pointed out to them the very many reasons for having peace and love between them and the Christians. Chief among them is that there is such great agreement concerning divine worship: Christians believe in one God and worship only him, [a fact] that the Saracens themselves will be compelled to believe when they listen to explanations for divine unity expounded before them with seriousness.[37]

Juan's arguments in favor of reconciliatory dialogue with Muslims were not well received by most of his peers, unfortunately. But one exception was his friend Nicholas of Cusa, who replied to Juan's letter with hearty agreement: "It seems to me that we must deal with the infidels in exactly the way that I see to please your most reverend paternity, and I have written a little book about this, which I entitled *De pace fidei*."[38]

Nicholas of Cusa, like Juan, demonstrated an important willingness to consider that there may be "more to the story" about Islam (and other religions). He was one of the most important leaders of the Catholic Church in his day, serving as a bishop, cardinal, and papal legate, and even traveling to Constantinople to try to negotiate an end to the schism between East and West. He was a complex and speculative thinker who was ahead of his time in many ways; his *De pacei fidei* may be one of the most interesting works on interreligious dialogue ever written.[39] Nicholas argued that dialogue with other religions—including Islam—is not only worthwhile but can help us to arrive at deeper understanding about God. Furthermore, he believed in interreligious dialogue as a means to achieve reconciliation and peace. Like Juan of Segovia, he argued for engagement with the Ottomans, rather than violence, in hopes that

> the sword will cease, as will also the malice of hatred and all evils; and all men will know that there is only one religion in a variety of rites [*una religio in rituum varietate*]. But this difference of rites cannot be eliminated; and perhaps it is not expedient that it be eliminated, for the diversity may make for an increase of devotion, since each region will devote more careful attention to making its ceremonies more favourable.[40]

It is the very plurality of religions that, to Nicholas, can help us to understand our own religion's truth more deeply, and bring about an "increase in devotion."[41]

Like Nicholas and Juan, we live in an age when Muslims are frequently perceived as a security threat, and there are many calls for a violent response. It is true that our historical predecessors' prescriptions may be unrealistic and undesirable in our own day—Juan's focus on conversion as the primary goal of interreligious dialogue is problematic after Vatican II's *Nostra Aetate*, for instance. Yet their firm insistence on the idea that Christians should approach Muslims for conversation—rather than just at the point of a sword—is extremely important. Both of these thinkers can provide an invitation to consider how today, too, we might respond to Islam in a way that is more authentically Christian, and therefore reconciliatory.

Conclusion

Today, Christians and Muslims interact in many contexts throughout the world under circumstances quite different from those faced by medieval Christians. Yet there is a common challenge of trying to live together in society with members of a religion that has both common ground with and key doctrinal differences from Christianity. One of the dangers today is an essentializing discourse that portrays Christians and Muslims as always, inevitably, in conflict throughout history. Here is where *ressourcement* can be helpful, and thus this essay is much indebted to the research of medieval historians. The figures that we have touched on in this chapter offer a more complex historical picture of Christian relations with Islam. That does not mean these historical figures are representative of Christian history in general, nor does it mean they are necessarily models for how Christians should think and act in the twenty-first century. However, by examining the complexities of the past, we have a better chance of honestly addressing the complexities of our contemporary situation as well. In that regard there are a few themes that emerge that may help us along the path of social reconciliation today.

First, one challenge faced by societies then and now is that of basic ignorance about the "other." There is a real need, in many educational contexts, for foundational, nonproselytizing teaching about religions. And Christians of all stripes would do well to imitate the genuine intellectual curiosity about Islam that is modeled by people like Nicholas of Cusa, who knew there had to be more to the story about Islam. Intellectual engagement with Muslims is a key way in which the thinkers examined here have shown respect and sometimes even conciliatory attitudes. Careful reading of the Qur'an and serious interreligious dialogue are vital ways of cultivating mutual understanding and diminishing the kinds of ignorant, derogatory, and divisive rhetoric that so often appears in media discourse about Islam today.

Second, even as we learn more about the "other," it is also important that we retain the sense that we still do not have the whole story, either about our neighbors or about God—perhaps a sense of what Nicholas of Cusa called "learned ignorance." This kind of humility, a willingness to defer judgment, can be an important building block of reconciliation. An example of this humble agnosticism can be found in a very early Christian response to the emergence of Islam, written by Jacob of Edessa in the late seventh century. He writes to respond to a specific pastoral concern: If a Christian becomes a Muslim, does that conversion invalidate his baptism? If he converts back, should he be rebaptized? His response is very interesting:

> It is not right for a Christian who becomes a Hagarene or a pagan to be [re]baptized. He had been born anew by water and by spirit according to the word of our Lord....But concerning whether he had been stripped of grace of baptism because he became a Hagarene, I have this to say: Concerning those things whose giver is God, it is not ours to say whether they are taken away, or indeed stripped, from whoever received them... [God] looks for their return and penitence because he does not want the death of a sinner.[42]

One sees a similar humble agnosticism in some of the medieval treaties concluded between Muslim and Christian states, which simply began with the preface, "In the name of God the Beneficent, the merciful. May God Bless all the prophets and have peace upon them."[43] Who is a true prophet? That is ultimately up to God.

This sense that certain things are best left between God and the "other" can create space for coexistence and perhaps even reconciliation. God's grace and the gift of prophecy are not under the control of either religious or political leaders. Human knowledge in both political and theological matters is flawed and partial. Reconciliation is vital in human societies precisely because we cannot achieve a perfect understanding of matters either on earth or in heaven. And thus we must hold space for the other, for the places where there may be more to the story, and finally, for the grace of God.

Reflection Questions

1. What elements of the history discussed in this chapter are the most surprising to you?
2. Martin Luther thought it was important to be aware of both the weaknesses *and* the strengths of an opponent's position. How might this be relevant in other contexts?
3. Sometimes individuals and groups choose to focus on the ways they differ from the "other." Other times they may choose to focus on common ground. What are some of the factors that might shape these choices? In circumstances where reconciliation is needed, how might we help people to focus on common ground, rather than disagreement?

Notes

1. I would like to gratefully acknowledge the research assistance of Liam Maguire and Hanaa Khan for this chapter.

2. In 2004, France passed a law banning "conspicuous religious symbols" from public buildings such as schools and town halls. It was generally seen as targeting Muslim women's headwear for exclusion from the public sphere. A more recent law passed in 2010 banned covering one's face anywhere in public.

3. See Kenneth Baxter Wolf, *Christian Martyrs in Muslim Spain* (Cambridge: Cambridge University Press, 1988); and Jessica A. Coope, *The Martyrs of Córdoba: Community and Family Conflict in an Age of Mass Conversion* (Lincoln: University of Nebraska, 1995).

4. Charles L. Tieszen, *Al-Masāq* 24.1 (2012), citing *Liber apologeticus martyrum*, 12, in *Corpus Scriptorum Muzarabicorum*, ed. Juan Gil (Madrid: Instituto Antonio de Nebrija, 1973), 2:384.

5. Tieszen, citing Eulogius, *Memoriale sanctorum*, I.20, in *Corpus Scriptorum Muzarabicorum* 2:383.

6. Tieszen, citing *Alvarus, Indiculus luminosus*, 10; *Corpus Scriptorum Muzarabicorum* 1:282–83.

7. Kenneth Baxter Wolf, "Christian Views of Islam in Early Medieval Spain," in *Medieval Perceptions of Islam*, ed. John Victor Tolan (New York: Garland, 1996), 85–109, at 107n53.

8. Wolf, "Christian Views of Islam in Early Medieval Spain," 96, citing Eulogius, *Liber apologeticus martyrum*, 12, in *Corpus Scriptorum Muzarabicorum* 2:481.

9. Wolf, "Christian Views of Islam in Early Medieval Spain," 96, citing Eulogius, *Liber apologeticus martyrum*, 12, in *Corpus Scriptorum Muzarabicorum* 2:481.

10. Wolf, "Christian Views of Islam in Early Medieval Spain," 96, citing *Liber apologeticus martyrum*, 17–18, in *Corpus Scriptorum Muzarabicorum* 2:486.

11. According to the Southern Poverty Law Center, "Since 2010, 201 anti-Sharia law bills have been introduced in forty-three states. In 2017 alone, fourteen states introduced an anti-Sharia law bill, with Texas and Arkansas enacting the legislation." See https://www.splcenter.org/hatewatch/2018/02/05/anti-sharia-law-bills-united-states (accessed May 8, 2018).

Also, Donald Trump's reelection campaign website includes a survey called "Listening to America 2018." One of the questions asks, "Are you concerned by the potential spread of Sharia Law?" https://action.donaldjtrump.com/listening-to-america-2018-survey (accessed May 8, 2018).

12. For a helpful discussion of the question from a contemporary Christian perspective, see Miroslav Volf, *Allah: A Christian Response* (New York: HarperCollins, 2001).

13. Sidney H. Griffith, "The Monk in the Emir's Majlis," in *The Majlis: Interreligious Encounters in Medieval Islam*, ed. Hava Lazarus-Yafeh, Mark R. Cohen, Sasson Somekh, Sidney H. Griffith (Wiesbaden, DE: Harrassowitz Verlag, 1999), 13–65, citing Robert Caspar, "Les Versions du dialogue entre le Catholicos Timothée I et le calife al-Mahdî (IIe/VIIIe siècle), 'Mohammad a suivre la voie des prophètes,'" *Islamochristiana* 3 (1977), 107–75, at 150.

14. Daniel Madigan, "Christian–Muslim Dialogue," *The Wiley-Blackwell Companion to Inter-Religious Dialogue*, ed. Catherine Cornille (Hoboken: Blackwell Publishing, 2013). Blackwell Reference Online, April 26, 2017, citing Alphonse Mingana, "The Apol-

ogy of Timothy the Patriarch before the Caliph Mahdī," *Bulletin of the John Rylands Library* 12 (1928): 137–298; reprinted in *Woodbrooke Studies*, vol. II (Cambridge: W. Heffer, 1928), 1–162, at 59–60.

15. Joseph Kenny, trans., "Saint Thomas Aquinas: Reasons for the Faith against Muslim Objections," *Islamochristiania* 22 (1996): 31–52.

16. In a section entitled "How to argue with unbelievers"—an interesting title that itself implies the value of arguing with, rather than merely killing, unbelievers—Thomas writes, "First of all I wish to warn you that in disputations with unbelievers about articles of the Faith, you should not try to prove the Faith by necessary reasons. This would belittle the sublimity of the Faith, whose truth exceeds not only human minds but also those of angels; we believe in them only because they are revealed by God." Kenny, "Saint Thomas Aquinas," 31–52.

17. Though they are rare, there are some Christian apologetic texts that show intimate knowledge of the Islamic tradition. For example, Thomas Burman discusses the twelfth-century *"Tathlîth al-wahdânîya,"* written by a Mozarab (Arabic-speaking Christian) priest in Al-Andalus. Interestingly, this priest used hadith in his apology for Christianity and drew on the debate within Islam about the attributes of God in order to show why the Trinity was plausible. See Thomas E. Burman, "'Tathlîth al-wahdânîya' and the Twelfth-Century Andalusian-Christian Approach to Islam," in *Medieval Christian Perceptions of Islam*, ed. John Victor Tolan (New York: Garland, 1996), 109–28.

18. Philip Krey, "Nicholas of Lyra and Paul of Burgos on Islam," in *Medieval Christian Perceptions of Islam*, ed. John Victor Tolan (New York: Garland, 1996), 153–74, at 155.

19. Jason Busic, "Polemic and Hybridity in Early Modern Spain: Juan Andrés's "Confusión o confutación de la secta Mahomética y del Alcorán," *Journal for Early Modern Cultural Studies* 12, no. 1 (Winter 2012): 85–113, at 97.

20. Busic, "Polemic and Hybridity in Early Modern Spain," 104.

21. Sarah S. Henrich and James L. Boyce, "Martin Luther—Translations of Two Prefaces on Islam: Preface to the *Libellus de ritu et moribus Turcorum* (1530), and Preface to *Bibliander's Edition of the Qur'ān* (1543)," *Word & World* 16, no. 2 (1996): 250–66, at 258–59.

22. A positive, even idealized portrait of al-Andalus may be found in Maria Rosa Menocal's *The Ornament of the World* (Boston: Little, Brown, 2002). For a helpful overview of various other perspectives, see Anna Akasoy, "Convivencia and its Discontents: Interfaith Life in Al-Andalus," *International Journal of Middle East Studies* 42, no. 3 (August 2010): 489–99.

23. Samuel Huntington, *The Clash of Civilizations and the Remaking of World Order* (New York: Simon and Schuster, 1996).

24. Jarbel Rodriguez, *Muslim and Christian Contact in the Middle Ages: A Reader* (Toronto: Toronto University Press, 2015), 321–30, excerpting *The Travels of Ibn Jubayr*, trans. R. J. C. Broadhurst (London: Jonathan Cape, 1952).

25. Donald J. Kagay, "The Essential Enemy: The Image of the Muslim as Adversary and Vassal in the Law and Literature of the Medieval Crown of Aragon," in *Western Views of Islam in Medieval and Early Modern Europe: Perception of Other*, ed. David R. Blanks and Michael Frassetto (New York: St. Martins, 1999), 119–36, at 124.

26. Kagay, "The Essential Enemy," 124.

27. Kagay, "The Essential Enemy," 124.

28. Kagay, "The Essential Enemy," 124, citing Robert Burns, *Islam under the Crusaders: Colonial Survival in the Thirteenth Century Kingdom of Valencia* (Princeton: Princeton University Press, 1973), 135. Burns writes, "Hoping to persuade the Murcians to surrender, [James] reminded them how he had treated their northern neighbors in Valencia over the past three decades. 'They knew very well that many Saracens lived in my country,' he said; 'my dynasty had kept them of old in Aragon and in Catalonia, and I in the kingdom of Majorca and of Valencia….All kept their law just as well as if they were in the country of the Saracens; these were come at my mercy and had surrendered to me….I did not wish their death or destruction, but wished that they should live for all time.' He desired them to keep 'their mosques [and] their law, just as they had undertaken in their first treaties.'"

29. Burns, *Islam under the Crusaders*, 179.

30. Burns, *Islam under the Crusaders*, 188, citing *Llibre dels feyts*, chap. 445.

31. Burns, *Islam under the Crusaders*, 183.

32. Anne Marie Wolf, "Juan de Segovia: The Lessons of History," in *In the Light of Medieval Spain: Islam, the West, and the*

Relevance of the Past, ed. Simon R. Doubleday and David Coleman (New York: Palgrave MacMillan, 2008), 33–52, at 35. See also Anne Marie Wolf, *Juan de Segovia and the Fight for Peace: Christians and Muslims in the Fifteenth Century* (Notre Dame: University of Notre Dame Press, 2014).

33. Wolf, "Juan de Segovia," 45–46.

34. Wolf, "Juan de Segovia," 35.

35. Wolf, "Juan de Segovia," 38–39.

36. Juan of Segovia, "De mittendo gladio divini Spiritus in corda sarracenorum," trans. in Wolf, *Juan de Segovia and the Fight for Peace*, 247.

37. Juan of Segovia, Letter to Nicholas of Cusa, December 2, 1454, trans. in Wolf, *Juan de Segovia and the Fight for Peace*, 257.

38. Nicholas of Cusa, Letter to Juan de Segovia, Dec. 29, 1454, cited in Wolf, *Juan de Segovia and the Fight for Peace*, 137–38.

39. For more on Nicholas, see Joshua Hollman, *The Religious Concordance: Nicholas of Cusa and Christian-Muslim Dialogue* (Leiden: Brill, 2017); and *Nicholas of Cusa and Islam: Polemic and Dialogue in the Late Middle Ages*, ed. Ian Christopher Levy, Rita George-Tvrtković, and Donald Duclow (Leiden: Brill, 2014).

40. Inigo Bocken, trans., "Nicholas of Cusa and the Plurality of Religions," in *The Three Rings: Textual Studies in the Historical Trialogue of Judaism, Christianity, and Islam*, ed. Barbara Roggema, Marcel Poorthuis, and Pim Valkenberg (Leuven: Peeters, 2005), 163–80.

41. One wonders if this idea arises from Nicholas's reading of the Qur'an, as it is strikingly reminiscent of the Qur'anic idea that God has intended for there to be a plurality of religions, so that they can "compete in virtue" (e.g., Qur'an 5:48).

42. Michael Philip Penn, *When Christians First Met Muslims: A Sourcebook of the Earliest Syriac Writings on Islam* (Oakland: University of California Press, 2015), 168.

43. Alauddin Samarrai, "Arabs and Latins in the Middle Ages," in *Western Views of Islam in Medieval and Early Modern Europe: Perception of Other*, ed. David R. Blanks and Michael Frassetto (New York: St. Martins, 1999), 137–45, at 140.

CHAPTER 7

Conversion of Memory and Hope for Peace

THE PEACEMAKING HOMILIES OF ST. BERNARDINO OF SIENA, 1427

Kristin M. Haas[1]

In the time of Franciscan friar St. Bernardino of Siena (1380–1444), the cities of what is now Italy faced a serious challenge to peace in the form of factional violence. Factions struggled for social control and political influence, displaying their emblems and carrying out revenge. For many in St. Bernardino's Siena, identity with one of several factions mattered more than care for those on the margins, fidelity to Christ, or concern about the next life. Bernardino, born in a town southwest of Siena, was a traveling preacher who sought to make peace through conversion of hearts, and he was called home to Siena a number of times to preach peace. In 1427, he preached to the people of Siena for six weeks, and a verbatim account of his preaching was kept by a "pious and literate cloth cutter" named Benedetto.[2] While rituals of peacemaking often accompanied such preaching visits, this reflection focuses on the preaching itself.[3] Bernardino's preaching points to the meaning of such rituals and resituates the violence theologically and existentially so as to bring about the collective conversion of the Sienese.

The message Bernardino shares with Siena in 1427 is that peace is the fruit of individual and collective conversion. He delivers his urgent but hopeful message in a way that touches the audience's collective memory and proposes to reshape their desires and commitments, taking for granted an intrinsic connection between the mysteries of the Christian faith and the peace so badly needed. Informed by his rigorous education, Bernardino's preaching in the vernacular brings alive familiar teachings, observations specific to Siena, and evocative rhetorical elements borne of his own pastoral creativity to inspire conversion away from hatred, faction, and violence toward a city of peace. The theological themes of creation and freedom, the brokenness of human relationships, and the hope for conversion remind the people of their identity in Christ rather than in the factions and fashions of this world. The homilies are deeply theological yet contain immense rhetorical and spiritual sensitivity. They seek to convey a new narrative about the violence and about the future, to cultivate in the Sienese a conscious desire for and commitment to peace.[4]

Preaching in Siena, 1427

By the time he returned to Siena in 1427, Bernardino was experienced in this peacemaking ministry. He came for that purpose, he says, by invitation of both the local bishop and the pope.[5] While Bernardino addresses a seemingly expansive range of issues, such as gossip, backbiting, marital conflict, economics, vanities, and more, he sees them all as connected to social reconciliation. Indeed the peace Bernardino preaches is a peace that spans politics, social norms, interpersonal relationships, marriages, and even a person's own eyes, mind, and heart.

Bernardino's methods are perhaps simple, but he seeks a lofty goal. First, he prays that his preaching will bring peace to Siena, so that "you will cast off all these parties and these divisions, in order that there may ever be peace among you, concord, and unity."[6] Second, Bernardino explains, "I have done it all for the honor and glory of God, and for the good of your souls and for your salvation."[7] This hope comes from his own fatherly commitment to Siena. He even affects some fatherly impatience: "As I have said to you, I have done this for you as if you were indeed my own children; and I tell you further that if I might get you by the hair I would set you in peace, each and all."[8] How did Bernardino pursue this goal? The next sections explore the themes of creation, sin, and conversion as Bernardino relates them to his audience through the lens of social reconciliation.

The Call to Peace: Remembering Creation, Harmony, and Freedom

Just as creation is the foundation for Christian Scriptures and theology, it is a cornerstone to the overall logic of Bernardino's message, though this often remains implicit. Indeed, in the Christian tradition, right relationship is at the foundation of the created world. Peace is not alien to the world; violence is, and violence is to be blamed on sin, not on the nature of things. Bernardino's preaching insists to the community that they are created free, that they are capable of peace, and that the call to peace with God and one another is indispensable. One of the opening homilies is about the character of creation itself, especially the free will of human beings. Bernardino explains the peaceful relationship between humanity and other creatures in order to say that human beings remain free:

> God made all things and established the order of them....The earth performs its duty above all by giving of its increase to sustain humanity; likewise fire, likewise water, likewise the heavens, all things that he made, he made for the sake of humanity. And if God has made all things for humanity and for our good, how can you believe that we are forced to do only...as the planets or the constellations direct us?[9]

Against the idea that human actions are determined by astronomical events, Bernardino asserts that human beings can choose to make peace. As we will see, free will forms the foundation of Bernardino's call to repentance, forgiveness, and conversion toward peace. Cynthia Polecritti highlights "the preacher's firm belief that people could change, thanks to the power of free will."[10]

Bernardino invokes creation in a more specific way when condemning the specific problem of slander. To explain the purpose of speech, he interprets the physical qualities of the tongue: God "has given you two ears and one tongue, so that you may hear more than you speak," and "the color of it is red, like fire. What does fire signify? Charity. So should the tongue…speak with charity."[11] These clever interpretations of the body likely help the Sienese to remember Bernardino's message, but they also reflect the view that the created world points toward charity. From the influence of the cosmos on free will to the color of the tongue, Bernardino's thought takes a strong foundation in the character of creation.

As a Franciscan, Bernardino draws on St. Francis himself as a model of relationships within the created order. According to Bernardino, Francis imitated Christ so closely that he shared the original harmony of the created order, even amid a fallen world. St. Francis exercised a gentle, nonconflictual relationship of governance

> over air, over land, over fire, and over water….Further, concerning the fishes, we have it that when he spoke they stayed to listen, and so likewise the birds….Moreover we have it that once a hare fleeing before the dogs, sought safety in the bosom of Saint Francis, and after they had passed on he let it go away.[12]

St. Francis's love was so pure that he "was granted the first innocence, as Adam was before he sinned."[13] Thus Siena, too, can "remember" when creation was a peaceful place and experience anew the capacity of creation for peace. The way to taste that original innocence is to imitate Christ in simple love, in poverty rather than worldliness.[14]

On the whole, the city of Siena was far from this Franciscan ideal of perfect harmony with creation. Yet the city had not always been so ensnared in the division and violence it now faced; at least in an ideal or primordial way, the foundation of the city itself was peaceful. As Polecritti argues, Bernardino reminded his audience of their identity as *citizens of Siena* rather than as members of factions.[15] Thus Bernardino provides something like a "creation story" for Siena, which serves to remind his listeners that they, too, could hope for peace.

In sum, then, the logic of Bernardino's preaching begins with creation. The world, at some primordial level, is capable of profound peace among human beings, God, and the natural world, and human beings are free to pursue that peace.

Sin: Remembering the Real Meanings of Violence

If the world is capable of peace, why is peace so elusive? This leads us to Bernardino's interpretation of the gossip, factions, and outright violence that were all too common in Siena. The first time Bernardino explicitly discusses Siena's division and factions he does not mince words, saying that the hatred between factions is exactly the opposite of Christian love, which is the condition for peace. Echoing his emphasis that human beings are created with freedom, Bernardino suggests that hatred thrives on the hidden choices in each person's heart. In a characteristically evocative metaphor, Bernardino compares this hatred to a thistle, which looks very innocent in winter or spring:

> [In the spring, the thistles are] all green; you will see the flowers growing on them, you will find them all pleasant, sending forth sweet odors. And so they grow up little by little. And how has the thistle grown up with the other green things? It grew from a very tiny thorn, and by little and little the thorn grew and hardened. When it was very young had you put your foot upon it, you would not have pricked yourself. Go, put your foot upon it when it is grown and hardened, see how you feel it![16]

Bernardino uses this metaphor to explain how choice and habit form a person's desires. Like a thistle, invisible at first, a person's choice to welcome hatred can lead him or her into full-fledged violence:

> So I wish to say of a people who cherish hatred and who consent to division and factions…by little and little the love of one faction increases and the hatred of the other, and then they harden in this love and this hatred. And when they are very hard, like the thistle in August…[you] desire the death and the destruction of the contrary faction; and you hate the contrary faction so that not only do you have no charity for it, and love it not as yourself, but, far otherwise, you hate it to the death and are murderous.[17]

Indeed, Siena and many other Italian cities had found themselves in serious conflict, driven by partisan identity and vendettas between factions. At all levels of society, there was pressure to choose one side or the other—families had loyalties, as did entire city-states, and there were some swing states, so to speak. They were entrenched in social sin, a downward spiral by which individual actions lead to social structures and cultural norms that entrench successive generations in specific, oppressive patterns of social behavior. These norms become easier to perpetuate than to escape.

Images: A New Memory of the Violence and a Revulsion to Sin

What medicine does the saint offer in response to this downward spiral? Having discussed free will, the possibility of peace, and the roots of violence in each person's heart, Bernardino spends many homilies unpacking evocative images that he hopes will reveal the reality of the violence both literally and spiritually, thus challenging the audience's desire to participate in acts of revenge.

First, Bernardino depicts the literal, societal effects of the factional hatred. For example, he addresses the women specifically to remind them how many evils have proceeded from these factions, how many women have been slaughtered in their own cities, in their own houses, how many have been disemboweled! Likewise, how many children have been killed for revenge upon their fathers....What do you think of this, women? More yet! I hear there have been certain women so rabid in their devotion to faction, that they have put spears into the hands of their baby sons, so that these might by murder avenge these factions.[18]

These damaging consequences of violence are unmistakable from the outside. Yet for those caught up in the conflict, their feelings of outrage, wounded pride, and catharsis can push the resulting victimization and grief into the background. Here Bernardino rhetorically provokes the women to see the hatred in their hearts, which is liable to fester into sin that is literally mortal to its neighbors—and which causes them a great deal of grief in the first place. Indeed, this theme, that vengeance, vanity, greed, and inequality constitute "occasions of loss and damage to your city,"[19] is a constant refrain throughout the homilies.

In addition to these tragic social consequences, Bernardino depicts the alarming sacramental and spiritual realities of the violence. To reveal a sacramental meaning of the division into factions, Bernardino contrasts it with the eucharistic celebration, the sacrament of thanksgiving and unity in Christ. Amid their culture of partisan identities and vendetta, Bernardino observes, the Sienese look at each other with eyes of suspicion so that they even project division onto inanimate objects:

You know this [division] reaches even to the man who is paring his peach, or cutting his garlic open. When a man pares a peach in a certain way, some bystander will say "He is Guelph or Ghibelline!"...Now do you not see that you have brought it about that every man and every woman, every boy, even the fruits, are "Guelph" or "Ghibelline"?[20]

How ridiculous! In a skillful moment of preaching, Bernardino must have made his divided audience "agree" by laughing at themselves. Immediately, however, Bernardino reveals the seriousness of the division in relation to the Eucharist: "Two things only remain which you have not made 'Guelph' or 'Ghibelline,' though perhaps you would do well to make them partisan, too. Do you know what they are? Bread and wine; and if you made these partisan, you would never eat them, in order not to have to do with the contrary faction."[21] Bernardino sees that the citizens' partisanship threatens the integrity of the eucharistic celebration, the prayer of the church as the one Body of Christ. As for the Corinthians to whom the Apostle Paul wrote (1 Cor 11), this division is a scandal in relation to the eucharistic celebration and thus a major spiritual problem for the community.

Finally, Bernardino points out the spiritual meaning of Siena's divisions: It is idolatry to make one's life revolve around factions and vendettas. For hearts not able to love, Bernardino suggests, this idolatry that causes so much suffering now will only bring more suffering in the life to come. Bernardino explains that this form of idolatry is the work of the devil, who

> made men take up certain devices when they were divided into different factions, and he made them love and honor and reverence these devices so that they were held more dear than any other thing, and they were loved more than God. As everyone then can see clearly, whoever holds with a faction or bears the device of a faction cannot suffer that any ill be said of this party, and it grieves him, he remembers the offence that has been done as if it had been done to God; and so in a hidden manner are the devils adored.[22]

Rhetorically, of course, this account of sin and faction sets up a common enemy, the devil himself. Further, this fascinating theological reflection serves to reveal the preeminent spiritual meaning of the social division in Siena: idolatry. The devil has found a way to be "adored": not in idols, as of old, but in the culture of the factions, which take the place of God in people's lives.

Bernardino says such idols are adored in Siena more than "in all the rest of the world together."[23] When it comes to idolatry, Bernardino condemns in particular the images and banners of the factions, the visual elements by which they perform their identities. What is the reason for this condemnation? The visual identifiers serve to perpetuate vendetta, enflaming memories of division. The same premise about images also explains Bernardino's effort to reveal so provocatively the social, sacramental, and spiritual-eschatological meaning of the factional divisions in Siena. The images he wants to burn into Siena's memory are of hidden thistles, factions among fruit, slaughter and grief, and the adoration of devils rather than the glee of factional emblems and dreams of revenge.

Bernardino's treatment of Siena's division does not shy away from implications for the afterlife. When it becomes idolatrous, division from one another entails division from God as well: "If devils have been adored by these partisans, and if they have never done penance for this, into what place do you think they [the dead partisans] have fallen?"[24] They "all go to the home of the devil" and "all go to the home of destruction" who spend their lives destroying the lives of others.[25] In short, "this matter of 'Guelph' or 'Ghibelline' is an invention of the devil, in order to get your souls."[26] The eschatological implications of each person's choice for peace or faction, and the certainty that God will reward and punish these choices in time as well, form major themes in Bernardino's preaching, certainly meant to jolt his audience into desiring change.[27]

Is this apocalyptic rhetoric simply a scare tactic to manipulate people into making peace? If it were, the result would certainly not be true peace but "negative peace"—a state of divine deterrence in which the absence of violence is maintained by threat. Yet positive right relationship is precisely what Bernardino seeks and sees so desperately lacking in Siena. Though he waxes too sure about the fate of all partisans, it is not wrong to suggest that those who perpetrate such violence might want to consider what those actions mean in relation to their eternal life or death. Furthermore, there is a strong scriptural warrant for prophetic denunciation of what does such harm to the vulnerable.

In short, then, Bernardino depicts a world in which violence is the result of sin, both individual and social. As in Genesis, where the sin of Adam and Eve spiraled into the murder of Abel and all subsequent violence, the malformed desires of the Sienese lead to all the lamentable violence they experience. By situating Siena's present violence within a new narrative of created freedom and peace, a fall into idolatrous factions, and a hopeful future, Bernardino helps those who are listening to desire something new.

Peace as a Fruit of Conversion to Christian Charity

What, then, are the people of Siena to do? Can they escape the violence, given how deeply entrenched is the cycle of hatred, revenge, and division? Bernardino admits that King David longed for peace but could not find "that true happiness which he desired" in the things of the world.[28] If not even one person can find individual peace, how can a whole city reconcile its factions? Yet Bernardino exhorts the people to seek a positive, integral peace: "See that you be always one of those who seek peace: peace with men, peace within your own soul, and peace with God."[29]

Peace is possible, to Bernardino, because the people of Siena remain free. The Sienese realize this freedom when they remember themselves within the story of creation and sin, a story in which violence is optional, rather than within the story of revenge, of offense and counteroffense. Within this narrative, the first step toward peace is individuals' choice to convert their hearts away from vengeful hatred and toward a commitment to peace, forgiveness, and reconciliation with enemies. This new way of life is, in short, charity, the love that enables one to care for the other and to forgive.

The conversion to charity is born of freedom, but it is hardly an autonomous, individual project. According to Bernardino, peace is possible to individuals, not through their pure effort but through their choice to open their hearts to a new way, receiving this way of peace as an unmerited gift. This new way of life consists in belonging to Christ, who entered our human history of violence in order to break its power. Yet belonging to Christ is incompatible with belonging to factions, just as the factions cannot be both vengeful and charitable at once.[30] Bernardino explains that it is a scandal to say, "I belong to the 'Guelphs' or to the

'Ghibellines.'"[31] On the contrary, a person "cannot have greater charity within himself than when he says: I belong to Christ."[32] Belonging to Christ and imitating his charity, however, lead to the cross. For Christ and those who belong to him rather than to factions: "Greater love has no one than this, that a man lay down his life for his friends."[33] The conversion to peace, then, is synonymous with participation in Christ. It entails belonging to Christ and walking in the footsteps of his perfect charity, as St. Francis had done, always preferring to endure violence rather than perpetrate it.

The Cries of the Victims: A Dangerous Memory

How does Christ propose or provoke this conversion of heart? In Bernardino's preaching, one important moment for conversion is hearing the cries of the innocent victims. The victims are important in a dramatic story of conversion set in nearby Crema, where factions have brought the town to a crisis. Ninety men and their families face banishment. Bernardino tells the Sienese that he preached without reserve about the violence there:

> In my preaching I spoke of the unceasing cries of the innocent before God, against those who have made them suffer punishment for no fault of theirs, asking for vengeance against those who have persecuted them. And these words entered into their [the citizens'] hearts so deeply that they called a council, in which there was such harmony that it was marvelous; and in this it was decided that each of those [exiles] might return to his home [rather than be banished].[34]

The cries of the innocent stir the hearts of the citizens to compassion and repentance. This compassion is a sharing in the compassion and charity of Christ and thus a movement toward conversion. Indeed, the cries of the innocent echo the voice of Christ, who is supremely innocent, and who says that whatever one does to the least of these is done to him (Matt 25:45). The remembrance of victims—the memory of suffering, as Johann Baptist Metz calls it—provokes the citizens' turn outside themselves in freedom. This is not merely a recollection of events, or a sterile rehearsing of the fact of violence. As Metz explains in general terms,

> There is another kind of memory: dangerous memories, memories that challenge. These are memories in which earlier experiences flare up and unleash new dangerous insights for the present. For brief moments they illuminate, harshly and piercingly, the problematic character of things we made our peace with a long time ago and the banality of what we take to be "realism"....They are memories that one has to take into account, memories that have a future content.[35]

In Bernardino's story, the daring attempt of the citizens of Crema to call a council, "peace talks" of a sort, tells us that this homily did not only scold the community for tolerating violence. At its core, rather, was a fundamental challenge, a "dangerous memory" with startling "future content." Indeed the news that their city has taken steps into this future entails "future content" for the exiles who, in their turn, find it joyful and even unbelievable. Bernardino continues his homily:

> Then leaving Crema I went to a village perhaps ten miles away, and I talked to one of those exiles, who had left in Crema great possessions of his, which were worth about forty-thousand florins. And he asked me: How does the matter stand? And I said to him: By the grace of God you may return to your house, because I know well what they intend [i.e., to make peace]. He laughed in mockery of what I said to him, but in a little while came a messenger from Crema who told him that he could return at will to his own house. And hearing this, he could not eat, or drink, or sleep, because of the joy that he felt....So great was the gladness he felt that he could not speak.[36]

The joy of this exile is the joy of mercy; his release from exile is the fruit of others' heeding the cries of the innocent. Their conversion becomes contagious:

> And listen to a wonderful thing: when he was returning to his house, he [the exile] found in the Piazza his enemy, who when he saw him ran and…wished to lead him home to supper with him. And another who was in possession of the house where he lived, at once, while they supped, cleared the house of all his possessions, and left there those of this other man; and whoever had anything of his, sent it to that house of his,—at once, his bedstead, his coffers, his table-cloths, his bowls, his casks, his silver…so that the very same evening he was led into his own house and slept in his own bed in the midst of his own possessions.[37]

Remembering the cry of the innocent leads, in this story, to a new possible future of peace for the city and of merciful return for the exile. All the social, legislative, and cultural transformations that are needed for peace begin with the openness to the voice of Christ heard in the cries of the victims.

Those who think themselves too strong for peace, Bernardino says, should turn their attention to Christ as the paradigm of forgiveness. In remembering Christ, those who refuse to forgive encounter the one who forgives the greatest possible offense: "You hear many who eject poisonous venom, saying that a man debases himself if he makes peace with one who has injured him. Alas! Have you never thought of what God did? Was God cowardly, then? Was it cowardice in him when he pardoned those who offended him? Oh, he never sought anything but peace!"[38] In sum, while violence is the result of nurturing the thistle of hatred, and of the evolution of that hatred into an idolatrous form of belonging, the remedy is belonging to Christ. It is possible for the Sienese to forgive, love, and have peace in their own fallen city through participation in the forgiveness, charity, and peace of Christ.

Aids to Conversion:
The YHS and the Kiss of Peace

Although the moment of conversion may be dramatic, Bernardino insists that belonging to a faction or to Christ grows stable only through small, daily choices. The starting point for either path, toward entrenched violence or integral peace, is a tiny thistle or a hidden choice to hear the voice of Christ. After the dramatic story of the man from Crema and the good news of a "resolution by [Siena's] government to achieve '*pacem et unionem*,'"[39] Bernardino brings the discourse down to earth with practical advice. The Sienese should "proceed by little and little, from good to better" in the spiritual journey, since "it is better to go with great slowness" so that the change will become habit.[40]

Bernardino provides practical advice on how to aid these small, daily choices. For example, fasting, penance, and responding with patience strengthen the resolve of a person to make peace.[41] Bernardino also provides a practical alternative to Siena's "idols," the banners of the factions. As Cynthia Polecritti observes, Bernardino brought along to his preaching a banner with the name of Jesus in the form of the letters *YHS*. She explains, "Bernardino hoped that the YHS, its golden letters and rays surrounded by a blue field, would become a substitute for factional emblems."[42] Bernardino gives the people a visual aid, an icon of their new form of commitment to Christ. This is the positive expression of Bernardino's belief that human desire is formed by images, that "we remember better the things which we see than the things which we hear."[43]

Though the journey to peace relies on gradual steps rather than theatrics, Bernardino does have a place for intense moments to express publicly the initial commitment to social reconciliation before God and neighbor. Perhaps the most memorable moments in Bernardino's preaching series were the ritual "bonfires of vanities and mass peacemakings."[44] These rituals signified the intention both to reject the latest material fashions (another cause of war, Bernardino insists) and to pursue peace with their neighbors.[45] At the culmination of his preaching, indeed, Bernardino instructs the men and women to go and "set yourselves in peace" at local churches:

> When you [women] leave the sermon and go home, see that you go into San Martino, entering thus by the Porrione, and let this going into the church be to show that you are at peace with every one; and present this peace and offer it up in the church, all who can enter. And when you find yourselves together there with those towards whom you have borne hatred, you will set yourselves in peace with one another, and see that you leave nothing unfinished in this respect. And if you cannot all enter the church, pass across the Piazza as a sign that you offer and will accept peace....
>
> Likewise, I say to you, men, go, and offer up peace to the Virgin Mary in the Duomo, in order that she may preserve you in peace, may protect you from those dangers which threaten you while you have hatred in your hearts. And then when you find yourselves there together with those to whom you bear hatred, you will set yourselves in peace with one another. Now see that you leave nothing unfinished in this respect.[46]

These peacemaking rituals were expected to bear fruit both for social reconciliation and for people's relationships with God. As for social reconciliation, each person should commit to do his or her part. Bernardino encourages women to convert their support of the factions into support of peace; as Polecritti writes, Bernardino "felt that Sienese women, the 'silent partners' in factional conflict, should be deeply involved in civic peacemaking, even if they could not legislate change themselves."[47] Likewise, Bernardino discusses the necessary role of political leaders in dispute resolution. In addition, he seems clearly to care about the legislative aspect of peacemaking, given the announcement during his visit of the "resolution by [Siena's] government to achieve '*pacem et unionem*.'"[48] Bernardino expects that the leaders and experts will be transformed along with the rest of the community and discern in their own practical wisdom how to shape laws, procedures, and other social norms in accord with peace. These social transformations flow from the spiritual aspect of the peacemaking ritual, the people's conversion from factional hatred to the charity of Christ. The spiritual fruit of conversion is prudence, gratitude, humility, obedience, compassion, and great fervor.

Perhaps to encourage further peacemaking and suggest specific actions the Sienese could take, Bernardino shares the beautiful result at Perugia, which bore the fruits of forgiveness, repentance, and resolve.[49] In a sense, the memory of others' conversions at Crema and Perugia is another kind of dangerous memory: real, hopeful events in nearby towns challenge the present complacency of Siena. Yet it seems Siena's conversion to Christian charity and to peace remained incomplete, even at the end of Bernardino's preaching there in 1427. Indeed, in the same homily, Bernardino dares and even begs the Sienese to complete their commitment to peace:

> In comparison to what your neighbors have, I would say that there remain yet many "peaces" to be made [in Siena];…Alas! For the love of God and one another. Ay me! Do you not see what will come upon you if you delight in the ruin of one another? Do you not perceive that you are ruining yourselves? Oh! Amend for the love of God….Love one another.[50]

Even with the aid of powerful stories, the YHS banner, and the ritual peacemaking, Siena's conversion toward the peace of Christ remains incremental.

Insights for Today

Modern Western deliberation tends to forget the importance of personal conversion as an aspect of seeking peace, and we prefer instead to seek change through the manipulation of social and political structures and of culture, communication, and even the material world. Pope Francis, interpreting Romano Guardini, calls this way of thinking the "technocratic paradigm." It plays out when a society relies too heavily on technical or technocratic means to solve problems that are also moral, cultural, and political in nature, such as climate change.[51] Bernardino's emphasis on human freedom and the ongoing possibility of conversion serves as a corrective, reminding us that, as Pope Francis says, both individual and collective conversion is needed, rather than individual or technical means alone:

> A healthy relationship with creation is one dimension of overall personal conversion, which entails the recognition of our errors, sins, faults and failures, and leads to heartfelt repentance and desire to change....Nevertheless, self-improvement on the part of individuals will not by itself remedy the extremely complex situation facing our world today....Social problems must be addressed by community networks and not simply by the sum of individual good deeds....The ecological conversion needed to bring about lasting change is also a community conversion.[52]

By connecting individual conversion to social reconciliation, Bernadino certainly embodies an impulse toward the kind of communal conversion that Pope Francis proposes in *Laudato Si'*. While perhaps Bernardino's eschatology tends to focus more on the individual, the substance of his proposal includes the vision of an integrally peaceful Siena. This proposal includes the provocation of communal memory with the "dangerous memories" of the cries of the innocent victims. Such memories confront individuals *and* the community as a whole with a choice as to their future: to side with the victims or the perpetrators, to belong to Christ or the factions, to live in harmonious peace or in idolatrous division.

Did Bernardino bring about peace, then, in the end? Did people attend his rituals? Did the rate of violence fall and were new laws enacted? These are worthwhile questions, but it is difficult to apply any empirical forms of evaluation to events from 1427. In the first place, it is impossible to say in any scientific way whether the Sienese were better off thanks to Bernardino's preaching. We cannot prove the counterfactual, and we cannot even interview the Sienese to get their stories. As for the "kiss of peace" and related agreements common in this era, Polecritti rejects another scholar's conclusion that these were merely "mystical rites which were in the last analysis inconsequential."[53] She insists that the rites carried "an importance that went beyond absolute 'success' or 'failure.'"[54] Polecritti is right to insist on the relevance of the rites, but she also seems to suggest that their impact was shallow and passing; these "ephemeral peacemakings were a way of reminding people that change was possible, if only for one beautiful moment...[like] images which were 'real' and yet idealized depictions, outlining a world which could never be."[55]

Yet if for Bernardino conversion is "not so much the quick descent of grace as an educational process,"[56] and "a slow process of education, designed as a step-by-step course in how to live well,"[57] even small reductions in violence may be important. Might not the ritual itself be effective precisely *as* a symbol, not in a manipulative way but as part of the "process which gradually strengthens the will"?[58] Bernardino's goal is the peace of Siena, the salvation of its citizens, and the glory of God,[59] and yet he seeks this lofty goal in just the way Polecritti describes, "little by little."

Bernardino's preaching of a "dangerous memory" addresses itself subversively to the individual heart and interrupts the collective memory of the community. There may well have been beautiful effects of this preaching that remain undetected. The one essential result that Bernardino sought was love—precisely the kind of result that often remains hidden, preferring to receive violence than undertake it, to forgive in one's heart, and to give alms in secret. It is through stories and testimonies that we learn to notice love, and Bernardino does give us evidence that his preaching made a difference at Crema and Perugia, not least to the citizens who remembered the cry of the innocent and called a council to make peace, and to the exile who returned home full of joy.

We who "listen" to Bernardino's preaching today should attend to the way his preaching presents theological content in relationship to his social context. When it comes to the *social context*, Bernardino's sermons are of interest because our societies are not immune to cultures of violence and economic injustice like those that plagued fifteenth-century Siena. How many people in the relatively prosperous West choose to spend leisure time displaying a partisan identity through images on social media rather than meeting and advocating for those with no such leisure? How

147

many of us work to build bridges instead of sneering smugly or despairingly with friends who agree? Does our relationship to the earth lead to harmony, or to the maintenance of our own social status? These challenges are not wholly different from those facing Siena in the fifteenth century.

Second, Bernardino's *approach to preaching* makes these homilies particularly rich for us today. Bernardino's homilies normally began before dawn, when he could not take a lively audience for granted. The evocative images, then, helped to make his points compelling to the audience—not only keeping them more attentive, but moving their hearts with the truths he preached. These images convey Bernardino's frank discussion of social issues, the spiritual journey, and the way to hope. The images helped to form the memory, identity, and desire of Bernardino's audience in accord with the theological narrative of the Christian faith they held, and so, too, in accord with peace.

Finally, and most centrally, there are lessons for us in the actual *content* Bernardino proposes to this audience. In seeking to shape the memory, identity, and desire of his audience, he appeals to a specifically Christian pattern of creation, sin, conversion, and redemption. Bernardino challenges the factions' narratives by deploying afresh these familiar theological categories, reinterpreting the divisions in their city, their own identities, and their future. Having remembered that they were created in freedom, the Sienese may now begin to face the ugliness they have wrought. Their memories are those of violence and grief, but Bernardino provides the reminder that before violence, in the core of their human nature, there exists the capacity for peace and freedom. In the same way a society can devolve into cycles of hatred and revenge, it can in Christ pivot back to freedom, desiring instead the delightful freedom of peace in charity.

Aware of the deep entrenchment of sin, Bernardino does not pretend to bring immediate perfection, nor does he think the right processes and policies in the formal sphere are sufficient to bring about true and lasting peace. What he offers to Siena and to us, instead, is a model of peace that suggests the importance of memory, conversion, and responsibility. Peace is not the product of a technical program or policy alone. The peace of Siena, Bernardino says, relies on the slow drama of free choice by individuals and communities to receive and abide in the charity of Christ, leaving behind hatred and vendetta for the sake of peace.

Reflection Questions

1. Do people in your context struggle to believe what Bernardino preaches about the goodness of creation and the idea that humans have free choice? What might you say about creation if you were in a role like Bernardino's today, reminding a group of people about the basic possibilities and limitations of their world?

2. How do people in your context understand the cause of division, partisanship, or violence? What insights could Bernardino's preaching provide about its meaning, and what would you like to add to his account of sin and violence?

3. How does peace come about, from Bernardino's theological perspective?

4. What would it mean to have a collective conversion toward social reconciliation? You may wish to explain the role of individual free choice, memory, identity, desire, ritual, and responsibility in collective conversion.

5. Bernardino treats eschatology (the last things) largely as an individual reward or punishment. What effects does he glean from this way of thinking? Are there other sources for eschatological hope that could provide a richer account of hope as both individual and collective?

Notes

1. I would like to express deep gratitude to the organizers of the seminars that led to this volume. Thanks in particular to Jay Carney, who both invited me to discuss the project in the first place and introduced me to St. Bernardino of Siena.

2. Cynthia L. Polecritti, *Preaching Peace in Renaissance Italy: Bernardino of Siena and His Audience* (Washington, DC: The Catholic University of America Press, 2000), 182.

3. This study refers briefly to these rituals, which have been studied in themselves most recently and thoroughly in Katherine Ludwig Jansen, *Peace and Penance in Late Medieval Italy* (Princeton: Princeton University Press, 2018). See also Jenny Benham, *Peacemaking in the Middle Ages: Principles and Practice* (New York: Manchester University Press, 2011); Kiril Petkov, *The Kiss of Peace: Ritual, Self, and Society in the High and Late Medieval West* (Boston: Brill, 2003) and "Kiss and Make Up? Ritual Peacemaking in Frankish Morea and Its Narrative Reflections," in *War and Peace: Critical Issues in European Societies and Literature 800–1800*, ed. Albrecht Classen and Nadia Margolis (Berlin: de Gruyter, 2011), 293–311; and James A. Palmer, "Piety and Social Distinction in Late Medieval Roman Peacemaking," *Speculum* 89, no. 4 (2014): 974–1004.

4. This study does not address some problematic aspects of Bernardino's preaching; these have been treated most notably in Franco Mormando, *The Preacher's Demons: Bernardino of Siena and the Social Underworld of Early Renaissance Italy* (Chicago: University of Chicago Press, 1999).

5. Bernardino of Siena, *Saint Bernardine of Siena: Sermons*, ed. Don Nazareno Orlandi, trans. Helen Josephine Robins (Siena: Tipografia sociale, 1920), Homily Selection XXVII.4. Polecritti notes that Bernardino certainly was invited to preach in Siena by the local government (Polecritti, *Preaching Peace in Renaissance Italy*, 183). Quotations from Bernardino's homilies at Siena are adapted from the 1920 translation. This lively English translation includes some constructions and terms that have fallen out of use, such as "thou" and "thy" for "you" and "your." I have made slight edits in accord with the idiom of twenty-first century English, maintaining the integrity of meaning and syntax.

6. Selection XXVII.4.

7. Selection XXXII.7; he also notes his concern about salvation in VIII.1.

8. Selection XXXII.7.

9. Selection I.2.

10. Polecritti, *Preaching Peace in Renaissance Italy*, 240.

11. Selection VII.1.

12. Selection XXIV.2.
13. Selection XXIV.2.
14. Selection II.3.
15. Polecritti, *Preaching Peace in Renaissance Italy*, 189.
16. Selection VIII.2.
17. Selection VIII.2.
18. Selection VIII.6.
19. Selection XXVII.14.
20. Selection VIII.3.
21. Selection VIII.3.
22. Selection VIII.3; see also XI.3, 4 on the same theme of idolatry.
23. Selection XVII.2.
24. Selection XVII.2.
25. Selection XI.3, 4.
26. Selection VIII.3.
27. Polecritti treats these eschatological themes in detail in her sequential reading of the homilies of 1427 (*Preaching Peace in Renaissance Italy*, 191–225).
28. Selection XXXI.1.
29. Selection XXXI.7.
30. Selection VIII.2.
31. Selection VIII.5.
32. Selection VIII.4
33. Selection VIII.4, see Polecritti, *Preaching Peace in Renaissance Italy*, 211–12.
34. Selection VIII.8.
35. Johann Baptist Metz, *Faith in History and Society: Toward a Practical Fundamental Theology*, trans. J. Matthew Ashley (New York: Crossroad, 2007), 105–6.
36. Selection VIII.8.
37. Selection VIII.8.
38. Selection XXXI.8; see Polecritti, *Preaching Peace in Renaissance Italy*, 235.
39. Polecritti, *Preaching Peace in Renaissance Italy*, 206, citing a study by Martino Bertagna on the government resolution, "Vita e Apostolato senese di San Bernardino," *Studi Francescani* 60 (1963): 60–65.
40. Selection IX.1, 5; see Polecritti, *Preaching Peace in Renaissance Italy*, 207.

41. Selections IX.7, X.

42. Polecritti, *Preaching Peace in Renaissance Italy*, 8. Perhaps ironically, given his intention to replace idolatry, Bernardino was twice accused of perpetrating idolatry through such banners; investigations found his activity to be entirely legitimate.

43. Selection XI.4.

44. Polecritti, *Preaching Peace in Renaissance Italy*, 7.

45. Selection XXV.2.

46. Selection XXXI.9.

47. Polecritti, *Preaching Peace in Renaissance Italy*, 204.

48. Polecritti, *Preaching Peace in Renaissance Italy*, 206, citing the study by Bertagna.

49. Selection XXXII.5.

50. Selection XXXII.7.

51. Pope Francis, *Laudato Si'*, 2015.

52. Pope Francis, *Laudato Si'* 218–19. In the latter ellipsis, Pope Francis is citing Romano Guardini, a critical influence on Francis in this document and elsewhere.

53. Jacques Heers, *Parties and Political Life in the Medieval West*, trans. David Nicholas (Amsterdam: North Holland Publishing Company, 1977), 205, cited in Polecritti, *Preaching Peace in Renaissance Italy*, 3.

54. Polecritti, *Preaching Peace in Renaissance Italy*, 3.

55. Polecritti, *Preaching Peace in Renaissance Italy*, 241–42.

56. Polecritti, *Preaching Peace in Renaissance Italy*, 190.

57. Polecritti, *Preaching Peace in Renaissance Italy*, 239.

58. Polecritti, *Preaching Peace in Renaissance Italy*, 190.

59. Selection XXXII.7.

CHAPTER 8

Three Lessons from St. Alphonsus Liguori's Analysis of Restitution

Julia A. Fleming

One possible resource that classical Roman Catholic moral
theology can offer to a dialogue on social reconciliation is an
account of a form of justice known as restitution. Restitution and
reconciliation are not identical. It is easy to imagine circumstances
in which restitution occurs, but no reconciliation follows. For that
reason, restitution represents only a possible first step toward
reconciliation. Yet restitution poses some of the same challenges
as reconciliation—sometimes in a more limited form that makes
them easier to analyze. As a result, a Christian study of social
reconciliation can draw helpful insights from the values and
concerns that our predecessors have emphasized in their analyses
of restitution.

The legacy of Roman Catholic ethical thinking on restitution
is quite extensive, so our discussion will focus upon the treatment
of the subject created by the Neapolitan theologian Alphonsus
Liguori (1696–1787).[1] In book 3 of his *Theologia Moralis*, Alphonsus
devotes an entire chapter to the thorny topic of restitution.[2] He
acknowledges that restitution poses particularly challenging ethical problems, and admits that he has changed his mind about
some conclusions that he had accepted or rejected in earlier editions of his text.[3]

The *Theologia Moralis* is a textbook designed to train priests to evaluate the sins that people confessed to them within the sacrament of penance. Following the literary conventions used in such manuals, Alphonsus's long chapter summarizes, develops, and weighs in upon the questions regarding restitution raised by his predecessors and contemporaries. His text thus provides a valuable summary of the state of the question at the end of the eighteenth century. By my rough count, Alphonsus invokes at least 155 different theologians and canonists in this chapter in addition to his citations from Scripture, church councils, Vatican documents, and canon law.[4] In the discussion that follows, the phrase *Alphonsus and his sources* will serve as a reminder that he inherited or borrowed many of these arguments and conclusions from other theologians.

To set Alphonsus's moral analysis in context, our discussion will begin with a brief introduction to his life and the structure of his chapter on restitution. Next appears a definition of restitution and the identification of its central purposes. After these preliminaries, our discussion will highlight the paradox of restitution as it appears in Alphonsus and his sources. On the one hand, these theologians view restitution as an obligatory act of justice; on the other, they recognize that restitution in the strict sense is often impossible, or even undesirable. Then we will briefly review five of the strategies Alphonsus and his colleagues employed to resolve that paradox. These strategies suggest three lessons for a dialogue on social reconciliation: (1) the importance of acknowledging our finitude (i.e., our human limitations); (2) the necessity of respecting the needs and human dignity of all parties; and (3) the significance of the search for equilibrium between the parties that restitution seeks.

Introduction to the Life of Alphonsus Liguori and to His Text

Alphonsus Liguori was born in Naples in 1696, the first of eight children in a family belonging to the kingdom's lesser nobility. His father, Giuseppe, an officer and eventually a commander in the Royal Galleys, had high hopes for his eldest son's career and marriage. Alphonsus studied law at the University of Naples, where he received his doctorate in both civil and canon law in 1713. After a period of legal apprenticeship, he began to practice in the courts. In 1723, however, Alphonsus abandoned his legal career to seek the priesthood. Since Naples had no seminary at the time, candidates for ordination received part of their training by their required participation in one of the city's priestly confraternities (i.e., organizations devoted to good works and to worship). Alphonsus joined the group devoted to apostolic missions, and it was in the context of his work with this group that he experienced a call to serve in missions of preaching, catechesis, and sacramental administration to the rural poor.[5]

Eventually Alphonsus became the founder of a religious order dedicated to that type of pastoral work, although the legal status of his community, the Congregation of the Most Holy Redeemer (commonly known as the Redemptorists), remained precarious in Bourbon Naples (and at some points, in the Vatican) throughout his lifetime.[6] Chosen against his will for the episcopate in 1762, Alphonsus served as a bishop for thirteen years before the pope finally accepted his resignation for reasons of health. He returned to his community's house in Pagani, where he died in 1787. He was canonized in 1839, recognized as a doctor of the church in 1871, and named as the patron saint of confessors and moral theologians in 1950.[7]

In addition to his pastoral work as a priest, religious superior, missionary, and bishop, Alphonsus was a prolific and best-selling author, especially in the areas of spirituality and moral theology. His publications in ethics began in midlife, after he addressed a topic of practical interest to missionary communities in the Kingdom of Naples—whether the common rural custom of cursing the dead represented blasphemy![8] When Alphonsus decided to write a textbook on moral theology, he followed a practice common at the time: expanding and commenting on an earlier work by another author. Alphonsus chose a popular seventeenth-century handbook for confessors by the Jesuit Hermann Busenbaum, the *Medualla Theologia Moralis*.[9] Alphonsus's annotation, published in 1748, became the first edition of a work that he eventually called the *Theologia Moralis*, a massive study of ethical questions that

Alphonsus revised and expanded throughout his career. Nine editions appeared during his lifetime; the last was published in 1785, two years before his death.[10]

In the critical edition of the *Theologia Moralis*, Alphonsus's chapter on restitution appears within his treatment of sins against the seventh commandment, where it is sandwiched between the chapters on theft and contracts.[11] The chapter on restitution has seven sections. The first defines *restitution* and asks who has an obligation to perform it. The second addresses the obligations of those involved, in some way, in the wrongful deeds of others, while the third considers whether such participants (as individuals) are bound to proportional or complete restitution of the damage. Section 4 analyzes whether restitution is necessary if one person impedes another from attaining some good. Section 5 identifies restitution's recipients. Section 6 considers categories of injuries conceivably subject to restitution, including harms to material property, life and bodily integrity, virginity, marital fidelity, reputation, and other spiritual goods. The final section focuses on the circumstances surrounding restitution, including those that excuse or modify the obligation to make it. Alphonsus's discussion of the topic, therefore, is extensive and wide-ranging.

Restitution's Definition and Purpose

Restitution, for Alphonsus, is an act of justice that seeks to repair damage inflicted upon one's neighbor through one's unjust action or inaction. Not limited to cases of deliberate harm, restitution nonetheless applies only when (a) the victim has suffered real damage and (b) that damage violates some right that the victim enjoys, for example, to life, bodily integrity, reputation, or property. This could be either a right to something that the person injured already has (e.g., life) or a right to obtain something in the future (e.g., on the basis of a contract).[12] Thus, fantasizing about or even plotting to harm someone is wrong, but does not require restitution as long as the victim remains unscathed.[13] Similarly, assuming that one uses neither force nor fraud, one can deprive others of something beneficial without owing them restitution if they have no right to the benefit per se. Convincing someone to give a job to one candidate rather than another is an obvious example.[14] In short, for Alphonsus and his sources, violations of justice can require restitution; violations of the other virtues, especially charity, do not.[15] (It is important to pay attention to this distinction, because twenty-first century usage often employs the terms *unjust* or *unfair* more broadly to describe actions with negative consequences that do not involve violations of rights in the strict sense).[16]

While judges and other authorities can require persons to offer restitution in the public sphere, Alphonsus presumes that the command to offer restitution can also come from one's confessor. The legal duty to make restitution and the moral duty to make restitution are thus distinct, albeit related and often overlapping, obligations.[17] Persons can have a moral duty to make restitution even if they have no legal obligation to do so.[18] Sometimes, however, restitution becomes a moral obligation only after it becomes a legal obligation. In Alphonsus's view, someone who has damaged another's reputation does not have to pay compensatory damages before receiving an order to do so from a judge because the offender is not restoring reputation itself, but mitigating the harm that has followed from lost reputation.[19] Similarly, a citizen who violates restrictions about the use of public lands, but causes only minor damage, is not obliged to make restitution until the fine is assessed. (One can rationally assume, Alphonsus concludes, that the community did not intend to impose any greater moral burden in these circumstances than paying any required fines).[20] Thus the restitution that one is legally obliged to make can be smaller than, greater than, or the same as what one's moral duty requires.

Alphonsus and his sources also conclude that, under some circumstances, restitution is necessary for accidental as well as deliberate harm.[21] This is particularly true when those in a position of trust neglect their responsibilities.[22] To illustrate the point, Alphonsus mentions public officials who fail to guard communities from wild animals, bandits, and soldiers; councilors and canons who look the other way during corrupt elections; tutors and guardians who do not protect the interests of those under their care; and servants who neither prevent nor report the loss of their masters' properties.[23] In each case, restitution is obligatory because (1) the agent could have acted and (2) the agent had a special responsibility to do so.

Finally, Alphonsus does not list the possible goals of restitution or rank the various goals that appear within his analysis, including punishment and deterrence.[24] Clearly, restitution's most obvious goal, as suggested by the definition itself, is to make reparations to one's injured neighbor. As an act of commutative justice, restitution pursues equality: what its agent or agents return should correspond, as much as possible, to what the original victim has lost.[25] As we shall see, however, the practical limits to achieving this goal, as well as the potential risks to the common good from attempting to do so, complicated the ethics of restitution. Indeed, Alphonsus's discussion suggests instead that restitution's most basic goal—the goal that remains applicable when others cannot be achieved—is the restoration of some form of equilibrium between the offender and the injured neighbor.[26]

The Paradox of Restitution

Restitution created a paradox for Roman Catholic ethics. On the one hand, general consensus regarded it as a duty for those who had seriously violated others' rights, and indeed, as necessary for salvation.[27] Penitents who were able to offer restitution but refused to do so could not be absolved, even if they claimed that they would perform the duty at the end of their lives or instruct their heirs to make amends. (There were exceptions if immediate restitution would cause great harm, or if the confessor realized that the penitent was in good faith and that trying to change his or her mind would be fruitless.)[28] In general, however, theologians warned confessors that restitution should precede absolution. Among Alphonsus's sources there was considerable debate about whether a penitent who promised to make restitution as soon as possible could be absolved before doing so—and how many times, if ever, the confessor should accept such a promise as genuine![29]

This possibility of refusing to absolve raised the stakes significantly for the theological analysis of restitution. This was particularly true for theologians like Alphonsus, who argues that confession gives penitents a "right to absolution, which cannot be denied" unless they are indisposed.[30] It is also worth noting that, in some times and places during the early modern period, failure to receive absolution could become a public as well as a private matter, not least because such denial rendered penitents unable to receive the Eucharist during Easter season as required by canon law. (Patrick J. O'Banion makes this point with an illustration from sixteenth-century Spain, where the names of those who had failed to fulfill their Easter duty were read aloud at Mass and posted in parish churches.)[31] Given the spiritual and social implications of denying absolution, therefore, confessors needed the ability to distinguish cases that required restitution from those in which restitution was optional.

In addition, the duty to make restitution might fall upon persons other than the primary offender. Like Aquinas, Alphonsus identifies a variety of forms of complicity that could render one liable for restitution, from ordering or encouraging another's bad act, to failing to prevent it or keeping silent about it.[32] When more than one person was involved in an injury, each might be obliged to make part of the restitution in proportion to the role that he or she had played in the offense. Under some circumstances, however, each participant could be liable for the entire damage.[33] In addition to accomplices, persons who had unwittingly benefited from the original bad act, such as the good-faith purchaser of stolen property, or a debtor's heirs, were sometimes bound to make restitution.[34] In fact, theologians even asked whether employees could legitimately accept payment from employers in very serious debt, since paying those wages would limit the employers' capacity to repay their creditors. Although theological consensus in that case favored the rights of the employees, the fact that the question was raised at all illustrates how seriously Catholic moralists took the duty to make one's neighbor whole, and how broadly they extended the range of persons conceivably subject to that duty.[35]

Yet despite his insistence upon the necessity of restitution, Alphonsus, drawing upon his contemporaries and his predecessors, describes a plethora of circumstances in which undoing the harm to the original victim is either impossible or undesirable. Some injuries, by their nature, exceed human capacities for restitution, including losses of life, limb, reputation, or bodily integrity.[36] Thus, while a judge or confessor can require someone who has wounded another unjustly to make payments to the victim, such compensation, strictly speaking, addresses the material damages associated with the injury (e.g., medical expenses) rather than the injury itself.[37] Even when the thing taken from the neighbor can be returned, the person who should make restitution may no longer have it or may not know the owner's identity.[38] However much the penitent wishes to make amends, circumstances can render the fulfillment of the desire physically impossible.

Moreover, the penitent's ability to make restitution to the injured party was not the confessors' only concern. Under some circumstances, theological consensus concluded, attempting to make restitution would inflict excessive harm upon penitents.[39] Debtors and their families, for example, have no moral duty to starve, steal, or prostitute themselves to make their lenders' whole.[40] According to Alphonsus, common opinion also excuses debtors if they cannot make restitution without surrendering what is necessary to live in a state of life that they have justly acquired: thus, workmen may keep the tools of their trade, and nobles, their horses and servants.[41] In a more homely illustration of disproportionate harm, Alphonsus's sources concede that when the expense of returning a stolen item far outweighs its value, the duty to make exact restitution sometimes disappears.[42]

In addition, Catholic moralists concluded that restitution could be wrong or unduly dangerous under some circumstances. If one foresees that the owner will use what one returns—a weapon, for example—to harm an innocent third party, restitution would be a sin rather than a duty.[43] Another illustration of excessive danger appears in Alphonsus's treatment of restitution for adultery, or (more accurately) the obligations of a woman who realizes her husband is not the biological father of her child. (The potential restitution problem in this case arises because the child stands to inherit some of the putative father's property at the expense of his biological heirs). Alphonsus mentions strategies that the wife could use to restore the inheritance to her husband's biological children—strategies that range from confessing the truth to convincing the child to enter a religious order. However, several of his sources conclude that these are rarely obligatory. In most cases, the risks to the mother and child of revealing the truth outweigh the financial harm to other parties.[44] Making other persons whole is not an absolute good, nor does its achievement override every other consideration.

Thus Alphonsus, like the thinkers upon whom he relies, recognized that restitution could raise problems of competing values and the conflicting yet legitimate interests of the various parties involved. What confessors needed were strategies for doing justice to all sides—in a sense, for respecting everyone's dignity—even when opposed interests seemed to promote contradictory resolutions. How could one find justice for everyone involved in cases where the solution seemed to render some legitimate concerns unattainable?

Strategies

In fact, Alphonsus's sources developed several different strategies for resolving such dilemmas.[45] One of them might be called the *irrationally unwilling argument*. Rational persons, Alphonsus assumes, must accept certain losses because their avoidance or the attempt to make restitution for them would inflict greater harms upon others. As an example, if marauding soldiers have ransacked my home, my neighbors who were forced into service as human pack mules to carry my goods away do not owe me restitution, for they had no duty to risk death to prevent my losses.[46] Alphonsus would describe me as "irrationally unwilling," if I do not accept my neighbors' participation in the theft, given the risk to their lives.[47] In such cases, no restitution is required. Similarly, several of Alphonsus's sources agree that the poor have no moral obligation to pay sales taxes at the cost of providing food and other necessities for their families. (Some authors add that officials can remit such payments on account of poverty when it is presumed that the prince would do so.)[48] Here again the theologians assume that the losers in the transaction—the prince and the tax collectors—should act according to reason and are irrationally unwilling if they do not. Acknowledging that reality can fall short of this ideal, Alphonsus asserts that debtors are excused from restitution when what they have done, according to a rational standard, should satisfy the creditors, even if the creditors are not content with the outcome.[49]

A second interesting strategy for managing the paradox of restitution invokes the limited nature of private property. This appears, for example, in a case where someone finds another's possessions but has no reasonable hope of tracking down the original owner, even with due diligence. (Alphonsus mentions the case of ordinary coins, where the lost objects have no identifying marks.) In these circumstances, he argues, the property reverts "to the primeval law of nature." Private property is a human convention, a development of social utility. When circumstances make it impossible for the owner to use the lost possessions, the convention disappears and property reverts to its original state. While human law may specify who is entitled to derelict property, natural law does not.[50] Because there is no owner, there is no duty of restitution.

Alphonsus applies the same argument to a very different scenario—the debtor living under circumstances of extreme necessity.[51] In these dire circumstances, the right of private property yields to the right of common use. It is not that the debtor is morally excused from paying the creditor. Instead, the resources literally cease to be the property of the creditor. Interestingly, Alphonsus's sources believe that this is true even when the creditor is in extreme need as well. Under emergency circumstances, the convention of private property no longer holds and the debtors have no duty to give up what they need to survive, even in the face of the original owner's need. No restitution is due because private property is a limited right. (Some authors make an exception for the case in which denying restitution would push the creditor into extreme necessity, since it is the failure to make restitution that moves the creditor into crisis.)[52]

While these two strategies conclude that no restitution is necessary in particular cases, Alphonsus and his sources sometimes substitute other forms of assistance for restitution. In cases where the nature of the loss renders strict restitution impossible, for example, Alphonsus and his sources frequently invoke what one might call the *duty of remediation*. No one can restore another's life, limb, or virginity, for example, so there is no duty of restitution in the strict sense of the term. But the offenders can provide resources for their victims' families or for their medical care.[53] A married or ordained man who has seduced a girl by promising marriage can provide a dowry so that she can marry someone else.[54] None of these responses is *restitution*, since none restores what was lost (or its equivalent). However, they can alleviate, to some degree, sufferings associated with the loss.

On the other hand, Alphonsus and his sources often treat the necessity of restitution as delayed rather than annulled.[55] To give a modern illustration, someone who rightly refuses to return car keys to a drunken friend is still willing to restore them once the owner recovers. The prudent friend is delaying, not denying, restitution.[56] This strategy also appears in cases where it is less likely that restitution will ever become possible. Thus debtors unable to meet their obligations have a moral right to delay repayment, although they must make good on their debts if their financial circumstances improve.[57] The presumption behind this approach is not that circumstances will necessarily change, but that we cannot be sure that they will not change. Considering this uncertainty, the rights of the party with a claim to restitution remain, even if the other cannot, or indeed should not, make restitution at the present time.

Perhaps the most interesting modification of this kind substitutes one recipient of a necessary restitution for another. Suppose that I am in possession of stolen property, but am unable, despite my best efforts, to determine its true owner.[58] In that case, the theologians advise, I can make recompense by directing my restitution elsewhere, that is, by giving the money to the poor or to a holy place such as a church or hospital.[59] Alphonsus even identifies this as a "general rule" for resolving uncertain debts.[60] While the tradition gave this approach no special name, one might reasonably call it *alternative restitution* as opposed to an *exact restitution* offered to the original injured party.

Alternative Restitution

For Alphonsus and his sources, alternative restitution offers a reasonable solution when circumstances prevent restitution to the original victim. Canon law provided an obvious precedent, since clerics who had neglected the liturgy of the hours were required to make restitution, and one option for doing so was to give part of their income to the poor.[61] Yet for our purposes, what is even more interesting than this practice is the theory behind it. How could giving what had been someone else's property to the poor constitute *restitution*? In fact, this practice rested upon several important principles.

First, the Catholic ethical tradition assumed that one person should not profit from another's unjust loss.[62] One finds frequent references in Alphonsus to the duty to return what has made one "richer [*ditior*]," even in cases where the unjust acquisition of another's property was inadvertent.[63] For example, soldiers might believe that they are fighting in a just war, and yet realize afterward that their cause was unjust. Are they obliged to return the booty that they received in payment? In this case, Alphonsus maintains, they are obliged to restore only the unspent booty that has increased their wealth.[64] Interestingly, Alphonsus does not invoke any notion of "filthy lucre" in explaining this principle: there is no sign that he regards the possessor as contaminated by the unjust acquisition. Instead, the focus is on rebuilding equilibrium. The unjust possessor—even a possessor in good faith—should not benefit from another person's injury. Giving up the unjust acquisition means returning to the level of wealth that one would have had without it. Thus a person who has unwittingly received stolen goods as a gift, and who has learned the truth only after selling them, should return the profits. "It should be enough for you," Alphonsus observes, "not to have less than before."[65] Alternative restitution represented a logical means for such divestiture when the original owner was unknown.

But what about those unfairly deprived of their property? How does alternative restitution to the poor make the original owners whole? Alphonsus and his colleagues assume that any spiritual benefits of the gift accrue, not to the person making the donation, but to the property's original possessors.[66] Such a gift, the theologians argue, reflects the owners' "presumed will."[67] If they cannot have their property, at least they can enjoy the spiritual fruits of the almsgiving. Thus alternative restitution essentially encompasses two spheres: the first serves the bodies of the poor, while the second serves the souls of those who have lost their possessions.

As indicated by the phrase *presumed will*, Catholic moralists concluded that alternative restitution is the remedy previous owners ought to desire, and Alphonsus invokes this assumption to resolve the problems of debtors who cannot name their creditors and thieves who cannot identify their victims, as well as finders of lost property who cannot return it to its owner.[68] In each case, it is *presumed* that the owner would give consent to the alternative restitution. The ethics of restitution, therefore, does not encompass only the injurer or unjust possessor; it also sets limits for what those who have suffered a loss can reasonably expect.

Thus Alphonsus and his sources developed a variety of strategies for handling conflict situations regarding restitution. Some remediated the damage through other strategies, while others delayed restitution, assigned it to another party, or even argued that its pursuit was irrational given the surrounding circumstances. What these strategies reflect is the conviction that the result must somehow do justice for everyone involved, even when justice does not equal exact restitution for the injured neighbor. It is this conviction that can illuminate our discourse on social reconciliation, for the commitment to justice in conflict situations is one that reconciliation and restitution share.

Lessons for Social Reconciliation

Alphonsus Liguori's analysis of restitution is a product of its times, and some of its case resolutions, particularly regarding their treatments of class and gender differences, do not fare well under modern scrutiny.[69] Alphonsus's treatment of restitution is no vaccine against the modern challenges of social reconciliation. However, this tradition does suggest three important values for a dialogue on social reconciliation: the importance of acknowledging our limitations, the necessity of attending to the needs and human dignity of all parties, and the value of the quest for equilibrium that restitution pursues. In each case, application of these lessons requires that we first distinguish the eighteenth-century context from our own.

Realistic Assessment of our Limitations

Because Alphonsus and his sources developed their treatment of restitution with an eye on the confessional, their focus was on the responsibility of individuals, since the sacramental encounter between priest and penitent was a private one. As their treatment of cooperation makes clear, these theologians realized that the duty to make restitution could be corporate as well as individual and could fall completely or proportionally upon each member of the offending group, depending upon the nature of his or her participation. However, even in the case of group wrongs, penitents confessed their sins individually. The confessor's role was to help each person recognize his or her obligations, and performing that role effectively demanded a realistic assessment of human limitations in general and of the penitent's circumstances. No one, Alphonsus might have said, has a duty to do what is impossible.

There is a stark difference between the confessional context and the quest for social reconciliation, which encompasses many persons with varying degrees of responsibility—or no responsibility—for the communal fracture. And yet the value of acknowledging human limitations is perhaps even more important for social reconciliation than for assessing the obligations of individual penitents to make their neighbors whole. Surely any process of reconciliation requires frank acknowledgment that only God can heal some wounds. This does not absolve persons of responsibility, but it does warn against the hubris that can turn the pursuit of "reconciliation" into an act of moral and social self-interest.

We know that we cannot and should not whitewash past wrongs, and that truthful reconciliation demands the admission that they cannot be undone. In many cases of communal brokenness, we must avoid the temptation of thinking that we could ever do enough to wipe the slate clean. No reparation can offer adequate recompense for genocide or slavery.[70] No attempted restitution will make the victims whole, especially in cases where they and the original perpetrators are long dead.[71] It is easy to imagine how the quest for restitution could trap us like the ghosts in George Saunders's *Lincoln in the Bardo*—spirits who remain with their decaying corpses because they cannot admit that they have "crashed upon the shore," and lost the power to effectuate some deeply desired change in the world they once inhabited.[72] Where restitution is concerned, we ignore the risk of hubris at our peril. The same, I suspect, is true of social reconciliation.

Here, however, it is important to remember that restitution, in the technical sense, was not the only form of amelioration available to Alphonsus and his sources. Honest grief for what is impossible should be the first step, not the last, in the quest for social healing.[73] Our confession of finitude calls us to creative imagination about other options like the early modern theologians' theory of alternative restitution to the poor.[74] Frank and realistic admission of our limits thus represents a liminal step in the journey toward social reconciliation.

Concern for the Human Dignity of all Parties

Throughout their analysis of cases that might impose a duty of restitution, Alphonsus and his sources pay careful attention to the rights and dignity of all the parties involved. Certainly their approach assigned greater weight to the rights of the offended than to the needs of the offender, and one of the consistent points of disagreement among these theorists was how much the first outweighed the second.[75] Yet the consequence of imposing a duty of restitution upon the offender was never an irrelevant concern. This attention to the needs of all persons involved constitutes a second important legacy for contemporary thought about social reconciliation.

In developing this claim, one must first acknowledge the difference in temporal range between Alphonsus's restitution scenarios and contemporary divisions in the human community. While Alphonsus and his colleagues did address cases of restitution involving the heirs of the original parties, their analysis does not consider cases stretching over multiple generations and centuries. In contemporary problems requiring social reconciliation, a schism often endures between the descendants of the offended and the offenders, since the original parties to the injury may be long dead. Moreover, the cumulative effects of estrangement can lead to injustices on both sides so that each group can accurately cite examples of its own victimization. Restitution, under these circumstances, becomes an even more complex ethical issue than it was in the circumstances that Alphonsus envisions.

Nevertheless, we have much to learn from the attention to all parties that marks early modern assessments of the need for and appropriate forms of restitution. These theologians' insistence that alternative restitution benefited the souls of the deprived and corresponded to their presumed will, for example, arises from a conviction that such persons can never be dismissed as the losers of history. Any just response must provide restitution in some way for the aggrieved—even if it is restitution in a very limited or alternative form. We share our early modern predecessors' conviction that death does not erase a person's dignity, especially in reference to one's good name. We believe that it matters how we remember the dead and that justice requires us to name offenses against them as offenses. In fact, one might reasonably ask whether the effort to bring the truth to light represents a favored mechanism of restitution in modern Western cultures, especially in cases where the original victims are gone.[76]

Yet if the early modern tradition confirms that we must never overlook the offended, it also reminds us that offenders never lose their dignity. For Alphonsus and his sources, restitution is not obligatory when it causes excessive harm to those who must offer it, nor do debts to a neighbor override the duty to provide basic care for oneself and one's dependents. While early modern treatments of restitution make many distinctions between the innocent and the guilty, they are firm in acknowledging the human dignity of the latter. Contemporary ethics of social reconciliation must not lose sight of this reality, which can be all too easily obscured in the face of legitimate outrage. The idea that every person is more than his or her worst act is not a bromide, but a basic principle of theological anthropology that our anger sometimes buries in the quest for retribution. Yet retribution is not the basic goal of restitution in Alphonsus's treatment of that topic, which emphasizes instead the restoration of equilibrium between the offended and the offender. This distinction provides a starting point for a final insight from the tradition on restitution.

The Meaning of the Effort to Restore Equilibrium

Within Alphonsus's analysis of restitution, restoring equilibrium is arguably a more basic goal than punishing the offender, or even insuring complete recompense for the victim's losses. In fact, restitution often did not or could not return those who had suffered to their original state. This raises an interesting problem: what precisely is being restored in restitution? Despite its name, no one, either in the eighteenth century or today, would regard it as the moral equivalent of a time machine. And yet, Alphonsus and his sources interpreted it as an act of justice, the reestablishment of a just equilibrium between the persons involved. But what kind of equilibrium is restitution intended to restore?

If anything, this is an even more acute problem in a twenty-first century dialogue about social reconciliation than it would have been for eighteenth-century confessors. By the time that a process of social reconciliation bears fruit, the beneficiaries may well be separated from the original communities by many generations. Even if it is possible to recreate the distribution of goods (including land and resources) that existed before the fracture, this reverse does not relieve the sufferings of the dead. Why then does the effort to restore equilibrium matter, and what exactly does it mean?

First, the attempt to restore equilibrium through restitution is an acknowledgment of the shared humanity, the shared subjectivity, and the shared moral agency of the various parties involved. The *equilibrium* that restitution attempts to restore is, at root, a reaffirmation of that shared humanity. It claims the others as people like us, with identities beyond their status as victims or as perpetrators.[77] What restitution restores, in a very fundamental way, is respect. In that sense it meets a basic definition of *justice*—giving all persons their due.

Second, our stumbling efforts to make restitution, even in an alternative form, or to alternative recipients, acknowledge that the progress of history is God's, even though we exercise our freedom within it. I can choose to do evil, here and now. But I cannot control how history, which encompasses my evil act, will play out because its arc is in God's hands. If the resurrection of Jesus is the promise of where history is going, then I am called to do as much as I can to write a postscript to the story of my evil act, or to the evil acts of others, such as my ancestors. An attempt at restitution is testimony that evil will not have the last word. I cannot undo the past, but I can try to reorient it within a new trajectory—the trajectory of healing that waits for God's completion. Restitution is my deference to God's plan of salvation. The equilibrium that restitution pursues is less a matter of goods that the parties exchange than a witness to who the parties are—children of the God whose eschatological redemption is strong enough to heal any wound and flaw.

Conclusion

Responding to a critic who claimed that missions produced only temporary improvements in human behavior, Alphonsus observed, "Whoever has had experience in these matters knows full well how many family feuds are healed during a mission, how many evil practices are rooted out, how much restitution is made, how much hatred is dispelled."[78] This comment seems, appropriately, to situate restitution within the sphere of social reconciliation. One may justify a similar conclusion based on Alphonsus's systematic treatment of restitution in the *Theologia Moralis*. Following his sources, he insists upon the necessity of restitution. When circumstances make strict restitution impossible, undesirable, or dangerous, Alphonsus advocates alternative strategies to reestablish some form of equilibrium between the parties or those connected with them. This indicates that reconciliation with God and neighbor is the goal that restitution is ultimately intended to serve. For a dialogue on social reconciliation, therefore, Alphonsus's analysis of restitution provides valuable reminders regarding finitude, respect, and our vocation within salvation history.

Reflection Questions

1. How would you define *restitution*, as it is explained in this chapter, in your own words, and why is it different from *reconciliation*?

2. Why does the author argue that restitution represented a paradox for classical Roman Catholic theology? Summarize the argument in your own words.

3. Choose three of the five strategies that Alphonsus and his sources used to resolve the paradox of restitution. Give an example of how either a person or group might use each of these strategies to deal with a contemporary problem.

4. The author warns that the search for social reconciliation can become distorted, so that it becomes a search for "moral and social self-interest." What do you think that this means? Can you cite evidence to support this from two other chapters in the book?

5. Look back at O'Keefe's chapter on reconciliation with creation. Do you think that it is possible or necessary for human beings to make restitution to the material world? Why or why not?

Notes

1. I have used Gaudé's critical edition of the Latin text in Léonard Gaudé, ed., *Opera moralia Sancti Alphonsi Mariae de Ligorio, doctoris ecclesiae: theologia moralis*, ed. nova, 4 vols. (Rome: Ex typographia Vaticana, 1905–12). Gaudé primarily uses the 9th edition of the *Theologia Moralis*, which was published in 1785. See Gaudé, *Opera moralia*, 1:xlii.

2. *Theologia Moralis*, lib. 3, tract. 5, chap. 2 (2:52–173). Because of the density of the Latin text, I will cite the internal subsection numbers followed by the corresponding volume and page numbers in parentheses. Thus this section begins with no. 547 (2:52). All translations from this text are my own.

3. *Theologia Moralis*, no. 547 (2:54).

4. For background on his range of sources in the work, see Pierre Hurtubise, *La casuistique dans tous ses états: De Martin Azpilcueta à Alphonse de Liguori* (Montreal: Novalis, 2005), 192–95. Alphonsus's dates (1696–1787) place him outside of the most creative phase of case resolution, which Albert R. Jonsen and Stephen

Toulmin have described as the period of "high casuistry," extending from 1556–1656. See *The Abuse of Casuistry: A History of Moral Reasoning* (Berkeley: University of California, 1988), 137–38.

5. Alphonsus was ordained in 1726. For background on his life, see Frederick M. Jones, *Alphonsus de Liguori: The Saint of Bourbon Naples, 1696–1787* (Westminster, MD: Christian Classics, 1992), 9–11, 15–21, 29–35, 41–45, 54, 58–61, 66–67, 74–76. See also Hurtubise, *La casuistique dans tous ses états*, 182–86. For a short presentation on Alphonsus with helpful bibliography, see Renzo Gerardi, *Storia della morale: Interpretazioni teologiche dell'esperienza cristiana. Periodi e correnti, autori e opere* (Bologna: EDB, 2003), 399–404.

6. See Jones, *Alphonsus de Liguori*, 96–99, 108–13, 130–32, 164–72, 214–23, 228–32, 447–73.

7. See Jones, *Alphonsus de Liguori*, 358–62, 439–41, 484–87.

8. See Jones, *Alphonsus de Liguori*, 203–5.

9. See Jones, *Alphonsus de Liguori*, 207. On Busenbaum, see Gerardi, *Storia della morale*, 366–67.

10. On the various editions, see Gaudé, *Opera moralia*, 1:xiii–xxiii; on Alphonsus's contribution, see Hurtubise, *La casuistique dans tous ses états*, 186–203; Gerardi, *Storia della morale*, 400–404.

11. *Theologia Moralis*, lib. 3, tract. 5, chap. 2 (2:52–173). The first chapter, on theft, extends from 2:27–51, while the third chapter, which begins on 2:174, concerns contracts.

12. *Theologia Moralis*, no. 547 (2:52).

13. On the general principle, see *Theologia Moralis*, no. 584 (2:75).

14. *Theologia Moralis*, nos. 547, 585 (2:54, 75–76).

15. *Theologia Moralis*, nos. 547, 582 (2:54, 73–74).

16. E.g., students sometimes characterize a professor whose grading scale is higher than those used by his or her colleagues as "unfair." But from Alphonsus's perspective, this would only be true if the institution required all instructors to use the same scale. Perhaps the professor is too demanding, but he or she has not violated demands of justice since the student has no "right" to be graded according to a common scale under these circumstances.

17. Note, e.g., the distinction between theological and juridical guilt in *Theologia Moralis*, nos. 549 and 554 (2:54, 56–57) as well as its practical application in no. 696 (2:161).

18. E.g., if I cheat my employees out of just wages, I have a moral obligation to pay them, even if the employees have no way to prove their claims and the obligation is legally unenforceable.

19. *Theologia Moralis*, no. 660 (2:136).

20. *Theologia Moralis*, no. 614 (2:94).

21. *Theologia Moralis*, no. 556 (2:57). Note that the obligation is more stringent for formal injury than for material injury.

22. *Theologia Moralis*, nos. 564, 573, 696 (2:62, 69–70, 161).

23. *Theologia Moralis*, no. 573 (2:69–70).

24. *Theologia Moralis*, nos. 550, 675 (2:54, 150). Note that he mentions punishment explicitly, while the deterrent function is implied in the canonical provisions that he cites.

25. See *Theologia Moralis*, no. 627 (2:106). For an example emphasizing equality, see no. 607 (2:89).

26. The term *equilibrium* is my own.

27. Alphonsus's definition of restitution describes it as "ad salutem necessarius necessitate praecepti" (*Theologia Moralis*, no. 547 [2:52]).

28. *Theologia Moralis*, no. 681 (2:153).

29. *Theologia Moralis*, no. 682 (2:153–54).

30. "Jus certum ad absolutionem, quae non potest ei denegari, nisi aliunde sit indispositus" (*Theologia Moralis* no. 669 [2:143]). Thus Alphonsus believes that when there is a probable opinion that a penitent is not bound to restitution, the confessor must absolve and cannot demand that the penitent follow a more probable opinion requiring it. For background on this debate, including references to Alphonsus, see Jonsen and Toulmin, *The Abuse of Casuistry*, 164–75; Jean Delumeau, *L'aveu et le pardon: Les difficultés de le confession XIIIᵉ–XVIIIᵉ siècle* (Paris: Fayard, 1990), 133–67; Jean-Louis Quantin, *Le rigorisme chrétien* (Paris: Le Éditions du Cerf, 2001), 71–106, 146–52.

31. *The Sacrament of Penance and Religious Life in Golden Age Spain* (University Park: Pennsylvania State University, 2012), 37–38. Note also O'Banion's comments about the impact of Jansenism (which encouraged the denial of absolution) upon Easter communion in France (174).

32. *Theologia Moralis*, lib. 3, tract. 5, chap. 2, nos. 557–78 (2:58–70). This represents an entire section of the chapter. For Aquinas's list of cooperators in acts requiring restitution, see his *Summa*

Theologiae II–II, q. 62, art. 7 (Madrid: Biblioteca de autores cris-tianos, 1953), 3:404. Alphonsus's second *dubium* begins with an identical list. *Theologia Moralis*, no. 557 (2:58).

33. *Theologia Moralis*, no. 579 (2:71).

34. *Theologia Moralis*, nos. 607–9 and no. 689 (2:89–90, 157). See also the discussion regarding the responsibilities of an executed criminal's heirs at no. 705 (2:173, n.e.).

35. *Theologia Moralis*, no. 694 (2:160). There was some debate about whether such servants were bound to leave their jobs. Number 695 (2:160–61) similarly asserts that the wives and chil-dren of debtors are entitled to financial support, even if it means that the debtors cannot repay their creditors.

36. *Theologia Moralis*, nos. 626–27, 660 (2:105–6, 136). The gen-eral rule in such cases appears in no. 660.

37. *Theologia Moralis*, nos. 627, 631 (2:106, 110).

38. See the distinction between material and formal injury in the case where one no longer possesses the property at *Theologia Moralis*, no. 556 (2:57). On the case of unknown owner, see no. 589 (2:78).

39. See, e.g., nos. 655, 697, 698 (2:133, 161, 162).

40. *Theologia Moralis*, no. 698 (2:163).

41. *Theologia Moralis*, no. 698 (2:162). Note that this is distinct from the case where a person has fallen into debt through the pursuit of luxuries.

42. *Theologia Moralis*, no. 598 (2:83–84). The sources disagree about the extent of the discrepancy necessary, however. Cf. no. 677 (2:151–52).

43. *Theologia Moralis*, no. 697 (2:162). This assumes that the agent can forego restitution without suffering equivalent or greater harm.

44. *Theologia Moralis*, no. 653 (2:130–32).

45. I will address only a few of particular interest for social rec-onciliation.

46. *Theologia Moralis*, no. 571 (2:66–67).

47. "Irrationalibiliter invitus" (*Theologia Moralis*, no. 571 [2:66–67]).

48. *Theologia Moralis*, no. 616 (2:98–99). See pages 96–97 for the more debated question of the responsibilities of those who were not paupers. For background on these unpopular taxes, see

William Daniel, *The Purely Penal Law Theory in the Spanish Theologians from Vitoria to Suárez*, Analecta Gregoriana 164 (Rome: Gregorian University, 1968), 139–40.

49. *Theologia Moralis*, no. 696 (2:161).
50. "Primaevum jus naturae" (*Theologia Moralis*, no. 603 [2:87]).
51. *Theologia Moralis*, no. 698 (2:163).
52. *Theologia Moralis*, no. 701 (2:168).
53. *Theologia Moralis*, nos. 631–33 (2:110–12).
54. *Theologia Moralis*, no. 640 (2:115).
55. *Theologia Moralis*, nos. 598, 697 (2:83, 161)
56. Cf. *Theologia Moralis*, no. 700 (2:164)
57. *Theologia Moralis*, no. 699 (2:163).
58. *Theologia Moralis*, no. 589 (2:77).
59. *Theologia Moralis*, nos. 589–90 (2:77–79).
60. "Regula…generalis" (*Theologia Moralis*, no. 595 [2:81]).
61. *Theologia Moralis*, no. 672 (2:144).
62. *Theologia Moralis*, no. 608 (2:90).
63. *Theologia Moralis*, no. 556 (57). Alphonsus expresses the general rule in this way: "Quisquis intulit injuriam damnosam, etiam materialem tantum, tenetur restituere; sed nonnisi id quod ex alterius re adhuc habet, vel quo ex ea factus est ditior" (no. 556 [57]). See also nos. 607 and 608 (2:89–90).
64. *Theologia Moralis*, 609 (2:90).
65. "Satis debet esse tibi, non habere minus quam ante" (*Theologia Moralis*, no. 609 [2:90–91]).
66. *Theologia Moralis*, no. 589 (2:77).
67. "Praesumptam voluntatem" (*Theologia Moralis*, no. 603 [2:87]). See also no. 687 (2:156).
68. *Theologia Moralis*, nos. 687, 589, 603 (2:156, 77, 87).
69. See, e.g., the assumptions about class and gender evident in the discussion of a nobleman's withdrawal of a fictitious marriage proposal to a social inferior. See *Theologia Moralis*, no. 643 (2:120–22).
70. See the important analysis of Jennifer Harvey, *Whiteness and Morality: Pursuing Racial Justice through Reparations and Sovereignty* (New York: Palgrave Macmillan, 2007), 144.
71. See, e.g., Donald Shriver, "Repairing the Past: Polarities of Restorative Justice," *Cross Currents* 57 (2007): 209–17.

72. George Saunders, *Lincoln in the Bardo: A Novel* (New York: Random House, 2017), 96, 97.

73. See Bryan N. Massingale, *Racial Justice and the Catholic Church* (Maryknoll, NY: Orbis Books, 2010), 96–129.

74. For a contemporary illustration of such an ethical challenge, see Rachel L. Swarns, "Georgetown Confronts Its Role in the Nation's Slave Trade," *New York Times* (April 17, 2016).

75. See, e.g., the debates over the level of damage necessary before thieves could be excused from returning stolen property and over the comparative rights of debtor and creditor when both were in grave rather than extreme need. See *Theologia Moralis*, nos. 598 and 703 (2:83–84, 170).

76. For two recent illustrations of such projects, see Timothy B. Tyson, *The Blood of Emmett Till* (New York: Simon and Schuster, 2017); and David Grann, *Killers of the Flower Moon: The Osage Murders and the Birth of the FBI* (New York: Doubleday, 2017).

77. See Miroslav Volf, *The End of Memory: Remembering Rightly in a Violent World* (Grand Rapids, MI: Eerdmans, 2006), 177–81.

78. Cited in Jones, *Alphonsus de Liguori*, 248.

III

MODERN AND CONTEMPORARY CASES

CHAPTER 9

The Sacrament of Anointing during Northern Ireland's Troubles

John Kiess

On January 30, 1972, a priest named Edward Daly from Derry, Northern Ireland, was returning from a funeral when he heard "two or three shots ring out."[1] Four British armored cars began to speed down the street, and Daly remembers everyone starting to run.

> As I was entering the courtyard, I noticed a young boy running beside me....He seemed about 16 or 17.... When we reached the centre of the courtyard, I heard a shot and simultaneously this young boy, just beside me, gasped or groaned loudly....I took a handkerchief from my pocket and waved it for a few moments and then I got up in a crouched position and I went to the boy. I knelt beside him. There was a substantial amount of blood oozing from his shirt....I put my handkerchief inside the shirt to try and staunch the bleeding. Then a young member of the Knights of Malta, Charles Glenn, suddenly appeared on the other side of this boy. He immediately set about treating the wound. I felt that I should administer the last rites to the boy and I anointed him.[2]

During a lull in the shooting, Daly and the other man decided to carry the boy down the street to find an ambulance. A widely circulated photograph of Daly waving his handkerchief (Exhibit 1) became one of the enduring images of the conflict in Northern Ireland, capturing both the depths to which the conflict descended and the compassion it generated in those who lived through it. When Daly and the others reached the corner of Waterloo and Harvey Streets, they noticed the boy was no longer breathing. "Then a patrol of soldiers appeared," he recalls, "and told us to clear off and I asked the people to calm down and kneel down and offer a prayer. The soldiers moved away. I remember one of the women screaming down the street after them shouting, 'He's only a child and you've killed him.'"[3]

Exhibit 1. Father Edward Daly escorting Jackie Duddy, January 30, 1972 (reprinted by permission of Mirrorpix).

Daly went on to anoint several other victims that day, as did many priests over nearly three decades of a conflict that came to be known as "the Troubles." A struggle over the fate of the six counties of Northern Ireland and whether they should remain British territory or become part of the Republic of Ireland, the Troubles claimed over three thousand lives before it concluded with the signing of the 1998 Good Friday Agreement. In addition to the violence committed by British security forces, paramilitaries on both sides engaged in targeted killings and bombings, prompting countless occasions for priests to deliver pastoral care to the wounded and dying. Two priests, Fathers Hugh Mullan and Noel Fitzpatrick, were killed in crossfire while attempting to anoint victims in Belfast.[4] In perhaps the most well-known instance, a Redemptorist priest named Father Alec Reid anointed a British corporal killed by the IRA, a moment immortalized in a famous David Cairns photograph (Exhibit 2). Throughout the conflict, priests performed anointings in far less dramatic circumstances: in family homes, hospitals, and church services.

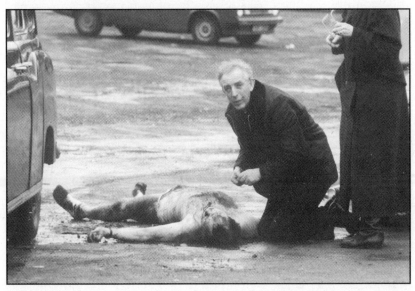

Exhibit 2. Father Alec Reid anointing Corporal David Howes, March 19, 1988 (reprinted by permission of News UK & Ireland Ltd).

Along with the sacrament of reconciliation, the sacrament of anointing is one of the Catholic Church's two sacraments of healing. Known for many years as "extreme unction" because of its association with the end of life, the sacrament underwent significant revision during the liturgical reforms of Vatican II, which restored its wider application to anyone suffering from a serious illness or condition.[5] This is reflected in the *Catechism*'s description of the effects of the sacrament, which include the "strengthening, peace, and courage to overcome the difficulties that go with the condition of serious illness or the frailty of old age," and, where possible, restoration of health.[6] The sacrament retains an important role in pastoral contexts of injury, death, and dying. The *Catechism* speaks of the strength to overcome "discouragement and anguish in the face of death," the forgiveness of sins, and preparation for passing over to eternal life.[7] Principally, the sacrament unites the afflicted person to Christ's passion for the good of the person, the sanctification of the church, and "the good of all men for whom the Church suffers and offers herself through Christ to God the Father."[8]

Against the backdrop of the Troubles, one gains a deeper appreciation of many of these dimensions of the sacrament, but in this chapter, I want to focus on this last one, the way the sacrament serves the good of all for whom the church suffers. Drawing upon interviews with priests who administered the sacrament during the Troubles, I explore what anointing reveals about the importance of liturgy and sacrament in responding to the destabilizing effects of political violence and building peace. While liturgy has emerged as a central lens for approaching Christian ethics in recent years, it remains a neglected focus in peace and conflict studies, where attention tends to concentrate upon macrolevel processes such as negotiations, elections, and transitional justice.[9] In a conflict as heavily ritualized and fraught with symbolic meaning as the one in Northern Ireland, the importance of sign and sacrament is difficult to ignore. Paramilitary and state actors resorted to violence to exploit symbolic linkages between individuals and their communities of belonging. Undermining ordinary assumptions about the dignity and worth of the human body, such violence threw into sharp relief the importance of the practices that sustain these assumptions. Anointing emerged as one such practice, serving in the words of Father Daly as an "act of contradiction" that helped to reinstill and safeguard the dignity and worth of the body at precisely the point it was most threatened. In some instances, the sacrament did more, witnessing to a broader communal horizon that transcended the ecclesial and political divisions of the conflict. Viewing the Troubles through the prism of anointing helps us better appreciate an overlooked dimension of peacebuilding, one that takes place at the local level of everyday life, involving the determination of ordinary civilians to continue to perform the practices that inform our deepest beliefs and give peace its density, texture, and stability.

The Logic of Political Violence in Northern Ireland

Appreciating this requires saying more about the logic of political violence in Northern Ireland. In his important book *Formations of Violence*, Allen Feldman explores the symbolic character of violence during the Troubles, a symbolism that grew out of the deeply embedded sectarianism of Northern Irish society and the perceived limits of resolving territorial disputes through conventional political means.[10] Focusing specifically upon patterns of violence in Belfast, Feldman draws attention to the riots of 1969 and the role they played in remapping the city along sectarian lines. Marches aimed at securing civil rights for Catholic/Republican communities were met with countermarches and forced dislocations, pushing groups into ethno-nationalist enclaves and establishing a strong link between ideological affiliation and residence. While the ultimate question of the political status of the six counties remained in abeyance, each side modeled their vision of the future at the microlevel of the neighborhood. There the political utopia of a United Ireland or British Ulster could be witnessed in the flags and murals adorning the streets and the accents and clothing of its residents.

For Feldman, this "sectarian retrenchment" of Belfast and other cities set in motion a set of symbolic associations that gave political violence a new rationale.[11] Once individuals became associated with particular neighborhoods, space emerged as a primary lens for deciphering identity. To enter the Republican Falls or Loyalist Shankill was to pass into a uniform space that encouraged outsiders to see all its residents in the same basic terms. Feldman compares this dynamic to the literary trope of synecdoche, where the part's relationship to the whole renders it a symbol of the whole.[12] Given that many of the features that marked space also marked the body, ideologically coded bodies became invested with the spatial "aura" of their communities—where a person's body was, there, too, was his or her community. As an example, Feldman points to the highly charged marching season when groups such as the Protestant Orange Order would parade through the streets of Belfast, often provoking the hostile reaction of residents in opposing neighborhoods. In the body of the marching Orangeman, adorned in the colors and insignia of Ulster identity, an alien space became palpable, threatening to take over the sanctuary space of those watching, not through physical dislocation, but through the symbolic assault of his body.[13]

Paramilitary violence exploited this dynamic, contesting space virtually at the level of the senses through the violent objectification of the body. By violently "staging" the victim's body, paramilitary actors could make it represent their own spatial constructs to expand the perceived reach of their imagined community. As Feldman puts it,

> The transfer of political performance from the level of entire communities and residential systems to the individual body in the sectarian murder is both a ritualistic transfer from whole to part and a rationalization of political violence....The discovery that the brutal killing of a single individual is commensurate in its political and polluting impact to the forced movements of entire communities, that terror has its own circuits of amplification that do not require material destruction on a large scale, is an essential discovery of paramilitary practice.[14]

Feldman shows how this link between body and space informed paramilitary violence at every level, beginning with the selection of targets. Once ideological affiliation became associated with residence, a paramilitary group could identify victims based upon where they lived. Feldman notes the prevalence of the practice of the "doorstep murder," in which a paramilitary group entered an opposing neighborhood, knocked on the door, and killed the first person who answered.[15] The randomness of the attack exploited the relationship between part and whole, and because any house could have been chosen, everyone in the neighborhood experienced the attack as a personal attack on them.

After exploiting the body's association with space to identify the victim, the paramilitary actor then set about severing this link by establishing a new relationship of part and whole, replacing the victim's community with the paramilitary's own. Through the stripping of clothing, the use of torture, disfiguring mortal wounds, or other such violence, the paramilitary actor symbolically "unmade" the victim so that the corpse could bear new meaning. "The body that was emblematic of territoriality and ethnicity," Feldman writes, "is inverted by violence into a sign of deterritorialization."[16] The assailant's use of a mask is essential in this process, as it dissolves the killer's own personal identity into the more abstract agency of his paramilitary organization or community of belonging; as a result, the victim's body bears the trace not of a single intruder, but a broader collective force. The act of violence "reproduces within the heart of the sanctuary space the territorial signs of an opposed ethnicity," effectively moving the physical border separating the two communities into the neighborhood, to the body itself.[17] By defiling the part, the whole is polluted.

Feldman argues that the British state was not above descending to this level of symbolically charged violence. Through its controversial policy of internment, the British Army rounded up suspects and subjected them to interrogation and torture, breaking down their bodies and returning individuals to society to circulate as markers of state sovereignty. It is not coincidental, Feldman argues, that the famous 1981 hunger strike that resulted in the deaths of ten imprisoned members of Republican paramilitaries was finally decided at the level of the body.[18] It was at the level of the body that meaning and belonging were ultimately contested in Northern Ireland.

While the Troubles is often framed as a struggle over the political status of the six counties of Northern Ireland, Feldman's analysis directs our attention to the way these territorial ambitions played out locally through the symbolic effects of violence. With conventional politics at a stalemate and the sectarian structure of urban space firmly entrenched, both paramilitary actors and the British state found themselves locked in a symbolic contest over the meaning of the body and its capacity to shape perceptions about space and belonging. Territorial control demanded the violent objectification of the body, the reduction of the body to a symbol communicating ideological meaning. It required deflecting attention away from the uniqueness of the body to what it represented, in essence requiring that one forget that it was the body of a person at all.

An Act of Contradiction

Narratives of anointing in Northern Ireland repeatedly emphasize the role of the sacrament in bringing attention back to the embodied nature of human personhood. Father Edward Daly, whose account of anointing Jackie Duddy we observed earlier, remarks, "Paramilitaries don't speak of the person. They speak of 'targets' or the 'enemy.' The sacrament of anointing is an act of contradiction to this."[19] If armed actors attempted to objectify the body through symbol and euphemism, priests stress how the sacrament undermined such attempts by focusing attention on the dignity of the victim. Father John McManus of St. Malachy's, Belfast recalls the night he lost a friend in a pub bombing:

> The parish priest arrived, and he went over and prayed with him, and anointed him. That actually focused us right away off "who did this?" Just the parish priest walking along—just an elderly man, walking on his own, going over to him, on his own, kneeling down there, doing it nice and quiet—that focused everybody right away. It took your mind off "what are these soldiers?" and "These Brits won't let us in" and focused us directly on the person who was dead, and the fact that he was actually *dead*. It focused our minds there…on what were the priorities then, praying for the person who had died, not revenge or whatever the case may be.[20]

McManus notes that the usual response to such violence is, "Who did this?" which, as we saw earlier, is the desired effect of paramilitary violence, deflecting the community's attention away from the victim toward the agent of violence and his community of belonging. The effect of the anointing here, however, "focused us directly on the person who was dead," and the fact that he "was actually *dead*." Anointing keeps attention focused on the body, creating an opportunity for those gathered to pause, reflect upon, and lament what just happened. The simple movements of the priest ("walking along...kneeling down...doing it nice and quiet") have a way of calming the situation, slowing time down long enough for the weight of the loss to set in. This causes the onlookers to give up their initial impulse ("revenge") and consider a different course ("praying for the person who had died"). The anointing takes just a few moments, but it is enough to begin to diffuse the situation and subvert some of the initial effects of the attack.[21]

The role of the sacrament in facilitating a deeper reckoning with loss is reflected in other testimonials. Canon Brendan McGee of St. Patrick's Belfast recounts,

> I will always remember two occasions....The first was when a number of British soldiers opened fire on Finaghy Road in West Belfast, killing a Catholic man named [Patrick] McVeigh....They called me out and I knelt down beside McVeigh and anointed him. Then I went off to see his wife and told her, and then I started making arrangements for the funeral. That night when I was going to bed, I took down my trousers, and my knees were covered in blood. That affected me terribly— seeing the blood of another man on my knees.
>
> And then when I was made a parish priest out at Greencastle, the same thing happened. A number of Loyalists came into a house there and shot a man dead. Then his wife lifted him up and had him on her lap, and they came back and shot him again. Then they called me, and...I knelt down beside him and anointed him, and then talked to the wife, and eventually got my way home. That night when going to bed, there was blood on my knees again—where I had knelt in his blood. That affected me terribly, kneeling in another man's blood. It was nearly as if I had caused it, but I hadn't

caused it. It was like the blood crying to heaven, you know, that's what it says in the Bible: "the blood cries out." I heard that....[22]

Here anointing not only focuses attention upon the body but immerses the priest in the bodily condition of the victim. McGee draws so close as to kneel in the blood of the victim; his body—his knees—bear the marks of the encounter. This contact facilitates extended exposure to the claim of these wounds upon him and the church. If the attack aimed to silence the victim and make his inert body convey the symbolic meaning of the paramilitary group, here the sacrament allows the victim to speak in the voice of his own blood, crying out like Abel cries to heaven in Genesis. One fratricide hauntingly evokes another, the primordial crime renewed; like Abel, the victim demands acknowledgment. To hear this cry for acknowledgment demands proximity. It demands that one draw close, that one kneel, reach out one's hand, feel and touch the wounded body, and allow oneself to be marked by his or her blood. It demands that one draw close enough to say, "I heard that."

Here and elsewhere, the element of touch is integral. Canon Robert Fullerton of Holy Rosary, Belfast, captures the importance of touch this way:

> Christ didn't cure people [in the abstract]. He reached out and touched them....He stretched out his hand and with spittle and mud anointed the eyes....It's that contact with humanity, not standing back, which is hugely important to people....I think the whole idea of touch, reaching out to touch, says an awful lot at the end of the day about the importance of the individual, and the body, and the sacredness of the person....The very fact that you touch people means something: connecting, respecting and loving. It's the very opposite of people who won't shake hands.[23]

The practice of anointing recalls that when Christ healed, he almost always did so through touch. To those ostracized by their infirmity—the lepers, the deaf, the blind, the lame—Christ extended his hand. Touching the untouchables, he refused to confine himself within the existing social conventions that regulated with whom he could come into contact. It was through touch that he redrew social boundaries and introduced a new freedom of movement unbound by the spatial limitations associated with sickness and injury. The sacrament of anointing is born from the same freedom. Jesus sends his disciples out into a divided world to cast out demons and anoint the sick with oil (Mark 6:13). The epistle of James asks, "Are any among you sick? They should call for the elders of the church and have them pray over them, anointing them with oil in the name of the Lord" (James 5:14). To those ostracized by their sickness, to those isolated in hospital beds, to those injured and dying, the church reestablishes contact through touch. In the context of Northern Ireland, the sacrament created a movement toward, rather than a retreat from, the injured and dying body, its practitioners refusing to follow the cues of paramilitary violence that would restrict their movement. In touching victims, priests and the laity who accompanied them restored the body to the fellowship of the living.

Agents of political violence seek to incapacitate our sense of touch. This is obviously the case with those individuals who are maimed and killed, who are deprived of all living sense, but as we have seen, political violence in Northern Ireland also aimed to dominate the senses of the living, policing their movements through the symbolic effects of violence. The objectification of the body was meant to keep communities from mingling, mixing, and touching, while also discouraging individuals from seeing the body as anything more than a surface for the projection of meaning. Anointing affirmed just the opposite, that we are never merely surfaces, but *bodies* capable of sense, movement, rhythm, and gesture; fully enfleshed beings who contain depth and interiority, vulnerable to, but also capable of being enriched by, all that surrounds us. That the church anoints at all is an acknowledgment that we are "earthen vessels," subject to sickness, injury, and death; bodybound creatures in need of care, attention, and healing.[24] The sacrament itself is irreducibly bodily: one can only touch with a body, and one can only be touched with a body. We touch not in the abstract but in the particular: to touch is to touch *this* person. Touching thus brings us back to our uniqueness, the fact that there is only one of us, which makes us irreplaceable, more than an interchangeable part of the whole. This is why Paul speaks of the church not through the metaphorics of synecdoche, but as one body with many members: "If the whole body were an eye, where would the hearing be? If the whole body were hearing, where would the sense of smell be?" (1 Cor 12:17). Rather, for Paul, each part is indispensable, with the weakest clothed with greatest honor. Such regard for the weak grounds the church's ministry to the sick and vulnerable: "If one member suffers, all suffer together with it" (1 Cor 12:26). Each part is affected by the strength or weakness of all the other parts, making the well-being of one person dependent upon the well-being of the others.

If touch affirms the uniqueness of the body, it also says something about its worth. As we have seen, political violence approaches the question of worth in terms of symbolic value. The body is valuable as a symbolic commodity, a function of the space or ideology it represents. The logic of anointing presents a different standard of worth. The first indication of this is the disproportion of the act itself. It is not just in touching, but going as far as to apply oil, that anointing conveys the worth of the body. Anointing says the body deserves care; it says the body is worthy of attention. Jesus's body is worth so much to Mary that she is willing to spend a year's wages on the perfume she uses to anoint him (Matt 26:6–13); it is the very economic recklessness of the act that conveys just how much his life is worth. Similarly, an act as seemingly futile as applying oil to the dying in a conflict zone suggests, by its very practical uselessness, just how much it is really worth.

A further testament to the worth of the body is suggested in the risk that priests took in ensuring that anointings were performed. That Daly would risk his life to anoint Jackie Duddy says something about how much Duddy's body is worth to him. The two priests who died anointing victims says the same. Father Gerry Reynolds of Clonard Monastery in West Belfast puts it this way, "I think the sacraments, and going to anoint the person, and the priest risking his life to go and anoint the person, is really wanting to say there is a divine quality about this person who has been killed. I think that is the meaning of it. That's why the priest would risk his life to go to the person who was wounded...it goes back to 'God loved the world so much that he gave his only son.'"[25]

At the same time, priests emphasize that the sacrament is not simply something shared between the priest and the person being anointed. Canon Fullerton notes, "You would have lay people who would stay with the injured or dying person. That's the other side. It wasn't just us. There were other people there comforting the person….There was a community of people there."[26] As the *Catechism* suggests, anointing is, like any sacrament, "a liturgical and communal celebration," intended for the good of the church and all those for whom the church suffers.[27] Addressing the importance of the sacrament for the victim's family, Fullerton observes, "The family would be interested, of course, in what exactly you did for the person, that you were there, that you prayed with them, that you anointed them. A lot of prayer isn't possible, but they would be comforted and reassured by the fact that you were there to administer the sacrament, absolution and anointing."[28]

If the objectification and devaluation of the body brought terror to a community, anointing's recovery of the dignity and worth of the body brought a measure of peace. Father Bernard Magee of County Down reflects, "We anointed. That was it. That was our job—to love the people, to prepare people for death and meet their God….We were there to bring the peace of God to the area."[29] Earlier we observed how anointing directed a potentially hostile and vengeful crowd to take stock of what had been lost. It calmed them down. It slowed them down. A response to violence that does not respond in kind, anointing helped to dissipate tension, and in this instance, introduced a reprieve from the cycle of violence.

This connection between anointing and peace brings into view the central role that liturgy and ritual play in constituting the everyday peace that most of us take for granted. We take liturgy and ritual for granted precisely because they are routine, part of the background and texture of our lives that allow us to focus on other, more conspicuous things that vary day to day. Because we are not ordinarily conscious of these routines, we tend to privilege extraordinary acts of peacemaking: the negotiated settlement, a declaration of amnesty, or a truth commission. When the extraordinary circumstances of conflict make such routines harder to practice, however, we become aware of them in a new way. We see how peace in fact rests on simple, everyday things that ordinary people practice all the time. Thus, when Father Bernard Magee says, "All through the Troubles we carried on as normally as possible. We said mass at the usual times....When they were dead, we went out to the people, we comforted the people," he is pointing to the deep architecture of peace, the concrete sacraments and practices that substantiate our deepest convictions about human worth and stabilize our existence as embodied creatures.[30]

Anointing across Boundaries

We have seen how, amid the extraordinary circumstances of conflict, anointing helped to reconstitute aspects of the ordinary by reinforcing assumptions about human worth and dignity. But of course, any attempt to recover the ordinary amid the extraordinary will reflect something of those extraordinary circumstances, with implications for the future shape of the ordinary.[31]

Let me return to the photo of Father Alec Reid anointing the British corporal (Exhibit 2). On March 19, 1988, Reid, a Redemptorist priest based at Clonard Monastery in west Belfast, was walking in a funeral cortège on the Andersonstown Road when a silver car suddenly interrupted the procession. Just three days earlier, a Loyalist paramilitary volunteer named Michael Stone disrupted another funeral, leaving the entire Republican community on edge and wary of another attack. The men in the car, off-duty British corporals David Howes and Derek Wood, were mistaken for Loyalist paramilitaries and dragged from their car into a nearby park, where they were stripped and beaten. Reid came upon the scene when the men were lying facedown on the pavement. They were surrounded by members of the IRA, who, leafing through one of the corporal's wallets, discovered they were not paramilitaries but British soldiers. Reid left the scene to find help before hearing gunshots.[32] Rushing back to the men, he found their bodies strewn across the pavement, and one of them still appeared to be breathing. He attempted to resuscitate him, and unable to do so, proceeded to anoint him. The photo captures the moment just before the anointing, with Reid kneeling beside the corporal's prostrate body, oils in hand, and the blood of the dying man streaked across his face.

The corporal in the photo is not Catholic. Or put differently, when Reid anointed him, he had no reason to believe that he was Catholic. All he knew was that he was a member of the British military, an agent of the state that opposed the Republican aspirations of many of his parishioners. Beaten and bloodied, abandoned as a spectacle for others to see and shun, the corporal's body had been violently staged like many before him, rendered a sign of territorial control, announcing that this space was not the British Army's to patrol. His body did not belong there, and the point of the killing was to restore communal boundaries and keep bodies in place. Only Reid didn't stay in place. He moved toward the corporal's body, knelt down, and anointed him. His free movement attests to the operation of a different imaginary, a different set of obligations that propelled him toward the victimized body, toward the threshold of the conflict and across it. Anointing had become, by this point, second nature to him, something instinctual, the obvious thing to do when faced with a sick, injured, or dying person. If in ordinary circumstances that instinct manifested itself in the form of anointing members of his own ecclesial community, in the extraordinary circumstances of the Troubles, which brought him face-to-face with victims on the other side of the conflict, that instinct took him beyond those boundaries.

Ordinarily, of course, Reid would not have been permitted to anoint someone who was not Catholic. The 1967 Ecumenical Directory is clear on the matter:

> Celebration of the sacraments is an action of the celebrating community, carried out within the community, signifying the oneness of faith, worship and life of the community. Where this unity of sacramental faith is deficient, the participation of separated brethren with Catholics, especially in the Sacraments of the Eucharist, Penance and Anointing of the Sick, is forbidden.[33]

Yet the Directory goes on to say,

> Nevertheless, since the sacraments are both signs of unity and sources of grace, the Church can for adequate reasons allow access to those sacraments to a separated brother. This may be permitted in danger of death or an urgent need (during persecution, in prisons) if the separated brother has no access to a minister of his own communion.[34]

Here the exception is grounded in the recognition that sacraments are not only signs of unity but also sources of grace, and in emergency situations, when one is deprived of one's own pastoral care, the view here is that the divisions of the church should not prevent one from accessing God's grace. The administration of the sacraments to separated brethren in such circumstances suggests that God's grace is not ultimately bound by our sinfulness. That it is an emergency that justifies the exception is especially fitting in the case of anointing, given that the purpose of the sacrament is to provide grace *in extremis*—at precisely those moments when we are at risk of falling out of the care and company of the ones we love. In such exceptional situations, the grace of the sacrament exposes our ecclesial divisions as contingent, reminding us that they are not permanent and should not be mistaken for the normal course of things.

Robert Schreiter speaks of the way that ritual and sacrament enable us to imagine the world in new or different ways.[35] Reid's anointing reflects a different imagination of the present in that it is not captive to the prevailing spatial boundaries or bodily disciplines imposed by political violence. It also reflects a different imagination of the future in that it allows us to glimpse a set of possibilities previously unimagined. From this vantage point, Reid's anointing exposes the scandal of disunity, but it also makes us long for a deeper unity: the unity of the church, wherein Protestants and Catholics can share full sacramental fellowship with one another, and the political and social unity of Northern Ireland. In Reid's anointing we see the contours of a different Northern Ireland come into view, a Northern Ireland that does not see the loss of life as belonging to one side or the other, but as shared. We see a vision of Northern Ireland that can perceive the dignity of the body regardless of identity, a body that is not confined to sectarian neighborhoods, a British body that comes into contact with an Irish body, a Unionist body that can come into contact with a Republican body, and citizens that can imagine a life together so intimate that they touch. That is something of what the sacrament helps us imagine and long for in this moment of brokenness.

It is not coincidental that the same man who anointed across political and ecclesial boundaries also became a key player in the Northern Ireland peace process. Reid was instrumental in setting up an early backchannel between Sinn Féin, the political wing of the IRA, and the more moderate wing of Irish Nationalism, the Social Democratic and Labour Party (SDLP).[36] At Clonard Monastery, he mediated secret talks between the leaders of both groups, Gerry Adams and John Hume, at a time when the thought of talking to the IRA was still highly controversial. These meetings yielded the blueprint for what eventually became the Good Friday Agreement. As his fellow Redemptorist Michael Kelleher observes, "Alec Reid was a no-man's-land figure, a threshold man; in his life he traversed the peace-line walls of Belfast."[37] His gifts as an imaginative, outside-the-box mediator grew out of the same ethos that led him to anoint the British corporal. Sacramental formation made him a peacemaker, and the peace process he helped shape reflected the spirit of the sacraments he celebrated.

It is not a phenomenon that was limited to Reid. At Clonard, one can see how formation in the sacraments inspired other priests to become bridgebuilders, as witnessed, for example, in the Clonard-Fitzroy Fellowship, an initiative aimed at facilitating cross-community dialogue and prayer between Catholics and Presbyterians across the Falls/Shankill divide.[38] The same sacraments likewise shaped countless laypersons as well, who were among the most vocal leaders in these and other initiatives. Sacraments such as anointing not only mediated core beliefs about the body but also formed people in the habits and dispositions necessary to sustain the everyday work of peacebuilding. This sacramental formation made such individuals partisans not of party or ideology but of the victim. As Reid put it, "I represent the next person who is going to be killed in this trouble. That was the line I took, that I don't belong to any political party. The only interest I have in this thing is the interest of the next victim."[39]

Conclusion

The sacrament of anointing during the Troubles served in the words of Father Daly as an "act of contradiction," undermining the violent attempt to objectify and devalue the human body. By focusing attention on the victim, anointing invited a deeper reckoning with the reality of the conflict and a deeper accounting of its cost. It called Northern Irish society back to the dignity of the human person. It made people aware of the bodily wounds of their nationalist and loyalist idolatries, and in some extraordinary cases, it prompted a reexamination of the boundaries of their own belonging and whose bodies they could see and care for. Finally, it constituted one concrete practice that sustained peace amid violence, serving as the rough ground upon which the broader peace process could take root and flower.

Reflection Questions

1. What is the relationship between identity, space, and the body in Northern Ireland? Are similar dynamics observable in your own context?
2. Anointing points to the centrality of touch in responding to the destabilizing effects of violence. In what other ways might the senses be important to peacebuilding and reconciliation?
3. What does anointing reveal about the importance of ritual and sacrament to peacebuilding? What other sacraments might be important in this respect?
4. What is the "deep architecture of peace"? In addition to rituals and sacraments, discuss other practices that might foster peace at this level.

Notes

1. Edward Daly, *Mister, Are You a Priest?* (Dublin: Four Courts Press, 2000), 191.
2. Daly, *Mister, Are You a Priest?* 192–94.
3. Daly, *Mister, Are You a Priest?* 196.

4. For more on the circumstances of their deaths, see David McKittrick et al, *Lost Lives* (Edinburgh: Mainstream Publishing, 2004), 82–83, 216–17.

5. See Vatican II, *Sacrosanctum concilium* 73, in *Vatican Council II: The Conciliar and Post-Conciliar Documents*, ed. Austin Flannery (Northport, NY: Costello Publishing, 1975), 22. See also Pope Paul VI, *Apostolic Constitution on the Sacrament of the Anointing of the Sick* (November 30, 1972), reprinted in *The Rites of the Catholic Church* (New York: Pueblo Publishing, 1976), 578–81. For more background on the sacrament, see Lizette Larson-Miller, *The Sacrament of Anointing of the Sick* (Collegeville, MN: Liturgical Press, 2005); Charles W. Gusmer, *And You Visited Me: Sacramental Ministry to the Sick and the Dying* (New York: Pueblo Publishing, 1984); James L. Empereur, *Prophetic Anointing: God's Call to the Sick, the Elderly, and the Dying* (Wilmington, DE: Michael Glazier, 1982); Genevieve Glen, ed., *Recovering the Riches of Anointing* (Collegeville, MN: The Liturgical Press, 2002); M. Therese Lysaught, "Vulnerability within the Body of Christ: Anointing the Sick and Theological Anthropology," in *Health and Human Flourishing: Religion, Medicine, and Moral Anthropology*, ed. Carol R. Taylor and Roberto Dell'Oro (Washington, DC: Georgetown University Press, 2006), 159–82; and Thomas Talley, "Healing: Sacrament or Charism?" *Worship* 46, no. 9 (1972): 518–27.

6. Catholic Church, *Catechism of the Catholic Church*, 2nd ed. (Vatican City: Libreria Editrice Vaticana, 2000), §1520.

7. *Catechism of the Catholic Church* §1520.

8. *Catechism of the Catholic Church* §1522.

9. For approaches to Christian ethics that emphasize the centrality of liturgy, see Stanley Hauerwas and Samuel Wells, eds., *The Blackwell Companion to Christian Ethics* (Oxford: Blackwell Publishing, 2004). Robert J. Schreiter discusses the lack of attention to ritual and sacrament in peace research in "The Catholic Social Imaginary and Peacebuilding: Ritual, Sacrament, and Spirituality," in *Peacebuilding: Catholic Theology, Ethics, and Praxis*, ed. Robert J. Schreiter, R. Scott Appleby, and Gerard F. Powers (Maryknoll, NY: Orbis Books, 2010), 226. For a powerful account of the role of the Eucharist in countering state violence, see William T. Cavanaugh, *Torture and Eucharist* (Oxford: Blackwell Publishing, 1998).

10. Allen Feldman, *Formations of Violence: The Narrative of the Body and Political Terror in Northern Ireland* (Chicago: Chicago University Press, 1991).

11. Feldman, *Formations of Violence*, 27.

12. Feldman, *Formations of Violence*, 59.

13. Feldman, *Formations of Violence*, 57–58.

14. Feldman, *Formations of Violence*, 78–79.

15. Feldman, *Formations of Violence*, 71–77.

16. Feldman, *Formations of Violence*, 73.

17. Feldman, *Formations of Violence*, 78.

18. Feldman, *Formations of Violence*, 218–69.

19. Bishop Edward Daly, interview by author, June 3, 2005, Cambridge, telephone conversation.

20. Father John McManus, interview by author, May 20, 2005, Belfast, digital recorder.

21. Emmanuel Katongole's contribution to this volume underscores the importance of registering loss and creating space for lament in reconciliation. See his "*Memoria Passionis* as Social Reconciliation in Eastern Africa," 268–87.

22. Canon Brendan McGee, interview by author, May 15, 2005, Belfast, digital recorder.

23. Canon Robert Fullerton, interview by author, May 20, 2005, Belfast, digital recorder. Hereafter Fullerton interview.

24. See *Catechism of the Catholic Church* §1420. The scriptural reference is 2 Corinthians 4:7.

25. Father Gerry Reynolds, interview by the author, May 14, 2005, Clonard Monastery, Belfast, digital recording.

26. Fullerton interview.

27. *Catechism of the Catholic Church* §1517.

28. Fullerton interview.

29. Father Bernard Magee, interview by the author, May 22, 2005, Castlewellan, digital recording. Hereafter Magee interview.

30. Magee interview.

31. Veena Das draws particularly helpful attention to this dynamic in the context of post-Partition India, tracking the way that ordinary routines bear the impact of, and serve as means of negotiating, the legacy of political violence. See *Life and Words: Violence and the Descent into the Ordinary* (Berkeley: University

of California Press, 2007), 59–94. Building upon Das, Fiona Ross examines the challenges (and ambiguities) of reconstituting the ordinary in post-apartheid South Africa, noting that "attempts to re-establish the ordinary draw from cultural repertoires that are not neutral and may have detrimental effects." For this reason, she prefers to speak of the "recreation of the ordinary," which "draws attention to efforts toward a *desirable* ordinariness, rather than simply the *possible* ordinary or the *permissible* ordinary available to those enduring apartheid." See Ross, *Bearing Witness: Women and the Truth and Reconciliation Commission in South Africa* (London: Pluto Press, 2003), 141. On this latter point, see also William O'Neill's contribution to this volume, where he cautions against conceiving reconciliation merely as the restoration of the *status quo ante* (225–47).

32. See Reid's recounting of the event in Martin McKeever, *One Man, One God: The Peace Ministry of Fr Alec Reid C.Ss.R* (Dublin: Redemptorist Communications, 2017), 33–35.

33. Catholic Church, *Ad Totam Ecclesiam: Directory Concerning Ecumenical Matters*, part 1 (May 14, 1967), no. 55, in *Vatican Council II: The Conciliar and Post-Conciliar Documents*, ed. Austin Flannery (Northport, NY: Costello Publishing, 1975), 499.

34. *Directory Concerning Ecumenical Matters*, 499.

35. See Schreiter, "The Catholic Social Imaginary and Peacebuilding," 228.

36. For an account of this role, see McKeever, *One Man, One God*, 13–75. See also Eamonn Mallie and David McKittrick, *The Fight for Peace: The Secret Story behind the Irish Peace Process* (London: Heinemann, 1996).

37. Michael Kelleher, "Preface," in McKeever, *One Man, One God*, 3.

38. For background on this initiative, see Ronald Wells, *Friendship towards Peace: The Journey of Ken Newell and Gerry Reynolds* (Dublin: Columba Press, 2005), 48–77.

39. *14 Days*. Directed by Diarmuid Lavery. BBC One, 2013. Such partisanship for the victim helps to explain how Reid could function as a trusted representative of the Republican/Nationalist community, on the one hand—representing their grievances to both the British and Irish governments—while being perceived

as a credible bridgebuilder by Protestant leaders such as Harold Good and Ken Newell, on the other. For more on how he sought to balance the demands of mediation, reconciliation, and justice, see his May 19, 1986, letter to John Hume, reprinted in McKeever, *One Man, One God*, 112–29, as well as the reminiscences of Good and Newell, reprinted in the same volume, 81–83, 102–4.

CHAPTER 10

Healing the Breaches

THE CHURCH'S PRAXIS OF SOLIDARITY THROUGH SOCIAL
NETWORKS IN SOUTHERN PERU IN THE CONTEXT OF
POLITICAL VIOLENCE, 1980–1992

Stephen P. Judd, MM

The Persistence of the "Colonial Wound" and the Emergence of New Social Actors in the Time of Political Violence in Peru

Peru was a country wracked by terrorist violence and repression by state-sponsored armed forces for twelve years, from May of 1980 until September of 1992. This outbreak of violence directly or indirectly affected the lives of all the inhabitants in the three regions of the country—the coastal cities, central *sierra* highlands, and tropical lowlands jungle areas—that then made up a population of twenty-eight million inhabitants. The Maoist-inspired terrorist group known as *Sendero Luminoso* (*Shining Path*) or the *Partido Comunista Peruano-Sendero Luminoso* (PCP-SL) was the group responsible for 60 percent of the seventy thousand deaths during the subversive conflict against the democratically elected Peruvian state during the tenure of Presidents Fernando

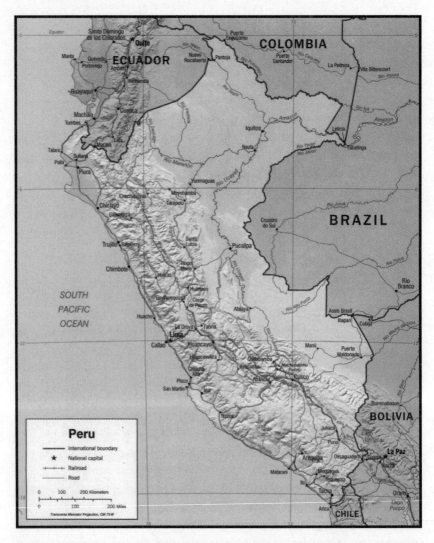

Belaunde Terry (1980–85), Alan Garcia (1985–90), and into the first years of the presidency of Alberto Fujimori (1990–2000).

According to the exhaustive and comprehensive final report of the independent *Comisión de la Verdad y Reconciliación* (CVR) Truth and Reconciliation Commission, members of state-controlled police and armed forces accounted for nearly 30 percent of the victims. Another terrorist group, the *Movimiento Revolucionario Túpac Amaru* (MRTA), claimed upward of 10 percent of the casualties. Not easily documented is the level of disruption, social displacement, and trauma caused by living with fear and uncertainty in a militarized and sharply divided country. Every Peruvian to a greater or lesser degree suffered, and continues to suffer, the consequences of the years of political violence.[1]

The response of the Catholic Church in Peru, as well as other institutions in civil society, reflected the challenge of addressing the social fault lines in a country still in the process of formation of a national identity. The country was still deeply marked by the "colonial wound"—a sharp racial and class divide that developed during the colonial period, the post-Independence period, and the Republican period of the mid-twentieth century.[2]

Some significant and influential sectors of the Catholic Church across the country fully embraced the reforms of the Second Vatican Council (1962–65) and tried to implement the renewal begun at the Medellín (Colombia) and Puebla (Mexico) Conferences of Latin American Bishops of 1968 and 1979. These more progressive sectors were shaped by visionary leaders and the theological movement known as liberation theology, with its focus on the preferential option for the poor. Other dioceses, however, especially those in the areas most affected by the violence, did not experience the same level of renewal.[3]

One progressive church sector, located in the South Andes Region of the Departments of Cusco and Puno and extending to the Bolivian border, was an exception to the rule. There, an emerging and renewed church presence closely identified with the Quechua and Aymara indigenous people of that region, provided an example of a church response committed to living out the option for the poor with a unique sensitivity to building an inculturated Christian community in a collegial fashion. This regional church's visionary and prophetic leaders included many missionaries from the United States and several European countries, along with a committed nucleus of Peruvian diocesan clergy and religious women and men, as well as a cadre of lay leaders formed in this period of renewal. This church community was deeply inserted into the life of the Andean people, embracing their cultural values, their indigenous worldview, and the defense of human rights.[4]

Over the past fifty years, the church in this region was continuously engaged with every sector of the local and national civil society in its commitment to integral human development, and to the people of this impoverished and physically remote region of the southern Andes called the *Surandino*. When the violence first appeared there in the early 1980s, the church mounted an instantaneous response in solidarity with human rights organizations, local indigenous communities, grassroots *campesino* federations, political parties, and local governments. This resulted in long-lasting, effective networks of social cohesion. The accumulation of social capital built up over many years complemented an effort to work for social change in a peaceful, nonviolent way. The fact that the level of violence in the Puno and Cusco departments never reached the proportions that it did in other areas may be attributed to this vast and intricate social network of religious and civil society organizations that functioned together in a coordinated fashion.

The actions of the *Surandino* church stand out as a significant case study of how a vast and diverse social network, in its formal and informal dimensions, was operative in those years of social turmoil and disruption. Church personnel, working with structures that were well-adapted to the particularities of this sociocultural reality, made this possible through an application of the principles of Catholic social teaching (CST) in close relationship with the people and their organizations. By comparison, in other areas of Peru the same kind of social networks were either nonexistent or not as fully operative as they were in Cusco and Puno.

Reviving Historical Memory: Factors behind the Emergence of Political Violence in Peru during the I980s

The terrorist movement PCP-SL had many of its roots in the extreme poverty and social exclusion found in the most remote and isolated areas of the mountainous regions of central and southern Peru. However, these factors do not fully explain the emergence of such a violent movement that cost so many lives and caused the displacement of so many people, especially the rural indigenous

poor. The sources and outcome of this complex historical process cannot be limited to one simple explanation. Many of its origins can be traced to social conditions in the peripheral mountainous provinces in the Central Andes region of the country.

The *Sendero Luminoso* movement was led by its self-proclaimed leader and founder, university philosophy professor and Communist Maoist ideologue Abimael Guzman, and the conflict lasted from 1980 until 1992. The high death toll was due to the terrorist actions and scorched earth political operations of the *Shining Path*, but the violent repression of state security forces intensified the climate of violence. However, equally disruptive were the long-term effects of the displacement of thousands of poor rural inhabitants from their small villages and towns to more populous department and provincial capitals and coastal cities. Later during this period, the violence and conflict spread to urban areas and the north central jungle region of the country, resulting in a social disruption of disproportionate dimensions whose effects remain embedded in the collective consciousness and memory of the Peruvian people to this day. Finally, in September of 1992, state security forces of the authoritarian government of President Alberto Fujimori captured Guzman and the other leaders of the movement, tried them, and sentenced them to life imprisonment.

As the Truth and Reconciliation Commission documented exhaustively in its conclusions in 2004, a variety of sociological and cultural factors explain the beginnings of the *Shining Path*. The movement emerged among newly awakened rural professors and dispirited rural youth in a state university located in the capital city of the Department of Ayacucho. This was an area characterized by chronic underdevelopment and extreme poverty centered in and around small- and medium-sized cities like Ayacucho and provincial towns located in remote and peripheral mountainous regions of the country.[5]

The profile of students enrolled in newly opened state universities in the 1960s grew to record numbers, introducing an important new demographic. At these universities, a generation of students of indigenous Quechua descent—in many cases the first in their families to gain access to a university education—was actively recruited by a core of charismatic professors led by the PCP-SL founder, philosopher Abimael Guzmán. The ideologues of the *Shining Path* paid special attention to those students preparing to become elementary and secondary teachers in rural schools, where they would be pursuing their profession in difficult, underpaid conditions.

Initially, some outside observers of developments in Peru erroneously explained the emergence of *Sendero Luminoso* as a kind of manifestation of a mythical indigenous uprising. In their explanations it may have been a twentieth-century reenactment of *Pachakuti*, a social upheaval long associated with short-lived native rebellions in Peruvian history from colonial times. In our view, nothing could be further from the truth. As soon became apparent, the extremist Marxist ideology was based on a doctrinaire and authoritarian approach to social change, and embodied little of the rich Andean mythical worldview or symbolic ritual actions that define daily life and the agricultural cycle of ancient and contemporary festivals in the Andean region.

In seeking to overturn and destroy any remnant of the indigenous past in a violent way, the movement fashioned itself on more modern and recent violent movements like that of Pol

Pot in Cambodia. Simply put, the PCP-SL sought to destroy the (arguably) flawed structures of civic life in Peru and its diverse indigenous peoples' civilizations in order to rebuild it on a vague, authoritarian, and destructive model of a presumably egalitarian but ultimately totalitarian society. Rather than calling for a return to a restored *Tawantinsuyo*—the Inca Empire that existed for 150 years before the Spanish Conquest—the movement adopted a violent ideology with an unabashed devotion to Mao's widow, Jiang Qing, and the "Gang of Four" featured in wall paintings across the affected zones.

The movement arose at a critical turning point in recent Peruvian history. For twelve years (1968–80), a reform-minded military government had overseen a transition to formal democracy. Unlike the many other national security states of the same era in neighboring countries, the Peruvian Revolution of the Armed Forces offered another pathway to political and social transformation from 1968 through 1975. Under President Francisco Morales Bermudez, the military government set in motion the process of a return to formal democracy and raised expectations in the populace for substantial changes. At the same time, fragmented leftist political parties were redefining themselves according to a new political discourse. That discourse was emboldened by the populist rhetoric and slogans about the ways that the agricultural and other reforms were falling far short of the goal of redefining the land ownership patterns inherited from the colonial past. Factionalism, divisions, and internal struggles characterized this resurgence of leftist political parties beginning in the late 1970s.

Ultimately, the democratic reforms did not respond to the deep-seated structural fissures and fault lines in institutional life that allowed for the persistence of inequality and racial and cultural exclusion of the vast majority of Peruvians. These factors limited their access to basic human services and their participation in forging a united nation. The residue of the "colonial wound" remained a major obstacle, particularly the colonial patterns of land ownership based on the dominant hacienda system. Agrarian reforms, for example, were mostly centered on the larger and more productive coastal rice- and sugar-growing estates. Meanwhile, vast expanses of cattle-raising haciendas in the highland sierra were only partially restructured into government cooperatives. This left the economic condition of the Peruvian *campesino* small landholder virtually unchanged and on the margins of the more economically developed regions of the country. Nevertheless, as the Truth and Reconciliation Commission noted in its final report, many of the *campesinos* who became followers of the PCP-SL ideology had actually benefited in some way from the reform-minded military government, particularly with regard to education.

The forces of the PCP-SL frequently targeted small provincial town government officials and local power elites, particularly in remote areas. Police stations and army posts were virtually nonexistent in these isolated towns and hamlets, leaving the local populace at the mercy of the armed columns of the PCP-SL. School teachers, store owners, and merchants were often herded together in the plazas of these towns for makeshift extrajudicial "trials" and then summarily executed by the terrorists in the presence of shocked townspeople.

These actions of the PCP-SL are key to understanding the massive movement of peoples from the countryside to the coastal cities in Peru in the 1980s. The acceleration of this migratory movement underway since the 1950s also contributed to a new awareness among highly organized slum dwellers in the so-called *pueblos jovenes* (young towns), makeshift squatter settlements that sprouted up on the outskirts of large cities like Lima and Arequipa but in smaller provincial urban areas as well. As migrants increasingly occupied large expanses of coastal desert terrain, a range of activist community organizations emerged where none had previously existed. These eventually coalesced into a vibrant but often fragmented social movement that advocated for the claims of the disenfranchised masses. They sought a better way of life and access to the basic services of electricity, water, and education that had long been denied to them.

The Process of Renewal of the Post-Conciliar Peruvian Church

In this context of myriad societal transformations, the Peruvian Catholic Church experienced a significant period of renewal in the aftermath of the Second Vatican Council (1962–65). This renewal reflected the transformation of the Latin American Church exemplified by the episcopal conferences in Medellín, Colombia, in 1968; Puebla, Mexico, in 1979; Santo Domingo, Dominican Republic, in 1992; and more recently, the Fifth Conference held in Aparecida, Brazil, in 2007.[6] As far back as the 1950s, the institutional Catholic Church started to become a modernizing force for social change in a sharp departure from its traditional and conservative role of supporting the European-oriented upper classes. At the Medellín Conference in 1968, Peruvian theologian Gustavo Gutiérrez, the highly acclaimed founder of the liberation theology movement, served as the theological advisor for the esteemed Cardinal Archbishop of Lima, Juan Landázuri Ricketts, and influenced the writing of several key conference documents.

Strong pastoral leadership by a cohort of bishops influenced by the Vatican II spirit combined with a vibrant missionary movement from the United States and Europe found inspiration in the emergence of liberation theology in the late 1960s in the social context of internal migration and the sprawling growth of coastal cities. Many of these nascent church movements grew out of commitments to the principles and methodologies of Catholic Action in Europe and the application of the church's social teaching that emerged in some areas among progressive Catholic professional elites.

The link between the overall social and political context and the emergence of an activist church can be traced to the devastating earthquake that occurred in May 1970 in the north central region of Peru that decimated the coastal city of Chimbote and several smaller cities. The experience of Chimbote was emblematic of the changes writ large occurring in the country—internal migration, small-scale industrialization in fishing and steel production, and a newly invigorated church with a large influx of U.S.-based missionary groups living out the spirit of the reforms of the Second Vatican Council. Significantly, it was in Chimbote in July 1968 that Gustavo Gutiérrez first coined the term of a "theology of liberation" at three public lectures in the presence of foreign missionaries and church pastoral agents from within and outside of Peru.[7] A notable presence at the talks was the indigenous novelist José María Arguedas, the writer who most accurately chronicled the social and cultural changes sweeping the country of Peru

from an indigenous worldview. Chimbote was a microcosm of the changes sweeping the entire country, captured so well by the title of one of Arguedes's signature novels, *Todas las sangres* (All the Blood Lines). It is no coincidence that the novel was written while he resided in Chimbote.[8]

While the earthquake literally and figuratively revealed deep social and economic fissures and fault lines in Peruvian society, it also provided an opening for the Catholic Church. Many religious pastoral agents were recruited to aid in the earthquake relief efforts in the region. For some, particularly those from more traditional religious orders, the experience of discovering another reality of the country far from the secure and isolated Catholic enclaves of Lima raised questions about religious life. In Chimbote, both the emergence of new social movements and new options for renewal in the Catholic Church found expression.

A Renewed Church Presence Based on a Culture of Solidarity with a People Who "Die before Their Time"

The church in the southern region of Puno and Cusco soon became a kind of laboratory for the applications of the principles of Catholic social teaching and liberation theology by a cadre of leaders, missionaries, and pastoral agents imbued with the Vatican II spirit of collegiality. Over the years, they developed an application of CST to a particular reality, along with a missionary spirit sensitive to inculturation and the Andean cultural matrix and worldview. This bore fruit during the social turmoil and crisis of the 1980s.

Already in the 1940s and 1950s, the Maryknoll Fathers, Brothers, and Sisters in the South Andes and in urban areas laid the foundation for the church's unique presence before and after Vatican II. Then in 1968, encouraged by the renewal begun at the Medellín Conference, Maryknollers and other foreign missioners began innovative lay formation programs and empowerment through human development and social communications projects that anticipated the renewal of the global and Latin American Churches.[9] All of these shifts and projects envisioned a protagonist role for indigenous people as social change agents, and sought to keep isolated communities connected to one another despite physical and territorial distances. A deep commitment to the project of inculturation of the Gospel resulted in the founding of the *Instituto de Pastoral Andina* or the Andean Pastoral Institute (IPA) in 1969. IPA conducted groundbreaking research and carried out the formation of church pastoral agents through courses, workshops, and scholarly publications that set out "to discover the indigenous soul" of the Quechua and Aymara peoples of the region in the spirit of collegiality.

IPA played a key role in convening formal and informal spaces for pastoral formation, reflection/analysis, and action among a vast network of participating church groups and civil society and political organizations. Early on it developed an operative model of the practice of social networking. This, in turn, gave rise to

211

currents of theological reflection based on liberation theology and indigenous theological expressions among the peoples and communities of the Southern Andes region. Grassroots observation combined with the application of pioneering anthropological research produced a rich storehouse of scholarly documentation to account for the unique experience of missionary communities and visionary church leaders committed to a transformational encounter with the indigenous people of the region.

The church of the South Andes began a pattern of establishing connections to a vast and diverse social network of local and national human rights and development groups. More awareness of issues of human rights and the peoples' right to organize in independent *campesino* federations gave birth to a generation of new social actors. These groups aided in the consolidation of a powerful nonviolent method of social change as they renewed the age-old demand of the Andean peoples for a radical restructuring of the patterns of land ownership to reverse centuries-long trends of feudal social relationships.

An esteemed Puno intellectual, geographer, and later senator Emilio Romero (1899–1993) was an important figure in reimagining a long-neglected, nation-building role for Puno and the South Andes.[10] A contemporary of the great socialist thinker of the period, José Carlos Mariátegui (1898–1930), Romero first envisioned a new protagonist role for the indigenous peoples in the transformation of the Peruvian reality as far back as the 1940s. Romero saw the major problem of Puno as one of "distance and not just the physical distance, but the human factor of the distance between peoples" to explain the chronic underdevelopment that afflicted this marginalized region.[11]

More than any other institution, the Catholic Church of the past fifty years helped to close the gaps between peoples that Romero first noted.[12] Physical and human distances between the indigenous inhabitants, emergent and newly awakened insurgent groups, and the modern day heirs of the elite landowning class contributed to the climate of political violence in the 1980s. Healing the breaches and fractures that separate people, as did the church during this period of the late twentieth century, was seen as one of the constructive ways to achieve the long sought goal of social justice and ultimately, social reconciliation.

Turning Points in the 1980s

Several key events in the 1980s helped to define the church's prophetic role amidst political violence in the region. In 1986, two outstanding pastorally minded bishops—Salesian Julio González, former bishop of Puno, and the Maryknoll prelate of Juli, Albert Koenigsknecht—died suddenly and accidentally. Their tragic deaths were preceded a few years earlier by the accidental deaths of Prelate Luis Dalle of Ayaviri and Archbishop Luis Vallejo of Cusco. Each of these losses became moments of public grief but also validated the significance of the Southern Andes experience of a collegial church whose leaders were closely identified with the people, their culture, and their struggle for dignity, human rights, and social justice.

During the APRA government of President Alan Garcia in the mid-1980s, church support for the *campesinos'* land claims coalesced around the pastoral document *La tierra: don de Dios, derecho del pueblo* (*The Land: God's Gift, the People's Right*). This document applied the principle of solidarity from Catholic social thought to the situation of growing political violence in the region. Together with a series of other prophetic documents and pronouncements during this period, this document shows the emergence of a popular kind of magisterium that sought to read the "signs of the times" amidst the realities of the South Andes Region.

Theologian Gustavo Gutiérrez, who had longstanding ties to the region, also helped shape theological responses to events there. To capture the tenor of the times in the early 1980s, Gutiérrez produced writings focused on spirituality in the time of violence: *Beber en su propio pozo* (*To Drink from Our Own Well*) and a reflection on the Old Testament Book of Job, *Hablar de Dios desde el sufrimiento del inocente* (*On Job: God-Talk and the Suffering of the Innocent*).[13] Gutiérrez frequently visited the Southern Andes region of Cusco and Puno in the 1980s. In 1986, he participated in a public forum organized by the leaders of the *Surandino* Church called *Puno quiere la paz* (Puno Wants Peace). Earlier in the year his op-ed piece in the Lima newspaper, *La República, Aún estamos a tiempo*, further dramatized the dire straits in which the country found itself after three hundred suspected terrorists were summarily massacred in Lima's most notorious prison, *El Frontón*. This op-ed captured the dark mood of the period but sent a message that "there was still time" to reverse the spiral of violence that enveloped the entire country. While underscoring the structural injustices embedded in the country's political institutions, he also highlighted the hopeful response of the poor, their organizations, and social movements. Gutiérrez's role cannot be overestimated in this decisive and pivotal year when the violence intensified and peaked in every region of the country.

Meanwhile, church leaders strongly and steadfastly supported the just claims of the people for land redistribution through their independent organizations. Because of its role as an advocate for a nonviolent approach to this social justice issue, the church's message clashed with the tactics of an authoritarian and doctrinaire terrorist group like *Sendero Luminoso*. Church institutions like the Rural Education Institutes (IER) in Ayaviri and Juli, or *Radio Onda Azul* in the Puno region became catalysts for social change and resistance to terrorist armed groups but were also targets of terrorist aggression. Church and civil society mobilizations in solidarity with church pastoral agents were a response to the two *Sendero* attacks in Juli and Ayaviri in 1981 and 1989 against the IERs. Moreover, they highlighted the significance of the church's capacity to convene wide sectors of Andean societies in efforts to repudiate the violence in the defense of life drawing on the existence of networks of social capital and solidarity built up over many years. At both marches following the attacks one could witness the strong bonds of reciprocal respect and identification between people, civil society, and church institutions in their commitment to defend life.

Creating and Nurturing a Culture of Solidarity

The establishment of a close-knit coordination of "Vicariates of Solidarity" in each of the four church jurisdictions—Ayaviri, Puno, Sicuani, and Juli—helped facilitate the church's networking with civil society. The Vicariates served as the nexus to human rights groups, political parties, *campesino* organizations, and local, national, and international intellectuals to form a wider social network working in concert to build a culture of solidarity. The Vicariates coordinated in an effective way with this wider constellation of social networks to provide human rights education and formation, legal assistance, accompaniment of families in recovering the remains of family members from mass executions found in common graves, interventions with police and government agencies, establishing creative communication networks, visits to remote communities where pastoral agents were at great risk, and national and international connections. Not the least of these services was the careful documentation of the violation of human rights, regardless of whether the violations were carried out by terrorist movements, armed forces, or government officials. Local radio stations like *Onda Azul* in Puno complemented the human rights advocacy and formation services given by the Vicariates to connect the most isolated of the communities in the region as the level of violence intensified.[14]

Though it clearly rejected the violence perpetrated by the *Sendero Luminoso*, the church nevertheless experienced political violence at the hands of government forces. Church support for the struggle to restructure and restore land to the communities set the stage for a confrontation with local power elites despite the once promising dialogue between the region's bishops and the government of President Alan Garcia in 1985 and 1986. Mobilization by the communities and the *campesino* federations coalesced into a large-scale movement that resulted in planned invasions and takeovers of the lands held by government-supported and state-owned land cooperatives. There were untold risks for the church in assuming this catalyst role, both from the *Sendero Luminoso* and from government responses.

When violence did occur, large public convocations and marches for life and peace called by a united church and other members of this vast social network highlighted the church's quick response in solidarity. For instance, in 1981, after the August 15 attack on the Rural Education Institute in Juli, over seven thousand people from all over the South Andes region gathered for an Andean ritual blessing of the desecrated ground. From the Rural Institute the marchers, led by each of the bishops and prelates of the jurisdictions, marched together to the town square of Juli. Significantly, each bishop walked side by side by the people from his particular place—Ayaviri, Sicuani, Puno, Juli, and Cusco. A subsequent march for life was also held in response to two unsuccessful assassination attempts against the Juli Maryknoll prelate Albert Koenigsknecht. In May 1989, an attack on the IER "Waqrani" of the Prelature of Ayaviri caused extensive damage to the experimental farm, machinery, newly harvested potato crop, and buildings for this center, a focal point for the organized land invasions by the *campesino* organization called FUCAM. In response, people from all over the South Andes region arrived in trucks and buses to demonstrate a united front in solidarity with their brothers and sisters.

Nothing symbolized the coordinated efforts of the church during those critical years more than the organization of a *Semana Social* (Social Week) to articulate its solidarity in building up a frayed social fabric. The week was headlined by its keynote speaker, Cardinal Archbishop Roger Etchegaray, president of the Vatican Commission on Justice and Peace and special envoy of Pope John Paul II. Inviting such an internationally known figure raised further opportunities for international solidarity in response to what had occurred in this remote corner of the Peruvian highlands.

There were a variety of other ways in which church leaders and pastoral agents took advantage of national and international solidarity networks. They drew on Maryknoll's connections in Washington, as well as reaching out to European groups such as *Misereor* and *Adveniat*—the German Church's project funding agencies. These connections provided valuable resources for advocacy and the defense of human rights and enabled an organized response to natural disasters like the drought and floods that afflicted the region in the years 1982–84.

Resistance and Resilience through Cultural and Symbolic Capital toward the Creation of New Sociocultural Imaginaries

Another important factor in the resistance to violence during this time were the many aesthetically creative and artistic responses from the rich cultural heritage of the Andean people. While the sources of social and economic capital were disconnected and cut off, the Quechua and Aymara people of the region drew upon this cultural and artistic heritage and their ritual cycle of fiesta celebrations as important forms of resistance to a culture of systemic violence. The artistic creativity of the people through initiatives like the *Talleres de fotografía social* (TAFOS) demonstrated a creative resilience on the part of the people to draw upon cultural traditions as well as new technology. The photographic workshops came about when celebrated German professional photographer Thomas Mueller arrived in the area in the 1980s. Mueller handed a small camera to one of the *campesinos* in the high ranges of the Andes in the department of Cusco. When he then developed the photographs of the surrounding countryside, he recognized the uniqueness of the indigenous *campesino* perspective that captured angles and scenic horizons unknown to his Western-trained eyes.[15] The TAFOS photography collection, produced and documented by the small farmers and leaders of popular organizations, offers a truly unique glimpse into the drama of the turbulent years in the country. With the passing of years, this collection stands out as a living memorial to the peoples' stamina and resistance to the political violence.

Despite claims to the contrary, the PCP-SL could never penetrate or weaken the strongly woven cultural matrix of the Andean cosmovision and its worldview marked by the communal solidarity of Quechua and Aymara indigenous communities. Church pastoral agents accompanied people in the rural communities in the exercise of their everyday lives of the agricultural cycle ritual of planting and harvest festivals that renewed the spirit and nourished their resilience to withstand threats and onslaughts against human dignity in a climate of fear. This bedrock of cultural resistance coalesced at critical moments in the struggle to recover ancestral land claims and as a bulwark of resistance against the violent alternative of armed insurgents. Never once to our knowledge in the South Andes did the threat of terrorist violence break the rhythms and patterns of celebrations of patron saint feast days throughout the region. According to Peruvian historian Victor Maqque, in the late colonial period of the Tupac Amaru insurrection against Spanish rule, peasant communities continued to participate in local agricultural cycles, social struggles, and litigations against abuses.[16] Likewise, in the more recent period of struggle, ritual celebrations and communal meetings and assemblies went on uninterrupted despite the danger. Grassroots popular organizations and movements flourished. Likewise, taking a cue from the people, the church, through parish groups and institutions, rarely if ever cancelled meetings, courses, workshops, and public events.

During the years of this tragic social conflict, artistic and musical expressions were paradoxically able to grow and flourish. This is a little-known part of the narrative of solidarity and resistance to the violence of this period and is evident in the artistic creations of artists like Cusco artist Antonio Huillca. His paintings were commissioned by the South Andes Church for yearly calendars and posters and demonstrate the deep reservoir of symbolic capital and social solidarity operative in the social networks. Another form of artistic expression is seen in the medium of the sculptured altar *retablos* from Quechua artisans in the most conflicted areas of the central Andes around the city of Ayacucho.

Community musical and dance competitions also translated the surrounding acts of violence into signs of endurance and resilience. These examples stand out as a creative witness to the human spirit to capture the essence of the struggle to affirm life and human existence against a backdrop of unbelievable cruelty. What these artistic media along with the TAFOS photographs so graphically portray is what the writer Arguedas called the Peruvian peoples' capacity for "infinite forms of creativity." For church workers, these art forms demonstrated a deep awareness of the strong identification with the paschal mystery of the life, death, and resurrection of Jesus.

Postscript to a National Trauma, Viewed from the Heights of Mount Kunurana by the "People of Memory, Resistance, and Hope"

The capture of *Sendero Luminoso* leader Abimael Guzmán and his imprisonment along with his cohort of followers in 1992 did not spell the end of the trauma of the *Sendero Luminoso* saga. Armed groups continued to operate in the tropical areas of Peru for many years afterward, aided and abetted by the networks of drug traffickers in the coca-growing region of the Upper Huallaga Valley. In addition, there remained a large population of prisoners from all sides of the conflict. Many of the leaders of the terrorist movement were imprisoned in newly built prisons around the country like the infamous Yanamayo center high in the Andean city of Puno. But a significant portion of the prison population at this center was made up of people who had been falsely accused, or innocent young people coerced into joining the *Sendero Luminoso* movement. Thus the prison population in Puno provided a composite picture of different sectors caught up in the conflict—a section of hard-core, committed members of the PCP-SL, a section of MRTA militants, and another section made up of the falsely accused, repentant, or compromised youth. As they awaited sentencing through the long and often corrupt and inept judicial process, they were watched over by military and police guards, many of whom had participated in assassinations, forced detentions, and other atrocities. Visits to Yanamayo prison outside the city of Puno that I made along with local human rights groups in the late 1990s raised growing awareness of the need for healing the wounds left by such a prolonged period.

Ten years elapsed before the formation of the CVR Truth and Reconciliation Commission in 2004 to carry out investigations into the causes and consequences of the conflict. The Peruvian populace was so weary and traumatized by the twelve years of continuous violence that few were ready to launch these investigations in the immediate aftermath. However, once initiated, the CVR investigation gained support and momentum. Ultimately, the final tally of the numbers of victims by the CVR surpassed and surprised even close observers like church pastoral workers and national and international human rights organizations, who had been unaware of the depth or extent of the destruction. The building of a victims' memorial in Lima with grants from the German government stands as an important witness to the historical memory of the years of violence and points toward the formidable task of building an environment of social reconciliation in Peru.

Meanwhile, in the aftermath of the political violence, the Vicariates of Solidarity turned their attention to a more general defense of human rights and life issues. Social networks in church jurisdictions were consolidated and turned their attention to the care of creation by challenging the mechanisms of environmental destruction, particularly the unrestricted and unregulated mining interests that impinged on the sacred ground of indigenous communities and threatened their natural resources. However, neither this shift in focus, nor the influx of newly appointed conservative church leaders, diminished the credibility or the historical memory of a people and a church in solidarity in a time of violence.

Efraín Morote, rector of the state university in Ayacucho, wrote a novel about life in the remote and marginalized sierra region of Ayacucho that he titled *Los pueblos sumergidos* (*The Submerged Towns*). (Ironically, he was the father of Guzman's lieutenant and accomplice Osmán Morote.) It was to these "submerged towns" on the periphery that the leaders of the South Andes Church made a deep commitment. These prelates and pastoral agents took up the struggle for human rights and the dignity of the poor in these remote areas in a remarkable way. Despite the complex factors involved, their courage helped the church to become an exemplary force for social justice and peaceful change.

One person who epitomizes the work of the church in this period is the late Dominican bishop of Puno, Jesus Calderón. During the height of the violence, he earned the admiration of all sectors of the Puno community for his strong defense of human rights and for his leadership throughout the region during a time of institutional crisis on every level. By building trust with every sector of Puno society, Bishop Calderón left behind a memory of a church in solidarity with the people—people now able to begin the long road of transforming every relationship, no matter how fragmented by the "colonial wound."

In indigenous belief, the snowcapped mountain peaks in the Andes region carry a mystical and symbolic connotation. One of these peaks is the majestic, seventeen thousand-foot Mount Kunurana, situated near the dividing line between the departments of Cusco and Puno, and visible from both sides in a striking interplay of light and shadow. This imposing peak was significant during the violence and land struggles of the 1980s not only because of its physical proximity, but also because of the belief of the people that it is an *Apu* or hill-spirit divinity that watches over and protects them. For many, *Kunurana* became the symbol of the peoples' struggle to reclaim their ancestral lands, merging this struggle with the mythic Andean worldview. The manifestation of the presence of the divine spirit dwelling there in Mount Kunurana makes it an enduring symbol of the ongoing challenge to close the breaches separating people from each other in the South Andes. And it stands as a symbol of the strength of the Andean peoples' "memory, resistance and hope," which were so evident to those of us privileged to have accompanied them.[17]

Within a highly politically charged environment, the Catholic Church was able to contribute to the creation of a vast social network of civil society organizations, which served as a counterforce to offset the effects of the political violence generated by extremist armed groups. This constellation of civil and church organizations is built on the accumulated resources of human, social, and symbolic capital present among the Andean peoples and their rich cultural and communitarian ethos and traditions. These networks were empowered by a church committed to intercultural dialogue, Catholic social teaching, and the ongoing renewal in the spirit of the Second Vatican Council. All these factors and variables serve to underscore the importance of social networks to create a more just society committed to solidarity and reconciliation despite the residue of the "colonial wound."

Reflection Questions

1. How can we apply the lessons learned from this case study of social networks in Peru to other countries in similar conditions of violence and systemic injustice?
2. Are there other examples of countries that experience the phenomenon of a "colonial wound" in the way Peru has, and if so, in what ways have they faced it?
3. The Catholic Church in Peru contributed to develop and strengthen a network of solidarity and healing of a deep-seated social wound. What other institutions and organizations could contribute in similar situations of conflict?
4. Other countries and societies have sought to bring about Truth Commissions to instill a "never again" message. Why have such efforts been accused of being too political?
5. What is the role of spiritually symbolic actions and ritual expressions as responses to political violence?

Notes

1. Steve Stern, ed., *Shining and Other Paths: War and Society in Peru, 1980–1995* (Durham NC: Duke University Press, 1998) offers the most incisive chapters on the social conflicts and political violence during the period. The abbreviated version of the final report of the Truth and Reconciliation Commission, entitled *Hatun Willakuy*, has been an invaluable resource in my research. The term *colonial wound* has been employed by noted scholars like Walter D. Mignolo in his seminal study, *The Idea of Latin America* (Malden, MA: Blackwell Publishing, 2008).

2. Stephen P. Judd, *The Emergent Andean Church: Inculturation and Liberation Southern Peru, 1968–1986* (doc. diss.; Graduate Theological Union, Berkeley, CA, 1987). Esteban Judd Zanon, *De apacheta en apacheta: testimonio de una vida de fe en el Sur Andino peruano* (Cochabamba, Bolivia: Editorial Verbo Divino, 2015). Firsthand personal missionary experiences from 1975 to 2002 are documented in both the dissertation and book memoir.

3. Cecilia Tovar, ed., *Ser Iglesia en tiempos de violencia* (Lima: Centro de Estudios y Publicaciones, 2006). This book is a valuable compendium documenting eyewitness accounts of church pastoral agents from diverse regions of the country. For the Southern Andes region, several colleagues and I participated in extensive interviews by the author of the chapter in this volume by Lupe Jara.

4. Jeffrey Klaiber, *La Iglesia en el Perú* (Lima: Fondo Editorial PUCP, 1988). To date this is one of the most comprehensive overviews of the development of the option for the poor in the Peruvian Church, along with the role of the church as a social actor in the country. Also, see the PhD dissertation by Stephen P. Judd, *The Emergent Andean Church: Inculturation and Liberation in Southern Peru, 1968–1986* (Graduate Theological Union, Berkeley, CA, 1987).

5. CVR, *Hatun Willakuy*, 56–57.

6. John Eagleson and Phillip Scharper, ed., *Puebla and Beyond* (Maryknoll, NY: Orbis Books, 1979). Alfred T. Hennelly, ed., *Santo Domingo and Beyond: Documents and Commentaries of the Latin American Bishops' Conference* (Maryknoll, NY: Orbis Books, 1993).

7. Gustavo Gutiérrez, *A Theology of Liberation* (Maryknoll, NY: Orbis Books, 1971). The book was republished in 1988 for a *festschrift* for Gutiérrez, held at Maryknoll in 1988.

8. José María Arguedas, *Todas las sangres* (Buenos Aires: Losada, 1964).

9. John J. Considine, *Proceedings of the Lima Methods Conference of the Maryknoll Fathers* (Maryknoll, NY: P.O.N.Y, 1954).

10. Esteban Judd Zanon, "Integración andina con integridad: el legado de Emilio Romero y la Iglesia sur andina," in *Allpanchis. Puno nuestra tierra* No. 53 (Cusco, Perú: Instituto de Pastoral Andina, 1999).

11. See *El Descentralismo*, first written in 1937 and republished in 1987 in Lima (*Tarea*), this seminal work on the human geography of the southern Andes points up the need for decentralization of

the Peruvian government political structures to address the social and economic exclusion of the country's indigenous population located in remote highland provinces. For more on the strong connection between the work of Romero and the church of the southern Andes, see my article cited earlier in n. 10.

12. Judd, *De apacheta en apacheta.*

13. Gustavo Gutiérrez, *We Drink from Our Own Wells: The Spiritual Journey of a People* (Maryknoll, NY: Orbis Books, 1984). Gutiérrez, *On Job: God-Talk and the Suffering of the Innocent* (Maryknoll, NY: Orbis Books, 1988).

14. Lupe Jara in Tovar, *Ser Iglesia en tiempos de violencia,* 441–623.

15. *Talleres de fotografía social* (TAFOS). This collection of several thousand black and white photographs taken during the years of political violence in the South Andes is now located in an archive at the Pontifical Catholic University of Peru in Lima. Several photographs from this collection appear in this article.

16. Victor Maqque, "'En mi Voz y de todo el común': bases de la cultura política en el Altiplano Tardo-colonial," *Antropología Andina Muhunik* 2, no. 2 (July–December 2015): 50.

17. My own experience is summed up in an open letter that I wrote in 2011, on the occasion of the Centennial of the foundation of Maryknoll, which was published in many national and church outlets in Peru. In it, I underscored the peoples' spirit of tenacity and resilience, a deep reservoir of "spiritual stubbornness." I expressed my gratitude for the bonds of solidarity forged during times of natural disasters, struggles in overcoming adversity, and in a time of political violence. This encounter of church and people produced an extraordinary witness of faithfulness to living out the gospel through the application of the tradition of the church's social teaching by a courageous exercise of solidarity in living out the preferential option for the poorest of the poor. Esteban Judd, *Carta abierta de agradecimiento al pueblo peruano,* published in *La República* and church publications in Lima, Peru, October 2011.

CHAPTER II

"Do You See This Woman?" (Luke 7:44)

WHITE PRIVILEGE AND THE POLITICS OF MASS INCARCERATION

William O'Neill, SJ

"Life is not tragic," wrote Camus, "merely because it is wretched."[1] Yet certainly it is wretchedness, not tragedy, we see today in our criminal justice system. In these pages, I will (1) first say a word about our dominant retributive view of crime and punishment. I will then (2) consider the implications of adopting an alternative restorative perspective. I conclude (3) with a brief reflection on the surplus of religious meaning—how distinctively religious attitudes and beliefs invite us to imagine otherwise. My reflections throughout are informed by my pastoral ministry at the Federal Women's Prison in Dublin, California, where I have ministered for the past fifteen years.

In his *Spiritual Exercises*, St. Ignatius invites us to imagine ourselves in the Gospel text, to engage in a "composition of place." Let us set the stage by placing ourselves in Luke's Gospel—in the enacted parable of Luke 7:36–50:

> One of the Pharisees asked Jesus to eat with him, and he went into the Pharisee's house and took his place

at the table. And a woman in the city, who was a sinner, having learned that he was eating in the Pharisee's house, brought an alabaster jar of ointment. She stood behind him at his feet, weeping, and began to bathe his feet with her tears and to dry them with her hair. Then she continued kissing his feet and anointing them with the ointment. Now when the Pharisee who had invited him saw it, he said to himself, "If this man were a prophet, he would have known who and what kind of woman this is who is touching him—that she is a sinner." Jesus spoke up and said to him, "Simon, I have something to say to you." "Teacher," he replied, "speak." "A certain creditor had two debtors; one owed five hundred denarii, and the other fifty. When they could not pay, he canceled the debts for both of them. Now which of them will love him more?" Simon answered, "I suppose the one for whom he canceled the greater debt." And Jesus said to him, "You have judged rightly." Then turning toward the woman, he said to Simon, "Do you see this woman? I entered your house; you gave me no water for my feet, but she has bathed my feet with her tears and dried them with her hair. You gave me no kiss, but from the time I came in she has not stopped kissing my feet. You did not anoint my head with oil, but she has anointed my feet with ointment. Therefore, I tell you, her sins, which were many, have been forgiven; hence she has shown great love. But the one to whom little is forgiven, loves little." Then he said to her, "Your sins are forgiven." But those who were at the table with him began to say among themselves, "Who is this who even forgives sins?" And he said to the woman, "Your faith has saved you; go in peace."

"Do you see this woman?" Jesus's question to Simon betrays the Pharisee's retributive "moral squint":[2] Surely, were he a prophet, Jesus would see who and what kind of woman this is who is touching him—that she is a sinner, thereby rendering him ritually unclean, even as she washes his feet. Judgment precedes mercy in an economy of exclusion, doubled here as the sinner is a woman. But Jesus's question inverts the moral order, inviting us to do the same. "Do you see this woman?"—not a figure or cipher of transgression in this house of murmuring men, but as *this* woman, who loves so richly, whose faith is saving, who leaves with the blessing of divine *shalom*, "peace."

"Do we see this woman?" As I noted earlier, at the federal prison, the women incarcerated fall under Simon's gaze: sinners, unclean, who must be set aside; they are, in Gutiérrez's words, "nonpersons" in our regnant, social narrative.[3] "Do you see this woman?" The sentences we "mete and dole" blind us to the fact that, for many of the women at the federal prison, the primary victims are their children and parents.[4] So let me say a word about our retributive rationale, the politics of retribution.

The Politics of Retribution

According to recently published figures from the U.S. Bureau of Justice statistics, inmates incarcerated in prison or jail number 2.2 million, a 500 percent increase over the last forty years. This is the highest official rate of incarceration in the world (at 731 per 100,000 population).[5] Almost 25 percent of those incarcerated globally are in America's prisons and jails. Including those in probation or on parole, the total number of citizens under the aegis of corrections departments now reaches 7.1 million, an increase of almost 300 percent since 1980. Today, one out of every 137 Americans is incarcerated, an increase due less to changes in crime rates than to changes in sentencing law and policy.[6]

Disaggregating for race and ethnicity, "black men are nearly six times as likely to be incarcerated as white men and Hispanic men are 2.3 times as likely. For black men in their thirties, 1 in every 10 is in prison or jail on any given day." One in four "born since the late 1970s has spent time in prison." Though 37 percent of the U.S. population, minorities comprise 67 percent of those incarcerated. "Overall, African Americans are more likely than white Americans to be arrested; once arrested, they are more likely to be convicted; and once convicted, they are more likely to face stiff sentences."[7] In 2010, the rate of incarceration for black women was

2.9 times higher than the rate for white women; the rate for Hispanic women was 1.5 times higher.[8]

Such racial and ethnic disparities in incarceration stem from a witches' brew of compounded social disadvantage, discriminatory policing practices, biased prosecutorial discretion, and sentencing.[9] And the stigmatization of felons and their families persists after incarceration, limiting access to employment, social welfare, and housing. Felony disenfranchisement deprives "1 of every 13 African Americans" of the right to vote.[10] Such systemic inequities, writes Michelle Alexander, perpetuate the "New Jim Crow" of "racial caste" and "racialized social control."[11] In Adam Gopnik's words, "Mass incarceration on a scale almost unexampled in human history is a fundamental fact of our country today…as slavery was the fundamental fact of 1850. In truth, there are more black men in the grip of the criminal-justice system…than were in slavery then."[12]

The dramatic increase in prison populations over the past half century stands "in sharp contrast to that of the preceding fifty years, during which time there was a gradual increase in the use of incarceration commensurate with the growth in the general population."[13] So, too, our current incarceration practices differ markedly from those of other Western democracies with comparable crime rates. Amnesty International reports that the "USA stands virtually alone in the world in incarcerating thousands of prisoners in longer-term or indefinite solitary confinement."[14] Racial and ethnic minorities disproportionately suffer the ultimate sanction, capital punishment, where "poor and marginalized groups have less access to the legal resources needed to defend themselves." Since the reinstitution of capital punishment in 1973, 160 U.S. prisoners sent to death row have later been exonerated. Others have been executed despite serious doubts about their guilt.[15]

Punitive attitudes prevail in what William Stuntz calls the "harshest" judicial system "in the history of democratic government," despite evidence of other mitigating factors underlying decreases in violent crime.[16] Repaying the offender's "debt to society" favors neither reparations for victims (recognizing victims' positive rights), nor reintegration of the offender into community. Indeed, as Ta-Neshi Coates observes, with hyperincarceration of minorities, "rehabilitation was largely abandoned in favor of retribution"—a policy of "penal harm...to make offenders suffer."[17] Social bonds are further attenuated as punishment is officially privatized. Crime may not pay but punishment increasingly does, creating incentives for higher incarceration rates.[18] And yet several recent studies confirm that massive, long-term incarceration fails to deter crime or recidivism. The point of diminishing returns was reached long ago.

The Justice Department itself acknowledges the failure of reintegration. Half of all former state convicts will be incarcerated again within three years of their release. "Sixty-two percent of...confined youth...have previously been in custody. Among those, 40% have been confined 5 or more times."[19] As John Tierney observes, "Some social scientists argue that the incarceration rate is now so high that the net effect is 'crimogenic': creating more crime over the long term by harming the social fabric in communities and permanently damaging the economic prospects of prisoners as well as their families. Nationally, about one in 40 children have a parent in prison. Among black children, one in 15 have a parent in prison."[20]

A similar punitive stance favors summary apprehension, detention, and deportation of the some 11.2 million undocumented migrants—"illegal aliens" in the United States.[21] In the fiscal year 2014, "the total number of persons detained by the Department of Homeland Security (DHS), Immigration and Customs Enforcement (ICE) agency had risen to 425,728," more than doubling the rate of fiscal year 2001.[22] Under the draconian policies of the Trump administration, immigration arrests have increased by 40 percent since 2016.[23] Despite promises of reform, the overwhelming majority of "those detained are held in jails or jail-like facilities...at a cost of over $2 billion."[24] In my ministry at the Federal Women's Prison in Dublin, California, the majority of the women I serve are poor migrants, some of whom will be summarily deported after completing their sentence. Federally mandated minimum sentences forcibly separate mothers from their children for years, their punishment exacerbated terribly by the punishment thus inflicted on their children. It is not surprising to hear a woman pray for her child who is now also incarcerated. Yet the crimes for which the women stand convicted are typically nonviolent drug offenses.[25]

A Punitive Rationale

Roman Catholic bishops have joined other religious leaders in opposing such a punitive regime.[26] Yet their words fail to disturb our undogmatic slumbers. Why? Rehearsing the complex genealogy of retributive practices in the United States would exceed the limits of my essay. My aim here is more modest: to trace several related themes figuring into America's retributive moral squint.

In modern liberal polities constituted through the legal fiction of a social contract, crime typically appears as a voluntaristic legal construction, an offense against the collective will of the body politic. For the early contract theorists, meting and doling punishment figured among the raisons d'être of the modern state. In the Lockean tradition, powers to enforce or punish are no longer diffused through intermediate associations of the medieval *civitas*; citizens cede their natural right of punishment to the state. For Thomas Hobbes, crime is principally an offense against the sovereign's rights and punished accordingly. And for Kant, legal punishment is just deserts for violating the social contract; justice is entirely retributive. Even where other strands of liberalism temper retribution, the rubrics of "just deserts" prevail, as adversarial adjudication of guilt and punishment vindicates the formal (procedural) rule of abstract right. Reaffirming the coercive prerogatives of the bureaucratic state, punishment restores "the reciprocal contractual relationship between obedience to the law and benefits received from living under the law."[27]

Yet, from the beginning, the "reciprocal contractual relationship" is vitiated by an economy of systemic exclusion. Racial bias and white privilege, writes Cornel West, "permeated the writings of the major figures of the Enlightenment."[28] The "peculiar institution" of slavery and the heritage of Jim Crow in its aftermath belie the very legitimacy of a contract founded on the will of the governed in the exchange of natural rights or liberties. Indeed, from the beginning, appeal to self-evident rights masked systemic distortions in the collective will to punish, that is, in determining the nature of offense and the debt to be repaid. Neither is the masking incidental, for if natural liberties underwrite the contract, their systemic denial must be "naturalized." And so, exclusion is

230

rationalized in the name of abstract right: first by a divinely sanc-
tioned belief in the natural inferiority of slaves; then with the
demise of chattel slavery, the continued criminalization of black
and brown bodies. In Coates's trenchant words, "Nearly a century and a half before the infamy of Willie Horton, a portrait
emerged of blacks as highly prone to criminality, and generally
beyond the scope of rehabilitation. In this fashion, black villainy
justified white oppression—which was seen not as oppression
but as 'the corner-stone of our republican edifice.'"[29] Here is our
country's "original sin"; the perduring myth of what Coates,
citing the white supremacist Hinton Rowan Helper, calls "the
crime-stained blackness of the negro."[30]

Yet the systemic distortions of our will to punish go further.
For if the state's bureaucratic prerogatives discipline citizens, no
less so do they penalize "aliens," whose bodies (and not mere
behavior) become "illegal." The economy of exclusion signified by
the social contract proceeds apace as "criminals" or "illegal aliens"
are denied the very "right to have rights." What Hannah Arendt
says of forced migrants pertains no less to all those suffering the
"loss of home and political status" (e.g., through mass, or perhaps
better, hyperincarceration and felony disenfranchisement). Such
loss, says Arendt, is tantamount to "expulsion from humanity
altogether." The "alien" is not the exemplar of humanity in general (the generalized other)[31] but, like the criminal, "a frightening
symbol of difference as such."[32]

Such symbols, then, are "naturally" stigmatized, divested of
moral standing. In M. Shawn Copeland's words, "A white, racially
bias-induced horizon defines, censors, controls and segregates
different, other, non-white bodies."[33] At play here, I believe, is a
perverse dialectic where our punitive regime constructs its own
object: the alien becomes "illegal," the young black man, the
"gangbanger," the "criminalblackman."[34] As Alexander argues,
our ostensibly impartial, "colorblind" criminal justice system thus
rationalizes, and effectively erases, its racial and ethnic partiality
or bias.[35] In constructing criminal bodies, the state absolves itself.

So, too, the symbolization/stigmatization of difference, whether
of illegal aliens or criminals, likewise blurs the lines between retribution and vengeance or scapegoating (the sublimation of vengeance) in our punitive regime. The will to punish, independent

of consequential considerations, remains a potent force in polities where social bonds are already frayed and violence naturalized. Vengeance, especially against "frightening symbols of difference" seems to have its own cathartic rationale: difference is feared and punished, reproducing (essentializing) the very differences we fear and, consequently, punish.

A Restorative Squint

How, then, do we respond to the moral myopia of our carceral regime? For, as we argued, its systemic distortions vindicate our economy of exclusion, criminalizing young black and brown bodies. In the face of what Father Greg Boyle calls a "lethal absence of hope," no mere reformist sentiments will suffice.[36] We must, then, imagine otherwise. And in recent years, restorative justice has emerged as an alternative moral squint in Roman Catholic social teaching. In their pastoral letter "Responsibility, Rehabilitation, and Restoration: A Catholic Perspective on Crime and Criminal Justice," the U.S. bishops write,

> An increasingly widespread and positive development in many communities is often referred to as restorative justice. Restorative justice focuses first on the victim and the community harmed by the crime, rather than on the dominant state-against-the-perpetrator model. This shift in focus affirms the hurt and loss of the victim, as well as the harm and fear of the community, and insists that offenders come to grips with the consequences of their actions.[37]

One of its leading theorists, the Mennonite theologian Howard Zehr, describes restorative justice in a similar vein as "a process to involve, to the extent possible, those who have a stake in a specific offense and to collectively identify and address harms, needs, and obligations, in order to heal and put things as right as possible."[38] For proponents of restorative justice, victim-offender reconciliation programs (VORPs), sentencing circles, or family group conferences (FGCs) represent an effective alternative to prevailing regimes of retributive justice.[39] Yet the distinction fails to do full justice to what is entailed by "putting things as right as possible" in restorative practices, programs, and rationales. Neither retributive nor restorative justice is, after all, a rigidly limited conception.[40] Some interpretations of retributive justice include restorative elements, while restorative practices need not exclude retributive sanctions. Indeed, proponents of restorative justice differ as to whether restorative practices should replace, complement, or be integrated within criminal justice systems.

Perhaps the crucial question is just what is being restored. Advocates of transformative justice seek not only amelioration of correctional practices (victim-offender reconciliation) but also redress of the social structural violence abetting crime in institutional racism. Such structural criticism overlaps with non-Western uses of restorative justice (e.g., the South African Truth and Reconciliation Commission). The massive crimes against humanity signified by apartheid in South Africa precluded a strict, juridical adjudication of individual guilt and punishment. Yet despite these considerable differences, a family resemblance holds among conceptions of restorative justice. While punitive practice in the United States views crime primarily as a legal offense against the body politic, restorative justice sees crime as a breach of *ubuntu*— our natural sociality. In the words of Archbishop Desmond Tutu, chair of the South African Truth and Reconciliation Commission,

> Retributive justice—in which an impersonal state hands down punishment with little consideration for victims and hardly any for the perpetrator—is not the only form of justice. I contend that there is another kind of justice, restorative justice....The central concern is not retribution or punishment but, in the spirit of *ubuntu*, the healing of breaches, the redressing of imbalances, the restoration of broken relationships. This kind of justice seeks to rehabilitate both the victim and the perpetrator, who should be given the opportunity to be reintegrated into the community he or she has injured by his or her offence.[41]

233

What might such restorative practices entail juridically, ethically, and theologically? How might such non-Western wisdom, as in Tutu's appeal to *ubuntu*, inflect both ethical and theological interpretations, for example, Roman Catholic social teaching? Let us begin with Tutu's "turn" in a spirit of *ubuntu*, to the "healing of breaches."

Now, in interpreting such breaches, both Tutu and modern Catholic social teaching invoke the modern concept of human rights. Here, basic human rights are less properties of sovereign selves, abstracted from the ensemble of social relations (as in modern liberalism), than the moral grammar of civic discourse in pluralist polities. Rights talk is less talk about rights than the talk rights make possible (e.g., testimony of both victims and offenders in reconciliation programs). Narratively embodied, rights reveal the breach of social bonds (i.e., the systematic distortions of racial and ethnic bias in constructing the "illegal alien," the "gangbanger," the "criminalblackman," the "nonperson"). This is the critical, or *deconstructive*, use of rights rhetoric—a moral squint letting us see crime but, no less, the systemic inequities of white privilege and racial caste in society and, tragically, as James Cone argues, in the very "life of the Church."[42]

In this richer, communitarian interpretation, moreover, rights imply correlative duties of forbearance and of provision and protection.[43] Rights are not merely a grammar of dissent disclosing systemic racism and ethnic bias; we must also redeem the *cri de coeur* "never again." We must seek to heal the breaches, to restore or establish a regime in which basic human rights are suitably redeemed and protected. To the critical, deconstructive use of rights there thus corresponds a *constructive* use in refiguring public narrative. As in modern Catholic social teaching, basic human rights generate structural imperatives to redress systemic deprivation as in the new "Jim Crow" of hyperincarceration—our own domestic apartheid of punitive segregation.[44]

As in the transformative conception of restorative justice, the question of systemic redress of social inequity thus looms large. What must be restored is not the *status quo ante* but the rights-based common good of mutual respect and recognition necessary, in Alexander's words, for "a thriving, multiracial, multiethnic democracy free from racial hierarchy." For "the failure to acknowledge the humanity and dignity of all persons has lurked at the root of every racial caste system."[45] Our rights talk must be rich enough to name both victim and offender while essentializing neither. Indeed, under the rubrics of the common good, our moral entitlement to indiscriminate respect justifies preferential treatment for those whose basic rights are most imperiled, or, in the words of Albert Camus, our taking "the victim's side" where victims include those unjustly suffering under our carceral regime.[46] Such a discriminate response finds expression in the graduated moral urgency of differing human rights and in the differing material conditions presumed for their realization.[47] A regime of rights must thus embody a legislative or juridical preference for victims of racial, ethnic, and gendered violence, and differential material entitlements corresponding to the differing prerequisites of agency.

Prevailing social arrangements, including hyperincarceration, must be assessed considering the *telos* of such a regime. A consequentially sensitive note is sounded: What policies and social arrangements best protect the basic rights of the most vulnerable, including liberties of effective participation for those so often consigned to the margins of history? As in the South African TRC and Catholic social teaching, the restorative turn entails not only consequential (forward-looking) assessments of deterrence and rehabilitation but also structural (legal, juridical) transformation of prevailing inequities, as in racial and ethnic disparities in sentencing and incarceration that culminate in effectively disenfranchising minorities.

Finally, the deconstructive and constructive hermeneutical uses of rights combine in *reconstructive* interpersonal redress. For mutual respect enjoins not so much recognizing the generalized other but generalized respect for the concrete other—the victims of systemic racial and ethnic bias. As Alexander reminds us, justice, to be just, cannot be "colorblind." Neither are crimes primarily an offense against abstract right. Crimes may indeed be legion, but they are always transgressions of the ineluctably unique, concrete other. While our prevailing incarceration system neglects both victim and offender, restorative practices provide a social stage for interpersonal redress, emphasizing effective participation of victim, offender, and the local community affected by crime. Those who suffer rights violations through state-sponsored violence or criminal behavior acquire ancillary positive rights: of legal/juridical recognition (that harm has indeed been done), of provision (e.g., health care, counseling), and of reparation (including restitution, where feasible). Still, Primo Levi reminds us that even legal punishment cannot exact a just "'price' for pain."[48] Offenders, conversely, acquire ancillary positive duties: of confessing to the harm done, of rehabilitation, and of reparation through, for example, victim-offender reconciliation programs, sentencing circles, or family group conferences.[49]

In integrating interpersonal and systemic redress, restorative justice looks beyond the rubrics of commutative justice, to which it is often assimilated on the analogy of retributive justice.[50] Indeed, in identifying systemic distortions of racism, ethnic bias, and white privilege, and redressing both interpersonal and systemic inequities, such justice seeks to restore the social bonds at the heart of a distributively just social order. Yet neither interpersonal nor systemic redress dictates a univocal practice. Rather, differing practices of restorative justice turn, in part, on the respective emphases placed upon systemic and interpersonal redress and the nature of the harm or crime itself. Informal victim-offender programs may be unsuitable for crimes of sexual or spousal abuse. Neither, as in the example of the federal women's prison, can we always assume a simple demarcation of victim and offender. Systemic and interpersonal redress must be taken together in a dynamic and fluid deliberative praxis.

In a similar vein, the systemic aims of deterrence are qualified by the ethical exigencies of personal redress, such as victims' rights and offenders' duties. Moreover, since persons never cease to matter, the basic rights of offenders retain their moral force: cruelty is never permissible, vengeance never justified. Assessments of deterrence must themselves be rights based, integrating both forward- and backward-looking considerations. Where less coercive measures than protracted incarceration (e.g., VORPs, FGCs) serve the purposes of deterrence and reparation, they would necessarily be preferred. "Here," as Tutu reminds us once again, "the central concern is not retribution or punishment but, in the spirit of *ubuntu* [and, we may say, Catholic social teaching on social solidarity], the healing of breaches, the redressing of imbalances, the restoration of broken relationships."[51]

A Surplus of Religious Meaning

"Do you see this woman?" To see with a restorative squint is to see the place of systemic distortion, social sin from the perspective of solidarity and the mediating option for the most vulnerable. I will speak here from my own faith tradition; but much of what I say, I believe, finds resonances in our other great traditions. Solidarity—covenant fidelity—bonds us in freedom to these sisters and brothers. The option for the most vulnerable lets us see them not as "frightening symbols of difference," but in all their truth, says Simone Weil, "exactly like me," albeit "stamped with a special mark by affliction."[52] The restorative squint tutors our imagination, as what Jean-Marc Éla called a "pedagogy of seeing":[53] the ineluctably unique, concrete Other, my neighbor, not criminals, but mothers and grandmothers, "exactly like me." And for Luke what we see, finally, is not merely a beloved sinner but the very model of disciple in Luke's Gospel. Indeed, we see just how profoundly the moral order is inverted as the despised other, the sinful woman, proves to be the true host.[54]

And there are moments, places of grace, where we "see" such an inversion taking flesh. My own prison ministry has been inspired by one of my former students, Father Greg Boyle, SJ, whose work with gang members led to the founding of Homeboy Industries. "In Africa," writes Father Boyle, "they say 'a person becomes a person through other people.' There can be no doubt that the homies have returned me to myself. I've learned, with their patient guidance, to worship Christ as He lives in them."[55] In the spirit of *ubuntu*, Homeboy Industries incarnates the threefold hermeneutic elaborated earlier: a critical pedagogy of seeing that integrates both interpersonal and systemic aspects of restorative justice. As pastor of Dolores Mission, one of the poorest Catholic parishes in the city, Father Boyle witnessed the devastating consequences of gang violence in the late 1980s. Seeking an alternative to incarcerating "our way out of this problem," he initiated programs of day care, alternative schooling, and job training that culminated in the founding of Homeboy Bakery in 1992 and Homeboy Industries in 2001. Serving fifteen thousand men and women each year, Homeboy Industries is now the largest gang intervention, rehabilitation, and reentry program in the world.[56]

"First be reconciled to your brother or sister," says Jesus in Matthew's Sermon on the Mount; "and then come and offer your gift" (5:24). Saint Ignatius places us before the crucified Jesus, and in him, as Ignacio Ellacuría reminds us, the crucified people:[57] To see Christ in the crucified presumes, even as it transcends moral deliberation—the threefold hermeneutic of rights previously elaborated. For in Christ we are always already in communion with the *anawîm*; the disciple's solidarity implies not merely taking the victim's side (the essential requirement of ethics), but, as Father Boyle says, "kinship,"[58] taking the victim's side as our own (in Karl Rahner's terms, the formal, existential demand of love[59]). Bryan Massingale thus bids white Christians, in humility that is also prophetic, to enter into the lament of their oppressed black sisters and brothers.[60] The distinctively Christian virtue of solidarity with the *anawîm*, of entering into lament, thus defines the disciple's horizon of discernment; for "to be a Christian," says Gutiérrez, "is to draw near, to make oneself a neighbor, not the one I encounter in my journey but the one in whose journey I place myself."[61] And such living response begins with invitation; for we must first be guests, and only then learn to be hosts in the beloved community.

On the Feast of La Señora de Guadalupe, the women at the federal prison enact the drama of Mary's appearance to Juan Diego. Mary appears, the story tells us, to a people stripped of their culture, language, and religion—speaking in their language, clothed in their garb, and resplendent with their religious symbols. And for the imprisoned women, these frightening symbols of difference, the story is lived again. For they, too, have suffered the loss of everything: their culture, self-esteem, status as mother. All these have been taken from us, they say in the liturgy, but not our faith, not the words of Mary who speaks, mother to mother, of what it is to lose a child. And although I play the part of the bishop who first dismisses Juan, they are the hosts, the true presiders that day in our Mass, a liturgy of restorative justice. And

I am humbled at such faith that has suffered more than I can imagine—faith that leads mothers with years still on their sentences to sing a song, "*mujer libre*" (free woman) for those finally leaving. Had I suffered as they, I truly wonder if I could sing; but I am privileged to join in their song.

Only in confessing a crucified love do we come to see. In putting ourselves in the sinful woman's place, we must come to see as she sees. Why has she shown such great love? Surely it is because she has been greatly loved—the parable within the parable shows this, that one who is forgiven much, loves much, loves enough to brave the censoring gaze, the murmuring; loves enough, to see only Jesus. "Do we see this woman?" How we answer is finally revelatory, not only of who she is but of who we are. For our punitive regime, I argued, a perverse dialectic of fear and punishment leaves us with only frightening symbols of difference. For disciples, conversely, the healing of breaches entails not only a hermeneutics of rights, but, as Father Boyle reminds us, a saving dialectic of kinship in which guest becomes host and host, guest. And at the heart of our kinship is Christ, true guest and true host—Love's word spoken in the silence of Calvary to a crucified people, love suffering because it is love. So, it is the beatitudes, the blessings of Matthew's Sermon on the Mount at the beginning of Jesus's ministry, that are fulfilled in the final parable of Matthew 25:31–46. For in seeing and ministering to the stranger, the hungry, the prisoner—these frightening symbols of difference—we see and minister to Christ. The beatitudes are fulfilled in the one who speaks them as guest becomes host again and Christ summons those blest by his Father to the eschatological fiesta.

Conclusions

In this brief essay, I've proposed that restorative justice forms the moral squint, the hermeneutic we bring to discernment. The biblical injunction to "act justly" tutors our imaginations, letting us "see this woman" as one bound down by social sin. We are summoned, as the woman in Luke's tale, to do justice in the "healing of breaches." Yet for disciples, such justice is marked by love:

in electing how we are uniquely summoned to love tenderly, compassionately in a dialectic of kinship. And so, little by little, we, the beloved community, are invited to walk humbly with the crucified God, whose love does infinitely more than we can ask or imagine (see Micah 6:8). Like the woman of Luke's tale, we must keep our eyes on Jesus. Finally, we come to see in our work of restorative justice, in doing what she did, washing one another's feet, that it is God who labors—who writes, in flawed words and stubborn sounds, the story of our lives as gospel.

Reflection Questions

1. Many U.S. citizens remain indifferent to mass incarceration or justify it on retributive grounds. Like the women in Luke's Gospel (7:36–50), those incarcerated are regarded as "sinners," receiving their just deserts. What prejudgments or prejudices underlie such judgments?

2. The legitimacy of our criminal justice system rests in its perceived impartiality. Yet social critics like Michelle Alexander argue that our criminal justice system is far from being "color-blind." How do race and ethnicity intersect with mass or hyperincarceration?

3. How might a biblical conception of justice as covenant fidelity let us imagine otherwise? What key biblical passages, parables, or stories might serve as a restorative pedagogy?

4. How might the biblical vision of a restored community be translated into the secular idiom of politics in a religiously pluralist polity like our own? Consider, in particular, how the essays of this collected volume might contribute to such a prophetic witness.

5. Liberation theology interprets biblical justice in terms of a "preferential option for the poor"; yet many regard any preference based on race, ethnicity, class, or gender as unfair. How, then, can we speak of such an option for those most vulnerable in our midst, especially those suffering incarceration?

Notes

1. Camus writes that "it is the failing of a certain literature to believe that life is tragic because it is wretched." Albert Camus, *Lyrical and Critical Essays*, trans. Ellen Conroy Kennedy (New York: Alfred A. Knopf, 1968), 201.

2. The phrase "moral squint" is from Robert Bolt, *A Man for All Seasons* (New York: Random House, 1990), 19.

3. Gustavo Gutiérrez, *The Power of the Poor in History: Selected Readings* (London: SCM, 1983), 193.

4. The allusion is to Tennyson, "I mete and dole/Unequal laws unto a savage race."

5. Bureau of Justice Statistics, summarized by The Sentencing Project, "Fact Sheet: Trends in U.S. Corrections," accessed September 1, 2017, www.sentencingproject.org/wp-content/uploads/2016/01/Trends-in-US-Corrections.pdf.

6. Bureau of Justice Statistics, summarized by The Sentencing Project, "Facts about Prisons and Prisoners," accessed August 22, 2012, www.sentencingproject.org.

7. The Sentencing Project, "Fact Sheet: Trends in U.S. Corrections."

8. The Sentencing Project, "Facts about Prisons and Prisoners." The number of women in prison has been increasing at a rate 50 percent higher than men since 1980. See also the Sentencing Project, "Fact Sheet: Trends in U.S. Corrections."

9. Hadar Aviram attributes such disparities to "racialized assumptions and practices that precede the incarceration stage: social disadvantage that produces violent crime; discriminatory policing practices; extensive prosecutorial discretion which is very resistant to judicial review; the everyday realities of lower courtroom practices; and the impact of race, and other demographic factors that intersect with it, on sentencing." "Why Are Racial Minorities Overrepresented in the Prison Population? A Systemic Institutional Inquiry," in *"Today I Give Myself Permission to Dream": Race and Incarceration in America* (San Francisco: Lane Center Series, 2018), 17–30.

10. The Sentencing Project, "Felony Disenfranchisement," accessed November 7, 2014, www.sentencingproject.org. The Sentencing Project reports that there were an estimated 1.17 million

241

people disenfranchised in 1976, 3.34 million in 1996, and over 5.85 million in 2010. The rate of felony disenfranchisement for Americans of voting age is more than four times greater than non-African Americans. Christopher Uggen, Sarah Shannon, and Jeff Manza, "State-Level Estimates of Felon Disenfranchisement in the United States, 2010" (July 2012), https://www.sentencingproject.org/wp-content/uploads/2016/01/State-Level-Estimates-of-Felon-Disenfranchisement-in-the-United-States-2010.pdf.

11. Michelle Alexander, *The New Jim Crow: Mass Incarceration in the Age of Colorblindness*, rev. ed. (New York: The New Press, 2012), 258. See Laurie M. Cassidy and Alex Mikulich, eds., *Interrupting White Privilege* (Maryknoll, NY: Orbis Books, 2007).

12. Adam Gopnik, "The Caging of America," *The New Yorker*, January 30, 2012, 73. Gopnik notes that in the last two decades, "the money that states spend on prisons has risen at six times the rate of spending on higher education" (73).

13. Ryan S. King, Marc Mauer, Malcolm C. Young, "Incarceration and Crime: A Complex Relationship," "The Sentencing Project," accessed February 24, 2010, www.sentencingproject.org.

14. Amnesty International, "Entombed: Isolation in the US Federal Prison System" (London: Amnesty International, 2014), 2.

15. Amnesty International, "Death Penalty," accessed March 1, 2018, https://www.amnesty.org/en/countries/americas/united-states-of-america/report-united-states-of-america/.

16. William J. Stuntz, *The Collapse of American Criminal Justice* (Cambridge, MA: Harvard University Press, 2011), 3.

17. Ta-Nehisi Coates, "The Black Family in the Age of Mass Incarceration," *The Atlantic* (October 2015), 19, https://www.theatlantic.com/magazine/archive/2015/10/the-black-family-in-the-age-of-mass-incarceration/403246/.

18. "Private prisons in the United States incarcerated 126,272 people in 2015, representing 8% of the total state and federal prison population. Since 2000, the number of people housed in private prisons has increased 45%." Sentencing Project, "Private Prisons in the United States" (August 28, 2017), http://www.sentencingproject.org/publications/private-prisons-united-states/.

19. See Stephen J. Pope, "From Condemnation to Conversion: Seeking Restorative Justice in the Prison System," *America* (Nov. 21, 2001): 13–16, at 13, 14.

20. John Tierney, "For Lesser Crimes, Rethinking Life Behind Bars," *New York Times*, December 11, 2012, A24.

21. Jeffrey S. Passel and D'Vera Cohn, Pew Research Center, "Unauthorized Immigrants" (December 6, 2012), www.pewhispanic .org/2012/12/06/unauthorized-immigrants-11-1-million-in-2011.

22. Justiceforimmigrants, "Immigrant Detention in the United States," accessed September 1, 2017, justiceforimmigrants.org/ 2016site/wp-content/uploads/2016/11/immigrant-detention -backgrounder-1-18-17.pdf.

23. "Blocking a Bad Immigration Law," *New York Times*, September 1, 2017, A20.

24. Human Rights First, "Jails and Jumpsuits: Transforming the U.S. Immigration Detention System—a Two-Year Review" (New York: Human Rights First, 2011), i.

25. Meda Chesney-Lind notes that "nearly half the women in the nation's prisons are women of color: notably 27 percent are African American and 17 percent are Hispanic. The number of Latinas incarcerated increased by 65 percent in the first decade of this century, a figure that reflects a general population increase, but also the increasing involvement of the criminal justice system in the criminalization of immigration, as well as policies and practices relating to the war on drugs." Meda Chesney-Lind, "'Remember the Ladies': The Problem with Gender-Neutral Reform," in *To Build A Better Criminal Justice System: 25 Experts Envision the Next 25 Years of Reform*, ed. Marc Mauer and Kate Epstein (Washington, DC: The Sentencing Project, 2012), 42–43, at 42.

26. For critical theological assessment by the National Council of Churches, see *Thinking Theologically about Mass Incarceration: Biblical Foundations and Justice Imperatives*, ed. Antonios Kireopoulos, Mitzi J. Budde, and Matthew D. Lunberg (New York: Paulist Press, 2017).

27. Roger Sullivan, *Immanuel Kant's Moral Theory* (Cambridge, MA: Cambridge University Press, 1989), 243.

28. Cornel West, *Prophesy Deliverance: An Afro-American Revolutionary Christianity* (Philadelphia: Westminster Press, 1982), 61.

29. Coates, "The Black Family in the Age of Mass Incarceration," 30.

30. Coates, "The Black Family in the Age of Mass Incarceration," 32.

31. See Seyla Benhabib, "The Generalized and the Concrete Other: The Kohlberg-Gilligan Controversy and Feminist Theory," in *Feminism as Critique*, ed. Seyla Benhabib and Drucilla Cornell (Minneapolis: University of Minnesota Press, 1987), 87.

32. Hannah Arendt, *The Origins of Totalitarianism* (New York: Harcourt, Brace & World, 1966), 297, 299, 301.

33. M. Shawn Copeland, *Enfleshing Freedom: Body, Race, and Being* (Minneapolis: Fortress Press, 2010), 15.

34. Kathryn Russell, *The Color of Crime* (New York: New York University, 1988), cited in Alexander, *The New Jim Crow*, 107. Coates writes, "Postbellum Alabama solved this problem by manufacturing criminals. Blacks who could not find work were labeled vagrants and sent to jail, where they were leased as labor to the very people who had once enslaved them." "The Black Family in the Age of Mass Incarceration," 31.

35. Alexander, *The New Jim Crow*, 236–44. See also, Ada Maria Isasi-Diaz's analogous *mujerista* critique in *En la Lucha / In the Struggle: A Hispanic Women's Liberation Theology* (Minneapolis: Fortress Press, 1993).

36. Gregory Boyle, *Tattoos on the Heart: The Power of Boundless Compassion* (New York: Free Press, 2010), xiv.

37. United States Conference of Catholic Bishops, "Responsibility, Rehabilitation, and Restoration: A Catholic Perspective on Crime and Criminal Justice" (Washington, DC: USCCB, 2000), 11.

38. Howard Zehr, *The Little Book of Restorative Justice* (Intercourse, PA: Good Books, 2007), 37.

39. See Gerry Johnstone and Daniel W. Van Ness, eds., *Handbook of Restorative Justice* (Portland: Willan Publishing, 2007); Andrew von Hirsch et al., eds., *Restorative Justice and Criminal Justice: Competing or Reconcilable Paradigms?* (Oxford: Hart Publishing, 2003); Gerry Johnstone, ed., *A Restorative Justice Reader* (Portland: Willan Publishing, 2003); Daniel W. Van Ness and Karen Heetderks Strong, *Restoring Justice*, 2nd ed. (Cincinnati, OH: Anderson Publishing, 2002); Howard Zehr, *Changing Lenses:*

A New Focus for Crime and Justice (Scottsdale, PA: Herald Press, 1990).

40. For differing rationales, processes, and programs, see Gerry Johnstone, *Restorative Justice: Ideas, Values, Debates* (Portland: Willan Publishing, 2002), 10–35, 161–71.

41. Desmond Tutu, *No Future without Forgiveness* (London: Rider, 1999), 51. "*Ubuntu*," says Tutu, "speaks of the very essence of being human." It "means my humanity is caught up, is inextricably bound up" in that of others. "We say, 'a person is a person through other people.' It is not 'I think therefore I am.' It says rather: 'I am human because I belong.' I participate, I share" (34–35).

42. James Cone, *Black Theology and Black Power* (Maryknoll, NY: Orbis Books, 1997), 72.

43. See *Pacem in terris*, nos. 28–39, 53–66, 132–41; *Gaudium et spes*, nos. 25, 30; *Dignitatis humanae*, nos. 6–7; *Populorum progressio*, nos. 22–24, 43–75; *Sollicitudo rei socialis*, nos. 38–40. See David Hollenbach, *The Common Good and Christian Ethics* (Cambridge: Cambridge University Press, 2002); Charles Curran, *Catholic Social Teaching: A Historical, Theological, and Ethical Analysis* (Washington, DC: Georgetown University Press, 2002); Kenneth R. Himes, ed., *Modern Catholic Social Teaching: Commentaries and Interpretations* (Washington, DC: Georgetown University Press, 2004).

44. See Walter H. Moberly, *The Ethics of Punishment* (London: Faber and Faber, 1968), 97–98, cited in Johnstone, *Restorative Justice*, 13.

45. Alexander, *The New Jim Crow*, 259.

46. Albert Camus, *The Plague* (New York: Alfred A. Knopf, 1960), 230. See William R. O'Neill, "No Amnesty for Sorrow: The Privilege of the Poor in Christian Social Ethics," *Theological Studies* 55, no. 4 (December 1994): 638–56.

47. See Gene Outka, *Agape* (New Haven, CT: Yale University Press, 1972), 20. See also, Ronald Dworkin, *Taking Rights Seriously* (Cambridge, MA: Harvard University Press, 1978), 227; and Aquinas, *Summae Theologiae* II–II, q. 31, art. 2.

48. Primo Levi, "The Symposium: Primo Levi," in *The Sunflower: On the Possibilities and Limits of Forgiveness*, ed. Simon Wiesenthal, rev. ed. (New York: Schocken Books, 1998), 191.

49. See Zehr, *Changing Lenses*, 197.

50. Commutative justice rectifies the transactions of legal individuals, whether voluntary (e.g., contracts) or involuntary (e.g., crime).

51. Desmond Tutu, *No Future without Forgiveness* (London: Rider, 1999), 51.

52. Simone Weil, "Reflections on the Right Use of School Studies with a View to the Love of God," *Waiting for God*, trans. Emma Craufurd (New York: G. P. Putnam's Sons, 1951), 115.

53. Jean-Marc Éla, "Christianity and Liberation in Africa," in *Paths of African Theology*, 143 (emphasis in original); cf. Laurenti Magesa, "Christ the Liberator and Africa Today," in *Faces of Jesus in Africa*, ed. Robert J. Schreiter (Maryknoll, NY: Orbis Books, 1991), 151–63.

54. "The word most often associated with hospitality in the LXX and the NT is *xenos*, which literally means foreigner, stranger, or even enemy. In its derived sense, however, the term comes to denote both guest and host alike. John Koenig, "Hospitality," in *The Anchor Bible Dictionary*, vol. 3, ed. David Noel Freedman (New York: Doubleday, 1992): 299–301.

55. Boyle, *Tattoos on the Heart*, xiv.

56. See https://www.homeboyindustries.org/why-we-do-it/ (accessed May 11, 2018).

57. Ignatio Ellacuría, "The Crucified People," in *Mysterium Liberationis* (Maryknoll, NY: Orbis Books, 1993), 580–604, trans. P. Berryman and R. Barr from "*El pueblo crucificado, ensayo de soteriologia historica*," in I. Ellacuría et al., *Cruz y resurrección: anuncio de una Iglesia nueva* (Mexico City: CTR, 1978), 49–82.

58. Boyle, *Tattoos on the Heart*, 71; Boyle develops the theme of kinship in *Barking to the Choir: The Power of Radical Kinship* (New York: Simon & Schuster, 2017).

59. Rahner, "On the Question of a Formal Existential Ethics," in *Theological Investigations* 2, trans. Karl H. Kruger (Baltimore: Helicon, 1963), 217–34. See Rahner, "The 'Commandment' of Love in Relation to the Other Commandments," in *Theological Investigations* 5, trans. Karl H. Kruger (New York: Seabury, 1966), 439–59; "Theology of Freedom," in *Theological Investigations* 6, trans. Karl and Boniface Kruger (New York: Seabury, 1974) 178–96; "Reflections on the Unity of the Love of Neighbour and the Love of God," in *Theological Investigations* 6, 231–49, at 240.

60. Bryan Massingale, *Racial Justice and the Catholic Church* (Maryknoll, NY: Orbis Books, 2010).

61. Gustavo Gutiérrez, "Toward a Theology of Liberation," in *Liberation Theology: A Documentary History*, 62–76, at 74.

CHAPTER 12

Lutheran and Catholic Hopes for Eucharistic Sharing

OPPORTUNITIES AND OBSTACLES

H. Ashley Hall

In 2016, something remarkable happened at the Churchwide Assembly of the Evangelical Lutheran Church in America (ELCA).[1] The Most Rev. Denis Madden, auxiliary bishop of the Archdiocese of Baltimore and cochair of the Lutheran–Roman Catholic dialogue in the United States, was invited to the podium by Bishop Elizabeth Eaton, the presiding bishop of the ELCA. Bishop Eaton presented Bishop Madden with a chalice; upon receiving it, Bishop Madden lifted the chalice into the air, declaring "I will wait for that day, not a long time in coming, I am sure, when we can share this chalice of the precious blood together. God has work for us to do as a body to bring Christ to the world. We can spread that word, we can share with joy those who know nothing of Jesus Christ."[2]

The context of such an extraordinary statement was the overwhelming approval of the Churchwide Assembly of *Declaration on the Way: Church, Ministry, and Eucharist*.[3] The *Declaration* is itself a survey of over fifty years of official bilateral dialogue on both a national and international level between Lutherans and Roman Catholics. Thirty-two points of consensus and convergence between the two communions are identified and described.

248

The title is indicative of the hope that, in outlining such consensus on these three central realities (church, ministry, and Eucharist), Lutherans and Roman Catholics are "on the way" to manifest unity at the altar. The document is now under consideration for wider approval by the Lutheran World Federation (LWF) and the Pontifical Council for Promoting Christian Unity (PCPCU).

There is much to commend the gesture of hope for eucharistic fellowship between Bishops Eaton and Madden and the people of the churches they serve. In 2013, the *Declaration on the Way* was preceded by *From Conflict to Communion*, which was issued by the Vatican and the LWF.[4] This document outlines the theological consensus by which Lutherans and Roman Catholics are able (even encouraged) to commemorate together the 500th anniversary of the Reformation. *From Conflict to Communion (FCTC)* is divided into six parts: the basis for commemorating the Reformation in an ecumenical age; new perspectives on Martin Luther; a shared account of the Reformation conflict; the basic themes of Luther's reformation in light of the last fifty years of Lutheran–Roman Catholic dialogue; a justification for a common commemoration of the Reformation; five ecumenical imperatives for moving forward; and finally, an appendix of resources.

Concomitant to *FCTC*'s urging for joint commemoration, a liturgy for *Common Prayer* was drafted and encouraged for use by Lutherans and Roman Catholics worldwide.[5] Indeed, in October of 2016, *Common Prayer* provided the liturgy for Pope Francis's visit to Lund, Sweden, where, with Bishop Munib Younan (President of the LWF), they led a joint commemoration to inaugurate the anniversary year. The emphasis within *FCTC* (and affirmed in the *Common Prayer*) is to present the Reformation as a story that is told together and told in a spirit of mutual repentance and reconciliation. The Reformation is, therefore, not so much "celebrated"—in which each side triumphalistically presents itself as simultaneously innocent victim and God-appointed victor—but "commemorated" in a spirit of thanksgiving for the reconciliation that has occurred and in hope that as the two communions have moved *from* conflict they might also be Spirit-led *toward* communion.

Therefore, one may rightly argue that the greatest ecumenical reconciliation in the last fifty years has been between Lutherans (the largest Protestant denomination in the world) and Roman

Catholics (the largest Christian denomination in the world). Two international agreements have moved the two churches toward a greater visible unity and concrete reconciliation at an institutional level. The first is the *Joint Declaration on the Doctrine of Justification* (*JDDJ*) (1999), which declared that the divisive issue of the sixteenth century is no longer a "church dividing issue."[6] The second is the previously mentioned *From Conflict to Communion*, affirming that Lutherans and Roman Catholics must move forward with a perspective of real and substantial unity and not division. With an eye to where this social reconciliation between two separated Christian communions might be heading, this essay will outline the process of dialogue and the principles of reconciliation that have allowed us to reach this point. In gesturing to the future, it will also be necessary to discuss the single greatest obstacle to this reconciliation: the issue of women's ordination. Here we reach the most profound paradox related to Lutheran–Roman Catholic reconciliation: according to the official teaching documents of both sides, many of the historical doctrinal conflicts that have divided Lutherans and Roman Catholics are no longer church dividing; rather, issues that have developed *since* the Reformation (the most neuralgic being the ordination of women) present obstacles to reunion.

The Eucharist

The restoration of eucharistic fellowship is the focus of Roman Catholic–Lutheran ecumenical work today. Lutheran–Roman Catholic dialogue on both the national (1968 and 1970) and international (1978) levels turned to the Eucharist as a topic quite early and noted remarkable consensus.[7] Such consensus is reflected in the common articles described in the *Declaration on the Way* (nos. 27–32) and *From Conflict to Communion* (nos. 140–61).

It is worth noting, however, that differences over the Eucharist were not the cause of historical division. Rather, the fracturing of eucharistic fellowship was the result of divergence on other issues of doctrine and praxis. To establish the theological foundation for unity and the hopes of eucharistic sharing, we can briefly outline the major points of convergence. First, there never has been a fundamental disagreement between Lutherans and Roman Catholics about what the Eucharist is: the true body and blood of Jesus Christ who makes himself sacramentally yet really present in the bread and wine. *FCTC* states, "Lutherans and Catholics can together affirm the real presence of Jesus Christ in the Lord's Supper: 'In the Sacrament of the Lord's Supper Jesus Christ true God and true man, is present wholly and entirely, in his Body and Blood, under the sign of bread and wine.'"[8] In this regard, Lutherans stand apart from other Protestants in the unambiguous affirmation of a real, objective presence and a change in the elements.[9] This shared, consistent affirmation by both churches is a justification for a generous measure of hope for the restoration of eucharistic sharing.

Historically, the most significant doctrinal conflict concerning the Eucharist was Martin Luther's rejection of the term *transubstantiation*. But in rejecting the term, the Lutheran tradition was not rejecting the reality the term attempted to affirm (i.e., the real presence). Indeed, Luther's arguments against *transubstantiation* were that the term—while clearly and emphatically describing a change in the elements of bread and wine—was inadequate in capturing the mode of Christ's presence. In order to affirm the real presence in a way consistent with orthodox Christology, Luther suggested that it was better to use the concept of a *sacramental union*, in which the bread and wine remain while the true body and blood of Christ adhere "in, with, and under" the elements (in the same way that the divine nature of the Logos did not eliminate the substance of Christ's humanity).[10] While the appropriate terminology was a point of contention, there are two things to note: first, the cause of this conflict is rooted in a shared value (namely, to preserve and defend the real presence and a change in the elements); second, Luther was not initiating a criticism so much as participating in the larger late-medieval Christian humanist criticism of Scholastic methodology and jargon. The Council of Trent definitively settled the question of terminology for those Christian humanists who were Roman Catholic.[11]

The primary differences between Lutherans and Roman Catholics are not found in what the Eucharist *is*, but around eucharistic practices. These include the following: reception of both kinds (i.e., bread and wine) in the Mass; the appropriateness of reserving the host for adoration (e.g., Corpus Christi parades); and the extent to which the Mass should be described as a sacrifice the priest makes to God or that Christ makes to his people. While my description has relegated these differences of praxis to a status of importance lower than the importance of the doctrine of the Eucharist itself, it cannot be concluded that these differences were trivial or inconsequential. In that time, the debate over the retention or reform of those practices was neuralgic, as they reflected the lived experience of devout Christians in the parish. With the passing of time and subsequent reforms (e.g., those ushered in by the Second Vatican Council or the liturgical renewal in Lutheran communities), the modern viewer might be tempted to cast a dismissive eye to zealousness with which the faithful of previous centuries quarreled over these issues. Even in the sixteenth century there were calls from both Roman Catholics and Lutherans to treat these matters as *adiaphora* (i.e., things neither commanded nor forbidden) and therefore calling forth mutual toleration. However, we should also not neglect the fact that the consequence of these debates helped to reinforce previous patterns of liturgy or reshape new ones. The conclusions become markers of identity around which groups will coalesce or react against. They help form the basis of divided communities, their identities, and markers of deeply held convictions.

At the risk of offering an inexcusably sweeping generalization, it can be said that—while significant—these differences were not insurmountable. Various interims initiated by the imperial diets of the Holy Roman Empire in the 1520s through the 1540s, allowed for the toleration of these varied practices (not to mention the toleration of married clergy!) in anticipation of an ecumenical council. Once solidified in the confessionalization of Europe and the institutionalization of a bi-confessional Holy Roman Empire in the Peace of Augsburg (1555), these diverse eucharistic practices become markers of conflicting Christian identity. And yet significant developments within both the Lutheran and Roman Catholic traditions have moved them closer together. The confessional renewal among Lutherans in the late nineteenth century, the liturgical renewal of both traditions in the early twentieth century, and the reforms of the Second Vatican Council have made all these issues around eucharistic praxis and piety either moot or noncontroversial. So while these divisions were significant in their time and can remain a distinctive element in practice today, these particular issues are not church dividing.[12]

The Practice of Dialogue and Reconciliation

The previous section, outlining the doctrinal consensus and reconciled differences on the Eucharist, documents the basis for a reasonable hope for visible unity at the altar between Lutherans and Roman Catholics. That is, in approving the conclusions of the previously mentioned ecumenical documents, both churches—at the highest and most official level—are affirming that the unity implied in the sharing of the Eucharist is built upon a foundation of explicit consensus on concrete doctrines and practices. Moreover, this consensus has not been reached in a momentary zeal (e.g., the 500th anniversary of the Reformation) or due to particular circumstances or personalities (e.g., the realities of religious life in the United States or the congeniality of Pope Francis). Instead, it is the process of nearly sixty years of sustained, intense, and intentional dialogue on an international level.

The already mentioned affirmation bears repeating because the reconciliation achieved to date is precisely under attack from critics who argue that such agreements are the result of rhetorical magic employed to create an ecumenical Potemkin village. One may legitimately argue that the consensus reached is insufficient for full reconciliation at the altar. Often, however, critics of these ecumenical agreements go further by attacking the legitimacy of the consensus statements themselves, often because these critics fail to understand (or appreciate) the method of ecumenical dialogue. In particular, a certain polemical stance views reconciliation through the lens of *repentance and recapitulation*, in which one side admits fault (or, primary fault or error) and appeals for a return to the good graces of the aggrieved party; the aggrieved party in turn responds with a Christian *noblesse oblige*. Under this way of thinking, the goal of ecumenical dialogue is to convince the other party of its error and to convert the other to one's own position, leading the heretical/schismatic party to repent and return "to the fold." This method amounts to a zero-sum game. For Lutherans of this polemical persuasion, this would mean that Roman Catholics should accept that their positions on the papacy, justification, ecclesiology, and certain pious practices are simply wrong and should be rooted out, essentially making the Roman Catholic Church now "Lutheran." Alternatively, for Roman Catholics of this polemical persuasion, this would mean that Lutherans would have to admit the error of their positions related to these controversial matters, essentially dissolving the Lutheran Church into the Roman Catholic Church. To be sure, the historical record of the sixteenth century presents us with theologians on both sides who advocated this view (e.g., Johann Eck and Jerome Emser on the Catholic side; Nicolaus von Amsdorf and Matthias Flacius Illyricus on the Lutheran side).

Yet the ecumenical dialogue of the last sixty years has taken an alternative model from the sixteenth century. Instead of seeking conversion and recapitulation, it has sought *mutual repentance and reconciled diversity*. Some conflicts within Christianity are simply irreconcilable. But among traditions that are close to one another (e.g., Roman Catholic/Orthodox; Roman Catholic/Lutheran), the differences may be real but no longer church dividing. This awareness of reconciled diversity often comes with the passing of time, after which (as mentioned earlier) the neuralgic issues are no longer so sensitive. There are moments where doctrinal controversy can be viewed from a point of shared conviction despite differing emphases. There are situations in which once church-dividing issues now pale in light of the diversity of thought tolerated within a particular tradition. In these instances, the goal of a dialogue is not to convince to but understand and (where possible) appreciate. In these instances, each party continues to hold the other accountable while also taking responsibility for one's own actions. In these instances, reconciliation is not only possible, it is morally imperative for those who seek to manifest the unity they already share in Christ. When the purpose and process of these ecumenical dialogues are appreciated, alongside the conclusions of these dialogues, then one can no longer dismiss them as a warm, fuzzy ecumenism that wants to forget the past. Rather, the documents in question here articulate an ecumenism that has made peace with the past and is oriented toward the future.

As one final prologue to examining modern Lutheran–Roman Catholic dialogue and to provide a brief historical example of the previously mentioned "alternative model" from the Reformation period, it should be noted that the first efforts at reconciliation occurred already in the sixteenth century. In 1530, Lutheran and Roman Catholic theologians met at an imperial diet under the auspices of Holy Roman Emperor Charles V. Weeks of dialogue around controversial topics rendered remarkable consensus; many bishops were agreeable to the draft of articles. However, full agreement could not be reached. The Lutherans presented their confession of faith (the *Augsburg Confession*). The Roman Catholic theologians responded with a *Confutation to the Augsburg Confession*, to which Lutherans wrote an *Apology to the Augsburg Confession*.[13] While reunion evaded participants, the *Augsburg Confession* and its *Apology* had the effect of uniting the Lutheran territories under an authoritative theological summary and are now included in the Lutheran Confessions. These two major texts of the Lutheran Confessions were formed in close dialogue with Roman Catholics. These same two documents have also repeatedly served as the basis of subsequent Lutheran–Roman Catholic dialogue. In 1541, another attempt to reach consensus, this time on the doctrine of justification, was held at Regensburg. Again Lutheran and Roman Catholic delegates reached remarkable consensus on the issue. Nevertheless, the proposed agreement failed, not because the wording was insufficient, but because neither side trusted that the other actually believed the words each had agreed to.[14] In this case the reconciled diversity achieved on the page did not reflect a true reconciliation of practice or emphasis when each side was deeply distrustful of the other's intention and sincerity.

The Principles of Dialogue and Reconciliation

The substantive ecumenical dialogues of the modern period between Lutherans and Roman Catholics began immediately after the Second Vatican Council. The Americans were the first to hold an official dialogue, starting in 1965. Though certainly not exhaustive, one can identify seven general principles for ecumenical dialogue.

First, the goal of any ecumenical dialogue is full and visible unity, especially around the eucharistic table. Every dialogue among separated Christians presumes the unity already shared in the person and work of Jesus Christ. While some traditions in ecumenical dialogue may be closer or farther apart, dialogue is imperative and the separation (no matter how justified) is a scandal. In the words of *Unitatis Redintegratio*, "Division [among Christians] openly contradicts the will of Christ, scandalizes the world, and damages the holy cause of preaching the Gospel to every creature."[15]

Second, each dialogue partner must be authentically themselves—that is, they must honestly reflect the diversity of thought within their communion on particular issues and must also be able to set personal opinions and preferences aside in describing the doctrines and practices of their church. This is true even when such teachings or practices are uncomfortable for the dialogue partner (though the goal cannot be to cause offense).[16]

Third, very early in the process of a bilateral dialogue between churches, there must be an effort to build an intentional community among dialogue partners. Here trust, vulnerability, speaking the truth in love, and the ability to bear one another's burdens is emphasized.[17] This takes time and sustained commitment. Fourth, while the purpose of dialogue is full, visible unity, the goal should not be conversion of the other (as stated earlier). Rather, the goal is mutual affirmation of ministries and ministers that would allow for eucharistic sharing—based on the previously established mutual recognition of baptism in each communion.

Fifth, the goal of the dialogue should be to affirm common statements on a topic. Sometimes that is easier, sometimes it is harder. To that end, there has been a noteworthy shift in the way the results of ecumenical dialogues have been produced. In the early days, there were short, common statements and then select, substantive academic papers or studies from dialogue participants on the topic.[18] In the present (Round XII) and three previous rounds of Lutheran–Roman Catholic dialogues, the common statements have become far more substantial, reflecting and emphasizing a consensus reached and vision shared. The task of a response from each side to the brief, common statement has moved to a drafting committee formed from members of each side who draft a common text for the review of the dialogue team and cochairs.[19]

Sixth, while the emphasis is on unity (what can be said together about a topic), of course differences exist. Here, the goal—where possible—is the possibility of a *reconciled diversity* or a *differentiated consensus*. This concept can be oversimplified, resulting in a "you're OK, I'm OK" approach to justify continued separations. However, properly understood, a reconciled diversity acknowledges (where possible) shared convictions that endure despite contrasting practices or perspectives.[20] The differences among Lutherans and Roman Catholics mentioned previously can serve as a good illustration of this. Sometimes we see that our diversity is, to borrow from comedian Mike Myers, the result of putting the "em*phasis* on a different syll*able*." So, for example, while Lutherans and Roman Catholics disagree on eucharistic adoration or Corpus Christi parades, Lutherans can acknowledge and affirm the notion of the real presence that undergirds such practices. Likewise, Roman Catholics can acknowledge the Lutheran concerns about historic abuses that prevent Lutherans from embracing these practices, and even acknowledge that those practices are not necessary to affirm a belief in the real presence.

Finally, where possible and concomitant with an appreciation for reconciled diversity, differences ought to be framed as an *exchange of gifts*.[21] The challenge and the opportunity presented here is to see in the other—even if practices diverge—a faithful foundation for his or her behavior. These are sometimes framed as "mutual affirmations and admonitions." A good illustration can be taken from chapter 4 of the *Joint Declaration*, "Explicating the Common Understanding of Justification." In addressing seven historically contentious topics related to justification (e.g., sin, sanctification, assurance of salvation, etc.) the chapter begins each subsection with a common statement, then continues, "Catholics affirm...but acknowledge from the Lutheran position..." and then "Lutherans affirm...but acknowledge from the Catholic position...." In this way, not only is the nature of the reconciled diversity articulated, a more nuanced consensus from the concerns of the other is both acknowledged and affirmed.

If we now turn to search for what these principles look like in practice, we might turn again to process and conclusions modeled by *From Conflict to Communion*. First, *FCTC* begins with honesty. The document is a frank assessment of historic realities and theological differences; it does not paper over either past or continuing disagreements. Its more substantial contributions, however, are in the characteristics that follow. The second characteristic is that the document models how to speak with integrity about our unique traditions and differences while remembering the imperative to explain our neighbor's actions in the kindest possible way. It is impossible to read the text without a growing awareness that the theological realities and necessities of the church today call us out of the polemical trenches of the past. Third, the document concludes with an articulated common mission and urgent witness to the Lord Jesus Christ; such that two churches—once so sharply divided—now see a common future and articulate a common path into the future God has prepared for us.

Likewise, the document calls for greater unity amid three new realities since the Reformation. The first is the *reality of an ecumenical age*. At no other time in history have the various denominations of Christianity engaged in not only serious theological dialogue but have done so with humility and with the goal of reconciling, not converting. It is simply not possible, if we wish to act with sincerity and in accord with the fruits of Spirit, to celebrate the 500th anniversary of the Reformation in a triumphal, polemical tone.

The second is the reality of the *global church*. To a certain extent, the church has always been global in scope. But the document names a particular missionary imperative: that we must do all that we can so that Lutherans and Roman Catholics in general, and in the growing, vibrant churches of the southern hemisphere in particular, are not burdened by the unresolved theological conflicts of the past. As paragraph 10 of *FCTC* affirms, "These churches do not easily see the confessional conflicts of the sixteenth century as their own conflicts, even if they are connected to the churches of Europe and North America…and share with them a common doctrinal basis."

The third and final reality presents a common challenge: the *increasing secularization* of European and American society in a post-Christian age and the *rise of new religious movements* (nos. 11–15). The problem of secularization can be partially addressed by demonstrating our visible unity and by demonstrating the power of the gospel and the work of the Holy Spirit to help Christians resolve their differences and work toward the work Jesus gave us to do. We are yoked in the new evangelism and therefore must act with sincerity and mutual respect so that perhaps "they may see your good works and give glory to your Father in heaven" (Matt 5:16).

Obstacles

The fact that such remarkable consensus on fundamental doctrines has been so thoroughly and broadly articulated is inspiring. So, too, is the expression of profound hope and real joy among Lutherans and Roman Catholics as to where this articulated consensus might lead us faithfully into the future church. However, there is very good reason to be cautious, even doubtful, about the possibility of an institutional reconciliation in the near future. But it is not the differences of the sixteenth century that divide us. Today, we are divided on contemporary issues: women's ordination and human sexuality (especially regarding the inclusion of men and women who are openly homosexual and in homosexual relationships). We do not have consensus here, in part because we do not have consensus in our own communions. The level of trust and vulnerability is simply not there to discuss these issues among ourselves—how can we hope to have a fruitful conversation across denominations? Are we not guilty of the same sin exhibited in 1530 and 1541, where an articulated consensus is possible, but we simply do not trust that our opponent means what they say or will not interpret it in a way that we find unacceptable?

For the purposes of this essay, I wish to focus on women's ordination. The differences over the ordination of women to holy orders must be set in the wider context of remaining differences between Lutherans and Roman Catholics on ordained ministry.

FCTC has reviewed the bulk of international dialogue on the subject and again found that substantial agreement exists on what ordained ministry is and what the ordained ministry does; they have even outlined the "reconciled diversity" and "exchange of gifts" possible on controversial issues (like the papacy).[22] *While there is profound agreement on what the ordained ministry is and what the ordained ministry does, there is no agreement on who may hold the office.* According to Roman Catholic doctrine, women are forbidden from the ordained ministry not as a choice by the church but, according to *Ordinatio Sacerdotalis*, because by the will of our Lord, the church has no authority to ordain women.[23] Whereas the ordination of a male Lutheran pastor can be considered valid but illicit because the sacrament was carried out by a bishop not in union with Rome (an administrative issue), the ordination of a female Lutheran pastor—from the current Roman Catholic point of view—is not only illicit but also invalid, since women are incapable of carrying the sacramental character of ordination.

It is clear, then, that this is as yet an insurmountable obstacle to eucharistic sharing. From the official Roman Catholic point of view, any Eucharist a male Lutheran pastor celebrates lacks the manifestation of full unity in the church—but that can be fixed. Any Eucharist a female Lutheran pastor celebrates is in fact no Eucharist at all. Moreover, one can see how this is simply an immovable issue: it would be impossible for Roman Catholics to say, "You can go to Communion in a Lutheran Church—as long as a male priest presides." Of course, there are Lutheran communions that also reject the ordination of women (e.g., the Lutheran Church-Missouri Synod), but they are not signatories on the major ecumenical breakthroughs (*JDDJ*, *FCTC*) that have made the hope of eucharistic sharing possible. Is it not possible for the two sides to just "dialogue" about it? Well, that will be most difficult under the current circumstances, as both communions have declared the issue closed and settled. Roman Catholics have a magisterial moratorium on the question, and Lutherans have said women's ordination is valid and we are not rehashing those arguments again.

Conclusion

So why continue to seek reconciliation? Why face these challenges with determination and dedication? Well, the "Declaration on the Way" itself gestures to some answers: because the gospel has power over sin and guilt; because the Lord frees us from our limitations; and because the Holy Spirit transforms our complacency and ignorance. When considered in this way, the document leads us to share a *common story*—a story that is really about the love of God made manifest in the grace of Jesus Christ historically and sacramentally in the church. Consider the power of the unified and unifying proclamation in a world that is not asking, "Should I be a Lutheran or a Roman Catholic?" but asking, "Why be Christian at all?"

It is a profound reality that—amid such an apparently insurmountable challenge like the ordination of women—both sides expect the dialogue to continue and have taken many public efforts to lift up the conclusions of the dialogue on this 500th Anniversary of the Reformation. As Lutherans and Roman Catholics, we move forward because of our shared history and core theological convictions. Moreover, we move forward not "in spite" of our differences (as if to forget or dismiss them) but "in the midst of" our differences—we are frank about who we are and where we sense the Spirit leading us. Our two traditions share a theological pattern language and deep instinct toward the incarnation and sacramental expression of the Christian faith. To be very clear, dialogue between the two traditions is done with integrity and honesty; it is not about "forgetting the past" or our current differences but reframing and rearticulating the past for the sake of the future. Through their shared baptism in Christ Jesus, Lutherans and Roman Catholics share a common calling, a common discipleship. Jesus speaks of the difficulty and danger of looking back once one has placed hands on the plow (Luke 9:62). How much more difficult is it, then, when two disciples cannot agree where to lead the oxen? Thus we are called to be reconciled (Luke 17:3; Heb 12:14) and to be diligent in seeking reconciliation (Matt 5:24). It is a reality of human life (which is to say, a reality of the church) that divisions and strife occur. Sometimes these divisions necessitate separation. At the same time, it is the mission of the church to be the instrument of God's own reconciliation. The gospel declares that through Jesus Christ, God and humanity are reconciled. Those who follow Christ are called to make manifest the same work of reconciliation in and through the Holy Spirit, even with our enemies. If Christians are not zealous for this task, how can the church expect others to believe the gospel it preaches?

To that end, let this essay conclude on a hopeful note. Aware of the conclusions of the dialogue—while they have been vetted by gifted theologians from around the world and received the highest endorsements from the teaching authorities in each communion—the framers of *FCTC* also crafted two documents: the first is a *Common Prayer* service to gather Lutherans and Roman Catholics together in a time of intentional prayer in mutual repentance, reconciliation, and thanksgiving for the unity we share—even as female clergy will help lead those celebrations. Second, an official *Study Guide* was created to help express these conclusions of the dialogue in a way that opens local dialogue between Lutherans and Roman Catholics in parishes around the world. We may hope that this call to common prayer and call to common conversation is the seed by which—through God's inscrutable and beneficent will—eucharistic sharing will someday become a reality. It is a difficult story to tell, but it is ultimately a joyful story to proclaim, and it is a faithful vision of the Body of Christ in the world. May we say with St. Paul, "All this is from God, who reconciled us to himself through Christ, and has given us the ministry of reconciliation" (2 Cor 5:18).

Reflection Questions

1. How is the ability to "tell the story together" a necessary condition for reconciliation? Why is this so? What stories are still too sensitive to tell in a mutually accountable way in the life of the church?
2. What role does "authenticity" play in reconciliation? Where are the opportunities and tension points in being both authentic to self/community and open to difference?
3. What are the opportunities and challenges presented

by a search for "reconciled diversity" in the work of reconciliation? What conditions are necessary to see our continued differences as "an exchange of gifts"?

4. This chapter addresses how some of the historical theological differences are no longer church dividing among some Christians, but the conflict over modern concerns (in this case, the role of women in church hierarchy) perpetuates old (or causes new) divisions. Are there other areas where it is not our past but new realities that hinder reconciliation with our neighbors and enemies?

Notes

1. The Evangelical Lutheran Church in America is (at roughly 4 million members) the largest Lutheran Church in the United States and member of the Lutheran World Federation. The Churchwide Assembly is the highest legislative body of the ELCA, meeting every three years.

2. See "Assembly: On the Way," *Living Lutheran* (August 31, 2016), https://www.livinglutheran.org/2016/08/assembly-on-the-way/.

3. *Declaration on the Way: Church, Ministry, and Eucharist* (Minneapolis: Augsburg Fortress, 2015). The document was drafted by a team of Lutheran and Roman Catholic theologians: Denis Madden (cochair), Mark Hanson (cochair); Brian Daley, SJ; Jared Wicks, SJ; Susan Wood, SCL; John Crossin, OSFS; Kathryn Johnson; William Rusch; Joy Schroeder; and Don McCoid. The impetus for such a summary was a suggestion by Kurt Cardinal Koch, who expressed hope that the 500th anniversary of the Reformation in 2017 might provide a survey of the progress made so far. The *Declaration on the Way* was approved by the Churchwide Assembly (by a vote of 931 to 9) in August of 2016, and the Committee on Ecumenical and Interreligious Affairs of the United States Conference of Catholic Bishops in October 2015.

4. *From Conflict to Communion* (Leipzig: Evangelische Verlagsanstalt, 2013); also available on the websites of the LWF and PCPCU. *From Conflict to Communion* was drafted by an international team of theologians (the Lutheran–Roman Catholic Commission on Unity)

in anticipation of the 500th Anniversary of the Reformation in 2017.

5. *Common Prayer* is available in subsequent editions of *From Conflict to Communion* (see the 4th rev. and expanded ed., 2016) and on the website of the LWF, accessed May 11, 2018, https://www.lutheranworld.org/content/joint-common-prayer-lutheran-catholic-common-commemoration-reformation-2017.

6. *Joint Declaration on the Doctrine of Justification* (Grand Rapids, MI: Wm. B. Eerdmans, 2000), accessed May 11, 2018, http://www.vatican.va/roman_curia/pontifical_councils/chrstuni/documents/rc_pc_chrstuni_doc_31101999_cath-luth-joint-declaration_en.html. Since being promulgated by the Vatican and LWF, other Christian denominations have adopted the declaration: The World Methodist Council (2006) and the World Communion of Reformed Churches (2017).

7. In 1978, the international dialogue produced a report on *The Eucharist: Final Report of the Joint Roman Catholic/Lutheran Commission*, available online at http://www.prounione.urbe.it/dia-int/l-rc/doc/e_l-rc_eucharist.html.

8. *From Conflict to Communion*, no. 154. The text offers a quotation from *The Eucharist*, no. 16.

9. *From Conflict to Communion*, no. 153, which in turn cites *The Eucharist*: "The Lutheran-Roman Catholic dialogue on the Eucharist was able to state: 'The Lutheran tradition affirms the Catholic tradition that the consecrated elements do not simply remain bread and wine but rather by the power of the creative word are given as the body and blood of Christ. In this sense, Lutherans could also occasionally speak, as does the Greek tradition, of a change' (Eucharist 51). Both Catholics and Lutherans 'have in common a rejection of a spatial or natural manner of presence, and a rejection of an understanding of the sacrament as only commemorative or figurative' (Eucharist 16)."

10. For a summary description of this position, see *From Conflict to Communion*, no. 143.

11. Council of Trent, thirteenth session (1551), chap. 4. See Heinrich Denzinger, *Enchiridion Symbolorum: Compendium of Creeds, Definitions, and Declarations on Matters of Faith and Morals*, ed. Robert Fastiggi and Anne Englund Nash, 42nd ed. (San Francisco: Ignatius Press, 2012) 394–95.

12. The reader will find greater detail of what is summarized in this paragraph in *From Conflict to Communion*, nos. 146–52, 157–61.

13. In these three texts, which are intentionally in conversation with each other, the reader can trace the areas of consensus, near-consensus, and conflict. For the *Augsburg Confession*, see Robert Kolb and Timothy J. Wengert, eds., *The Book of Concord: The Confessions of the Evangelical Lutheran Church* (Minneapolis: Fortress Press, 2000), 27–105; the *Apology to the Augsburg Confession*, Kolb and Wengert, *The Book of Concord*, 107–294. For the *Confutation of the Augsburg Confession*, see Robert Kolb and James A. Nestingen, eds., *Sources and Contexts of the Book of Concord* (Minneapolis: Fortress Press, 2001), 105–39.

14. Namely, though consensus statements about Creation, the fall, sin, and justification were reached, the Roman Catholic party implicitly understood papal primacy as the means by which God's grace was made efficacious in the world, a position Lutherans rejected. By this point in time, trust in and from both sides of the conflict had eroded and the participants were too far apart on the papacy and the pace of reform. See Peter Matheson, *Cardinal Contarini at Regensburg* (Oxford: Clarendon Press, 1972).

15. *Unitatis Redintegratio* (Decree on Ecumenism) (1964), no. 1.

16. E.g., in the meetings of the U.S. Lutheran–Roman Catholic dialogue, Mass is said alternatively according to each tradition. All of the participants of dialogue attend each other's Mass. In doing so, the participants reinforce their shared commitment to sacramental grace and common liturgical tradition; both experience the pain of fractured unity in that the participants cannot receive the Eucharist together. In saying the Mass, each party must be authentic to itself. In doing so, there may be elements that also prevent the full participation of the other. For instance, in the Roman Mass, the confession ("I confess to almighty God and to you my brothers and sisters...") presents no obstacles for Lutheran participation, until the lines "...and I ask the blessed Mary, ever virgin, and all the angels and saints...to pray for me to the Lord our God"—as the invocation of the saints was precisely a controversial matter in the Reformation. In this case we simply have a matter of difference (perhaps even conflict) when one party is authentic to itself, though no intentional offense is caused. This would stand in contrast to an act insisted by one

party as an intentional means toward excluding the other (e.g., a purely hypothetical case in which a Roman Catholic cochair would insist that each session began with reciting the rosary).

17. For a moving and thought-provoking description of this, see Margaret O'Gara, "Friendship in the Ecumenical Movement: Its Theological Significance," in *No Turning Back: The Future of Ecumenism*, ed. Michael Vertin (Collegeville, MN: Liturgical Press, 2014), 28–41.

18. As an example, see the previously mentioned *Eucharist and Ministry: Lutherans and Catholics in Dialogue* (Round IV), ed. Paul C. Empie and T. Austin Murphy (Minneapolis: Augsburg Publishing House, 1970). The document begins with "Common Observations on Eucharistic Ministry" (7–16), then reflections from each side (17–33), then twelve more chapters (forming the substance of this 325-page book) dealing with various biblical, historical, and systematic issues related to the dialogue and providing citation for the positions held by each side.

19. See, e.g., Lowell G. Almen and Richard Sklba, eds., *The Hope of Eternal Life: Lutherans and Catholics in Dialogue* (Round XI) (Minneapolis: Lutheran University Press, 2011).

20. See Harding Meyer, *That All May Be One: Perceptions and Models of Ecumenicity* (Grand Rapids, MI: Wm. B. Eerdmans, 1999); and Ola Tjøhom, *Visible Church, Visible Unity: Ecumenical Ecclesiology and the Great Tradition* (Collegeville, MN: Liturgical Press, 2004). Tjøhom (ibid., 85) articulates five characteristics of reconciled diversity that are helpful: reconciled diversity (1) embraces both basic agreement and remaining differences; (2) presupposes a differentiation between church-dividing and nondividing issues; (3) makes clear that these differences are not reduced to merely different perspectives but as an approach to be applied to each article of faith; (4) acknowledges the validity of one's own tradition while recognizing the validity of other expressions of faith; and (5) gestures not only to doctrinal agreement but also aims at a common Christian life together.

21. See Margaret O'Gara, *The Ecumenical Gift Exchange* (Collegeville, MN: Liturgical Press), 1998.

22. Nos. 162–94 (pp. 61–71).

23. See *Ordinatio Sacerdotalis* (1994), https://w2.vatican.va/content/john-paul-ii/en/apost_letters/1994/documents/hf_jp-ii_apl_19940522_ordinatio-sacerdotalis.html. Also see *Inter Insigniores* (1976), http://www.vatican.va/roman_curia/congregations/cfaith/documents/rc_con_cfaith_doc_19761015_inter-insigniores_en.html.

CHAPTER 13

Memoria Passionis as Social Reconciliation in Eastern Africa

REMEMBERING THE FUTURE AT MAISON SHALOM

Emmanuel M. Katongole

Maggy Barankitse's Dangerous Memory

In a testimony before Pope Francis, Lutheran bishop Mounib Younan, president of the Lutheran World Federation, and other dignitaries gathered at the joint prayer service to commemorate the 500th anniversary of the Lutheran Reformation (Sweden, November 2, 2016), Maggy Barankitse speaks about the victory of love over hatred. Reminding her listeners that the first crazy man was Jesus, she invites the audience to accept the unique vocation of love and to be "crazy for love."[1] The winner of the 2008 Opus Prize, the 2016 Aurora Prize for Awakening Humanity, and numerous other awards, Maggy has been described in many ways: as the "Mother Teresa of Africa," as a "crazy woman," and as the "Mother of Burundi." But since 2015, the mother of the nation lives exiled from her native county of Burundi, a victim of political persecution and now a refugee herself in Rwanda. Here, at the outskirts of Kigali, she works with Burundian refugees, setting up Maison Shalom Rwanda and building an Oasis of Peace—a regional center for peace and reconciliation in the Great Lakes Region.

Maggy's Burundian government has done all it can to kill her dream. They tried to kill her. They closed the headquarters of Maison Shalom. They shut down all of Maison Shalom's programs: the hospital, radio station, microfinance credit union, and other programs that sustained the local community of Ruyigi. They confiscated Maison Shalom's bank accounts and killed some of the children at Maison Shalom. Despite it all, Maggy retains her fundamental confidence: evil will never have the last word and love always wins.

What is the basis of this confidence? What drives this "crazy woman" and her relentless dedication to the refugees and the victims of Africa's power struggles, the poor, the marginalized, and the vanquished of history? What keeps her going amid so much loss, opposition, and so many threats to her personal security? What gives her confidence that evil will never have the last word? The simple answer is love. "I am a Christian," she notes, "and as Christian, I know that our human vocation is to love."[2] Elsewhere, as she notes, "love is not only our identity; it is our unique vocation....Love is the most beautiful calling of human beings. We are created out of love and to love."[3] But true as that answer no doubt is, it does not get to the heart of what drives Maggy, and how she discovered this noble vocation of love, which she seeks to realize in its full personal, social, and political dimensions. Neither does it explain why that vocation pushes her to identify with the poor, the suffering, and forgotten in Africa, nor how she is able to sustain the tenderness of that love on a daily basis amidst the ongoing realities of violence and hatred.

A great part of the answer to these questions—and in fact the key to Maggy's efforts of social reconciliation in Burundi and beyond—lies in her exercise of dangerous memory. The memory of remembered suffering, according to the German political theologian Johannes Baptist Metz, can be and is "dangerous." For unlike the memory that "bathes everything from the past in a soft, consoling light," this kind of memory can "unleash new dangerous insights for the present."[4] Metz refers to these memories of human suffering as "dangerous memories" to the extent that they are able to resist "premature and easy reconciliation with the 'given'" and are thus able to "interrupt" the logic of "the way things are." Accordingly, for Metz, the revelation of these dangerous insights is subversive because they "illuminate for a few moments and with a harsh and steady light the questionable nature of things we have apparently come to terms with."[5]

However, Metz also knows that the memory of suffering (*memoria passionis*) in and of itself does not stimulate hope for the future for the victims and vanquished. In fact, suffering can and does often lead to despair. For Christians, what saves suffering from leading to despair is the memory of the death and resurrection of Christ. Accordingly, for Metz, the memory of suffering becomes "dangerous" memory for Christians to the extent that Christians are able to remember the suffering in the world under a more determinative memory, namely the memory of the death and resurrection of Christ. Only in this regard does *memoria passionis* become not only dangerous (subversive, interrupting of the status quo), but also hopeful—making present the freedom of the resurrection in history. In this connection Metz argues that for Christians, the memory of suffering is dangerous not because it is a matter of looking backward "archeologically," but rather entails "forward memories" and as such "anticipates a future as a future of those who are oppressed, without hope and doomed."[6] That is why for Metz *memoria passionis* is always "*memoria mortis et resurrectionis Jesus Christi*"—whereby the remembered death and resurrection of Christ becomes the invitation into Christian praxis and solidarity with and on behalf of the "crucified peoples" (to use an expression popularized by Latin American liberation theologies). Accordingly, the memory of the death and resurrection of Christ introduces in history both a moment of resistance (a resolute "no" to the structures that sacrifice millions) and an element of the dangerous freedom of Jesus's resurrection. *Memoria passionis* as the twin memory of the suffering in the world on the one hand, and of the death and resurrection of Christ on the other, is the key to reconciliation in its many dimensions, including the social realm. For as Paul notes in 2 Corinthians 5:19, "*in Christ God [has reconciled] the world.*" More specifically, it is the notion of *memoria passionis* that is at the heart of the story of Maison Shalom, explaining Maggy's relentless activism on behalf of the suffering peoples of Burundi, her unwavering conviction that evil will never have the last word, and her confidence that love always wins.

In this essay, I will explore five interrelated dimensions of *memoria passionis* as exemplified in the life of Maggy Barankitse and the story of Maison Shalom. Exploring the five elements of *memoria passionis* as (1) twin memory, (2) dangerous memory, (3) social innovation, (4) remembering the future, and (5) eschatological hope will not only help to illumine Maison Shalom as an exemplary radiance of God's reconciling love in the world. It will also help to confirm that memory, the memory of suffering in particular, is the key to social reconciliation. For implicit in my analysis of Maison Shalom is an assumption that similar dynamics of *memoria passionis* are at work in other movements and initiatives for social reconciliation in Eastern Africa. Thus exploring the dynamics of *memoria passionis* in relation to Maison Shalom is an opportunity to display the inner logic that drives and shapes Christian social engagement in solidarity with the oppressed, the poor, the marginalized, and the victims of Africa's power struggles.

Memoria Passionis: Remembering Violence, Remembering Love

The story of Maison Shalom must be located within the broader story of political violence in Burundi, within which "ethnicity" was reinforced and reproduced as an unquestioned building block of Burundian society.[7] A German colony until 1919, Burundi came under Belgian rule that, using the same Hamitic mythology as in Rwanda, divided the country neatly into Hutu, Tutsi, and Twa identities and affirmed (as natural allies) Tutsi privilege while setting up a system of political and economic administration that marginalized the majority Hutu. Unlike Rwanda to the north, Burundi's independence in 1962 left the Tutsi in power, but the "ethnic" hatred between the groups set the framework for Burundi's postindependence history, which has been marked by political instability, a series of coups d'état, and massacres that have pitted Hutus and Tutsis in an endless cycle of revenge and counter-revenge. The fact that Burundi's ten million people speak the same language, and that more than 80 percent are Christian, with Catholicism as the dominant religion, seems not to make much difference.

In 1993, following the assassination of Melchior Ndadaye, Burundi's first democratically elected Hutu president, the country erupted in Hutu-Tutsi ethnic massacres and countermassacres. Although herself Tutsi, Maggy had adopted seven children, three Tutsi and four Hutu. Together with her children and other Hutu families, she sought refuge in the bishop's residence at Ruyigi, where Tutsi militias found her, set the place on fire, and killed seventy-two people. She was spared but was forced to watch the massacre of the seventy-two, including her close friend Juliette.[8] After the massacre, Maggy, crying and trembling, crawled into the chapel. Here, looking at the cross, she cried out, "Why, oh God? How could you allow such hatred? What kind of God are you? Mother told us that you are a God of love. Did she lie to us? And why was I not killed?"[9]

Two surprising gifts ("miracles" as Maggy calls them) emerged amid Maggy's anguish as she beheld the crucified God. First, Cloe, one of Maggy's adopted children, cried out from the sacristy, "Mama, we are all here, all of us are here." The children had escaped the massacre and were hiding in the sacristy. Second, with the gift of her children also came the gift of "inexplicable strength."

> I felt this incredible resistance inside me, like strength…
> as soon as I knew that my children had survived, I felt
> a strong will to live. I could think of one thing and only
> one thing: taking care of them, raising them beyond this
> hatred and bitterness that I came to see in their eyes.[10]

As this citation indicates, the strength was connected with a determination that eventually took on the sense of "a calling" to raise the children "beyond the hatred and bitterness" of the killers.

If the founding of Maison Shalom remains inescapably connected to the memory of the massacre in the bishop's compound, that memory is itself linked to the "*memoria mortis et resurrectionis Christi*" that Maggy contemplated in her anguished prayer before the chapel crucifix following the massacre. When Maggy first prays before the cross, her words take the form of lament. She engages in the practice of wrestling and arguing with God. Following the practice of Old Testament prophets and psalmists, she names the evils she has witnessed and calls God to account. Yet in that very act of arguing with God she discovers hope. While despair is a resignation that nothing can be redeemed, lament names the injustice at hand and calls on God to act. Insofar as Maggy understands her own suffering as part of the *"memoria mortis et resurrectionis Christi,"* her lament also becomes a confirmation of God's love—God's excessive love that is confirmed by the death and resurrection of God's Son.[11] If in Maggy's sorrowful lament she had questioned God's identity and love, now in the crucified God she began to glimpse the full extent of God's love, not simply as an action, but as the very identity of God, as well as our own identity. For as children of God, she realized, human beings are created by love and for love. Love is both our identity and our destiny. She was determined to raise children into the fullness of this love. This is how Maison Shalom was born, beginning with Maggy's seven children and twenty-five other orphans that had survived the massacre.

Memoria Passionis as "Resistance"

According to Metz, "Every resistance to oppression is nourished by the subversive power of remembered suffering."[12] Moreover, "The memory of suffering is always standing up against the modern cynic of power politics."[13] This is what makes the memory of suffering, according to Metz, "dangerous memory" in that it has the power to "break through the canon of the ruling plausibility structures and take on a virtually subversive character."[14]

Maggy's determination to restore, through love, the "dignity" and "image" of God's love that had been shattered by the hatred of ethnic politics, fomented her resistance to a number of things that had come to be taken for granted within Burundi's politics and social life. The resistance took many forms. First, she was able to see and point out the lie that assumed Hutu and Tutsi as "natural" identities. Our primary and natural identity is love, she pointed out. "We are crazy," she noted. "We are not afraid to kill one another. We have accepted hatred because of ethnicity, and we have forgotten the most noble gift of belonging to God's family."[15] Second, once she was able to name ethnicity as a lie, she was able to name the extent to which the lie had infected all aspects of Burundi's society, subverting even African ideals of community and solidarity to serve the story of hatred and vengeance. Third, she questioned the church's silence and "practical hypocrisy" by which the church had come to accommodate itself to the lie of ethnicity. "This is what allowed the massacre to take place even in sacred places by people who were Christians."[16] What kind of Christianity was this?

Maggy also called out the hypocrisy of the international community who is keen to provide "aid" and "relief" to so-called poor countries like Burundi while keeping in place the international economic and political structures that keep those countries dependent. "I told the World Food Bank, 'No we do not need food from the UN. We can cultivate our own food and vegetables.'"[17] She questioned the lifestyle of the political and church leaders who lived in luxury while millions of Burundians languished in misery. She met both government ministers and rebels and advocated for an end to war and violence. This is how Maggy came to be seen as a "troublemaker" and as the "crazy woman" of Burundi. On her part, the craziness was made possible by the strength and "incredible resistance I felt within me" emerging from the events of 1993. Moreover, the resistance was connected to the newly discovered identity and mission of love. "Love has made me a rebel" she says, and so "I must constantly say no to war, to hatred, to violence."[18] In the words of Metz, from the very start, Maison Shalom was born as a movement that sought to break through the plausibility structures that had made violence an inevitable aspect of Burundian society.

Memoria Passionis as Social Innovation: "Love Has Made Me an Inventor"

But if the memory of 1993 was a subversive memory, it was also a "liberating" memory that freed Maggy from all her fears, releasing extraordinary courage and fueling her innovativeness on behalf of the children. If the memory of 1993 had made her a rebel, it also made her an advocate of love. Recalling the events of 1993, she notes, "It was the needs of those children that drove and inspired me. I had these children in the beginning, and I had nothing to offer them. They needed love, they needed safety, and they needed food and clothing. I simply had to invent ways to help them."[19] Love, as she often says, "made me an inventor."[20]

The invention of love took many forms. First, she gathered children, mainly orphans around Ruyigi, her native village. Soon, she had over one hundred children. To date over thirty thousand children have been raised under Maison Shalom. Second, as the massacres turned into a full-fledged civil war, the work of Maison Shalom extended beyond Ruyigi, as she set up centers to welcome more children—both the victims of Burundi's civil war and children escaping from the 1994 Rwanda genocide. She opened houses for the children, settled them in schools, and set up businesses for them. In Ruyigi she built the children a cinema and even a swimming pool. These inventions were not only an effort to shield the children from the ravages of the violence, but they served to "demonstrate" an alternative to violence and the politics of hatred, while at the same time reflecting the boundless possibilities made possible by God's reconciling love. Accordingly, she insisted that her children had to live in homes, not orphanages. For Maggy there are no orphans in the household of God since "each person is created out of love as God's child and is meant to live in the house of God as a member of God's family."[21] When she built a cinema and swimming pool for the children, she responded to those who criticized her for wasting precious resources, "We are all princes and princesses in the household of God," and so children in Burundi should enjoy the same amenities as children everywhere.

Thus through Maison Shalom, Maggy sought to demonstrate the practical dimensions of the fundamental theological claim relating to our identity as God's children, which had been affirmed in the chapel in October 1993. Remembering that event was not simply a matter of recalling the past, but 'making present' the freedom and excess of God's reconciling love. It is for this reason that reconciliation and forgiveness were, from the very start, at the heart of the work of Maison Shalom. For it is forgiveness that introduces the "freedom" of God's reconciling love as a social principle in history in a manner that can break the endless cycles of violence. In Daniel Philpott's chapter in this volume, he argues that the ethic in which forgiveness is situated is one of reconciliation. He notes that reconciliation is a biblical form of justice—the restoration of right relationships. Through a forgiveness that restores relationships, Maggy is changing the social fabric of her community. As Justine, a child of Maison Shalom who lost her parents in one of the massacres, confirms, "Maggy gave us love and the grace with which we can overlook our sad experiences.... If I had not found her, I in turn would have become a killer."[22]

Thus through various events, activities, and opportunities for reconciliation, Maggy encouraged the children and the community to live into this freedom. As the experience of forgiveness and reconciliation came to be embraced among the children of Maison Shalom and the community, the work of Maison Shalom also extended to other social sectors within the community, including the setting up of a cooperative society, a hospital, and a radio station in Ruyigi. However, significant as these social services and projects are, Maggy rightly insists that Maison Shalom is not about these projects. Rather it is about the message: love is God's identity and our identity. The services and projects are merely the necessary social expression of love. It is the memory of 1993 that helps Maggy to remember this and thus remember the future rightly.

Remembering the Future: Keeping *Memoria Passionis* Alive

As the work of Maison Shalom in Ruyigi and beyond expanded and became more impressive, it attracted more visitors to Ruyigi. The visitors would be interested not only to meet Maggy but also to see the impressive hospital, the swimming pool, the businesses, and the other projects. As mentioned previously, Maggy is keen to remind visitors that Maison Shalom is not about the projects but the message: the message of God's reconciling love, and how this message is good news for all, but especially the poor. For this reason she always begins the tour of Maison Shalom by taking the visitors back to the bishop's compound and to the cemetery where she buried the seventy-two people. Here she narrates the events of 1993. After my third visit walking through this painful memory, I asked Maggy, "Why insist on going back to the gravesite?" "Part of that is for myself," she said. "The reason I must return to the gravesite is not to relive the trauma but that I may see the future more clearly."[23] Involved in this remark is the realization that one can only see the future clearly by remembering the past. And just as for Metz, remembering the past is not a matter of looking backward "archeologically," but also a future-oriented activity—a "forward memory" that anticipates a future as a future of those who are oppressed. The events of 1993 revealed her call to form a new community that reflects the story of God's reconciling love in the world. Remembering these events renews that call and energizes her solidarity with and her struggle on behalf of the children who are, so to say, the evidence of God's love.

Apart from the regular visit to the gravesite, there are two other ways in which Maggy sustains this "disciplined" memory that helps her to see the future more clearly. First, she spends an hour every day in quiet prayer before the Eucharist and the cross. For Maggy, the meditation is a daily opportunity to contemplate and "remember" God's excessive and self-sacrificing love manifested on the cross and in the gift of the Eucharist. Moreover, it is this remembering that connects Maggy's own suffering and the suffering in the world with God's own suffering. This in turn helps to place her story and the suffering in the world under a more determinative story—the story of God's reconciling love. This not only helps her to take her own and the world's suffering seriously, but also to see, just as in the case of Christ, that "evil will never have the last word."[24] Paradoxically, the memory of suffering is the basis of her confidence that love always wins.

The other disciplined practice of Maggy's *memoria passionis* is through the daily celebration and reception of the Eucharist. The latter not only renews her own inner spiritual life but also strengthens and sustains the call to pour herself out daily in solidarity with and on behalf of the suffering others. For Maggy, the Eucharist is a "spirituality that includes everything."[25] By this she means the Eucharist is not simply a "spiritual" reality (in the narrow sense of *spiritual* as opposed to *material*). Rather it is a way of seeing and living in the world—with, in the words of Metz, the dangerous "freedom" of what it means to be God's children whose true identity is love. The freedom is itself made possible by the death and resurrection of Christ, which the Eucharist remembers and represents. Thus just as in the visit to the gravesite or in the daily meditation before the cross, in the Eucharist Maggy remembers the drama, the bigger story into which her life and her calling is drawn. Placing herself in God's great drama allows Maggy to see more clearly the opportunities made possible by God's reconciling love. Finally, if the memory of 1993 helps Maggy to remember her calling and see the future, it also keeps her grounded in the face of so many daily challenges as she seeks to realize the future of God's reconciling love in the here and now, while recognizing that its full realization always lies beyond now, and beyond her.

Memoria Passionis as Hope

The overall impact of the foregoing discussion is to confirm that, as with Metz, Maggy's practice of memory is not simply a matter of looking backward. Rather it is a form of spirituality, which is to say a way of locating one's life within the ongoing drama of God's reconciling love in the world. Doing so involves a constant awareness of oneself as both the "recipient" of God's reconciling love and its "ambassador." As an ambassador, Maggy understands her call in terms of a constant struggle to fight and keep back the forces of darkness. Accordingly, she understands her daily work as one of "lighting small candles to fight the darkness."[26] Elsewhere she notes, "I wanted to be a little instrument to love."[27] In order to be such an instrument, Maggy constantly notes that Maison Shalom is not "her" project. "God is God," she notes, and "our lives belong to God."[28] Accordingly, she constantly warns that in the struggle against the forces of darkness, hatred, and violence, we must be careful "not to lose the tenderness" of God's love.[29]

278

Recent developments in Burundi, which led to the closing down of Maison Shalom and the sending of Maggy into exile, have tested Maggy's own ability not to "lose the tenderness" and yet to forge ahead with the struggle against hatred and darkness. In a recent public lecture at Notre Dame, she reiterated her conviction that evil will never have the last word. Pressed for "evidence" for this claim that love always wins, she pointed to herself and to Christ. "Look at me! I am angry, but I am not discouraged, for I know love always wins. Secondly, look at Christ: he was killed and buried, did he lose?"[30] She then named Paul's own experience in 2 Corinthians 4:8–10: "We are hard pressed on every side, but not crushed; perplexed, but not in despair; persecuted, but not abandoned; struck down, but not destroyed. We always carry around in our body the death of Jesus, so that the life of Jesus may also be revealed in our body." Accordingly, she also sees her exile as another chapter in the unfolding of the story of God's reconciling love. "Who knows," she notes, "perhaps God sent me into exile in order to expand the work of Maison Shalom outside Burundi, in Rwanda and beyond."[31]

Maggy's assessment of her exile as an "opportunity" for Maison Shalom is based on the expectation of miracles and unexpected gifts that is a constant theme in her self-understanding as an ambassador of God's love. Reflecting on Maison Shalom in 2009, she noted,

> There are always miracles in the Shalom House because I believe in love. I believe that nobody can stop me. I compare the Shalom House to a train that God conducts. Nobody can stop this train. He will still move it—because God is God. There will be some cars that will stop. But He will continue to gather Congolese, Rwandese, Europeans, saying, "come my children and build my dream."[32]

This is the drama within which Maggy understands her life and calling. And in just the same way that Maggy insists that Maison Shalom is not about the various projects (e.g., farm, cinema, swimming pool, hospital) but about the message—God's reconciling love—she also talks about being "possessed" and of "surrendering" to God's love. At a workshop in 2015, after listening to Maggy narrate her story, an obviously moved leader asked her how she would like to be known. Maggy responded, "I never thought every person must be known." The leader persisted and wanted to know how she would like to be remembered. Maggy's answer was simple: "That God is God." And then she added, "We are merely grass—*une herbe qui bruele*," a veiled reference to Psalm 90:6 that speaks about human beings as grass that springs up in the morning but by the evening is withered and faded.[33]

Involved in Maggy's response is the realization that she is simply a tiny fraction of the big drama of what God is doing in the world, and her efforts constitute but a tiny effort in the realization of God's reconciliation in the world. This also means that as inevitable as the "train" of God's reconciling love is, its full realization lies beyond her and beyond the here and now. In a 2017 interview at Notre Dame, Maggy invoked the words of Oscar Romero and noted, "We can only plant the seeds…the future belongs to God."[34] What these observations confirm is that whereas the story of God's reconciling love is real—and takes definite social and practical dimensions—social reconciliation is experienced as always broken, never complete, as an eschatological hope and an ongoing journey. The memory of the events of 1993 not only help Maggy to remember the telos of her work but keeps her grounded in the struggle, renewing her energy and innovativeness. This ensures that she neither despairs nor "loses the tenderness" in the face of various challenges and setbacks.

Conclusion: Examples of Dangerous Memory in Eastern Africa

The foregoing discussion of Maggy Barankitse's life and her work with Maison Shalom has confirmed several things. First, reconciliation, which is the story of God's love in history, is always social reconciliation. Second, social reconciliation is an ongoing journey with and on behalf of the oppressed, the suffering, and those without hope. Third, the key to this social engagement lies in memory, more specifically the memory of suffering. In this connection, Johannes Baptist Metz's notion of *memoria passionis* has provided a very helpful lens to understand the dynamics of social reconciliation in Eastern Africa. Our discussion here has helped to illumine five constitutive and interrelated elements of *memoria passionis* as they are exemplified in Maggy's life and work with Maison Shalom. But while the elements of *memoria passionis* as (1) twin memory, (2) resistance, (3) social innovation, (4) future memory, and (5) eschatological hope are clear in Maggy's story, my claim is that similar dynamics of dangerous memory are at work in other efforts of social reconciliation in Eastern Africa. By way of conclusion, we can only point to a few of these examples.

In 2002, David Kasali resigned his prestigious position as president of a famous Christian college in Kenya to return to his native Congo, amid the war, to establish a new university—*Université Chrétienne Bilingue du Congo* (UCBC) at Beni. Kasali's vision for UCBC is to form a fresh generation of leaders for Congo and Africa. The root of Congo's (and Africa's) problems, Kasali had come to realize, is the lack of principled and ethical leadership: "Our suffering in Congo is dependent on the type of leaders that we have. If we can prepare a new generation of leaders who are critical in their thinking, who are grounded in ethics of love your enemies and love your neighbors, and who say, 'Enough is enough,' then in the long run we will change to a sustained development that will do away with the relief work."[35]

However, it is the suffering in Eastern Congo during the years of fighting—fighting that eventually claimed the lives of tens of thousands of people, including David's brother and his twenty-eight-year-old niece—that triggered Kasali's decision to return to Congo. It is this memory, coupled with the memory of God's love, that Kasali had come to experience as a "love affair with God" when he accepted Christ, that propels him. This explains, on the one hand, UCBC's resistance to the violence in Congo ("enough is enough") and on the other, its focus on formation and social innovativeness in Beni and beyond.

Similar dynamics of "dangerous memory" are at work at St. Monica Girls' Vocational Training School in Gulu, Northern Uganda. The school provides a home for girls, many of them young mothers. These women are victims of twenty-five years of fighting associated with the Lord's Resistance Army, who killed, maimed, and abducted many young people to serve as child soldiers or sex slaves (serving as "wives" to the rebel commanders). Sister Rosemary Nyirumbi, member of the Sisters of the Sacred Heart of Jesus, has been the director of the St. Monica Girls Vocation Training School in Gulu since 2001. The winner of several awards including the 2007 CNN heroes award, the UN Women Impact award (2013), the Uganda Nalubaale Award (2014), and the 2014 *Time Magazine* "100 Most Influential People in the World," Nyirumbe understands her work at St. Monica as one of "giving love" and of "helping my girls experience the restorative and forgiving love of God."[36] For Nyirumbe, what makes this work possible and sustains it is the twin memory of suffering: the suffering experienced by her girls on the one hand, and the suffering of God on the other, which she contemplates daily as a sister of the Sacred Heart. At the center of her order's devotion is the image of the Sacred Heart, which is a symbol and expression of God's infinite love for humanity, made manifest especially in Jesus's suffering and death on the cross. It is this "suffering love" of God that Sister Nyirumbe seeks to make present to her girls through various social programs. She accordingly has noted, "I do whatever I do because I am a sister of the Sacred Heart….If I weren't religious, I would not be a Sister. That is why I am here." Or, as she put it most recently, "There is no other formula for love, humility and zeal…. This formula is not attractive because it is the cross. But there is no other classroom to learn about compassion, love and mercy than the Sacred Heart of Jesus….This is the highest PhD. We are students every day. We learn from the Sacred Heart of Jesus."[37]

A similar experience of *memoria passionis*—as the twin memory of suffering in the world on the one hand, and of the death and resurrection of Christ on the other—accounts for Archbishop John Baptist Odama's advocacy during the fighting in Northern Uganda, whose story is also discussed by Daniel Philpott in his chapter in this volume. Odama became archbishop of Gulu in 1999 at the height of the insurgency of the Lord's Resistance Army. The fighters of the Lord's Resistance Army (often referred to as "the rebels") waged war not only by ambushing government and military vehicles but also by attacking villages, burning down houses, abducting over twenty-six thousand children, and killing and maiming civilians.[38] Odama worked tirelessly to end the fighting, mediating between

President Yoweri Museveni's government and Kony's LRA. He traveled a number of times into the bush to meet with Kony and his commanders, appealing to and pressuring them to stop the fighting and then appealing to and pressuring the government to give up the Operation Iron Fist offensive and agree to peace talks with Kony. At the same time, he was a strong advocate for the displaced people, children in particular. He also helped to establish and lead the ARLPI (Acholi Religious Leaders Peace Initiative), an advocacy group working for peace made up of Protestant, Catholic, Muslim, and traditional religious leaders.

However, the sustaining factor in Odama's effort lies in his practice of setting aside Thursday as a time of prayer, fasting, and adoration. When asked why he takes Thursdays off, which he spends in the chapel in his residence, Odama responded, "So that I may not take myself too seriously. The mission of peace is not mine. I do not own it. It is owned by God, and I am merely the servant....Many times I do not know the next steps towards peace, but I know that steps to peace can be found."[39] Pressed on what he "does" the entire time he is in the chapel before the Eucharist and the cross, Odama talks about "listening." The time, he notes "keeps me focused, and I listen," and the listening "keeps me hopeful in the face of so much suffering." But Odama also talked about his Thursday practice before the Blessed Sacrament and the cross as a time of remembering. "I bring all names and faces of the suffering children and people I have met in the week before God, and then I look at the cross and see God's own suffering for humanity." Not unlike Maggy, Kasali, and Nyirumbe, this twin memory of suffering, far from being a reason for despair, informs, drives, and deepens his advocacy for peace with and on behalf of suffering people in Northern Uganda.

Finally, embedded in Maggy's story, as well as in the stories of Kasali, Nyirumbe, and Odama, is the claim that God's reconciling love makes possible a new world. Their stories reflect forms of advocacy and "inventions" (Maggy's "love has made me an inventor") out of that new world. However, also reflected in their stories is the scandalous and most radical claim Christians make—namely that God's reconciling love is "crucified love," pointing to the cross as the reality that uniquely reveals the excess of God's love. Standing amid war, violence, and suffering, these leaders have been drawn into the dangerous memory of God's crucified love as they contemplate the suffering around them. The *memoria passionis*, the twin memory of suffering, thus becomes the basis and motivation behind their advocacy and inventiveness on behalf of those without hope. In this case one can rightly refer to *memoria passionis* as hope—a strange hope indeed—for it is hope born from, within, and through lament. But in reality, that is the only hope there is for the world.[40]

Reflection Questions

1. Metz argues that memories of human suffering are "dangerous memories" because they "illuminate for a few moments and with a harsh and steady light the questionable nature of things we have apparently come to terms with." What would be an example of a dangerous memory in your own community? What might engagement with this dangerous memory illuminate?

2. What differences do Christian faith and Christian hope make in the life and work of the leaders described in this chapter?

3. Maggy Barankitse says, "Love has made me an inventor." What do you think she means by this? In what ways might this love, which inspires innovation and creativity, challenge conventional approaches to development and peacebuilding?

4. This chapter discussed five dimensions of Barankitse's *memoria passionis*. How did each of these five dimensions draw her into deeper solidarity with the oppressed? How might you apply these five dimensions of *memoria passionis* to your own sociopolitical location? What impact might this have on you and your community?

Notes

1. Maggy Barankitse, "When I Became Refugee, I Fled with My Biggest Treasure: Love," Public Lecture, The Lutheran

World Federation, November 2, 2016, https://www.facebook.com/lutheranworld/videos/1621443564822945/?hc_ref=ARSPHM3dlPQ3MNjUT8RHA9L579E3PxL_KuZ5XvBCsws O8s9y CEoukrToE-Thm9wp0_I.

2. Maggy Barankitse, interview with the author, Ruyigi, Burundi, January 17, 2009.

3. Emmanuel Katongole, *The Sacrifice of Africa: A Political Theology for Africa* (Grand Rapids, MI: Eerdmans, 2011), 176.

4. Johann Baptist Metz, *Faith in History and Society: Toward a Practical Fundamental Theology*, trans. James Matthew Ashley (New York: Crossroad, 2011), 105.

5. Metz, *Faith in History and Society*, 105–6.

6. Metz, *Faith in History and Society*, 206, as cited in Joas Adiprasetya, "Johann Baptist Metz's *Memoria Passionis* and the Possibility of Political Forgiveness," *Political Theology* 18, nos. 3–4 (2017): 237.

7. For a general background to Burundi's history, see Rene Lemarchand, *Burundi: Ethnic Conflict and Genocide* (Washington, DC: Woodrow Wilson Center Press, 1996).

8. For a full account of the story, see my *The Sacrifice of Africa: A Political Theology for Africa* (Grand Rapids, MI: Eerdmans, 2011); and *Born from Lament: The Theology and Politics of Hope in Africa* (Grand Rapids, MI: Eerdmans, 2017).

9. Katongole, *Born from Lament*, 229.

10. Katongole, *Sacrifice of Africa*, 171.

11. For a more extended discussion of the connection between lament and hope, see my *Born from Lament*.

12. Metz, *Faith in History and Society*, 106.

13. Metz, *Faith in History and Society*, 106.

14. Metz, *Faith in History and Society*, 105–6.

15. Katongole, *The Sacrifice of Africa*, 174.

16. Katongole, *The Sacrifice of Africa*, 175.

17. Maggy Barankitse, interview with the author, Ruyigi, Burundi, January 17–19, 2009.

18. Maggy Barankitse, interview with the author.

19. Maggy Barankitse, quoted in Norman Wirzba, *Way of Love: Recovering the Heart of Christianity* (San Francisco: Harper One, 2017), 186.

20. Katongole, *The Sacrifice of Africa*, 17.

21. Katongole, *The Sacrifice of Africa*, 176.

22. Katongole, *The Sacrifice of Africa*, 192.

23. Katongole, *Born from Lament*, 260.

24. Katongole, *The Sacrifice of Africa*, 191.

25. 49th Eucharist congress, KTOTV, "Témoignage: Madame Marguerite Barankitse," YouTube, May 30, 2012, accessed January 17, 2018, https://www.youtube.com/watch?v=97R3lGRhIoU. See also my "A Blood Thicker Than the Blood of Tribalism: Maggy Barankitse's Maison Shalom," in *The Journey of Reconciliation: Groaning for a New Creation in Africa* (Maryknoll, NY: Orbis Books, 2017), 159–66.

26. Katongole, *The Sacrifice of Africa*, 183.

27. Katongole, *Born from Lament*, 258.

28. Katongole, *The Sacrifice of Africa*, 180.

29. Katongole, *Born from Lament*, 258.

30. Maggy Barankitse, "The Courage of Giving Refuge," Public Lecture, University of Notre Dame, April 10, 2017.

31. Maggy Barankitse, interview with the author, Notre Dame, Indiana, April 11, 2017 (hereafter Notre Dame interview).

32. Katongole, *The Sacrifice of Africa*, 180.

33. Maggy Barankitse, interview with the author, Bethany House, Uganda, January 19, 2015.

34. Maggy Barankitse, Notre Dame interview.

35. "David M. Kasali: Being Transformed to Transform," Faith and Leadership, September 19, 2010, accessed January 17, 2018, http://www.faithandleadership.com/multimedia/david-m-kasali-being-transformed-transform.

36. Katongole, *Born from Lament*, 137.

37. Rosemary Nyirumbe, interview with the author, University of Notre Dame, March 9, 2015. At the time, she confessed, "I am not a very strong spiritual person, who spends a lot of time in quiet adoration. I have learnt over time that all my activities are prayer. The prayer is a form of self-emptying: it about the acronym Self: S (surrender); E (I am empty); L (it is your love); F (fill me; make me whole). So, throughout the day I keep on praying that prayer of SELF."

38. For a good introduction to the history of the Lord's Resistance Army in Northern Uganda, see Tim Allen and Koen

Vlassenroot, eds., *The Lord's Resistance Army: Myth and Reality* (London: Zed Books, 2010).

39. For a full discussion of Archbishop Odama, and for references to the citations here, see my "Archbishop John Baptist Odama and the Politics of Baptism in Northern Uganda," in *The Journey of Reconciliation: Groaning for a New Creation in Africa* (Maryknoll, NY: Orbis Books, 2017), 121–36.

40. I am grateful to my doctoral research assistant, Marie-Claire Klassen, for her keen editorial eye, revisions, and recommendations, which have made the essay both richer and smoother.

CHAPTER 14

The Surprise of Forgiveness in Modern Catholic Teaching and Practice

Daniel Philpott

Forgiveness is not politics as usual. Candidates for public office in developed democracies do not make forgiveness a plank in their campaign platforms. Politicians rarely advocate forgiveness on the floor of parliaments. Forgiveness has virtually no pedigree in Western political thought and little track record as a political practice over most of the history of the modern nation-state.

It has been a great historical surprise, then, to see forgiveness enter global political discourse over the past generation, which it has done in the context of a large wave of countries who have confronted injustices in the aftermath of the enormities wrought by war, dictatorship, and genocide. During roughly the same period, forgiveness rose in prominence in Catholic social thought, especially through the locutions of Pope St. John Paul II, who repeatedly commended forgiveness for politics. The rise of forgiveness in these two settings—globally diverse political orders and Catholic social thought—is in part related. In many settings of transitional justice, it has been Catholic or other Christian leaders who have urged forgiveness for political crimes publicly and urgently but not without controversy.

In this paper I explore forgiveness as a practice of political reconciliation rooted in Catholic social thought. I then seek to develop this teaching further, showing how forgiveness can be situated in an ethic of political reconciliation that can be practiced concretely in political orders. Finally, I aim to show the practicability of political forgiveness by pointing to a major episode of it on the part of victims of political violence in Uganda. In Father Katongole's chapter in this volume, he offers several examples in which forgiveness plays a strong role in social reconciliation: the *"memoria passionis"* of Maggy Barankitse in Burundi; the healing work of Sister Rosemary Nyirumbi in Northern Uganda; and the leadership of Archbishop John Baptist Odama in Northern Uganda. The case of Odama overlaps with my own field research. The practitioners of forgiveness in Uganda very much carried out what Odama was preaching.

Forgiveness in the Social Teaching of the Catholic Church

That popes would preach reconciliation and forgiveness comes as no surprise; both concepts stand at the center of the gospel message. It is far more novel for popes to advocate these practices in the political realm. The first instance of such advocacy in the era of the modern nation-state was Pope Benedict XV's urgent plea for European states to forgive one another in the wake of World War I, voiced in his encyclical of 1920, *Pacem, Dei Munus Pulcherrimum*. Benedict XV appealed to Jesus's teaching of charity and love for enemies and insisted that "the Gospel has not one law of charity for individuals, and another for States and nations, which are indeed but collections of individuals." Presciently he warned that "the germs of former enmities remain" and that "there can be no stable peace or lasting treaties...unless there be a return of mutual charity to appease hate and banish enmity."[1]

Benedict XV's teaching of political forgiveness remained isolated and largely forgotten until it was revived by Pope St. John Paul II in his second encyclical, *Dives in Misericordia* (Rich in Mercy), in 1980. True, certain magisterial teachings and actions that belong to the same family as forgiveness arose in the interim years, for instance, statements of repentance toward other Christian churches surrounding the Second Vatican Council. It was John Paul II, though, who taught forgiveness in the political realm. Again, there is nothing surprising about a pope teaching on mercy, except perhaps for the exclamation mark that John Paul II placed on the virtue, insisting that "loud cries of mercy" ought to be the "mark of the Church of our times."[2] Mercy was arguably the most important theme of his pontificate. Even more innovative, though, was his call in the final section of the encyclical for mercy to be practiced in the social and political realms. Mercy would not supplant or negate justice, which the Catholic tradition has long held to be the supreme virtue of political life, but rather would complement and even shape the meaning of justice. In the social and political realm, mercy would be expressed through reconciliation and forgiveness.[3]

The final sections of *Dives in Misericordia* were not anomalous. John Paul II would elaborate and develop his teaching of political forgiveness in his Message for the World Day of Peace in 1997, and then in 2002, only a few months after the attacks of September 11, 2001, when he appended to Pope Paul VI's well-known apothegm, "no peace without justice," the phrase, "no justice without forgiveness." He also urged forgiveness in the context of particular conflicts such as the war in the former Yugoslavia in the early 1990s. Resonant with the theme were also his many requests for forgiveness for the past sins of the church, totaling over one hundred mea culpas for over twenty-one different categories of wrongs, culminating in a litany of apologies in the years preceding the Jubilee Year of 2000.[4]

No mere Sunday school moralism, John Paul II's teaching on mercy, reconciliation, and forgiveness in the political realm was shaped by his history of living under Nazi occupation and then decades of Communist rule in Poland. In 1965, on the eve of the one thousandth anniversary of Poland's conversion to Christianity, John Paul, who was then archbishop of Krakow, joined Poland's other bishops in inviting Germany's bishops to practice reciprocal forgiveness for the two nations' entire mutual history. For this he earned the ire of Poland's Communist government.[5] John Paul II was also intensely aware of Jesus's revelations of mercy to Sister Faustina Kowalska, whom he later canonized.

John Paul II's successor, Pope Benedict XVI, took up the message of political reconciliation. It is often forgotten that he named himself not only for St. Benedict of Nursia but also for Pope Benedict XV, who, he told a general audience in St. Peter's Square, "was a prophet of peace who struggled strenuously and bravely, first to avoid the drama of war and then to limit its terrible consequences. In his footsteps I place my ministry, in the service of reconciliation and harmony between peoples, profoundly convinced that the great good of peace is above all a gift of God."[6]

Shortly before becoming pope, on the sixtieth anniversary of the Normandy invasion in June 2004, Benedict spoke of reconciliation between Germany and its allies after World War II in an address at a German cemetery near Caen, France. A Christian notion of reconciliation, rooted in the atoning sacrifice of Christ, he argued, motivated Catholic statesmen like Konrad Adenauer, Robert Schumann, Alcide de Gasperi, and Charles de Gaulle to promote European unity after the war.[7] Benedict proclaimed reconciliation often in political settings, including the war in Lebanon in summer 2006, the relationship between the church and the Chinese government, politics in Africa, and religious freedom. In his exhortation of 2007, *Sacramentum Caritatis*, he explained that justice, reconciliation, and forgiveness in service of social peace are implications of the Eucharist.[8]

Pope Francis has continued these themes. He has followed John Paul II in making mercy the central theme of his pontificate, even declaring a year of mercy. In his apostolic letter closing that year, *Misericordia et Misera*, he wrote of the social character of mercy and elsewhere has commended pardon and reconciliation in contexts of armed conflict.[9] In his 2014 *Message for the World Day of Peace*, Francis taught, "Only when politics and the economy are open to moving within the wide space ensured by the One who loves each man and each woman, will they achieve an ordering based on a genuine spirit of fraternal charity and become effective instruments of integral human development and peace," later adding, "this entails weaving a fabric of fraternal relationships marked by reciprocity, forgiveness and complete self-giving."[10]

Papal teachings on mercy, reconciliation, and forgiveness in the social and political realm amount to a development in the social teaching of the Catholic Church. These teachings innovate not only in their substance but also in their source. Previous papal teachings, at least since the influential writings of Thomas Aquinas, grounded politics and justice primarily in natural law while rendering the church as a contrasting realm of the supernatural. These new teachings, though, are rooted directly in the saving action of God as described in the Bible, not in moral norms known by reason. They envision politics participating in God's ongoing reconciliation of the world to himself.

Opposition to Forgiveness in the Wake of Political Violence

If recent popes have commended mercy, reconciliation, and forgiveness for the political realm, they have also left the world with manifold questions about praxis. Through what sorts of policies and measures, and in what circumstances, are these practices to be enacted in political orders? What is their relationship to justice? To judicial punishment? May heads of state carry out these practices in the name of collectivities?

Posing these questions sharpest are critics of reconciliation and forgiveness who direct their skepticism not usually at papal teachings but rather toward advocates and practitioners of these practices, including religious officials, in the past generation's global wave of political transitions. These critics are most commonly proponents of "the liberal peace," which sociologist Jonathan Van Antwerpen has called the global orthodoxy for dealing with past injustices.[11] Typically, they are officials and staff in the United Nations, Western governments, and NGOs; international lawyers; and academics. Rooted in Enlightenment thought, their vision of peace advances human rights, the rule of law, free markets, and judicial punishment, which they justify either on retributivist or utilitarian grounds. Among international lawyers and human rights activists involved in transitional justice, judicial punishment holds pride of place. If this is their theology, then the glass tower of the International Criminal Court in The Hague is their cathedral. The greatest mortal sin, to them, is blanket amnesty, to which they cry, *Nunca Mas!* (Never Again).

Proponents of the liberal peace and their intellectual allies raise several objections to the practice of forgiveness in the aftermath of dictatorship, war, and genocide. Some hold that forgiveness negates the justice of judicial punishment and contributes to a culture of impunity.[12] A related criticism is that forgiveness chokes off emotions of resentment and retribution, which they argue can be healthy responses to gross injustices and do not necessarily take the form of reckless revenge. Others insist upon the highly personal and inward character of forgiveness, which they say makes forgiveness inappropriate for political processes. Critics took to task the South African Truth and Reconciliation Commission of 1996–98, for instance, for pressuring victims to forgive, thereby disrespecting their autonomy, agency, and freedom to decide. Still another criticism is that forgiveness is an inherently religious value and thus should be kept out of the secular, public realm.

Some critics argue even more strongly that asking victims to forgive revictimizes them by placing further burdens upon them. In some versions of this criticism, forgiveness is possible only for the rare saint and it is dangerous to recommend it generally. Even several scholars who have taken reconciliation as their paradigm for approaching past injustices believe that forgiveness stretches the possibilities for reconciliation too far. "Rather than being reasonable and appropriate, urging forgiveness and the overcoming of resentment in contexts where wrongdoing is systematic and ongoing seems at best naïve and at worst a form of complicity in the maintenance of oppression and injustice," argues philosopher Colleen Murphy in a book where she presents a theory of reconciliation.[13] If forgiveness is going to be advocated in political contexts, then, it needs to be situated in an ethic that makes it morally plausible and backed up with evidence that it is actually practicable.

Forgiveness: A Practice in an Ethic of Reconciliation

The ethic in which forgiveness is situated is one of reconciliation. John Paul II made clear the close relationship of forgiveness to reconciliation in the closing sections of *Dives in Misericordia*. I argue further that reconciliation is equivalent to justice. This claim may grate in the ears of modern Westerners, for whom justice is a matter of rights, punishment, and the proper distribution of wealth. That reconciliation is justice, though, finds defense in Christianity's most important written source, the Bible. In this collection, Father Thomas Stegman shows the central place of reconciliation in the writings of the Apostle Paul, who links reconciliation's horizontal and vertical axes: reconciliation between persons flows from God's reconciliation of humanity to himself. For Paul, the fruit of reconciliation is righteousness, which, I argue, the Bible also translates as justice.

The righteousness to which justice in the Bible is best translated in turn means comprehensive right relationship: the entire set of obligations that people owe to one another, to the community, and to God. This righteousness is captured through Hebrew words, *tsedeq* and *mishpat*, and through various Greek words that begin with the *dik-* stem such as *dikaiousune*.[14] The justice of right relationship, as I will call this justice, in turn is virtually equivalent to the concept of reconciliation as it is found in the New Testament. Reconciliation, then, is a concept of justice.

That reconciliation and, still more, forgiveness would be thought of as justice again confronts the dominant mode of thinking about justice in the West, the mode that the liberal peace embodies. In the transitional justice settings of the past generation, reconciliation has often been posed as a challenger paradigm to the liberal peace; Antwerpen calls reconciliation the "heterodoxy" of transitional justice. If reconciliation is justice, though, how does it differ from the Western liberal conception? The dominant notion in the West, one that has shaped enlightenment liberalism, comes from Roman law, and is stated as "the constant will to render another his due." Due, in turn, implies what someone is owed or that to which he may claim a right, as well as what someone deserves, as with criminal punishment.[15] Rights and desert have each played a central role in Western thought since the Enlightenment.

Reconciliation, the justice of right relationship, need not reject rights and desert. Rights—subjective rights, involving claims to what is owed, are arguably grounded in natural law and arguably found

294

in certain passages in the Bible, for instance, ones that speak of the rights of the poor.[16] A case can be made that desert, too, has a foundation both in natural law and the biblical texts. If biblical justice encompasses right and desert, however, it is also wider than these concepts and includes obligations and practices that exceed and elude rights and desert—like forgiveness. A wide consensus of philosophers and theologians agree that forgiveness is neither something that a victim owes, nor even more something to which a perpetrator has a right or deserves. In a justice that is wider than these concepts, forgiveness may participate.

There are two senses in which the biblical justice of reconciliation exceeds what is due. First, it entails certain duties that promote right relationship but that enjoy no corresponding right. Many of these are wide duties, definable as ones whose discharge is open-ended with respect to the actions that they involve and the people toward whom they are performed. The biblical duties to love one's neighbor or to serve the poor, for instance, are constitutive of right relationship and involve respecting certain rights claimed by one's neighbor and the poor, but are not limited to respecting these rights and not specified as to how they are to be carried out. Does one expend one's finite resources on giving to the local homeless shelter or to the relief of refugees in war-torn Sudan? How much does one expend in light of other just claims on one's time and resources? The duty to serve the poor alone contains no answer to these questions.

There are other duties that involve no corresponding right but that are not exactly wide duties because their recipients and their constitutive behavior are clearly specified by the duty. Forgiveness is one of these. Again, it is broadly agreed that a perpetrator has no right to forgiveness. A case can be made, though—meaning that I would argue it but cannot fully do so here—that in Christianity, forgiveness is a duty. The Gospel of Matthew recounts Jesus commanding forgiveness at least twice (6:12–15). This command is more fully developed in the parable of a servant whose master forgives him his debt but who refuses to forgive his own servant's debt, a parable through which Jesus elaborates on his answer "seventy-seven times" to Peter's question, "How many times shall I forgive my brother or sister who sins against me?" (Matt 18:21–35 NIV). Jesus makes no distinction with respect to the nature or magnitude of the sin when he commands forgiveness. The Christian, it appears, is required to forgive a perpetrator who has no right to be forgiven. Jesus's own utterance of forgiveness from the cross exemplifies the teaching most vividly of all (Luke 23:34).

A second respect in which the justice of reconciliation (or right relationship) exceeds the boundaries of rights and desert is found in the Bible's use of the language of justice to describe the saving actions of God. These actions take place through God's repeated restoration of his covenant with Israel in the Old Testament and then through the new covenant, God's promise of forgiveness and salvation for the repentant sinner, fulfilled through the atoning sacrifice of Christ. Examples of justice language include Second Isaiah's references to a justice that is saving and renewing (see 45:8 or 45:21, for instance) and the Gospel of Matthew's (12:20) direct quotation of Second Isaiah (42:1–4) in its reference to Jesus as the "servant" who "brings justice to victory." The Apostle Paul's concept of justification is also arguably a use of justice language to describe God's atonement for sin and restoration of humanity through Christ. In this volume, Stegman indeed stresses the close relationship of reconciliation and justification in his chapter. Yet both Scripture and the heavy weight of Christian tradition have held that God's salvation of humanity is a gift and not something due: deserved or fulfilling of a right. Stegman, for instance, stresses God's initiative in the reconciling action through which God forgives us our sins. The Bible's most central expression of justice, then, falls decisively outside of the justice that is due. Forgiveness, which is part and parcel of God's saving justice—the justice that restores right relationship, namely reconciliation—thus participates in this justice.

How is the justice of restoring right relationship enacted in social and political contexts? Through practices that address the broad range of wounds inflicted on persons and relationships by perpetrators of injustice. This will to restore, motivated by pity, is the essence of mercy, which converges with justice in an ethic of reconciliation.[17]

Forgiveness is one of these practices. A victim enacts it by a willingness to overcome resentment toward her perpetrator and choosing to look upon her as a citizen in good standing. Forgiveness, then, is not merely a relinquishment but also a constructive act through which a victim wills to restore right relationship. It is this constructive dimension that makes forgiveness a practice of reconciliation. To be sure, forgiveness does not itself achieve full reconciliation. It is only one of several practices that restore right relationship, others of which include apology, acknowledgment, reparations, and just punishment.[18] Forgiveness itself might be performed partially. A victim's forgiveness may fail to be reciprocated by a perpetrator's acceptance, for instance, either because the perpetrator is unwilling or perhaps because she is missing or dead.

When forgiveness goes well, or even partially well though, it can contribute to restoring political orders that have been sundered by systemic injustices. As a practice of reconciliation, it does this by addressing several forms of wounds. First, it conspires to defeat what may be called the "standing victory of injustice"—the sense in which a wrong stands legitimated—by naming and condemning a wrong and then willing a future in which the wrong no longer has force or status. Second, forgiveness helps to restore the agency of the victim by enabling her to act as an engaged constructer of a better world and by helping her to overcome anger and resentment, admittedly a long-term process. Third, forgiveness may also help to restore the soul of the perpetrator, an important goal in a Christian ethic—by inviting him to become something other than what he was when he committed the crime. Fourth, when fellow citizens favorably acknowledge forgiveness, they help to overcome the social isolation of the victim and to build peace by commending the act to other citizens. Fifth, by willing right relationship with other citizens in the political order, the victim rebuilds respect for human rights, a critical component of just citizenship, especially in the aftermath of war and repression. Forgiveness can also help to break cycles of revenge and their attendant further violence and contribute to stable peace settlements and nascent constitutional democracies. It is well documented that the Catholic statesmen who launched European federalism (what eventually became today's European Union) in 1950 understood the venture as an exercise in Christian reconciliation and forgiveness in the wake of World War II.[19]

To note these benefits of forgiveness is not to claim that forgiveness is easy or common, especially in the aftermath of widespread violence and injustices. It is rather to outline how forgiveness may be viewed as a part of an ethic of political reconciliation that builds upon the teaching of social reconciliation that recent popes have offered the world. It also points to how some of the criticisms marshalled by skeptics of forgiveness can be answered. It shows how forgiveness can be conceived so that it is not at odds with justice but rather a part of justice. In addition, because forgiveness is one of several practices of reconciliation, it does not supplant other important measures that justice requires in times of transition: the uncovering of truth, reparations, acknowledgment of victims, apologies—and judicial punishment. In an ethic of reconciliation, forgiveness does not negate or call for the abandonment of accountability for war criminals or human rights violators but rather is compatible with punishment both in theory and in practice. In part, this compatibility is achieved through positing a restorative justification for punishment, an argument that I made in *Just and Unjust Peace* and that resembles the restorative justice that Father William O'Neill advocates in his chapter for this volume. Thus conceived, forgiveness and punishment each address a different dimension of right relationship and are often performed by different actors. To cite just one example, the widow of a South African antiapartheid activist offered forgiveness to Eugene de Kock, the head of the apartheid's police unit, the Vlakplass, at a hearing of the Truth and Reconciliation Commission even while de Kock served a 212-year prison sentence. De Kock accepted the forgiveness and expressed remorse even while he remained behind bars.

Objections will remain. Forgiveness wounds victims, is too difficult to ask of victims, and, simply, is rarely practiced. One can answer these objections by taking a close look at forgiveness in the laboratory of a major episode of violence.

The Practice of Forgiveness in Uganda

Resolving the civil war in Uganda was supposed to be a textbook case for the liberal peace. It was here that the first chief prosecutor of the new International Criminal Court (ICC), Luis Moreno-Ocampo, chose to make his first indictments in 2005, selecting five leaders of the Lord's Resistance Army (LRA), a rebel group that has fought a war with the armies of the government of Uganda since 1987. The war, which waned when the LRA's leader, Joseph Kony, and his followers were driven out of Uganda in 2009, took the lives of an estimated one hundred thousand people and displaced over 1.5 million. Kony was the subject of one of the world's viral YouTube videos, "Kony 2012," which told of his crimes and, echoing the liberal peace, called for his arrest.[20] As of this day, Kony is still on the run and only one of the five indictees, Dominic Ongwen, is being tried by the ICC.

A very different approach to peace was pursued by a group of religious leaders, the Acholi Religious Leaders Peace Initiative (ARLPI), which was founded in the late 1990s to advocate for an end to the war. A central figure in this founding and chairman of the ARLPI from 2002 to 2010 was the Catholic archbishop of Gulu, Uganda, John Baptist Odama. What is the central theme of Odama's and the ARLPI's approach to the conflict? Forgiveness.

Emblematic of the ARLPI's approach and a tangible fruit of its lobbying was the Amnesty Act that the Ugandan parliament passed in 2000, empowering thousands of child soldiers to leave the LRA and return to their homes and proving critical to the peace process. Led by Odama, ARLPI leaders paved the way for peace negotiations, traipsing for miles through the Ugandan bush to meet with Kony in person. ARLPI leaders, which represented Catholic, Anglican, and other Protestant Christians as well as Muslims, regularly urged their people to practice forgiveness and reconciliation.[21]

In an interview, Odama was asked how he could go out and meet with Kony, who had committed so many atrocities. He replied that he looked into Kony's soul and saw a human being there. Rather than punishment at the hands of the International Criminal Court, what Kony needs is repentance and salvation, Odama held.[22] He and his fellow religious leaders looked askance upon the ICC, which they viewed as an imposition on the part of Western powers and an obstacle to a peace agreement.[23]

Odama and his fellow religious leaders are advocates of the practice of forgiveness in the political realm, as John Paul II and other popes have called for. Have Ugandans taken up their call? One who did was Angelina Atyam, whose daughter the

LRA abducted along with about 130 other girls from a Catholic girls' boarding school in Lira in October 1996.[24] Beset by feelings of helplessness and anger, Atyam and other parents of abducted girls gathered regularly at the local Catholic cathedral to "work together, to pray together, to advocate together," as she put it.[25] Their anger, though, hindered their prayer. One day when the parents came to the words, "as we forgive those…" in the Our Father, they came to believe that God was calling them to forgive their daughters' abductors. Following this call, Atyam became a regular and outspoken advocate of forgiveness, urging it upon the other parents of the abducted girls as well as others who had lost loved ones in the conflict. She even found the mother of the soldier who held her daughter in captivity and, through her, forgave him, his family, and his clan. Subsequently, when this soldier lost his life in combat, Atyam wept and conveyed her sorrow to his mother.

Atyam's commitment to forgiveness did not negate her pursuit of justice. With other parents she formed the Concerned Parents Association, which campaigned for the release of the girls and brought international attention to their plight. When Kony heard about the publicity, he became worried and had one of his underlings communicate with Atyam that he would release her daughter if the organization would cease its advocacy. Atyam refused the offer. She would halt the campaign only if Kony released all the girls. Eventually, after spending seven-and-a-half years in captivity, Atyam's daughter escaped and was reunited with Atyam.[26]

Atyam forgave and became a leader in forgiveness.[27] She enacted what Odama advocated in Uganda and what recent popes have taught to the whole world. But how typical was Atyam among Ugandans? Was she rather a rare saint whom we might admire but whom it would be dangerous to look upon as a model for others? Is the recent teaching on political forgiveness from the Catholic hierarchy a tangible practice for communities on the ground?

I sought to answer this question by conducting a 2014 study of forgiveness in the aftermath of war in Uganda in close collaboration with the Refugee Law Project, a Ugandan NGO.[28] A survey of 640 inhabitants of five districts that have seen war asked them whether they have practiced forgiveness, how they regard forgiveness, what it means to forgive, why they would forgive, and related questions. In each district, two daylong focus groups took place in which about twelve participants discussed forgiveness, adding up to ten groups. Five in-depth interviews were carried out in each district as well, which, when added to interviews of Odama and Atyam, totaled twenty-seven interviews.[29] The five districts provided variation on language, religion, the circumstances of fighting, and many other factors. Of the 640 respondents, 593 identified themselves as victims of some form of violence. Respondents were presented with a long list of forms of violence that included violence against family members, the destruction of homes and other forms of property, as well as more direct assaults against bodily integrity.[30]

What did the survey find about forgiveness? In part, the survey queried respondents' attitudes. One question asked them, "What would you like to see happen to members of rebel groups who committed human rights violations?" as well as a question that was identical except that it substituted "members of the Ugandan military" for "rebel groups." Respondents were presented with a variety of possibilities including "capture and kill them," "have them compensate the victim," "have them confess," "grant them amnesty," and "forgive them," and they could choose more than one option. A solid majority of 60.94 percent answered "yes" to the "forgive" choice, whereas 39.06 percent answered "no." When the question asked about members of the Ugandan military, 53.91 percent answered "yes" to the "forgive" choice and 46.09 percent answered "no." Another question measured attitudes toward forgiveness by asking respondents whether they agreed to the statement, "It is good for victims to practice forgiveness in the aftermath of violence," to which 85.97 percent answered "agree," 8.71 percent answered "disagree," and 5.32 percent answered, "not sure."[31]

Other questions sought to measure the actual practice of forgiveness. One, posed only to victims of violence (593 respondents), asked directly, "Did you personally forgive the perpetrator of the act of violence against you?" Here, 68.3 percent of respondents answered "yes," 28.16 percent answered "no"; and 3.54 percent answered "don't know." A separate question asked people to judge the extent of the practice of forgiveness around them by asking whether they agreed with the statement, "People in my region have practiced forgiveness widely in the aftermath of armed conflict." Answering "agree" were 47.83 percent of respondents; answering "disagree" were 32.31 percent; while 19.97 percent answered "unsure."[32]

What are we to make of these numbers? Much depends on one's prior expectations about people's willingness to forgive. If one believes that only rare saints practice forgiveness, or if one shares in the skepticism or indifference to forgiveness that is widespread in the international community, then these numbers will appear startlingly high. That 68 percent of victims of violence would report practicing forgiveness, or that 86 percent would agree that forgiveness is a good thing in the aftermath of nightmarish war, are difficult attitudes to reconcile with the views of the liberal peace. Those without such prior skepticism may be less surprised by the results. They may note the substantial "noes" to the forgiveness choice toward rebels and even more so toward government troops as well as the 32 percent who disagreed that forgiveness was practiced widely in their region. Still, on balance, majorities favored, practiced, and reported the practice of forgiveness, and on some measures, did so in large majorities.

Might these results be quirks or the product of reporting biases? It is unlikely. The survey posed questions about attitudes and the practice of forgiveness in several different forms, all of which returned positive results regarding forgiveness. The results were also corroborated in the conversation that took place in the focus groups and interviews.[33] Paralleling the numbers, approval for and reports of the practice of forgiveness were far from unanimous. Participants offered reasons both for and against forgiveness. Favor toward forgiveness was widespread, though. Virtually no one argued that forgiveness was beyond the pale, unthinkable, or outside the boundaries of possibility in milieus where war had taken place, contrary to the views of even those Western analysts favorable to a reconciliation paradigm. In Uganda, forgiveness is a normal part of the regular practice of ordinary people in the wake of war.

When Ugandans approve of or practice forgiveness, what do they mean by it? From the focus groups and interviews emerged the common theme that forgiveness is a matter of the heart, a willed, inner act and not simply an outward performance. An interviewee from Luwero said, "Forgiveness comes from the heart. If you don't [forgive], your heart is always full with anger and instead of thinking about development, you are thinking about revenge."[34] In forgiving with their heart, victims performed two major actions. First, they decided deliberately to relinquish revenge, resentment, grudges, and payback. One focus group participant in Gulu commented, "Forgiveness is letting go the wrong things someone has done to you by trying to forget about it. It is [to leave] bad things and start doing good things."[35] Second, participants in the focus groups and interviews commonly voiced their view that forgiveness also involves an act of construction, one that to some degree restores relationship with the perpetrator. One interviewee in Amuria went so far as to say, "I wished the people who did all that to me the very best of luck and some of them died…the perpetrators are now very good friends of mine; we chat and talk about projects. I forgave them."[36] In many cases, forgiveness did not involve full restoration of right relationship. Some victims did not want to go this far. More often, victims were ignorant of the identity or location of perpetrators or else knew that they were dead. The survey showed that of victims who forgave, 71 percent answered "no" to the question, "Did you express forgiveness to the perpetrator in words," while only 28 percent answered "yes." The former victims forgave "from the heart," involving a willed act, but did not or could not express forgiveness to their perpetrator in words. As one interviewee in Amuria put it, "When we speak of forgiveness, I have forgiven them because they don't know me and neither do I know them, and God said that we should forgive wrongdoers."[37]

Other comments from the focus groups and interviews further rounded out the picture of what forgiveness is. One frequent comment pertained to what it is not: forgetting (though this was not unanimous; some thought forgiveness involves trying to forget). Many others stressed that forgiveness is not easy. It is "like swallowing a bitter pill," said one participant in Gulu. Still others stressed that forgiveness "takes time and a lot of courage," to quote the words of a participant in Gulu. Another said, "Years down the line [people involved in the war] forgive and reconcile. Even those who harbor grudges in their deathbed call perpetrators and forgive them. It therefore takes time to forgive." A focus group participant in Luwero also said of the time factor, "If you're hurt less you forgive quickly, but if you are hurt severely it takes you long to forgive." Some victims found forgiveness just too difficult. As one Luwero focus group participant put it, "I have never forgiven; I cannot forgive. To forgive someone who killed my father or mother!" Some focus group participants became more open to forgiveness through the experience of the focus group itself.[38]

One set of questions on the survey probed victims' views of transitional justice measures other than forgiveness: trials, apologies, reparations, truth-telling, and public recognition of suffering. These questions probe to what degree victims favor the priorities of the liberal peace, especially judicial punishment, and help to test the charge that a focus on forgiveness inappropriately places the burden of repair on victims. Ugandans do not reject judicial punishment, the measure for which the international community had made their country a prominent test case, nor do they appear to regard judicial punishment as intrinsically contradictory to forgiveness. To the question, "Is it important to you that persons responsible for abuses in Uganda are tried through the judicial system for their actions," an overwhelming 83 percent of respondents answered "yes," while 10 percent answered "no" and 7 percent "don't know." Respondents favored judicial punishment for leaders more than for ordinary soldiers. In contrast to Archbishop Odama, for instance, they would be willing to see Kony tried for his crimes.[39]

Yet if respondents favored trials and other measures of justice, they were equally of the view that these other forms of justice had not come to pass. Strong majorities of victims believed that perpetrators had not been held accountable; that victims of violence had not been adequately compensated; that leaders of armed groups had not adequately apologized for their crimes; that victims had not been given satisfactory opportunities to tell their stories; that not enough had been done to find out the truth; and that those who committed violence against them had not expressed remorse adequately.

Strikingly, though, victims were still willing to forgive despite other conditions of justice remaining unfulfilled, as the previously reported questions showed. In questions regarding attitudes toward forgiveness, survey respondents indicated favor for forgiveness being conditional upon apology and the telling of truth about violence. In practice, though, victims of violence who forgave reported doing so without conditions. Eighty-six percent of them reported that their perpetrators did not apologize before they forgave, while 96 percent reported that their perpetrators offered them no reparations and did not perform any act of repair. Ugandans, then, place high value upon forms of justice other than forgiveness yet do not seem to regard forgiveness as excessively burdensome in the absence of these forms of justice.[40]

What motivates high favor for and practice of forgiveness among Ugandans? Survey questions posed a series of questions about motivation to respondents who had practiced forgiveness. By far the strongest factor was religion. No less than 82 percent of respondents answered "yes" to the question, "Did you forgive because of your religious beliefs?" Ugandans are a religious people. Of the survey respondents, 78 percent report attending services once or more every week, while 81 percent report that "prayer is a regular part of my life"—both high readings by international standards. Of those surveyed, 37 percent identified as Roman Catholic, 26 percent as Anglican, and 23 percent as Muslim. To the question, "Which of the following is a good reason to forgive," 62 percent of the respondents to the survey answered "yes" to "because forgiveness is the teaching of Christianity," while 20 percent answered "yes" to "because forgiveness is the teaching of Islam"—percentages that correspond closely to the portion of the total respondents belonging to these religions. Participants in the focus groups and interviewees commonly associated forgiveness with religion.[41]

Ugandans are comfortable with religious leaders encouraging their followers to forgive, of which 97 percent expressed approval. Of those who practiced forgiveness, 70 percent affirmed that a religious leader had encouraged him or her to forgive. Ninety-four percent said that they were not pressured by a religious leader to forgive, in contrast to 6 percent who answered "yes." The fact that religious leaders are commending forgiveness with respect to politically motivated violence does not seem to bother Ugandans or provoke them to complain about the mixing of religion and politics. Ugandans do not seem to expect religion to remain separate from politics in the way that, say, citizens of the United States do.[42]

Those who forgave cited other reasons, too. Tribal traditions and family ranked highly, as did the desire for psychological peace. Many victims reported that they were far less angry and less anxious after they had forgiven. Said one participant in a Gulu focus group, "When you pile up wrongs in your heart, it painfully burns and hurts like heartburn. Forgiveness is good for health and peace of mind."[43] A large portion of respondents favored forgiveness because they believed it would bring peace to the community. A majority of 57 percent said that they forgave because it would help the perpetrator heal. Another factor that led victims to forgive in many cases was their recognition that perpetrators, usually children, were abducted into the LRA and forced at gunpoint to commit violence and atrocities. A total of 44 percent of victims answered "yes" to the question, "Did you forgive because you thought that the perpetrator was not responsible for his/her crime (for example, he/she was forced to commit it)?" While an even higher percentage of 48 percent answered "no" to the same question, 44 percent is still a high number. Combining Ugandans' motivations for forgiveness—religion and the promotion of peace in the community—we can say with confidence that Ugandans see forgiveness as a legitimate and important tool for building peace in the wake of colossal violence and injustice.[44]

Conclusion

Uganda is not the only site of forgiveness in political settings over the past generation. A discourse of forgiveness and at least some documented instances of its practice arose in South Africa, Sierra Leone, Northern Ireland, Germany, Guatemala, Chile, El Salvador, Timor Leste, and other settings. In many of these locales, forgiveness was associated with Catholic and other Christian churches. In many places, forgiveness was also contested and sometimes refused. This is to be expected of a practice that is fresh in political settings, challenges existing orthodoxies, and is loaded with questions, ambiguities, and dilemmas. Still, the fact that forgiveness has arisen unexpectedly in the social thought of the Catholic Church, and even more surprisingly in the actual practice of politics, testifies to the power of the gospel to spring up ever new as history unfolds. Victims of nightmarish crimes have exercised their Christian faith in following the teaching of Archbishop Odama that "forgiveness is a must for us if we want to heal our society."[45]

Reflection Questions

1. Why did forgiveness enter Catholic social teaching at such a late stage in history? What historical developments in recent years would favor or call for this teaching?
2. How would you evaluate the criticisms of political forgiveness that skeptics offer? Can the ethical practice of forgiveness accommodate these criticisms?
3. Are you surprised by the high rates of favor for and practice of forgiveness in Uganda? How does this compare to your own culture's approach to questions of forgiveness?
4. Do you think you could forgive the perpetrator of an act of wartime violence against you or a loved one? What if any impact would Christian faith have on your response?

Notes

1. Pope Benedict XV, *Pacem Dei Munus Pulcherrimum*, nos. 14, 1, accessed October 5, 2017, http://w2.vatican.va/content/benedict -xv/en/encyclicals/documents/hf_ben-xv_enc_23051920_pacem -dei-munus-pulcherrimum.html.

2. Pope John Paul II, *Dives in Misericordia*, no. 15, accessed October 5, 2017, http://w2.vatican.va/content/john-paul-ii/ en/encyclicals/documents/hf_jp-ii_enc_30111980_dives-in -misericordia.html.

3. Pope John Paul II, *Dives in Misericordia*, 14–15.

4. Messages for the World Day of Peace, accessed October 5, 2017, https://w2.vatican.va/content/john-paul-ii/en/messages/ peace/documents/hf_jp-ii_mes_08121996_xxx-world-day-for -peace.html and https://w2.vatican.va/content/john-paul-ii/en/

messages/peace/documents/hf_jp-ii_mes_20011211_xxxv-world
-day-for-peace.html; Luigi Accatoli, *When a Pope Asks for Forgiveness*, trans. Jordan Aumann (Staten Island: Alba House, 1998).

5. Luigi Accattoli, *When a Pope Asks Forgiveness: The Mea Cul-
pa's of John Paul II*, trans. Jordan Aumann (New York: Alba House,
1998), 48–51.

6. Catholic News Agency, "Pope Tells Why He Chose the
Name of 'Benedict XVI,'" accessed October 5, 2017, http://www
.catholicnewsagency.com/resources/benedict-xvi/life-and
-ministry/pope-tells-why-he-chose-the-name-of-benedict-xvi/.

7. Reprinted as "Acting in the Strength that Comes from
Remembrance: The Grace of Reconciliation," in Joseph Cardinal
Ratzinger, *Values in a Time of Upheaval*, trans. Brian McNeil (San
Francisco: Ignatius Press, 2006), 123–28.

8. Pope Benedict XVI, *Sacramentum Caritatis*, no. 89, accessed
October 5, 2017, http://w2.vatican.va/content/benedict-xvi/en/
apost_exhortations/documents/hf_ben-xvi_exh_20070222
_sacramentum-caritatis.html.

9. Pope Francis, *Misericordia et Misera*, accessed October 5,
2017, https://w2.vatican.va/content/francesco/en/apost_letters/
documents/papa-francesco-lettera-ap_20161120_misericordia
-et-misera.html; Pope Francis, *Evangelii Gaudium*, nos. 227–30,
accessed May 15, 2018, http://w2.vatican.va/content/francesco/
en/apost_exhortations/documents/papa-francesco_esortazione
-ap_20131124_evangelii-gaudium.html.

10. Message of His Holiness Francis for the Celebration of the
World Day of Peace, January 1, 2014, no. 10, https://w2.vatican
.va/content/francesco/en/messages/peace/documents/papa
-francesco_20131208_messaggio-xlvii-giornata-mondiale-pace
-2014.html.

11. Jonathan Van Antwerpen, "Reconciliation as Heterodoxy,"
in *Restorative Justice, Reconciliation, and Peacebuilding*, ed. Jennifer
Llewellyn and Daniel Philpott (Oxford: Oxford University Press,
2014), 77–117.

12. See the broad criticism of Amy Gutmann and Dennis
Thompson, "The Moral Foundation of Truth Commissions," in
Truth v. Justice: The Morality of Truth Commissions, ed. Robert I.
Rotberg and Dennis Thompson (Princeton: Princeton University
Press, 2000), 22–44.

13. Colleen Murphy, *A Moral Theory of Political Reconciliation* (Cambridge: Cambridge University Press, 2010), 11. See also Rebekka Friedman, *Competing Memories: Truth and Reconciliation in Sierra Leone and Peru* (Cambridge: Cambridge University Press, 2017), 49–51; and Ernesto Verdeja, *Unchopping a Tree: Reconciliation in the Aftermath of Political Violence* (Philadelphia: Temple University Press, 2009), 16–19.

14. On the relationship between justice and righteousness in the Bible, see Christopher D. Marshall, *Beyond Retribution: A New Testament Vision for Justice, Crime, and Punishment* (Grand Rapids, MI: Eerdmans, 2001), 35–59.

15. See, e.g., the arguments in John Finnis, *Natural Law and Natural Rights* (Oxford: Oxford University Press, 1980); Thomas D. Williams, *Who Is My Neighbor? Personalism and the Foundations of Human Rights* (Washington, DC: Catholic University of America Press, 2005); Nicholas Wolterstorff, *Justice: Rights and Wrongs* (Princeton: Princeton University Press, 2008).

16. See Proverbs 31:5, 8, 9; Ecclesiastes 5:8; Isaiah 5:23, and Lamentations 3:35.

17. On the definition of *mercy*, see St. Thomas Aquinas, *The Summa Theologica*, vol. 3, trans. Fathers of the English Dominican Province (Notre Dame: Ave Maria Press, 1948), 1311; John Paul II, *Dives in Misericordia*, no. 6. On restorative practices in the political realm, see Daniel Philpott, *Just and Unjust Peace: An Ethic of Political Reconciliation* (Oxford: Oxford University Press, 2012).

18. Again, see Philpott, *Just and Unjust Peace*, 4. The practices are not envisioned as necessarily performed in a particular order. Whether ethically justified forgiveness requires a prior apology is a matter of dispute. My own view is that the New Testament sanctions unilateral forgiveness (without prior apology).

19. See Brent L. Nelsen and James L. Guth, *Religion and the Struggle for European Union: Confessional Culture and the Limits of Integration* (Washington, DC: Georgetown University Press, 2015); and Alan Paul Fimister, *Robert Schuman: Neo-Scholastic Humanism and the Reunification of Europe* (Brussels: Peter Lang, 2008).

20. *Kony 2012*, accessed January 25, 2018, https://www.youtube.com/watch?v=Y4MnpzG5Sqc. The video received over 1 million hits.

21. More precisely, the ARLPI comprises Catholic, Anglican, Pentecostal, Orthodox, Seventh-Day Adventist, and Orthodox leaders, accessed August 23, 2017, http://www.arlpi.org/.

22. Refugee Law Project, *Forgiveness: Unveiling an Asset for Peacebuilding*, 2015, 30, https://www.refugeelawproject.org/files/others/Forgiveness_research_report.pdf.

23. As we shall see, on this score, Odama's views differ from the majority of survey respondents, who hold that forgiveness and judicial punishment are compatible and mutually desirable. Odama, however, strongly opposes the ICC. My own view echoes that of the respondents: judicial punishment and forgiveness are both important and desirable practices of reconciliation provided that they can be achieved. Although I am a strong admirer of Odama, on this issue, I respectfully disagree with him. Kony needs to repent, to be sure, but he also deserves prison.

24. See Marc Lacey, "Escape from Rebels Leads to a Reunion in Uganda," *The New York Times*, October 10, 2004, http://www.nytimes.com/2004/10/10/world/escape-from-rebels-leads-to-a-reunion-in-uganda-953340.html?mcubz=0.

25. Refugee Law Project, *Forgiveness*, 15.

26. Refugee Law Project, *Forgiveness*, 14–15. On Atyam's story, see also Emmanuel Katongole, *The Sacrifice of Africa: A Political Theology for Africa* (Grand Rapids, MI: Eerdmans, 2011), 148–65.

27. It's also worth noting that forgiveness was also a key part of Acholi rituals of reconciliation, the most extensive form of which are called *mato oput*. Odama and the other Acholi religious leaders strongly commended *mato oput* to their followers in Acholiland in addition to commending forgiveness on Christian grounds.

28. Refugee Law Project, *Forgiveness*. Field research took place between March and September, 2014.

29. The five districts included (1) Gulu, the city at the heart of Acholiland and the war in the north; (2) Yumbe of the West Nile region in northwest Uganda, which is heavily Muslim and has seen several insurgency movements since the fall of President Idi Amin in the 1970s; (3) Amuria, a city in the Teso subregion of Eastern Uganda; (4) Luwero, a region in Central Uganda where intense fighting took place in the early 1980s between the forces of Milton Obote's government and those of the guerilla army commanded by

Yoweri Museveni, who won the conflict and became president in 1986. See Refugee Law Project, *Forgiveness*, 5–9.

30. Refugee Law Project, *Forgiveness*, 11–13.
31. Refugee Law Project, *Forgiveness*, 13–14.
32. Refugee Law Project, *Forgiveness*, 14.
33. It should be noted that all ten of the focus groups and twenty-five out of the twenty-seven interviews were carried out by fellow Ugandans. The same was true for the survey, which was conducted completely by Ugandans. I, a Westerner, was present for only two of the focus groups and was not the primary leader of them. This eliminates the objection that the participants changed their message for a Western interviewer.
34. Refugee Law Project, *Forgiveness*, 15.
35. Refugee Law Project, *Forgiveness*, 16.
36. Refugee Law Project, *Forgiveness*, 16.
37. Refugee Law Project, *Forgiveness*, 15–18.
38. Refugee Law Project, *Forgiveness*, 18.
39. Refugee Law Project, *Forgiveness*, 18–25.
40. Refugee Law Project, *Forgiveness*, 21–22.
41. Refugee Law Project, *Forgiveness*, 25–32.
42. Refugee Law Project, *Forgiveness*, 27, 30.
43. Refugee Law Project, *Forgiveness*, 35.
44. Refugee Law Project, *Forgiveness*, 32–39.
45. Refugee Law Project, *Forgiveness*, 28.

Social Reconciliation in the Catholic Tradition

RESSOURCEMENT FOR A FULLER EXPRESSION OF CATHOLIC SOCIAL TEACHING

Robert Schreiter, CPPS

In the conclusion to his 1997 volume, *The Reconciliation of Peoples*, Gregory Baum lamented that social reconciliation had been accorded so little attention in the church—both in Catholic social teaching and among theologians in general.[1] This was coming at a time when there was dramatically increased interest in the topic around the world. After the collapse of the bipolar political order with the fall of the Berlin Wall in 1989 and the demise of the Soviet Empire in 1991, there had been a dramatic upsurge of armed conflicts around the world. What distinguished these conflicts from earlier ones was that most of these new wars were happening between factions within countries rather than between countries. As a result, the aftermath of these conflicts meant that assuring peace and rebuilding societies would entail finding ways to reconstruct a social order in which neighbors who had been enemies would now find ways to live together once again. This reconstruction of divided societies would require more than cease-fires and peace treaties negotiated at the national level.

The language of reconciliation came into greater prominence as the world faced the problem of resolving conflicts within nations rather than between them. Such language captured not only the need to redress the past, but the task of engaging the hearts and minds of the erstwhile combatants and the affected civilian populations so that they could build a new life together.

The language of reconciliation carried more a sense of aspiration than a definable program of how to reach such a new life together. It often became apparent that the roots of conflict reached further back in history than the immediate conflict itself. Moreover, the conflict itself frequently divided communities internally, leaving yet another set of wounds to be addressed.

For Christians, this renewed interest in reconciliation resonated immediately with a central narrative of Christian identity: God's reconciling the world to God's own self through the suffering, death, and resurrection of Jesus Christ. This sense of reconciliation was expressed especially in the Pauline corpus, as the chapter by Thomas Stegman outlines in this book. Yet most of the theological reflection on this central theme of Christian faith had focused upon the reconciliation of the individual sinner to God. The social dimensions of reconciliation seemed relatively unexplored.[2] To be sure, social and racial reconciliation had been a theme developed among U.S. black theologians in the early 1970s.[3] In the 1980s, it had been taken up by theologians in South Africa looking toward the end of apartheid. But there was also a reluctance by theologians to explore the theme of social reconciliation further in view of how some (usually those in political power) had used the language of reconciliation to quell efforts to pursue liberation and social justice. This had been the case with some of the military dictatorships in Latin America (notably in Argentina) and with the apartheid regime in South Africa.

At the same time, developments in Catholic social teaching contained elements that addressed aspects of social reconciliation in important ways. From John XXIII's encyclical letter *Pacem in Terris* in 1963, through the discussion of peace in *Gaudium et Spes* at the Second Vatican Council, to the annual papal Messages for the World Day of Peace from the 1970s onward, a body of theological reflection has grown that can be crafted into a theological proposal for the work of social reconciliation that engages the current needs and aspirations of a conflicted world. The salient themes arising from Catholic social teaching—the dignity of every human person, the preferential option for the poor, the imperative of human and social solidarity, the defense of human rights, the importance of the common good, and the care for creation—present important building blocks for a coherent theology of social reconciliation.

It has been this twofold problem—dealing with reconstructing societies that had been riven by armed conflict and the need to expand traditional Christian understandings of reconciliation—that has turned theologians to examine and build out a theology of social reconciliation that can meet the needs of our time. Over the last twenty years, other scenarios beyond dealing with post-conflict situations have gained the attention of those theologians working for social reconciliation. The increasingly polarized political and social situations in many Western countries, for example, challenge theologians to expand notions of social reconciliation to address these crises as well. The essays in this volume have been presented as drawing upon resources in Christian tradition—especially in its Roman Catholic accentuation—that might bring us closer to a theology of social reconciliation that both mines the experience of two millennia of Christian faith and helps illumine the social situation in which contemporary Christians find themselves. They do not represent a systematic theology of social reconciliation in themselves, but rather reflect a wisdom growing out of recurring themes that have surfaced at different times and places throughout history.

To see more clearly how these contributions from Christian history and contemporary experience might illumine the current situation, it might be helpful to begin with what might be called the "state of the question" in understanding how peace is built after a time of deeply dividing conflict. On that basis we can turn to what role the church might find itself being able to play in using its own resources in societies that are trying to find ways to live together once again. The Catholic Church takes up a special role in this regard since it is both a local and a global institution, with social, political, and pastoral parts to play in local and global settings.

314

Social Reconciliation Today: From a Liberal Peace to a More Comprehensive Vision

Daniel Philpott, a contributor to this volume, has delineated well here and elsewhere the current view in the larger world of how to build peace in divided societies.[4] The consensus around this matter has been called a "liberal peace" inasmuch as it derives from an understanding of the human being and of society mediated by the European Enlightenment. Here the key points revolve around the freedom of the individual and the inherent dignity of each human person, endowed with rights that are to be respected at all times and in all places. The rebuilding of a divided society then must focus on a praxis of seeking justice to both correct the violation of human rights of the past and to ensure the enactment of just laws within the framework of an international order. These rights have been presented most cogently in the 1948 United Nations' Declaration of Human Rights. The path from armed conflict to a restored peace, then, is marked by peace agreements that are then implemented through practices of transitional justice—formal actions within an established legal framework that will establish the truth about what has happened in the past, will call to account miscreants who have violated human rights and international law in the conflict, and will then work to restore the rule of law and repair to the extent possible within the social institutions of a divided society. In so doing, liberal peace builds the social framework for life together after a time of deep conflict.

In his work, Philpott has shown that the framework and procedures of liberal peace can indeed stabilize a volatile situation and meet public needs for order as it creates an environment governed by the rule of law rather than a raw exercise of power. Such an environment allows other social actors, at the national and international level, to interact in a nonviolent way with the actors in the erstwhile conflict. But the features of liberal peace—respect for human rights, retributive justice, the promotion of democracy and of free markets—still fall short of a more comprehensive program for social reconciliation. As he argues in

315

his chapter, the concepts of forgiveness and mercy must also be taken into account. This is the case not only at the macro level of the state, but especially also at the micro level of the face-to-face interaction of people in local communities. Already earlier, John Paul Lederach had noted that sustainable peace requires working both at the national level and at the community level, and the dynamics of the two levels are not entirely parallel. The national level works principally within the framework of law and procedural justice; the community level, with the framework of human relationships.[5] Growing out of his extensive experience in conflict transformation, Lederach has called for a more integrated approach encompassing both the national and community levels.

Philpott proposes an "ethic of reconciliation" to expand the liberal peace in order to make possible a closer integration of these levels. He finds key elements for this in the religious traditions of the Abrahamic faiths—notably in their understandings of justice, forgiveness, and mercy. Some critics have seen his proposal as violating the strict secularity of the liberal model that, in its Enlightenment bias, sees religion as part of the problem rather than part of the solution. But such a view overlooks religion as a source of resilience in local settings. As he shows here in his case study of forgiveness in Uganda, it is often religious values that help people in local communities come to the possibility of reconciliation.

It is against this background that we can now explore the insights into social reconciliation that the authors of this volume have been able to garner from Christian tradition.

Insights from the Catholic Tradition Contributing to a Theology of Social Reconciliation

At the outset, one must recall that the Catholic Church occupies a unique position for engaging social reconciliation. It is both a global and a local institution. At the global level it can interact with nation-states and in transnational settings. Jay Carney's discussion of the medieval Peace of God movement shows how the church could operate to contain social violence in Europe among armed elites and provide some measure of protection for the civilian population. As he notes, the lines between political and religious action are blurred here. Even though the liberal ethic of peace-building tries to keep them separated, there is still frequently such a blurring of the political and the religious today, especially in societies that are not secularized.

Laurie Johnston's account of Catholic-Muslim relations in the Iberian Peninsula retrieves additional perspectives about how efforts at reconciliation are always approximations; they rarely yield complete social reconciliation. She draws us more deeply into how shifting conceptions of the enemy "other" are essential to continuing processes toward reconciliation.

Philpott has pointed out the rich resources in Judaism, Christianity, and Islam for an ethic of reconciliation. Themes of justice, forgiveness, and mercy are replete in all three of these traditions. In my own experiences of working at reconciliation in the field with partners of other faiths, those parallels are richly obvious. What is distinctive about the Christian view of reconciliation is that the different elements that make up reconciliation are brought together in a unified narrative that is also the basic story of Christianity itself. It is articulated most succinctly in the New Testament in Romans 5:1–11. God created the world and all within it good, but humankind has fallen away from God. God in turn has chosen to reconcile this fallen world to God's own self, brought about by the incarnation, death, and resurrection of Christ. In all this, God is reconciling the world in a process that is not yet complete but will be so when all is gathered together in Christ.

To be sure, this distinctively Christian narrative is not accepted by Jews or Muslims, nor should we expect it to be. But what is most significant here is that reconciliation begins with a "vertical" axis, that is, the work of reconciliation is first the work of God, who initiates it and brings it to its conclusion. Human efforts, on the "horizontal" level, are (from a Christian perspective) only efficacious to the extent that they are anchored in God's reconciling activity. What this can point to is something that relates to the experience of working toward reconciliation today from secular as well as religious perspectives: it seems we always need some kind of outside "leverage" to bring about reconciliation. The deeply entrenched enmities that follow conflict and mistrust do not resolve themselves easily. This is caught in a truism sometimes articulated among workers for peace: what caused the conflict will not resolve the conflict. For Christians, it is this appeal to the founding narrative of Christian faith that provides this outside leverage; for secular actors, its analogue is an appeal to universal human rights. The point here is that in a pluralistic world there will likely not be a single common appeal to the nature of this leverage. But that communities seek such leverage is something each set of actors must consider.

Thomas Stegman's essay gives a comprehensive view of the Pauline understanding of reconciliation, which is at the basis of any Christian understanding of the concept. He notes how the vocabulary of reconciliation Paul adopted derived from a social context of the aftermath of war and contention in the courts. Paul's own experience of conversion and forgiveness, however, gives Christian reconciliation its distinctive character. That reconciliation is initiated by God gives Christian reconciliation its distinctive vertical dimension. This vertical dimension grounds the horizontal dimension: the church is to engage in a ministry of reconciliation (see 2 Cor 5:17–20), carrying the message and the ministry of reconciliation to the world.

A central part of that message of reconciliation is given in 2 Corinthians 5:17: "If anyone is in Christ, there is a new creation." A "new creation" indicates that reconciliation is not about returning to some *status quo ante*—as if we can go back to before the conflict, the divisions, and the suffering began. Reconciliation is about finding a way to take into account the past, yet move also to a new place. John O'Keefe adumbrates this here in his reading of Irenaeus's polemics with the Gnostics. Creation is given to us as a whole; and so the work of reconciliation cannot be seen as a single strategic program of course correction. The reconciliation that God will bring about is best seen as an "*oikonomia*," a more comprehensive ordering of things that can only be called a "new creation." And this new creation is not in the first instance a matter of technocratic management (a point reiterated also by others in this volume), but might be better considered as a "*mystagogia*," a being led into the deeper reality of things and of their transformation by someone far greater than ourselves. It is a result of the Christ as the "New Adam," a "force of divine stability in a destabilized creation…unleash[ing] the spiritual potential of the material creation." These elements of Irenaeus's vision point to initiation into a comprehensive, holistic mode of social reconciliation as a mystagogical task. Put another way, social reconciliation is more than strategic ambits for alleviating suffering and fostering harmony—important and necessary as all these things are. It entails also a spirituality, a particular vision and set of disciplined practices that sustain and deepen that apprehension of reality. It implies, too, that the work of social reconciliation is as much a work of the imagination as it is one of calculation. This is one of the most important insights the Catholic tradition brings to the contemporary work of social reconciliation.

More will be said about that later. But something further needs to be noted here about the new creation. The fact that it is signaled as a "new creation" implies its comprehensive and holistic character. Such an all-embracing character of social reconciliation is already being recognized in secular discourse as well. The effects of climate change on social conflicts now has to be part and parcel of any approach to working for social reconciliation as drought and natural catastrophe foster and compound conflict. An Irenaean vision allows us to gain a more applicable voice for embracing what it means to reconcile with the earth.

Moreover, this "new creation" is to be understood within the larger narrative of God's reconciliation of the world: it is an experience of "already but not yet," a process has begun but is far from fulfillment. The concrete experience of work toward reconciliation highlights the experience of reconciliation as an exercise in approximation, as Laurie Johnston points out. Emmanuel Katongole elaborates on this when looking at the many conflicts in contemporary East Africa. Transitional justice procedures are usually enacted within a limited framework of time. Social reconciliation, however, typically takes more than a generation if it is achieved at all. Such an open-ended process can seem disheartening to the actors involved, but if seen through the prism of a world that is intended by God to come back together through the agency of Christ, those actors can continue their efforts without losing hope. The hope that the eschatological vision requires and engenders gives the impetus to sustain our efforts at social reconciliation.

The "new creation" is enacted in social reconciliation by a transformation of the practices of social reconciliation, and what directs this enactment is what John Kiess has called here the "deep architecture" of reconciliation—the spirituality that flows from a sacramental imagination. Let us look now at the practices of social reconciliation that are illuminated by aspects of the Christian tradition, and then at the deep architecture of the spirituality that underlies them.

The Practices of Social Reconciliation

Four sets of practices stand out in processes of social reconciliation. They might be termed as (1) healing of memories, (2) truth-telling, (3) pursuit of justice, and (4) forgiveness. The chapters of this book offer insights about all four of these practices.

The Healing of Memories. Social reconciliation in its most simple sense is about healing the past and building the future. Healing pertains to the wounds that conflict and violence have wrought upon both victims and wrongdoers, and upon the whole society itself. For victims, this means restoring their agency (a point made here by Laurie Johnston); for wrongdoers, it entails repentance and commitment to a new way of living. Dealing with the past requires dealing with memories and the process of remembering. Emmanuel Katongole devotes a great deal of his presentation to memory, and especially the "dangerous memory" first articulated by Johann Baptist Metz and developed further on a variety of theological fronts. It is the "dangerous memory of the suffering and death of Jesus Christ"—whose death did not end in failure and being forgotten but in his being raised up by God. This dangerous memory challenges any narrative that violence and evil will ultimately prevail. It is that memory of what God has done in Jesus Christ that keeps even the worst of suffering from sliding into despair. Katongole elaborates on the dimensions of this memory in his telling the story of Marguerite Barankitse, who overcame devastating suffering to envision a "new creation" in Burundi. Stephen Judd outlines how acts of networking and solidarity closed the gaps of colonial and neocolonial wounds among the Aymara people in Peru, leading from division to solidarity. In social reconciliation, the memory of suffering is not erased or forgotten; to do so would be to enact violence upon victims once again. Rather, memory is transformed. We do not forget the past; we come to remember it differently—in a way that is transformative of our relation to the past and constructive for a different kind of future. Ashley Hall captures this in another way in reflecting on the efforts at reconciliation between Lutherans and Roman Catholics in the twentieth century. These two groups have come to commemorate the past, that is, a way to remember the past together (co-memorate), rather than remembering in a way that reinforces past divisions.

Truth-telling. There is an old adage that says that the first casualty of war is the truth. As positions widen and harden in the course of conflict, versions of the truth come to serve one's own side and denigrate that of the other. Over time in prolonged conflict, cultures of lies and cultures of silence are likely to emerge. Cultures of lies dehumanize opponents and justify aggression and repression. Cultures of silence block the truth from emerging and create climates of fear and isolation. Zachary Smith's masterful presentation on speech and silence in early monastic life underscores the powerful potential of both modes of expression. Speech can be deeply harmful, especially when it is intended to wound the enemy. Silence, especially the asceticism of monastic silence, can empower speech when it is rightfully employed. Contemplative silence, as Smith points out, can create the space where one can take stock of oneself and one's opponent in a safe yet stable space. In so doing it can overcome the damaging patterns of a culture of silence that represses truth.

The reflections on truth by the Truth and Reconciliation Commission in South Africa identified one of the most difficult forms of truth-telling. They called this form "dialogical truth," that is, narrating the past in such a way that both sides can recognize themselves in the story, both in their achievements and failings.[6] Ashley Hall points to a successful case of this in the Lutheran–Roman Catholic document *From Conflict to Communion*, in which both sides of the sixteenth-century Reformation can now tell that story together, and in so doing, each recognize their suffering, mistakes, and achievements. Dialogical truth is extremely difficult to effect, and there are few successful examples of it in contemporary peacebuilding literature. The pattern of dialogue that Hall traces here shows how it can bear fruit as mistrust between parties is lessened and truth-telling can gradually take hold. Achieving dialogical truth is one of the important ingredients in social reconciliation.

Truth-telling that overcomes division requires dialogue. For Christian reconciliation, dialogue is rooted in God's initiative, reaching out to a fallen creation that has turned away from God. As Pope Paul VI pointed out already in his encyclical *Ecclesiam Suam*, the model for dialogue begins in the dialogue that characterizes the inner life of the Trinity. Stephen Judd recounts how efforts at building networks of dialogue helped create the solidarity among the Aymara that brought them to a new creation. Kristi Haas's examination of the preaching praxis of Bernardino of Siena underscores how dialogue is necessary to bring warring factions together. Scott Moringiello's recounting of how Cyprian worked to overcome the divisions in Carthage provides yet another example.

Pursuit of Justice. Liberal peace focuses especially on retributive justice, which highlights violation of human rights and the legal order. An important contribution from the Christian tradition is its focus on restorative justice, which looks especially to the justice due to victims. William O'Neill, in his discussion of incarceration, speaks of a "restorative squint," a way of seeing that keeps the restorative dimension of justice always in view, even amid the punitive dimensions of incarceration as the outcome of retributive justice. Julia Fleming's presentation of Alphonsus Ligouri's reflections on restitution—an important part of restorative justice—brings our attention to how society requires establishing an equilibrium to balance contesting claims. Indeed, she points out how working toward equilibrium provides an important window on our shared humanity, a key element in bringing about social reconciliation.

Forgiveness. As Daniel Philpott has noted in his presentation, forgiveness has become a "surprise element" in peacemaking. Yet forgiveness in the Christian tradition is a central theme, emerging as it does out of an experience of God's mercy. Mercy creates a space of generosity and gratuity that allows a new creation to emerge. The teaching of Pope John Paul II in *Dives in Misericordia* and the entire pontificate of Pope Francis have given central place to mercy and forgiveness. Pope John Paul II famously said in his 2004 Message for the World Day of Peace that the two pillars of peace are justice and forgiveness. British theologian Leah Robinson has noted that in contemporary Christian theologies of reconciliation, one finds two emphases in the pursuit of social reconciliation: one emphasizes the importance of justice and liberation, and the other foregrounds mercy and forgiveness.[7] It should be noted that these emphases do not represent exclusive options. Robinson goes on to show how contexts may indicate that one approach may be more effective than the other. There has been a great deal of philosophical and psychological debate about the meaning and limits of forgiveness in the face of past injustice,[8] but the Christian understanding of forgiveness is opening new perspectives in social reconciliation. It has called into question human limits placed upon forgiveness by pointing to the infinite mercy of God. These insights into forgiveness represent an important advance for understanding and achieving social reconciliation that is now working its way into the broader discourse of social reconciliation.

The Spirituality of Social Reconciliation: The Deep Architecture

Because God is seen as the author of reconciliation, the church as bearer of the message and ministry of reconciliation must always be in constant and deep communion with God if it is to be an effective agent of reconciliation. Consequently, if it is to serve an *oikonomia* of reconciliation, the church has to have a vision from which it engages in social reconciliation. The contributions in this volume highlight four dimensions of that spirituality or "deep architecture" of social reconciliation: (1) the primacy of love, (2) the need for conversion, (3) the practice of contemplation, and (4) a sacramental imagination.

The Primacy of Love. Fundamental to Christian reconciliation is the belief that God reached out to reconcile the world out of love: "But God proves his love for us in that while we still were sinners Christ died for us" (Rom 5:8). It is love that is the foundation for peace, as Cyprian reminds us. And it is Christ's sacrificial love that invites us to overcome our divisions, as Bernardino of Siena preaches. It is love that creates the spaces of mercy that in turn make forgiveness possible.

Conversion. Central to a "new creation" is that all parties must change. Secular understandings of reconciliation certainly assert the importance of wrongdoers repenting and committing themselves to a new way of life. But the grace of reconciliation touches victims as well—evidenced in the healing of memories and the capacity to forgive. The conversion of victims is a delicate process; pressing change upon them too quickly can victimize them once again. But conversion makes it possible for them to make new space and fresh accommodation for their enemies, as Johnston pointed out. Conversion opens a renewed sense of agency that is a sign of reconciliation taking place in their lives.

Contemplation. Smith's treatment of monastic speech and silence, and the asceticism that focuses the spiritual subject, reveal a paradoxical but central aspect of the practice of social reconciliation; namely, the practice of contemplative prayer. If Christians believe that reconciliation is the work of God, then it requires contemplative prayer to be in communion with God's intentions and actions. In contemplative prayer, we center upon God and decenter ourselves. That is crucial if we are to be engaged in finding that "leverage" that will lift us out of the impasse that prolonged conflict has created. A "new creation" means being able to see and imagine otherwise. The power of contemplative prayer to heal is also seen in Katongole's presentation of Marguerite Barankitse's daily time spent in such prayer; this helped heal her memories and sustains her in the continuing struggle.

Sacramental Imagination. O'Keefe's reading of Irenaeus reminds us that reconciliation is more than a set of strategies. It is an *oikonomia.* Even seen from a secular perspective, what we are striving to do in reconciliation is somehow change the past, undoing as it were wrongdoing's ongoing damage to the present and the future. We cannot change the past, of course, but we can journey from the present to the past through ritual. The Christian celebration of the Eucharist is such a journey to memory. John Kiess's analysis of the use of the sacrament of anointing during the Troubles in Northern Ireland reminds us of how anointing of bodies counteracts the devaluation of life that armed conflict always brings. Moreover, he shows how the daily routines of liturgy create an ongoing perspective on everyday life by pointing to something larger and greater that should inform our sense of what is rightful and just.

This sacramental imagination—the capacity to see the world around us at once as it is (O'Keefe's reading of Irenaeus) and what it is intended to be (the eschatological vision explored by Katongole)—has implications beyond Catholic life. Social reconciliation is always about repair and transformation. That means a commitment to what is present and what has been: the current brokenness of things and the wounds inflicted in the past. But it must also mean a larger, dynamic vision that is part of a new creation, bringing us all to a new place.

The Catholic tradition brings a sense of holism, a commitment to both the macro and micro levels of human life, practices that foster the ongoing difficult work of reconciliation, and spiritual resources needed to sustain this work and imagine a different kind of future. The essays in this volume give us insight into all these aspects. Work toward a fuller theology of social reconciliation continues. It is enriched by engaging new conflicts and controversies that cry out for resolution. And it will continue to benefit from returning to resources within the Christian tradition to help focus upon possible avenues toward a genuinely "new creation."

Notes

1. Gregory Baum and Harold Wells, eds., *The Reconciliation of Peoples: Challenge to the Churches* (Maryknoll, NY: Orbis Books, 1997), 187.

2. For an historical overview, see Dirk Ansorge, *Gerechtigkeit und Barmherzigkeit. Die Dramatik von Vergebung und Versöhnung in bibeltheologischer, theologiegeschichtlicher und philosophiegeschichtlichter Perspektive* (Freiburg: Herder, 2009).

3. J. Deotis Roberts, *Liberation and Reconciliation: A Black Theology* (Philadelphia: Westminster Press, 1971).

4. Daniel Philpott, *Just and Unjust Peace: An Ethic of Political Reconciliation* (New York: Oxford University Press, 2012).

5. John Paul Lederach, *Building Peace: Sustainable Reconciliation in Divided Societies* (Washington, DC: United States Institute of Peace, 1997).

6. On dialogical truth, see John de Gruchy, *Reconciliation: Restoring Justice* (Minneapolis: Fortress Press, 2002), 155.

7. Leah Robinson, *Embodied Peacebuilding: Reconciliation as Practical Theology* (Bern: Peter Lang, 2015).

8. See, e.g., Bas van Stokkum, Neelke Doorn, and Paul van Tongeren, eds., *Public Forgiveness in Post-Conflict Contexts* (Cambridge: Intersentia, 2012).

Contributors

Editors

J. J. (Jay) Carney is Associate Professor of Theology at Creighton University, Omaha, Nebraska. He earned his masters of divinity from Duke University and his PhD in church history from The Catholic University of America. His research engages questions of political theology, social reconciliation, and modern Catholic history and theology in East Africa. He is the author of *Rwanda before the Genocide: Catholic Politics and Ethnic Discourse in the Late Colonial Era* (Oxford, 2014). As a Fulbright Scholar, he is currently working on two manuscripts concerning Catholic leadership in modern Uganda.

Laurie Johnston is Associate Professor of Theology and Religious Studies at Emmanuel College in Boston, where she also serves as Director of Fellowships. She is also a visiting scholar at the Center for Human Rights and International Justice at Boston College. She holds degrees from Boston College, Harvard Divinity School, and the University of Virginia. She is coeditor of two recent books, *Can War Be Just in the Twenty-first Century* and *Public Theology and the Global Common Good*, and author of numerous articles in the field of social ethics. She is a member of the Community of Sant'Egidio and serves on the steering committee of the Catholic Peacebuilding Network.

Julia A. Fleming is Professor of Theology and the current chair of the theology department at Creighton University. Dr. Fleming's research interests include the history of moral theology and Roman Catholic social ethics. Her recent publications include studies of Antonino Diana's casuistry regarding the disabled and contemporary developments in Catholic social teaching on the death penalty.

Kristin M. Haas is a PhD student in systematic theology at the University of Notre Dame. A graduate of Boston College (MTS) and Notre Dame (MA), she served as a pastoral leader and worked with the Catholic Peacebuilding Network and the Under Caesar's Sword project before returning to full-time academic work. Her research interests include ecclesiology and the doctrine of creation in twentieth-century thought.

H. Ashley Hall is Associate Professor of Theology at Creighton University. He completed his graduate education at Fordham University. His areas of research are the Reformation, the early church, and ecumenism. Hall is also an ordained pastor of the Evangelical Lutheran Church in America (ELCA) and delegate to the current round of dialogue between the ELCA and the U.S. Conference of Catholic Bishops.

Stephen P. Judd, MM, is originally from Butte, Montana. A Maryknoll missionary priest, he received his PhD from the Graduate Theological Union in Berkeley, California, in 1987. He has served in mission in Peru and Bolivia for forty years. He now resides in Los Altos, California, where he is engaged in mission education efforts and several writing and lecturing projects throughout the western United States.

Emmanuel M. Katongole is Associate Professor of Theology and Peace Studies at the University of Notre Dame. A Catholic priest of Kampala Archdiocese (Uganda), he previously served as the founding codirector of the Duke Divinity School's Center for Reconciliation. He is the author of books on the Christian social imagination and on Christian approaches to justice, peace, and reconciliation. Recent books include *Born from Lament: On the Theology and Politics of Hope in Africa* (Eerdmans, 2017); *The Journey of Reconciliation: Groaning for a New Creation in Africa* (Orbis, 2017); *The Sacrifice of Africa: A Political Theology for Africa*

(Eerdmans, 2011), and (with Chris Rice) *Reconciling All Things: A Christian Vision for Justice, Peace and Healing* (IVP, 2008).

John Kiess is Associate Professor of Theology and Director of the Office of Peace and Justice at Loyola University Maryland. He received his PhD in theology and ethics from Duke University in 2011. As a George J. Mitchell Scholar, he earned his MA in comparative ethnic conflict from Queen's University Belfast and MPhil in theology from Cambridge University. His research interests include moral theology, political philosophy, and the ethics of war and peacebuilding. He is the author of *Hannah Arendt and Theology* (Bloomsbury/T&T Clark, 2016), and his work has appeared in *Modern Theology, The Journal of Moral Theology,* and *The Christian Century*.

Scott D. Moringiello is Assistant Professor in the Department of Catholic Studies at DePaul University, where he teaches classes on Catholic theology and religion and literature. His research interests include the history of biblical exegesis, especially in the early church, and religious themes in contemporary literature.

John J. O'Keefe is Professor of Theology at Creighton University. His academic research focuses on ancient Christianity and the emerging field of environmental theology. O'Keefe is also a documentary filmmaker and cofounder of the Backpack Journalism project, a social justice filmmaking initiative. In addition, O'Keefe is currently working on a "deep mapping" project focused on the Nebraska Sandhills.

William O'Neill, SJ, is a member of the Society of Jesus and Emeritus Professor of Social Ethics at the Jesuit School of Theology of Santa Clara University (California). He is also a visiting professor at the Jesuit School of Theology, "Hekima" in Nairobi. His writings include *The Ethics of Our Climate: Hermeneutics and Ethical Theory* and book chapters and journal articles on human rights, social reconciliation, and immigration and refugee policy.

Daniel Philpott is Professor of Political Science at the University of Notre Dame. He is a scholar of religion and global politics who has specialized in reconciliation, religious freedom, theories of the political behavior of religious actors, and ethics and international relations. His books include *Just and Unjust Peace: An Ethic of Political Reconciliation* (Oxford, 2012) and his forthcoming monograph, *Religious Freedom in Islam? Intervening in a Public Controversy*. He is codirector of the project *Under Caesar's Sword: Christians in Response to Persecution* and has conducted faith-based reconciliation in Kashmir and the Great Lakes Region of Africa. He earned his PhD in political science from Harvard University in 1996.

Robert Schreiter, CPPS, is the Vatican Council II Professor of Theology at the Catholic Theological Union in Chicago. He has worked widely in postconflict peacebuilding in different parts of the world. He is past president of the American Society of Missiology and the Catholic Theological Society of America. Among his many authored and coedited books are *Reconciliation: Mission and Ministry in a Changing Social Order*; *The Ministry of Reconciliation: Spirituality and Strategies*; *Peacebuilding: Catholic Theology, Ethics, Praxis*; and *Mission as Ministry of Reconciliation*.

Zachary B. Smith is Assistant Professor in the Department of Theology at Creighton University. He researches the connections between Christianity and its cultural contexts, specializing in the late antique and Byzantine periods. His current projects revolve around the monks of the eastern Mediterranean. He is the author of *Philosopher-Monks, Episcopal Authority, and the Care of the Self: The* Apophthegmata Patrum *in Fifth-Century Palestine* (Brepols, 2018), and is the associate editor for the *Journal of Religion & Society*.

Thomas D. Stegman, SJ, a Jesuit from the USA Midwest Province, is Dean and Professor of New Testament at Boston College School of Theology and Ministry. His publications include *Opening the Door of Faith: Encountering Jesus and His Call to Discipleship* and *Written for Our Instruction: Theological and Spiritual Riches in Romans* (both from Paulist Press). He is also one of the coeditors of the *Paulist Biblical Commentary* and author of its commentary on Romans.